SON OF THE WILDERNESS

Son of the Wilderness

THE LIFE OF

JOHN MUIR

BY

LINNIE MARSH WOLFE

1947

ALFRED A KNOPF *NEW YORK*

THIS IS A BORZOI BOOK,
PUBLISHED BY ALFRED A. KNOPF, INC.

Manufactured in the United States of America. Published simultaneously in Canada by The Ryerson Press.

PUBLISHED JULY 16, 1945
REPRINTED THREE TIMES
FIFTH PRINTING, JANUARY 1947

TO

ROY N. WOLFE

IN MEMORY OF OUR SUMMER DAWNS
AND DAYS TOGETHER IN THE MEADOWS
AND GROVES AND ALONG THE TRAILS
OF THE YOSEMITE

THE MOUNTAINS *are fountains of men as well as of rivers, of glaciers, of fertile soil. The great poets, philosophers, prophets, able men whose thoughts and deeds have moved the world, have come down from the mountains — mountain-dwellers who have grown strong there with the forest trees in Nature's workshops.*

JOHN MUIR

PREFACE

WHEN, in 1939, Wanda Muir Hanna,[1] elder daughter of John Muir, talked over with me the task of writing his biography, she said: "Many people know of my father as a naturalist, but the world has never understood him as a man. I wish you would write of him from that point of view and tell of his human relationships." When I deplored the fact that I had not known him personally, Mrs. Hanna replied: "It is better so. If you had known him, you would have seen only one side of him, and he had many sides. No two people — even his closest friends — ever had quite the same idea of him." I have taken my cue from her words, striving mainly to see all the way around him and to lift a few veils that have obscured his rich life among men, thus, I hope, making him somewhat more than a disembodied voice crying in the wilderness.

In my researches before and since that time I have found Mrs. Hanna and her sister, Mrs. Helen Funk Muir,[2] ever willing to share their memories with me and to discuss frankly all phases of their father's life and character. I have talked also with his friends, and with his enemies as well. Few men of genius have escaped being maligned in their time, and John Muir, who championed unpopular causes, had his share of maligners. Wild stories were set afloat about him in an effort to destroy his influence. Some of these, unfortunately, are still extant. With a sincere desire to get at the truth, I dragged out every hypothetical skeleton from its closet and tracked down every wild story, only to find that they melted into thin air when brought face to face with well-attested facts. In this book I have related only that canard used for decades by the foes of conservation — and therefore of Muir — charging him with having ruthlessly cut down trees in the Yosemite in his sawmill days. In its obvious falsity it is typical of them all. In other instances, while not dignifying libels by specific mention, I have related facts that reveal their absurdity. Readers who have heard

[1] All notes will be found at the end of the volume, beginning with page 351.

these slanderous legends about Muir will recognize their refutations.

Early in 1937 the mass of Muiriana was turned over to me by his heirs, that I might edit some of his notes and journals for publication.[3] Eagerly delving into the thousands of letters in his files, and his innumerable notes, I gained substantial knowledge of the John Muir whom the world did not know.

Two years later, after I had been asked to write his life story, I set out to search into his beginnings. The war in Europe made it impossible for me to visit Scotland, although in doing so a few years before, I had gathered some impressions of his racial background. However, I did spend nearly a year in his old Wisconsin haunts, living in his boyhood home at Hickory Hill Farm, in Portage, in Prairie du Chien, and at the University of Wisconsin. I also followed him up into Canada, and then down to Indianapolis, to find what memories of him still lingered in those regions.

Out of all my garnerings east and west — an embarrassment of riches — I formed a fairly clear conception of the youth and mature life of John Muir, who with all his planes and contrasts was a strongly individualized, consistent human being. I came to the conclusion that, far from being an effeminate plaster saint, all sweetness and light, as some of his admirers have conceived him, he was in truth red-blooded and intensely masculine; a mystic, yet a realist with his feet on the ground; a lover of solitude, yet gregarious and often a prey to bitter loneliness; frugal in supplying his own needs, but lavishly generous to others; a man of puckish humor and of stern, dour moods. Infinitely gentle and understanding in his friendships, and toward the young, the old, and all defenseless creatures, he was blazingly intolerant of bigotry and every form of social callousness. Although mellowed in maturity and more humorous in his judgments, he was still a fighter, an arch enemy of all encroachments in the name of "progress" upon human or animal rights. Bailey Millard, the journalist, who knew him in his late years, said he was "wild as a Modoc and as unafraid," and as hard to tackle "as a grizzly."

As he grew beyond the narrow Scottish environment of his boyhood, all humanity became his clan, and his beliefs were as unfettered by institutions as the wilderness he loved. Deeply impregnated with that germ of democracy that brought millions of immigrants to America in the nineteenth century, he went out from the University of Wisconsin a pioneer of a new way of life. Other gifted sons of immigrants, sharing in that same urge toward freedom and equality, became sociologists, historians, and political leaders. It was John Muir's destiny to lead men back to a realization of their origins as children of nature. "In God's wildness lies the hope of the world," he said. He dared to dream of a day, and to work for it, when our Government would cherish this wildness as a perpetual heritage of raw resources for all the people, and a source of healing for body and spirit, and of faculties fostered into fulfillment by intimate communion with the Great Mother.

Muir, learning his economics from nature, found co-operation to be the universal law. "Everything is hitched to everything else," he declared. "Each for all and all for each." Man alone had become an alien, predatory element, bringing about unbalance in nature by his ruthless exploitation of the wilderness; just as in his boasted civilization, organized on the competitive, survival-of-the-strongest basis, he had brought unbalance in the form of wars, revolutions, and widespread human misery. Hence John Muir turned his back upon wealth and position, "to be true to my own instincts." That he might grow and ripen untrammeled in the heart of nature, he became "a tramp." In the fullness of time he came down from the mountains leading a crusade to release men from their shells and prisons in towns and houses, prisons of religion, politics, and commerce. "A supersalesman of Nature," someone has called him; his was a new voice in America.

Emphasis has been placed in this book upon Muir the pragmatist, the down-to-earth realist. Hence no extended effort has been made to portray him as a mystic and intuitionist except as these phases of his genius played their part in the events of his life. But truly he was a seer worthy of study. Here was a man who saw home to the heart of things and spoke as one having authority. The Divine Logos was with him from the beginning. His philosophy came not from plodding among syllogisms, but sprang full-grown from the Unconscious. The thoughts set down by him in his earliest journals, concerning life, death, and human society, remained granite truths to him to the end. In his scientific work as a geologist in the special field of glaciation, he was a reasoner as well. By following up his initial intuitions with years of painstaking investigation, he evolved theories more nearly modern than those of other scientists of his time working in the same field. Indeed, throughout his life intuition and reason went hand in hand, thus balancing and giving substance to his idealism.

Much more might be told of his innumerable warm friendships and his family life if space allowed. Because the latter has been a subject of misrepresentation, however, I have made a special effort to reveal him as a husband and father. My information has come from those best qualified to give it — his daughters, other relatives, and friends who saw much of his home life — and also from family letters. It all adds up to a consistent testimony. I have had no desire to prettify him, only to tell the truth. Prominence has been given to his wife for her selfless devotion. As his silent partner and "best counsellor," she deserves credit along with himself for the humanitarian labors of his maturity.

As to the last great controversy of Muir's public life, let me say that it is with sincere reluctance and no wish to arouse old local bitternesses that I have told the story of the Hetch Hetchy fight. But it has been impossible to omit that supreme struggle that consumed the energies of his last dozen years, cut down his literary output by several books, and shortened his life-span.

The whole story of his leadership in conservation would fill a large book by itself. Its highlights are related here. Only those who, inspired by his message, took up the cause and fought by his side through the years know how great a share his guiding hand played in the growth of the movement throughout the nation. "His work was not sectional but for the whole people," said Robert Underwood Johnson, "for he was the real father of the forest reservations in America."[4] And Enos Mills declared: "The grandest character in national park history . . . is John Muir."[5]

LINNIE MARSH WOLFE

Berkeley, California

ACKNOWLEDGMENTS

THE MEMORIES and assistance of scores of people in several states have gone into the background of this book. Among so many I can list only those outstanding in their contributions. For intimate family memories I owe most to John Muir's two daughters, whom I have mentioned in the Preface, and to Mr. Thomas Rae Hanna, his son-in-law; also to his nieces, Mrs. May Reid Coleman, Mrs. Helen Hand Moore, Miss Cecelia Galloway; and to his grandniece, Mrs. Marjorie Shone. Close to this inner circle are James Foster, Mrs. Jeannie Foster Guidinger, and Mrs. Maude Watson, related to the Muir family by marriage.

Special acknowledgments are due to William E. Colby, friend and co-worker of John Muir and Secretary of the Sierra Club, for much information and valuable criticism upon the portions of the manuscript dealing with conservation. I am equally indebted to François E. Matthes of the United States Geological Survey, for counsel and criticism upon those pages relating to Muir's scientific background and his glacial investigations.

For Muir lore in Wisconsin — still a living thing in that home of his youth — I give my sincere thanks to the Misses Jessie and Annie Duncan, Mrs. Daniel Brown, Chauncey Cairns, Harry W. Kearns, and other residents of Marquette County too numerous to mention; also to William Breese, Mr. and Mrs. Elisha B. Maltbey, Miss Mary Porter, and John Smith of Portage. Among those in Madison and at the University of Wisconsin who helped me uncover the past are Professor-Emeritus William D. Frost, Albert O. Barton, Professor F. A. Aust, Frederick L. Holmes, and the Misses Alice and Bettina Jackson. For long and patient aid in research I am indebted to the staffs of the University of Wisconsin Library and the Wisconsin State Historical Society Library and Museum, especially to Dr. Joseph Schafer, Dr. Louise Phelps Kellogg, Miss Alice Smith, and Mr. Charles E. Brown. Other residents of Wisconsin who have given valued aid are State Geologist E. F. Bean, Mrs. Frank Dreher, Mrs. Annabel Hinman, Mrs. Burr Jones, Mrs.

McBride Sumner, and Dr. Peter Lawrence Scanlon. To this group, as former residents of Wisconsin, also belong Miss Isabelle Thayer, later of Pacific Grove, California; Mrs. Grace Sterling Lindsley of Stockton, California; Mr. Charles G. Sterling of Wheaton, Illinois; and Mrs. H. J. Taylor of Berkeley, California, to whom I owe much for information and introductions in Madison.

Residents of Canada who gave generously of their time and knowledge are L. H. Beamer of Meaford, Archie Trout, and W. B. Dowkes of Owens Sound.

For memories of Muir's life and work in Indianapolis, I am deeply grateful to the Misses Ellen and Jane Graydon of that city, and to Samuel Merrill of Pasadena, California.

Among numerous friends of Muir or his family who have given me information of his life in the West are Mrs. Helen Swett Artieda, Frank Swett, William Magee, Charles Keeler, Dr. John Wright Buckham, J. E. Calkins, Norman Sisson, Mr. and Mrs. Carlton E. Durrell, Mrs. Helen Lukens Gaut, Gertrude Hutchings Mills, Robert Moran, Mrs. Marion Randall Parsons, Mrs. Brooks Palmer, Professor William Ritter, and A. C. Warner.

To National Park officials in Washington, D.C., and elsewhere in the park system I am grateful for access to valuable Government files in the nation's capital and for manifold courtesies in my research journey across the continent. I would especially mention A. B. Cammerer, former Director of National Parks; Major O. A. Tomlinson and Herbert Maier, Director and Associate Director of Region IV, and Dorr Yeager, head of the Regional Museum Laboratories; also Park Superintendents Frank A. Kittredge, Frank Bean, Colonel John White, John E. Doerr, and Preston P. Macy. Others who have aided me are C. A. Harwell, former Chief Naturalist of the Yosemite National Park, and Oscar Nelson, former Assistant Superintendent of Mount Rainier National Park.

Officials of the United States Forest Service in Washington, D.C., and the staffs of the Forest Products Laboratory at the University of Wisconsin, and the California Forest and Range Experiment Station at the University of California, have been most co-operative. Wallace I. Hutchinson, Assistant Regional Forester of California, has also been cordially helpful.

ACKNOWLEDGMENTS

For unfailing assistance through the years I wish to pay tribute to Milton G. Armstrong and Mrs. Isabelle Longbourne, who have painstakingly transcribed for me a mass of dim Muir manuscripts and notes. And for other valued services too varied to list here, I give my thanks to Mrs. William Frederic Badè; Francis P. Farquhar of the Sierra Club; Mrs. Anna George DeMille, daughter of Henry George; the Honorable Bertrand W. Gearhart, Congressman from California; Mrs. Mabel Young Sanborn, daughter of Brigham Young; Miss Harlean James, Secretary of the American Planning and Civic Association; and William G. Schultz, conservationist. Also indispensable has been the aid rendered by Miss Susan T. Smith, City Librarian of Berkeley, and her staff; Miss Mary Barmby, former Librarian of Alameda County, and her staff; and the staffs of the Library of Congress, the Bancroft Library of the University of California, and the Library of the Pacific School of Religion in Berkeley.

For permission to quote from published and unpublished writings I am grateful to Mrs. Enos Mills; Mrs. Charlotte Kellogg; Mrs. Charles Keeler; August Derleth, biographer of Zona Gale; Mrs. Sadie Mitchell, daughter of James Whitehead; Owen Johnson, son of Robert Underwood Johnson; Roland Harriman, son of E. H. Harriman; Mrs. Adeline Barrus Johnson, sister of Dr. Clara Barrus; Mrs. Mary McHenry Keith; her niece Miss Elizabeth Keith Pond; and Brother Cornelius, biographer of William Keith; also to Clifton J. Furness, Mrs. Vernon Bailey, and Mrs. Theodore Roosevelt, Sr.

Among the publishers who have allowed me to quote from published books, I am first of all indebted to the Houghton Mifflin Company for permission to refer extensively to the writings of Muir, and to those of John Burroughs and Thérèse Yelverton. Other publishers who have kindly permitted me to use passages are Little, Brown & Company, the Fleming H. Revell Company, Farrar & Rinehart, Inc., and the Sierra Club.

Finally I wish to express appreciation to Alfred A. Knopf, and to J. R. de la Torre Bueno, Jr., Wilson Follett, and Clinton Simpson, for helpful criticism and advice in preparing my manuscript for publication.

CONTENTS

ILLUSTRATIONS

ILLUSTRATIONS

ILLUSTRATIONS

SON OF THE WILDERNESS

PART I

1849–1860

A STERN HERITAGE

RAY DAWN was paling the tops of the smoke-shrouded mountains of southeastern Lanarkshire, Scotland. Murky shadows still smothered the moors and small crofts on the foothills below when out from a huddle of thatched farm cots stole the slender form of a youth with a pack on his back. He glanced sharply about to see that no one else was astir. Then without looking behind him he quickened his long-legged pace out of the gate and down the winding road that led toward Glasgow.

On this summer morning of the year 1825 Daniel Muir was running away from the home where he had lived since childhood with his sister Mary and her shepherd-farmer husband, Hamilton Blakley.

Mists veil the origin of the Muir family. We do know, however, that they belonged to the Gordon clan and must therefore have had their ancient home in northeastern Scotland between Inverness and the sea. And there is reason to believe they were swept southward during the clearances that followed the Jacobite uprisings of the eighteenth century.

The last uprising had been staged in 1745 when that Stuart known to legend as Bonnie Prince Charlie barged down into England with his pipers and kilted warriors to dethrone the Hanoverian King, only to be chased back to the Highlands two jumps ahead of the English troops led by the Duke of Cumberland, known as "The Butcher." The Duke, catching up with the ragged remnant at Culloden Moor, near Inverness, slaughtered nearly all of them. Then began a mopping-up campaign in which the clansmen were destroyed on a wholesale scale or driven out from their crags and glens, their hereditary crofts being converted into great sheep-raising estates to supply southern factory towns with wool and mutton.

The bolder clansmen who survived scattered over the earth. Some fiery spirits went to fight in Continental wars and revolutions. Others migrated to new lands to blaze trails for kinsmen to follow. But the mass of these land-loving people, including the Muirs, drifted southward, to languish in the coal mines and factories of Lanarkshire or find shallow rootage on barren rented plots in that or other Lowland shires.

True Highlanders as they were, the Muirs had an untamable passion for liberty. In Edinburgh one Thomas Muir was banished in 1793 for espousing the rights of the submerged classes. He died in exile and his body was brought back at the expense of the poor he had defended. Over his grave they placed a stone graven with words he had spoken at his trial: "I have devoted myself to the cause of the people. It is a good cause. It shall ultimately prevail. It shall ultimately triumph."

One branch of the Muirs found harbor in southeastern Lanarkshire on a small tenant farm, near the village of Crawfordjohn. From this region John Muir I, wanting to escape his narrow environment, enlisted in the British Army. Stationed in the manufacturing city of Manchester, England, he married an English wife, Sarah Higgs, and to them were born two children — Mary in 1793, Daniel in 1804. Both parents died soon after Daniel's birth, and the children were sent back to Lanarkshire to live and toil with their relatives. Mary watched over her brother from infancy, and when she married Hamilton Blakley, a neighboring sheep-farmer, she took the boy to live with her.

So Daniel grew up a restless, hot-hearted, tall, handsome lad, endowed with musical talent, a fine tenor voice, and deft hands that were always whittling and carving. With little outlet for his gifts, he sang while he worked, and sculped even the turnips in the fields into snowy little images of carts and horses.

When the Highland young folk gathered among the crofts to dance and sing, he joined them. His lusty voice and good looks soon made him a leader. But he liked best to listen to the screaming fiddles playing the mad old strathspeys and reels and marching airs of their ancestral glens. These were like strong wine in his blood, giving him dreams that teemed and surged against the narrow bounds of his existence. And they put an itch into his fingers to play a fiddle of his own.

One night he held one hungrily in his hands. Then, toiling after work hours, he made a fiddle for himself. The night it was finished he ran ten miles in a smother of wind and rain to a village store to buy cat-gut strings. Before long he could play all the psalm tunes, ballads, and wild northern airs he had ever heard.

During adolescence he found another outlet in religion. When fourteen he was "converted." Emotion, which he called "the ecstasy of the Apostles," flooded his soul, and he spent the rest of his life striving to recapture and retain it. The Bible became to him textbook and teacher — the only book a man needed from birth to the grave. At night by the light of a peat fire, he pored over the Scriptures, enthralled by the beauty and terror of the Old Testament and the Book of Revelation. The sulphurous preachments heard on the Sabbath, seared into his mind the same ineradicable pictures of a God of Wrath and a Lake of Fire. In all his after-seekings through the sects he remained a Calvinist in his conception of God.

Life on earth became an everlasting tug of war between God and Satan to possess man's soul. Salvation could be attained only by a perpetual state of emotional excitement, called "worshipping the Lord." To relax for one hour was to risk falling into hell-fire. Thus Daniel Muir became obsessed with "the devil-worship called Christianity," [1] which swept Great Britain and America in the nineteenth century.

But not even religion made him content with his lowly station. He wanted wealth and power, in the Old World inseparably tied up with landownership. But the whole structure of society and the laws of the land were against the rise of the common man. Only the near-sterile spots were rented to crofters, and the leases could be canceled at will by the owners. Even on their precarious holdings the farmers were often forbidden to cut peat for fuel, or pasture a horse. Women and little children toiled in the fields, doing the work of horses. Daniel's son John must have had in mind his father's

[1] All notes will be found at the end of the volume, beginning with page 351.

youthful environment and its effects upon character when he wrote: ". . . men that grow in hard countries, are gnarled, bent, stunted, full of individuality, but lacking in full-rounded symmetry."

However, seeking escape from these harsh, body- and soul-enslaving conditions, Daniel in his teens heard of America, where, he was told, vast tracts of land could be had for a song, with no leases and no masters, where any man with brains and energy could rise to be a laird. His imagination took fire. Every Highlander had "the wandering foot," he more than most. So in his twenty-first year he ran away in the dawn toward Glasgow, his Bible and his fiddle on his back, a few shillings in his jeans, his blue eyes deep-set and glowing in his bronzed and brown-bearded young face.

Arriving in Glasgow — that great bottleneck of wretched humanity — he walked the streets in search of a job to earn his ship fare to America. But there were no jobs open to able-bodied men. While he had been growing up on an isolated farm, vast world changes had come about. The Napoleonic Wars had made England the great mercantile nation of the earth; but when they ended, in 1815, British trade went into an abysmal slump. Ships rotted in all the harbors. Factories and mines were closed down. Every industrial city became a center of tumultuous, starving multitudes. Even the women and children who had toiled like slaves in the coal pits and at the spindles, because they were cheaper to hire than men, were laid off. The demobilized armies, unable to find jobs, stampeded and rioted through the country, threatening another Reign of Terror.

After seven or eight years trade began to revive. The expanding Empire had developed new markets in the Americas, Africa, and the Orient. The factories and mines of England and Scotland were reopened. Gold once more flowed into the country, making the mercantile class richer, but doing little to lighten the lot of the workers. They were forbidden to organize. Wages were low. Women were hired again, and children apprenticed into virtual slavery; while mobs of unemployed men still roamed and rioted for food.

One day while Daniel Muir was tramping the streets, faint and giddy with hunger — his last ha'penny gone — he came upon a sidewalk recruiting station, where sleek, well-fed redcoats lay in wait for such as he. He passed — then came back — and signed away his dreams of freedom.

Daniel, lithe, upstanding, about six feet tall, made an ideal soldier. Food and the braw uniform of a Scotch regiment soon restored his self-respect and converted the crude country boy into a dashing, masterful fellow. In 1829 he was sent as a recruiting sergeant to Dunbar, on the east coast of Scotland, to enlist other youths in the Army.

Sergeant Muir had lost nothing of his religious fanaticism. Indeed, he now practiced it with stern military discipline — a discipline that in future years would make of his home a concentration camp. On the Sunday after his arrival in Dunbar he made his way up Kirkbrae Hill to the Presbyterian Church, where he caused somewhat of a flutter among the lassies with his good looks, his fine regimentals, and the gusto with which he sang the Psalms.

The ancient and royal burgh of Dunbar was at this time a fairly prosperous town of perhaps 5000 inhabitants. Embosomed in an amphitheater of hills, its quaint, crooked streets straggled down to the beaches and harbor that lay just south of the mouth of the Firth of Forth and faced the North Sea. For centuries it had been known as "a fisher toon." Nature's economy had never failed to bring rich harvests through the seasons, of herring, crabs, white fish, and lemon sole. Stretching west and south of the town, the fat, alluvial farmlands of East Lothian yielded fine crops of corn, wheat, and potatoes. Coal, too, was mined in the vicinity.

But even with this natural wealth there was much poverty in Dunbar. Before the machine age the cottars had made a good living weaving on hand looms in their homes. But mass production had put them out of work. Cotton mills built in the war era had helped for a while; but in the slump that followed, these had been closed and never reopened. Many of the weavers had crowded into the cities to beg for work at any wage. Others were still in Dunbar, either starving or living upon the spasmodic charity of the more fortunate. Daniel Muir's son John was to be haunted all his years by the memory of the poor of Dunbar: bent, gnarled old people living like animals under hedgerows and haystacks and in fence corners, creeping out by day to beg or steal; the wan faces of children looking hungrily in at shop windows where food was displayed.

Before Daniel Muir had been long in Dunbar, he married a young heiress to a thriving grain-and-food store. But owing to her lack of training the business was rapidly declining when the canny young bridegroom persuaded his wife to buy his release from the Army that he might manage her affairs. Collecting what he could of the scrambled bills, he bought new stock and opened his doors to a strictly cash-and-carry trade. He soon established a reputation for that rigid honesty that was to make his name a household word in far-away Wisconsin. "Good scripture measure, heaped up, shaken together and running over, he meted out to all," his son John once said of him. Before long he was making money hand over fist.[2]

His first marriage was of short duration. His wife died, leaving him the sole heir to her property.

At some time before or after her death he bought a large three-story stone building on the High Street, in the best business district of the town. Enlarging his stock, he moved in on the ground floor.

Across the street was a similar three-story building bearing the sign: "Gilrye Place," chiseled into the stone tablet above the entrance. In the upper rooms of this house lived the owner, David Gilrye (pronounced *Gil-rī'*), a well-to-do retired flesher, or seller of meat, with his wife and daughters. Margaret was married to Captain John Rae. Since he was away most of the time on long trading voyages, she with their little girl, Maggie, lived in her father's house.

Ann, the younger daughter, was a tall, quiet, gray-eyed girl who loved nature and took long solitary rambles about the countryside. In a modest way she was gifted in drawing and painting and even wrote poetry.

David Gilrye, having shortened his family name of Gilderoy, had come to Dunbar in 1794 from Northumberland. The Gilderoys had sprung from the Highlands, where one roistering blade of the clan, in the time of Queen Mary, had won notoriety in Perthshire as "the Robin Hood of Scottish Minstrelsy." He with his wild followers had preyed upon the rich Clan Stuart, making such a pest of himself to all save romantic maidens that a reward of a thousand pounds was set upon his head. Percy's *Reliques* contains the lament of one of the fair ones left desolate by his execution.

Soon after coming to Dunbar, David Gilrye had married Margaret Hay of Coldstream, also of the Border country. The Hay family, originally a Highland clan, had scattered far and wide through the eastern Lowlands, intermarrying with their sturdy Saxon neighbors. From this stock stemmed many distinguished men — architects, engineers, soldiers, and leaders among the gentry. One Captain Hay, with his picked cavalry, had fought with Wallace to put the Bruce on the throne. The Marquis of Tweeddale, hereditary chieftain of the clan, served for many years under Queen Victoria as Lord-Lieutenant of Scotland. But the Hays were proudest of the fact that one of their blood had died a martyr to his Covenanting faith when King Charles tried by violence to foist the Episcopacy upon the Presbyterian Scots.

David and his wife had been blessed with ten children. But the white plague had ravaged their home, and eight lay in the kirkyard on the hill. Their two daughters, Margaret and Ann, however, both lived to hale old age.

Within a year after his first wife's death Daniel Muir was courting Ann Gilrye. This caused some buzz of disapproval among her friends. They felt the young merchant was beneath her in social station. Ann was a Hay, and the Hays were gentry. She could marry gentry, if she wanted to.

But the main opposition came from David, her father. Being an "Established man" himself, and an elder of the kirk, he was distressed when his voluble would-be son-in-law criticized orthodox doctrines and customs such as election and the patronage system. Moreover, Daniel was forever talking about zeal. Because the kirk folk weren't always praying and shouting to the Lord, he thought they lacked zeal. "Yon wants a body to think and act his way," said David. "An' ye don't, he says ye're nae a true Christian."

But the gentle Ann had a mind of her own. So early in the year

1833 Mr. Jaffrey, minister of the kirk, united them in marriage, and the young couple went to live across the street in the rooms above Daniel's store.

All went well, thanks to Ann's sense of her wifely duty to adjust her life to her husband's ideas, strange as some of them seemed. Scotchwomen were brought up to believe that under God a man was master in his own household. His decisions were not to be questioned.

Soon she learned that her husband didn't want any adornments in the house. He banned all pictures from the wall by quoting pontifically: "Thou shalt not make unto thee any graven image." All her pretty landscapes and exquisite pieces of cross-stitch needlework were "folderols" and had to be hidden out of sight or given back to her mother. When they sat down to a meal, she was told it was a sacrament; hence there must be no unseemly talk or jesting. Ann had a quiet, bubbling humor, and it was hard at first to quell it. But as time went on she spoke less and seldom laughed out loud, not sulking, but bottling up her thoughts and fun inside herself. At the center of her being was an impregnable citadel, and within that Ann Muir lived in tranquil independence. "I am always happy at the center," her son John often said in his years of stress and hardship. This stability was his most precious heritage from his mother.

She and her husband had one joy in common — the long high-walled garden stretching back from their house. In the midst of it stood a great spreading elm, while pear and apple trees were espaliered against the sunny stone wall. Low boxwood hedges bordered the paths. In this garden Daniel Muir gathered choice plants. He even helped his sister-in-law, Margaret Rae, make for herself a plot of lilies, for he had a poet's delight in the soft texture and color of flowers. Their loveliness was the Lord's gift, and no stern Biblical command inhibited him from loving and enjoying them. Ann, loving them too, worked happily with him in the garden until the babies began to come.

Children were born to Daniel and Ann Muir in fairly rapid succession. First, in 1834, came Margaret; Sarah two years later.

After another two years, on April 21, 1838, John was born. He bore, as in later life, a marked resemblance to his father, with his bright blue eyes and ruddy silken brown hair. As he grew older, he was like his father in other respects. He had the same eager, questing mind, the same impassioned, beauty-loving spirit, and the same deft hands. There was much of his mother in him too — something anchored as upon a rock. In other words, he was both Gael and Saxon. After still another space of two years David followed John. Three years later came Daniel, Jr. Finally, one morning in October 1846, John awoke in the dawn to find his father bending over him in great excitement. "Go ben ye're mither's room and see your twin sisters," he said. These were named Mary and Annie.

Very early in life John felt it his duty as the eldest son to shield his brothers and sisters from all harm. One of his first acts was to bite the doctor who vaccinated David. "I wasna gan to let him hurt my bonnie brither," he exclaimed angrily. He was like a tigress defending her young. He acquired more civilized methods later on, but throughout life he remained their strong protector and friend.

A sturdy, average middle-class family they were in those early years. They had servants, so nobody had to work very hard; and two doting grandparents across the street; also kind Aunt Rae, with her precious lily garden, which John looked upon as something "sacred and beyond price."

And always there was Mother, quietly wise and understanding. She was a refuge in all the ills of life. Her strong and tender arms healed the hurts of body and spirit — as when John thought he had swallowed his tongue; and when the "shining soldier" robbed the robin's nest in the elm tree and carried away the fledglings to be sold to buy beer.

Father, too, could be a delightful person. He loved his children, and their presence smoothed away many a frown and made him shout with jollity. Then Mother laughed too, a clear, ringing, wholesome laugh it did one good to hear. (At other times you had to see the quirk of her mouth to know she was laughing inside.) John recalled long afterward the fun that lighted up the household when Father came home in a happy mood. "There were sterner memories later on"; but not yet.

Sometimes on a holiday such as New Year's — Christmas was not made much of because it smacked of Papacy — they would beg Father to "lift the fiddle." Then, taking it out of its cloth shroud, he would play ballads and hymn tunes for them to sing. They all developed good voices and under his leadership became a singing family. In years to come this bound and kept them together in spite of temperamental differences. Father was always gentle when he tucked the old hand-made instrument under his chin. His eyes would shine, and his hands seemed to caress the thing of wood and strings. Sometimes in those early years he played the wild, braggart airs of his long-descended race, born among the stern, storm-swept tors and crags of the northland. But although John liked those tunes best, his father after a while refused to play them. He seemed to be trying to stamp out in himself and his children their pagan inheritance and to substitute for it a culture wholly Hebraic. Even his everyday speech became a composite of Biblical phrases. Not until he mellowed into a wiser old age did he again play the Highland airs. Someone who then heard him said it was an experience never to be forgotten.

But Daniel Muir failed utterly to crush in his eldest son, John, his ancestral instincts and emotions. The clouds of glory the boy came trailing into the world, no prison-house could ever shut away.

From the first there was rivalry between Margaret and Sarah as to who should be "John's Little Mother." It was the custom for the eldest daughter to mother the eldest son, and so on down the family. But even after David came, Sarah was unwilling to surrender her claim. A kinship of mind between these twain endured through the years. It was Sarah who first recognized something beyond the ordinary in her brother. "We expect great things of you, John," she often said. After he left home, it was to Sarah he turned in his letters for an understanding the others were unable to give.

Grandfather Gilrye was John's first teacher. As soon as the child was out of the cradle, his extraordinary vitality and ingenuity in escaping all bounds created a family problem. "The verra deevil's in that boy," his perplexed father would say. But his animal spirits found a partial outlet when his grandfather began taking him on walks. The grizzled, beetle-browed old man limping along on his cane, leading an impish little boy with a Glengarry cap awry on his tousled brown hair, became a daily sight on the High Street. Halting now and then and pointing his cane at a sign above a shop, Grandfather would name the letters and tell what they said. John never forgot. When they passed the Town Hall with its squat Flemish tower and dialed clock, Grandfather taught him the numerals and how to tell the time of day. The ancient horologe gave the boy a kind of clock complex. Later he began to whittle clocks of his own and harness their motor-power.

As his legs grew longer and sturdier, their walks extended. Often they ambled down to the waterfront to see the yawls and trawlers come in with their cargoes of shining fish. The boy liked to watch the great boats gently rocking off shore, their decks piled with ropes, nets, and creaking winches. And out there where the firth died in the sea, there was often a covey of sailing vessels waiting for wind and tide to carry them up to Edinburgh, while far out on the horizon, when the day was fair, they could see the schooners plying by, their white canvas bellying in the wind. At a very early age John began to whittle ships of his own to sail on pools. A little later he was drawing pictures of them on the flyleaves of all his school books.

As time went on, there were longer walks, along country roads, where John scampered about like a puppy. One day they clambered over a low stone dike into a field. Grandfather sat down on a haycock to rest. It was a day John would long remember; for as he paused in his gyrations, his ears caught a tiny, anguished "needle-sharp voice" from somewhere in the tawny, tangled heap. Instantly he was down on his knees frantically scratching away the old man's seat from under him. There in the hay he found a mother field mouse with a litter of naked pink babies clinging to her teats.

When John reached the age of three, he was sent to school. On that first day he set forth in jaunty kilt of Gordon plaid, carrying suspended from his neck a small green bag that flapped in the wind. It contained his first book — a primer costing four cents. Down the street he went, pulled reluctantly along by Margaret and Sarah to the high-walled Davel Brae schoolyard close by the sea. The girls left him at the primary building while they went on to the grammar school.

Mungo Siddons was a kindly old dominie who tempered his leatherin's to small boys and occasionally doled out currants and gooseberries to his charges. His morning sternness was mellowed as the day advanced by frequent trips to his own house, less than ten yards away, where, it was rumored, he fortified himself between classes "wi' a wee drap o' whuskey."

On this eventful day the dominie assigned John a seat midway down the room. But, not being used to such straitlaced inactivity, he squirmed and fidgeted about until pop went a button somewhere in his nether garments, with the result that when he sprang from his seat at recess and leaped out the door, his red petticoat fell unnoticed.[3] Somebody else spied it, though, and carried it up to the master. When school resumed, he held it high for all to see, and boomed: "Wha has lost his petticoat?"

An agonizing pause ensued while John wished the earth would open up and swallow him. Then a hand waved wildly, and a big boy bellowed: "It's Johnny Moor's. I saw him drap it." How John did hate that fellow as he stumbled up to claim his property!

The rigid discipline prescribed in Scottish schools was designed to turn out a tough-fibered race. "The whole educational system was founded on leather," John Muir once said. Hot-blooded youth however, contrived to make the most of each fleeting moment Someone said of Muir when he was a grown man: "He knew how to catch fun on the fly." Perhaps he learned how in the old Davel Brae school, for the wildest din and disorder broke loose the instant the dominie left the room. The floor became the arena of wrestling, rolling, panting boys, pommeling one another's faces — until at a given signal from the outpost they all sprang back to their seats, and a suspicious quiet reigned when the refreshed master entered, "clothed in awful authority," bringing his upraised stick down on his desk with a resounding whack as he roared *"Silence!"*

But it was out on the playground and up Davel Brae that "the ancient inherited belligerence in our pagan blood" had full play Opposing armies were quickly formed to settle the all-importan

ANN GILRYE MUIR
photo taken in 1863

DANIEL MUIR, *painted from memory after his death by his daughter, Mary Muir Hand*

Muir's birthplace, Dunbar, Scotland. Later the Lorne Temperance Hotel

question of who was "boss." An impudent stare or dare set up a status of strained relations, and before you could say Jack Robinson, the war was on. Sticks, stones, snow, or sand stuffed into blue bonnets made good ammunition. With this exhausted, they came to close grips, kicking, gouging, and tearing clothes. When both sides were out of breath and lathered with sweat and blood, one of the losers would shout: "Hi, I'll tell ye what we'll do wi' ye. You let us alone, an' we'll let ye alone!" Whereupon friend and foe went peacefully back to classes or home to tea.

Foot races were much in vogue. The steep road up Davel Brae was the favored course. When school was dismissed for the day, the boys and girls alike swooped out of the building like a flock of birds to the starting-place. Thanks to his nimble legs, John usually reached the top first. But one day that tomboy Agnes Purns caught up with him, passed him on the slope, and reached the goal a full yard ahead. To be beaten by a girl was almost as shameful as losing your petticoat. After that whenever he could slip out of the house in the evening before curfew, John might have been seen running up the brae, holding his breath. Before long he became champion of the racing matches.

At the age of seven or eight John Muir entered the grammar school, presided over by Dominie Lyon. Here the daily warfare began all over again on a more ferocious scale. If you were a new scholar, all the rest ganged up on you, and you had to meet every challenger. Almost as important as trouncing your opponent was being able to take defeat on the chin. "Ye mauna greet, You must not cry," was the code of every "gude fechter." When the dominie brought down the tawse on your bare hands or your back, you just stood and took it with the stoicism of a wild Indian at the torture stake. All this, of course, was good training for a boy who aspired to be a soldier. And what red-blooded young Scot didn't yearn to become another Wallace or Bruce or Bonnie Prince Charlie?

John and his mates were steeped in the heroic lore of their country. Some of it came from history books and readers. Most of it came from parents, servant maids, or one another. "The boys were always telling stories of wars," said John Muir. And not content just to tell them, these young Hotspurs had to choose up sides and fight them out on the actual spots where they had taken place. They couldn't have found a bloodier ground in all Scotland than "the royal red city of Dunbar."

For more than a thousand years the stronghold of Dunbar Castle, which the warlike Picts built after they drove back the Romans, had stood on its black basaltic rocks, facing the sea like a vulture, to guard the rich inland farms and the firth waterway that led to Edinburgh, the ancient Dunedin of the Gaels.

The boys knew all the legends of the castle. When they played among the haunted battlements, they could almost see the phantom ships of the English invaders sweeping in to besiege and destroy, or hear the ghostly hoofbeats of the horse of Edward II as he came fleeing from Bannockburn to take refuge in the fortress. Queen Mary and her wild man Bothwell, they could fancy, might still be living in North Tower as they had in those last tragic weeks before they met their doom of imprisonment with death at the end.

When the tide was out, the boys often explored the damp, winding caverns beneath the castle. Here they played games of dare which they called "scootchers." Dungeons were there that never saw the light of day until the sea, eternally gnawing, had broken down in places the thick, solid masonry. One of these was blacker and deeper than the others, and to descend into it, they decided, should be the biggest scootcher of all. Danger was a challenge to John Muir even at that tender age. Instinctive within him was a will to master every difficulty. So he climbed down into the infernal pit, finding handholds and footholds on the rough walls. He reached bottom and came up again. Henceforth he identified it with hell. One day, so the story goes, a servant girl scolded him for some naughtiness, telling him he would go to hell when he died. "Weel, an I do," answered John, "I'll climb out o' it. I ken I can, because I did!"

John Muir had imbibed Scotch balladry with the air he breathed. To the end of his life he could recite or sing all the ballads he had ever heard. Somewhere on a scrap of paper among his notes is scribbled in pencil: "My first conscious memory is of the singing of ballads, and I doubt not they will be ringing in my ears when I am dying."

But along with the romantic legends he had heard the stark prose of history. For the Scots have a streak of hard realism running parallel with their sentimentality. The centuries-long struggle of an indomitable people was a living thing as of yesterday. "The very thoughts of it do to this very day strike terror into them," said a historian of Muir's day. For the farmers and burghers of East Lothian got the brunt of every war until they were racially sick of the whole ghastly business. Each succeeding army of invasion or civil war, sweeping like a scourge over the countryside, levied money and provisions and often laid everything waste. Dunbar had been sacked times without number and had been burned to the ground at least twice. The yeomanry had been at the disposal of whatever chieftain was in control at the moment. Common folk were but pawns in the game.

The religious wars were no kinder than the political ones. Horrible atrocities were committed by Catholics and Protestants alike. The Covenanters were hunted down like wild beasts on the moors by the soldiers of Stuart kings on the throne of England, because they worshipped the same God in a different manner. Then came Cromwell.

Many a Saturday afternoon the Muir boys and their schoolmates gathered southwest of the town on the slopes of Doonhill, blood-soaked since the time of the Romans, to fight over again with sticks and stones that final battle in which the Cromwellians, with real swords, had mowed down their fellow Protestants "like stubble," slaughtering 3,000 of them, and taking 9,000 captive.

In the war games of his school days John Muir learned history the hard way. Fighting now on one side, now on the other, to avenge some ancient wrong, he earned the proud title, "a gude fechter." But a few years later he saw how foolish were the causes for which he and his ancestors had shed their blood. War, he said, was "the farthest-reaching and most infernal of all civilized calamities."[4] This was his feeling about the Civil War in America, for which he refused to volunteer. In old age when he related to some friends the story of those boyhood battles, he commented:

"And so a peace was declared something like that between Japan and Russia. They simply glared at each other, and then quit! That's about how most wars end, you know. They start talking about honor, or something or other, and declare this and so — a boys' war — a big boys' war — no sense in it!"

Home life in the Muir household was also designed to toughen the fiber. About the time John started to school, his father began to set him a daily stint of learning a hymn or a few verses from the Bible. At first the rewards were rather pleasant, as when he received a penny for reciting *Rock of Ages*. There were sterner days, however, when he forgot to learn his verses until the sandman caught up with him at night. Then came punishment swift and painful. Applied to the cuticle, it woke him up and stimulated his mind. This didn't happen often, thanks to Mother's reminders and the fact that a mere glance at a printed page would fix the words upon his photographic memory.

On winter evenings there was always a delicious interim between tea and supper when the Muir children scampered over to Grandfather Gilrye's to study their lessons. But John's prime objective was the food he knew Grandmother would have ready — oatmeal bannocks and jam, or a plate of caraway-seed cakes. Growing up into a tall, gangling boy with little fat on his bones, he was always ravenously hungry. Father believed a Spartan diet was good for the soul; so tea at home consisted of a cup of "content" — hot water with milk — and a half slice of unbuttered bread.

After the inner man had been satisfied, David and John settled down by the bright ingleside to study. The main feats of the evening were to learn and recite a huge assignment of French verbs and Latin declensions, and to write compositions in those languages. "Great Scott! It was queer Latin and French!" said John Muir long afterward.

After an hour or two of this they went home to a late supper of mutton broth and barley scones. Then came family worship, at which Father talked long and fervently to the Lord. It was hard for David and John to stay awake, although when they had gone to their garret room they were bursting with new energies. John, ever fertile in scootchers, hatched up a spooky one. Nearly every Scotch home of that period had its "ghost room." An old doctor had once owned the Muir house. Now that he was dead, it was said he came back nightly to his laboratory to dabble with retorts and test-tubes. The scootcher was to open the door of this room, dash in, and try to catch him at his spectral tasks. But when they got there, all was empty save for the tall medicine glasses on a high sideboard, gleaming in the moonlight. In later years John Muir was cynical about spiritistic phenomena. Perhaps his early delvings made him so.

The dormer window of the boys' room looked out upon the garden in the rear, and on a summer's night what could be more fun than to climb out over the sill and, with billowing nightgown, hang on by a hand or even a finger? Or scramble up the steep slates to sit triumphantly astride the ridge, sniffing the salt wind from the sea?

David was a timid boy, but he could seldom refuse to follow his masterful brother. John — always a Pied Piper — made everything seem easy and alluring. Sometimes David got into a jam, as the first time he tried to climb the roof. He hadn't gone far before he began to whimper: "I canna get doon. I canna get doon."

"Dinna greet, Davie, dinna greet. I'll help ye," soothed John. "Coom awa' doon. Put your foot in my hand, an' I'll pu' ye in." So with heels resting in John's cupped hands, he was lowered gently and hauled in.

On Saturday afternoons when the sun shone bright on the fields and hills back of Dunbar, there was a battle of wits in the Muir home. Daniel didn't want his sons to go out with the other boys. The gang they moved with had become a terror to the countryside. Farmers and gamekeepers drove them off with sticks and stones and had even threatened them with guns.

John, too, was learning to swear. A good resounding oath was sweet music in his ears. He never got over his addiction to purple language. His daughter Wanda, upon being asked: "Did your father swear occasionally?" chuckled: "Yes, volubly!"

So David and John were shut up in the garden. But high stone walls and locks were no bar to John's nimbleness, and by dint of pulling David up and easing him down, the two of them often got out while their parent was serving a customer in the store. They liked to go out Belhaven way, where the larks sang in the fields and the screaming gulls followed the plowman over the red tilth.

Often the sight of pedestrians ahead on the road sent them scuttling over dikes and hawthorn hedges to avoid "dandy doctors" who might be snooping about, seizing small boys for the dissecting-rooms of Midlothian. One day when John was quite small, he went out with Willie Chisholm, a lad older than himself and apparently his evil genius. They ran up a hill west of Dunbar overlooking the firth. Leaning over a low wall, they spied two men gathering dulse on the beach below. All at once Willie made the terrifying suggestion that they were "dandy doctors." "They'll be poppin' us into their bags," said Willie, "an' takin' us awa' to Edinbory!" Whereupon they threw themselves down on the macadamized road and crawled all the way back to town. It is not recorded what happened when they arrived home with bleeding hands and knees and ravaged clothing.

But the fear of skelpings never daunted John. As he grew older, he raced over the countryside, lay in tall meadow grass to watch the larks soar, scurried up trees to rob birds' nests, scaled orchard walls bristling with broken glass, to steal green apples, snatched turnips out of wayside gardens to devour them, dirt and all, and when he was thirsty, groveled on his belly to drink from some cool burn. And the utmost that parental wrath could inflict upon this particular "little fighting, biting, climbing pagan" failed to quench his joy in these escapades.

"He grew up savagely strong," a friend once said of him. Although he didn't know it then, he was building up a body of enormous endurance for mountain-climbing later on. And being far more observant of Nature in all her manifold phases than his mates, he was storing up beneath the threshold of consciousness a wealth of memories.

As Daniel Muir grew into maturity, he increasingly tugged at his religious moorings. The spirit of democracy was abroad in the world, volcanic and untamable; and having no political outlets, he, like thousands of other lower- and middle-class men in the islands, sought it in freedom of worship. In an age still dominated by a closed Calvinist theocracy, he dared to be an iconoclast as his son was to be after him in far greater measure. Believing passionately in liberty and equality for all men, Daniel disagreed violently with the Calvinistic doctrine of election, which proclaimed certain favored individuals were preordained by God to be saved while the rest of humanity was doomed to perdition. And he protested against patronage which made the Established Church dependent upon the nobility, who selected the ministers, paid their livings, and dictated their policies.

Before he had been long in Dunbar, he withdrew from the Presbyterian kirk to which his wife and her parents belonged. After that he joined each new seceding denomination that came to the town, with the hope of finding at last the democracy and zeal he was seeking, only to be disillusioned; for each group, believing it alone possessed the keys to the Kingdom, tended to harden into a new orthodoxy with a fixed, exclusive creed.

A family crisis arose when he got around to uniting briefly with the Episcopal communion. In years to come, Sarah could recall a solemn conference at which Grandfather Gilrye stamped up and down the room, pounding the floor with his cane, and shouting: "Yon will be joining the Papacy next!"[5]

This ultimate in scandalous behavior, however, was averted when the Disciples of Christ appeared on the horizon. Thomas Campbell and his son Alexander, two Scotsmen, had for some years been preaching in Ireland, Scotland, and America a return to primitive Christianity as a basis of love and unity. Having failed to bring down the walls of bigotry within the churches, Alexander Campbell organized his followers in America into a sect called the Disciples of Christ. Following the path of pioneering, he had carried his evangel of human brotherhood westward into Ohio and adjoining states, where it did much to infuse the new West with the spirit of democracy.

Meanwhile the movement started by him in Scotland had spread from the cities to the towns and villages and even down into England. Among the Edinburgh leaders was one Philip Gray, a stationer, a personal friend of Campbell. Gray had a brother in Dunbar, who organized a group in that town. Among them Daniel Muir found at last his spiritual home.

Campbell, returning to Scotland during the forties, added great impetus to the cause. Not only did he rouse his followers to a higher tempo of enthusiasm, but he planted in their minds a driving urge to emigrate to America as a land of religious freedom, a new Utopia.

Immediately Daniel's old desire to go to America flared up again. This time he wanted to get land and wealth to carry on the Lord's work of saving souls.

Since he was a British subject, his first vague plan was to go to Canada. Disciples were forming colonies in Ontario and other Eastern provinces. Besides he had only the haziest notion of North American geography, but he had faith God would lead him to the right place.

Not having learned that democracy as well as charity should begin at home, he did not consult his wife. He simply announced they were going, and Ann, being a dutiful spouse, silently accepted the inevitable.

Everybody in the Muir home was wild with excitement except Mother as she quietly sewed and packed. As for the old people across the street, they seemed to wither all at once into feeble age as they waited, helpless to avert this final separation. Ann and the children still went freely to the Gilrye home, but the old man and Daniel had long since come to a parting of the ways. Now, however, David Gilrye injected himself into his daughter's family affairs to stipulate that she and the younger children should remain with him until a substantial home was prepared for them in America. Daniel, consenting, formed a plan to go first, taking with him John, David, and Sarah. Margaret was to remain with her mother to help care for Danny and the twins on the later journey.

David Gilrye, disappointed in both his wandering sons-in-law, drew up an ironclad will that winter of 1848, providing that at his death his property should be safely invested and administered by three trustees. The proceeds were to be sent quarterly to Mrs. Rae and Ann Muir. At the death of either, her share of the principal was to be distributed among "the heirs of her body."

While Daniel searched for a cash buyer of his store, the children remained in school. Romantic legends, even war games, were forgotten in those days of frantic excitement over the discovery of gold in California. Dominie Lyon selected for their study stories of the New World. John was thrilled no end by accounts of the natural history of America. Most of all he was entranced by Audubon's description of the passenger pigeons that "darkened the sky like clouds." But when he read how, gathering to rest and rear their young in forests, they were beaten down with poles to be fed to hogs, he was roused to a fierce hatred of human cruelty.

On the night of February 18, 1849 Father had been away at teatime and had not returned when the boys went across the street to study. All was quiet by the ingleside when he burst in at the door — a most unusual proceeding. "Bairns," he announced, "you needna learn your lessons the nicht, for we're gan to America the morn!"

The household was early astir that bleak morning of February 19. A gray mist rolled up from the sea, which froze on their cheeks as they started from the street door. Grandfather and Grandmother Gilrye emerged from the fog, and they all walked down the High Street toward the railway station.

All was wild confusion on the Glasgow dock when Daniel and the three children arrived alongside the decrepit old sailing vessel that was to be their ocean home. Crowds were milling about, weeping, laughing, chattering: newly married couples with radiant faces, going out to found homes in the New World; middle-aged folk; even very old people, who had sold everything they had to get passage-money, their eyes shining with renewed hope; long-legged Highlanders dreaming of adventure; Irish, Germans, Scandinavians, and Frenchmen jabbering about the high wages they would get working on railroads and canals, or in the pineries of Maine and Michigan; gold-seekers from every nation on their way to California; Englishmen going out as emissaries of factory groups to take up land for colonists to follow. They were a cross-section of the shifting, landless hordes of Europe in one of the greatest mass movements of history, driven from their homelands by revolution, famine, and social inequalities — all seeking the gold that lies at the end of the rainbow.

Late that night, as the ship slipped down the Clyde, Daniel and Sarah stood by the rail looking their last upon their native land, while John and David, sprinting about the deck, had no thought for anything but the hoarse shouts of captain and crew, and the spreading of sails like great wings, as they headed westward into the Atlantic.

On the deck sheds were erected to shelter the cook-stoves, and here the next morning Sarah and her father valiantly tried to get breakfast for themselves and the boys. The tall, soldierly man and the bonnie red-cheeked lassie were so awkward about this that they quite won the sympathy of kindly Scotch matrons, who henceforth took an interest in the little family. They soon had need of it, for the first day out Sarah grew wan and took to her bunk. Before long, Daniel, too, succumbed to nausea. Only the boys remained well and omnivorous.

More than once during the six weeks and three days of the crossing they ran into stiff gales. Then the ship of hope became "an auld rockin' creel," and most of the emigrants almost wished she would go to the bottom. Food boxes slid about the decks, crashing into one another and knocking people down. Cooking was forbidden for fear of setting fires. No candles or lanterns were allowed at night. Below decks the smell of salt pork, potatoes, coffee, and whisky, together with the lack of sanitary provisions, gave rise to a stench that sent nearly everybody to the rail to "stretch the neck."

After a few days Daniel recovered sufficiently to stagger up from his cabin to dole out to his greedy boys the candy his wife had told him to give them, and attend prayer meetings on the lee side of the ship; for he had found a group of Disciples going out to found a colony in Ontario. But poor Sarah never rose from her bunk until they landed in New York Harbor. To the end of her life it made her ill to recall the horrors of that voyage.

Although Daniel Muir, like Abraham, "went forth . . . not knowing where he went," he was canny about keeping his ears open to talk about the New World and the best places to settle. Canada, he learned, was so densely forested that it would take all of a man's life to clear a small farm; whereas the "West" of the United States — particularly southeastern Wisconsin — had many "oak openings" where one could raise a fine harvest the first year. There was much excitement, too, about a canal planned to unite the Fox and Wisconsin Rivers. This single waterway would open up a passage for boats from the St. Lawrence to the Gulf of Mexico, making available to Wisconsin farmers the grain markets of Canada and the South of the United States. When the land-loving immigrants on board heard of this project, said to be already under construction, a dream of wealth rivaling that of the gold-rushers fired their hearts. Daniel Muir saw in this the hand of the Lord guiding him.

After a brief pause in New York he and his children journeyed up the Hudson to Albany. Here they boarded an Erie Canal packet to carry them westward through the winding Mohawk Valley. At Buffalo they met William Gray, brother of Philip Gray of Edinburgh, who also advised them to go to Wisconsin.

A few days later the little family landed from a lake steamer at Milwaukee. When the slower freight steamer arrived with their ponderous crates and boxes filled with antiquated farm machinery bought in Scotland, Daniel engaged a farmer with a stout team of horses to transport them to Kingston, in Marquette County, the region Gray had recommended. The spring rains had been falling in floods, melting the snow, when they set out, guiding their course with a compass through a sea of mud.

Often as they paused on their week's trek westward over the prairies, Daniel looked speculatively about him. Had he known anything about properties of soil, he would have settled there. For this was the richest land in Wisconsin. But along with most of the other early pioneers he had been told he must go on to find plenty of wood and water. They were headed for the region of shallow dying lakes, peat bogs, and an abundance of hardwood timber instead of grasses, where, as they were to find out to their cost, the top sandy soil of low organic content was thin and soon to be exhausted by intensive wheat farming.

Arriving at Kingston, Daniel engaged a room for his little brood, then rode on horseback ten miles to the farm of Alexander Gray, who, he had been told, knew the section lines and would help him find land. In his absence Sarah rested, while the boys, let loose, barged through the village, challenging congenial spirits to racing contests.

Alexander Gray, known to his neighbors as Sandy, had migrated earlier in the forties and had settled on a tract straddling the boundary between Marquette and Columbia Counties. A big-hearted typical pioneer, he welcomed later arrivals and helped them to find claims, build their houses or sod huts, clear the land, and plant their first crops.

With Gray following in a big wagon drawn by white oxen, Daniel returned to Kingston. When his goods had been loaded, he looked about to find a pony for the children. Back in Scotland he had promised them this, and he always kept his word. From a storekeeper he bought for thirteen dollars a little Indian bay which the boys named Jack.

At the whitewashed farmhouse of the Grays the travel-worn family found rest that night.[6] The men and boys slept in the haymow, while Sarah shared the one tiny bedroom with Mrs. Gray. In the morning Muir and his host set off northward to find land, Sarah, accustomed only to fireplaces, took her first lessons in stove cookery, and the boys, hardly waiting to eat breakfast, bounded out with war whoops to explore the surroundings. Through the meadows and down the road they raced, yelling like savages, long-legged John ahead by several leaps, little David panting along in the rear.

That night Daniel and Mr. Gray came home, having located a farm of eighty acres ten miles to the northwest near the Fox River. It had plenty of oaks and hickory timber and lay alongside a lake filled with fish. The next day with Gray's hired man and one or two neighbors they returned over the low trackless hills with machinery and several kegs of square nails brought from Scotland. Young bur oaks, cut down with broad-bladed axes, were chopped to the proper length for walls. White-oak saplings were then hewn on one side to make a puncheon floor. With these a one-windowed shanty was built on a sunny rise east of the lake, overlooking a meadow. This boggy, sloping meadow had many springs, all feeding the lake. Daniel Muir named his new estate Fountain Lake Farm.

On a bright May morning one of Sandy Gray's wagons, piled high with household goods and children, arrived at Fountain Lake Farm. But before the wagon had lumbered to a full stop, and before the boys and Sarah had time to look at their new home, or even the scenery, John spied a blue jay's nest in a tree near by. And before you could say Jack Robinson, he jumped down from the wagon, with David scurrying after him, and climbed up the tree to see the little green, speckled eggs and the beautiful mother bird that flew about them, swearing and screaming: "Thief, Thief!" This was their first discovery.

Had the future naturalist had all the world from which to choose his training-ground, he could hardly have found a richer treasure house than Fountain Lake, the boggy meadow, and the woods that embosomed them. "Nature streaming into us, wooingly teaching her wonderful glowing lessons . . . every wild lesson a love lesson, not whipped but charmed into us. Oh, that glorious Wisconsin wilderness!"

They often saw, rising from the trees on the west side of the lake, a curling blue feather of smoke from an Indian tepee. But the red men themselves were a terrible disappointment. They didn't wear war bonnets and paint, nor did they carry tomahawks. Ragged and dirty, they lived in filth. The American Indian was always a contradiction of John's idea that wild humans should be clean and beautiful like wild animals.

These neighbors often visited the farm. An old Winnebago would push open the door and grunt "Pork" or "Flour." Sometimes they brought fish to barter. One day when Sarah was alone, she saw a sinister-looking old savage sharpening a knife — or was it a tomahawk? — on the grindstone. Her heart was in her throat when he came to the door demanding the usual dole. She handed out what he asked for and was enormously relieved to see him walk peacefully away.

But there was nothing to fear from these cowed and beaten Winnebagos, living here and there in little groups upon the charity of the white settlers. As time went on, John learned the long story of treachery and cruelty perpetrated against them to get their land. The wretched people across the lake — most of them old — had literally crawled back from the reservation across the Mississippi to which they had been driven, to die and be buried in their homeland beside the Fox. At the south end of the farm in the "lower forty," John soon found a mound overlooking the lake, and on its edge a row of grass-thatched graves. There were other graves, too, on lower ground, and he was sickened to remember in later years that "we ploughed them down, turning the old bones they covered into corn and wheat."

Much work had to be done that first summer and autumn in clearing and planting the land. A huge breaking-plow, drawn by stout oxen, was used to cut through the bushes and root-bound sod with the efficiency of a modern war tank. Then the underbrush had to be dragged off and the severed tree roots grubbed out. Daniel saw a chance here to harness the energies of his two boys in pulling away the debris and burning it. It was fun to watch the big fires with their "great white hearts and red flames." But as they sashayed about, throwing on more brush to make the fire leap higher, their father, who worked twenty-four hours a day doing his duty as he saw it, called a halt to impress upon his offspring a solemn lesson. Out of his much-thumbed old Bible he read them lurid passages depicting the fate of a sinner: "And he shall be tormented with fire and brimstone in the presence of the holy angels, and in the presence of the Lamb. And the smoke of their torment ascendeth up for ever and ever, and they have no rest day nor night. . . ."[7] But the effect was nil, since "those terrible fire lessons quickly faded away into the blithe wilderness air."

After the planting was done, Daniel set about building a good frame house. Wanting the best of lumber, he went to Milwaukee, whence he brought back a load of fine white pine from the northern forests. A site had been chosen slightly to the east of the shanty, but still about a quarter of a mile from the section line that bounded the farm on the east. Some dour desire for aloofness and independence, brought down from feudal times, prompted the Scotch immigrants to build their houses far back from the road, and always on a hill with a wide view.

The carpenters who helped with the building called it "a palace of a house." And, indeed, for many a year it was the best in Buffalo Township. With two and a half stories, it had eight rooms, a wide front hallway, and a dignified entrance facing the road. In late October it was completed, and Sarah with housewifely pride put up white curtains and made the rooms gay with purple asters and goldenrod. Father never objected to flower decorations. In fact he had already made plots for flowers outside the house, planting seed he had brought from Scotland. And he helped Sarah put out lilac bushes before the front door.

About the only work John was called upon to do that first year was to help Sarah with the washing. A "blue Monday" it was indeed when tubs were brought in and soapy steam filled the air. Arguments arose in a shrill din of Scotch voices. The men in the fields, hearing the racket, would look up questioningly; and Daniel would say: "It's only Sarah and John fechtin' aboot the wash." [8]

Otherwise those months were a period of unadulterated joy to John Muir. With David at his heels, he was abroad at dawn, running barefooted in the furrows behind the plow, playing hide-and-seek among the tall corn, or riding the "pawny" Jack over the gentle hills. Once he was thrown off over Jack's head into a "kettle" back of the Indian mound. But nothing curbed his wild energies.

Best of all he liked to explore the boggy meadow, rosy with masses of pogonia and calopogon. Down by the lake he picked the purple heads of swamp thistles, and among the hills harebells and gowans like those of Scotland. He talked to them as if they were people, greeting them with: "Oh, you bonnie muggins! How did ye coom sae far frae hame?"

One day early in November Daniel Muir met at Milwaukee his wife, Ann, with Margaret, Danny, and the twins, who had celebrated their third birthday on shipboard. They arrived at the farm on the evening of November 7. On the next morning, although it was the Sabbath, when walks were ordinarily forbidden, Daniel, proud of his husbandry, took them for a stroll to see the field of winter wheat. They never forgot the lush greenness of it, and the deer grazing on the tender young blades.

By December the deep snows had blanketed the fields, the frozen lake, and the roads, making their huddle of farm buildings the one center of life and warmth in a vast white wilderness. No neighbor lived within four or five miles. Even the house was shut in by high snow walls, through which the men had to tunnel their way to the thatched barn to feed the stock. To reach the outside world each farmer had to dig himself out with an ox team hitched to a wagon and a plow behind the wagon. Gradually by community effort the primitive section-line roads were also plowed and packed for travel.

Before John had been long at Fountain Lake, he went with his father to Portage to get supplies. They followed the old Indian Trail — sometimes called "the River Road" — that passed the farm on the upper end. As the crow flies, the distance was perhaps not more than twelve miles. But tracing the trail around swamps that intervened, it was nearer sixteen.

On the way, within two miles of the town, they passed Fort Winnebago. Standing on an upland overlooking the Fox, it was built of logs and enclosed within a high stockade. The military had abandoned it only three years before the Muirs came.

Portage at this time was a picturesque, booming frontier town of several hundred inhabitants. Moccasined Indians padded along the streets, trading furs for trinkets, food, and fire-water. Cook Street, the main thoroughfare, was lined with saloons, dance-halls, stores, and taverns. Every stage, sweeping in with a grand flourish, brought a new aggregation of Yankee lawyers, real-estate sharks, gamblers, and pretty ladies to fleece the shifting population. Already it was a stopping-point for red-shirted lumberjacks and raft men on their way up and down the Wisconsin River between the northern pineries and the cities below. Immigrant farmers from a large radius of territory — Norwegians, Scotch, Welsh, Irish,

French, Germans, and Belgians — came here, as did the Muirs, to buy supplies, and the streets rang with the babel of their tongues. When John was a little older, he came to regard the tumultuous humanity he saw as part of a grand pageant of exploration and colonization that had passed and was still passing that way. He understood why the townsmen boasted of Portage as "the Key City of the West." Its unique position between two rivers made it so.

The Wisconsin, flowing south and west to the Mississippi, and the Fox, flowing north and east to Lake Michigan, approached within a mile of each other. Only a swampy strip of land lay between them. From time immemorial Indian tribes sailing up the Fox to the narrow boggy welt — "O-ning-ah-hing," the carrying-place, they called it — had shouldered their canoes and dog-trotted over it, to embark once more and glide down the great Wisconsin, only to be followed back by tribes from the West, bent on war or trade.

In the sixteenth and seventeenth centuries the *voyageurs* and *coureurs de bois* from New France in the north, were sailing and singing their way over the same waterways. At the carrying-place they established a trading post which they called "Le Portage." In 1634 Nicolet, the first official explorer, came as far as Green Bay, seeking new territory to annex to the crown of France. Thirty-nine years later Joliet and Father Marquette, more daring than Nicolet, sailed up the Fox, crossed Le Portage, and went down the Wisconsin to the Mississippi. For a century and a half this peaceful penetration continued, the French making friends with the Indians and trading with them on fairly equal terms.

Then came a sterner era when the English conquered New France and took over the lake-and-river routes to the south and west. Great fur companies invaded the territory, bent on stripping it of its wild-life resources. In the War of 1812, fought in part to end English encroachments in this region, Le Portage became a military camp, first of the British, then of the Americans. Thereafter the Northwest Territory passed finally into the possession of the United States.

Exploitation now went on more ruthlessly than before. John

Jacob Astor's American Fur Company, appropriating all the routes and trading posts, extended its commercial domain ever farther to the west. The Indians were no longer friendly, so Astor, to protect his fur interests, persuaded the Government to build a string of forts stretching from Green Bay to Prairie du Chien, a town founded by the French *voyageurs* near the confluence of the Wisconsin with the Mississippi. A few massacres and uprisings occurred. These were put down with much slaughter, and the lands of the Indians seized. John Marsh,[9] sub-Indian agent at Prairie du Chien, came up to Portage in 1828 to negotiate a "treaty" that fleeced the Winnebagos. Then Fort Winnebago was built. But since by this time the Indians had largely disappeared in that region, having been driven out or killed, the duties of the military consisted mostly in rounding up the feeble remnants and shipping them off in flatboats to a reservation across the Mississippi. All this recent history was very real to the boy John Muir, who had met at Fountain Lake some of those who had crawled home to die. Recalling in later years his youthful sympathy for the unfortunate natives "robbed of their lands and pushed ruthlessly back . . . by alien races," he said: "It then seemed to me . . . it was . . . only an example of the rule of might with but little or no thought for the right or welfare of the other fellow if he were the weaker."

As John grew up he learned more about the exploitation of the weak by the strong in Wisconsin. He learned how the rugged Yankee individualists got in on the ground floor and grabbed everything in sight, from the lead-mining region of the south to the valuable timberlands of the north. When Wisconsin became a state, in 1848, the Legislature — made up mostly of Yankees — was set up in Madison to work hand in glove with Washington in furthering their special interests. The immigrants of foreign races, having had no share in the political life of their native lands, and now living mostly in colonies, were too busy clearing and tilling the soil and attending religious revivals and camp meetings, to take an interest in law-making. Hence they were soon sold out by the shrewder American business men and politicians.

Then came the canal fiasco. Like the "cities on paper," shown to peasants in every town and hamlet of Europe to indicate an advanced stage of development in the New World, the canal formed a beautiful lure to attract immigrants. By every mountain pass and river path the land-hungry multitudes came pouring westward, hundreds of thousands of them through the years converging upon Wisconsin.

When the Muirs arrived, Portage was in the throes of the canal boom. In 1846 an obliging Congress had bestowed upon certain promoters a huge land grant to finance the canal and the dredging of the lower Fox. But as the years passed, no dredging worthy of the name was ever done and no canal was dug deep enough to float anything larger than a small steamboat. In 1854 the Fox & Wisconsin River Improvement Company took over, and after this through political pull, two more enormous grants were made. But little was accomplished beyond the fact that the company sold the land to the settlers — the Muirs among them — pocketed the money, and seized for themselves all water rights on the lower Fox.

So John Muir again learned history the hard way, not by playing games this time, but by being a part of it. As a result, from his boyhood on he hated with all the passion of his nature the injustices and cruelties perpetrated in the name of "progress." "Civilization" became to him a synonym for organized aggression, for everything that tended to crush individuality and stifle the aspirations of the human spirit. Aside from his love of nature, this did more than all else to send him out into the wilderness, to seek beauty, harmony, and freedom.

John had hardly passed his twelfth birthday, in April 1850, before his father put him to work plowing a field. His head hardly rose above the handles and he had to reach up to grip them. Guiding the heavy share, lifting it out of the ground at the end of the strip, and setting it straight for the return were back-breaking work. But " 'Tis dogged as does it," he said to himself grimly. This old folk adage of determination helped him over many a hump then and in later life. The hired men lauded him for his straight furrows and his speed, and praise, seldom bestowed by his father, was sweet to his ears. The glamour soon wore off, however. Before long he was set to other tasks — chopping down saplings, building snake fences, and grubbing out matted hickory and oak roots. As the season advanced, hoeing began, and went on from dawn till dusk all summer. David, Margaret, and Sarah were also given this work to do as something "easy." Daniel deployed them about the field among the potatoes and corn, no two on the same row lest they waste time talking. Often in the subtropical midsummer the ground was so hot the barefooted boys had to dig away the surface soil with their toes to find cool spots to stand on.

Farm work had begun in deadly earnest. Daniel, disappointed in the spotty character of his original tract, soon acquired a quarter section across the road to the east. As soon as one field was under cultivation, a new one was broken.

The Muirs all sacrificed much to the cause of making money to carry on the Lord's work, but beyond question the children paid the greatest price. John as the eldest son bore the brunt of the toil. As he grew toward manhood, his growth was stunted. Although he reached a height of five feet nine inches, in that tall family he was called "the runt." Only after he left home in his twenties did he add another inch to his stature. David, less strong to begin with, soon revealed a lack of stamina evident even to his father. Often in the midst of his work he became faint and dizzy. Daniel accustomed in his youth to seeing women toil in the fields, put his own daughters to the hardest labor. Sarah so strained her young body that she spent her mature life in precarious health. Margaret early slipped into a state of semi-invalidism, from which she never recovered.

A strong bond of comradeship developed between John and Margaret during their years of toil. Working as a team in the reaping, they accomplished prodigies of labor. He went ahead, swinging the gigantic cradle rhythmically in wide semicircles, cutting the golden grain stalks which the "fingers" on the grapevine handle laid flat in long rows. Tall Margaret, coming behind and bending over, gathered them up in her arms and bound them in bundles. Swiftly, silently they worked over the rolling hills. A sudden rain might come on to mildew the ripe grain before they could haul it to the barn and thresh it with flail and fanning mill. Sam Ennis, an Irish neighbor, said in later years: "Maggie was a wonderful worker. I remember once she raked and bound six acres of grain a day after the cradler. There's hardly a man who could do three acres today."[10] As to Daniel's share in the farm labor, Ennis commented: "He preferred preaching to working."

Buffalo Township filled up rapidly with Scotch immigrants. Among the first to arrive after the Muirs were Philip Gray of Edinburgh and his family. Less than a mile south of Fountain Lake Farm they took up land and built a log house. Gray and Muir, both being Disciples, began to hold religious services at their respective homes. James Mair, a Disciple from the Highlands, was another early arrival. Later Benjamin Whitehead, a Methodist minister, came with his family to swell the little colony of devout souls.

John and David Muir became friendly with the Gray boys, David and John. David Gray, two years older than John Muir, and educated in the schools of Edinburgh, had already shown marked literary talent. It was said he had taken prizes in poetry.

Philip Gray, although ill-fitted to be a farmer, did much to advance the community life. He established the first post office in his own house, helped build the first school, and set up at home a lending library. Unlike Daniel Muir he took a keen interest in the political affairs of his adopted country. He subscribed for the *New York Tribune,* and good periodicals as well as recent books found their way to his farmhouse. Mrs. Stowe's *Uncle Tom's Cabin,* along with Horace Greeley's anti-slavery editorials in the *New York Tribune,* made him and his family militant abolitionists. Together with the Whiteheads, it is said, they harbored runaway Negroes, helping them escape to Canada. David Gray, a few years later, as associate editor of the *Buffalo Courier,* did effective work against slavery.

Among the first new settlers came David Millar Galloway, a sturdy, black-haired young Scot with blue eyes that sparkled with fun and goodwill toward his fellow men. Frederick Jackson Turner, the historian, spending his youth in Portage and gaining there his impressions of democratic principles innate among the Scotch, must have had in mind such men as David Galloway when he wrote: "The Scottish race brought the true democratic germ to the new world, and were the nurses of it on the first frontier."[11]

George Galloway, David's father, was a tenant farmer in Fifeshire, Scotland. There he had married Jean Millar of the Gordon clan, to which Daniel Muir belonged. Always ahead of his time, he had devised methods of draining bogs and rehabilitating exhausted soil. Moreover, he was one of the first farmers in Scotland to use a barometer in agriculture, to foresee adverse weather conditions.

The Galloways had a sense of personal dignity that would not allow them to adopt the speech and manners of servility. And because of the undemocratic system of the Established Church they withdrew and became Disciples. David, following in his father's footsteps, was hotly rebellious against a society that put the earth and the fruits thereof into the control of the aristocracy. So when his father's farm lease was about to expire, he came to America to establish a new home for his parents and unmarried sisters.

Being a Disciple, he gravitated naturally to the Muirs. And while visiting them he took up a claim of eighty acres for himself on the other side of the township, and at the same time found land for his father a few miles to the north in Packwaukee Township. As he wrote home: "We'll have something to show for our labor, and we don't have to pay rent or call any man Master."

David Galloway was religious, but far more tolerant than any of the Muirs. His favorite poet, Burns, may have taught him that. If he preached anything, it was that people should have leisure for a happy family life — time to read and sing and play together and with their neighbors. Although he was nine years older than John Muir, a close friendship sprang up between them. Many a chance remark dropped by David when they were working in the fields gave the boy a wider horizon and became a part of his mature philosophy.

Courtships were slow in those days, but it became plain after a few months that young Galloway was in love with Sarah, and she with him. But his duty to his parents came first, so as soon as he had the Packwaukee farm well started, he went back to the old country to bring over the family.

As Marquette County became settled, schoolhouses, used also as churches, were built in every township. Most of the immigrants were Presbyterians, Methodists, Baptists, and Disciples; but creeds broke down on the frontier, and all met amicably together to listen to occasional circuit-riders or to lay speakers.

The Disciples, rebelling against the professional clergy that held sway in older churches, would have no "reverend dandies" in their sect. Hence the order of "preaching elders," of whom Daniel Muir was one of the foremost in rural Wisconsin.

His reputation as a speaker spread abroad, and to all who called upon him he gave generously, asking no reward. The story is still told [12] in a neighborhood where he often spoke that one day after the service was over, a group of deacons met in the churchyard to discuss ways and means of paying him something. "Mr. Muir is verra faithfu'," one argued. "He cooms a lang way, an' he gi'es us a guid sermon." "Hush, mon," objected a canny son of Scotland, "it's nae needfu' to pay him mooch. Mr. Muir likes to talk!" Apparently this argument prevailed, for there is no evidence he ever received a stipend.

As the Muir wagon drew up at a schoolhouse gate of a Sabbath morning, all weather, crop, and baby chatter of neighbors meeting after six days of isolation stopped. Daniel Muir, stern and priestly in his "blacks," fringed plaid, and chimney-pot hat, marched in, followed by his family and the whole hushed congregation.

Taking his stand by the teacher's table in lieu of a pulpit, he led them in hymn-singing, then closed his eyes and prayed for three quarters of an hour. Then after more singing he launched forth upon his "discoorse" — an hour-and-a-half-long test of endurance. He differed from most "exhorters," however, in that he spoke quietly without apoplectic contortions and pulpit-pounding. He stood with hands folded in front of him, head uplifted, eyes closed as in a trance. "We all stood in awe of him," said one who heard him often. "He seemed far removed from things of this earth, and ordinary folk like ourselves. He seemed truly a Man of God!" [13]

Ann Muir, "a stay-at-home body," was seldom seen except at church. Here she was regarded with that deference accorded in Scotland to "the Laird's leddyship." Some were inclined at first to believe "she felt hersel' a bit aboon common folk." The rumor that "o'er in the auld country she was a rich man's dochter" no doubt helped create this impression.

But her quiet kindness and genuine simplicity finally won their way, and to this day old families speak of her with warmth in their voices: "She was a real leddy, Mrs. Muir was." One who knew her well has described her as "tall, big-framed, strong-minded — a stronger character than any of her family. She was full of wit and wisdom."

John Muir early revolted against religion as he saw it practiced. The iron entered his soul when he saw pious people ruthless in their treatment of animals and human beings in their charge. His first active rebellion stemmed from his father's callousness in over-driving the horse Nob to get from one religious meeting to another. When the poor beast, slowly dying of pneumonia, followed them about the farm, as if dumbly pleading for help, he began seriously to question a religion so devoid of love. Another grief came when his father sold Jack to someone bound for the California gold mines. The money he got for the pony meant more to him than the happiness of his children.

The coming of the Whitehead family brought about an incident that further alienated John. Benjamin Whitehead, with a zeal for soul-saving equal to Daniel's own, had the reputation of cruelly beating his children and his unfortunate brother Charlie. "Uncle Charlie's troubles were pre-natal," James Whitehead once told John Muir. "He was born crooked and his limbs were broken that his defect might . . . be readjusted." [14] Possibly it was this inhuman method of adjusting "his defect" that left him crooked in mind as well. At any rate, Charlie, "a puir feckless body," went about pouring his sufferings at the hands of his righteous brother into the ears of sympathetic neighbors. John, ever tender of heart, was deeply roused. The climax came when Charlie tried to drown himself in Fountain Lake. He was dragged out alive, but died a few days later.

More than fifty years afterward, when Muir wrote his autobiography,[15] he threw aside his natural reticence in regard to family matters to strike a blow for the freedom of children from the domination of parents. When his brother David protested against his revealing the harshness of their own father and that of Benjamin Whitehead, he replied: "As I hate cruelty, I called attention to it." On another occasion, in defense of the same exposure, he said: "There is one thing I hate with a perfect hatred — cruelty for anything or anybody!"

In 1854 the Taylor family arrived from Scotland. In this group were an old grandam, two sons in middle life, a daughter in her thirties, and David, a grandson of sixteen. On a high boulder-strewn ridge just east of Daniel Muir's quarter-section they built a frame house of thin walls, which must have been bitterly cold to live in even in its best years. It still stands, a poor gray shell of a hut, with three downstairs rooms and a windowless attic reached by a ladder. But when the Taylors lived there, the walls of the lower rooms were lined with books — an excellent library of English literature. For they were people of culture. And Davie himself, with his big, luminous eyes and sensitive face, was a poet with more than a little of the authentic divine fire.

Almost at once a friendship sprang up between David Gray and David Taylor. So inseparable were they that the neighbors called them "the Twa Davies." They lived about a mile apart and, as David Taylor said afterward: "Had that mile been water, and that water the Hellespont, I have no doubt it would have been crossed." [16] Although they had to work in the day on their respective farms, the nights were their own. Each donned his best clothes and set forth to their rendezvous as to a king's banquet. They walked the roads and fields and sat on fences, declaiming the lines of Byron, Poe, Wordsworth, and Milton. Then before they went home in the dawn to the prose of farm work, they would recite their own most recent poems, each submitting humbly to the criticism of the other. But David Gray, who was to make for himself a name in American literature, acknowledged then, as he did to the end of his life, the greater genius of his friend.

While the Twa Davies roamed the countryside in nightly sessions, spouting poetry, John Muir, the wells of his genius still untapped, slept the sleep of exhaustion, and rose each morning to the prospect of endless, deadening toil.

But one day in the fall of 1854 when the crops were in and the plowing and planting done, he along with David Gray and David Taylor were picked by the township "pathboss" to build a corduroy road over a near-by bog which the two poets called "the Weird Swamp."

When they arrived in the early morning, their first job was to cut down tamarack saplings to lay a foundation for the road. This bottom layer was then to be crossed and crisscrossed with more trees and finally covered with a mass of brush and dirt until it was built high and firm above the swamp. John attacked the trees and soon had a large pile ready for use. He had a special technique that attracted much attention in the neighborhood. "He struck his axe straight into the trunk horizontally," recalled Sam Ennis. "Then by a swinging stroke upward he made the chips fly. He cut no V like the rest of us, and when his tree was down, it had a square, smooth end."

Whether the other boys did much effective work that day is doubtful, for the two young troubadours were singularly inept at manual labor. Besides they had business more important. Davie Taylor began by chanting certain poems. This soon slowed up John's wood-chopping. Poetry he had heard recited all his life, but never like this. The cadenced lines, sweet on the tongue, ineffable to the ear, sank into his heart and awakened something sleeping there. He had not known words could be so beautiful or mean so much. He stood like one enchanted, and when Davie paused, he could only cry out: "Go on. Go on!"

John Muir went home that night treading among the stars. A spark had been lighted that was to become a conflagration. Some deep ancestral passion for beauty, choked and smothered within him by years of drudgery, had been released. Fifty years later he said in *The Story of My Boyhood and Youth:* "I remember as a great and sudden discovery that the poetry of the Bible, Shakespeare, and Milton, was a source of inspiring, exhilarating, uplifting pleasure, and I became anxious to know all the poets, and saved up small sums to buy as many of their books as possible."

John Gray, brother of David — the same John Gray who in maturity became a financial backer of the young inventor Henry Ford — visited John Muir long afterward in California and heard the old naturalist pay tribute to the Twa Davies for the inspiration they had given him that day. He spoke of "the envious delight" with which he had listened to them, and said their talk gave him his "first spurring" [17] to read and learn from books.

When John was seventeen, his father bought more land. The thin soil of the original tract was exhausted by the intensive growing of winter wheat. And in a chain of sequences somewhat like that of the house that Jack built, they had felled the trees that homed the birds that would have eaten the larvæ that grew into bugs that ate the wheat. Moreover, the wholesale destruction of northern pineries had lowered the water tables under the whole state and dried up springs and creeks. Disastrous floods and droughts ensued. The grain, now produced in small quantities, was inferior in quality.

The Crimean War, beginning in 1854, created a demand for American wheat. Hence, since the canal dream had petered out, Wisconsin broke into a rash of railroad schemes, each one generously subsidized by Congress with land grants. In spite of this a throng of slick high-pressure boys went out to sell railroad stock and bonds. Cities, towns, and counties plunged into debt to invest. Six thousand farmers mortgaged their lands to buy stock.

Daniel Muir did not fall for this get-rich-quick scheme; but shrewdly he proposed to capitalize upon the war boom and the promised transportation. So he bought a half-section of virgin land six miles southeast of Fountain Lake, naming it Hickory Hill Farm.

John protested vigorously, for like David Galloway he believed men should live on small tracts and not strive to get rich at the expense of things more precious. "Living is more important than getting a living," he said.

But nothing could dissuade his father. Alexander Campbell had for some years been working his followers up to a feverish missionary zeal. Negroes and Indians in America and heathen in far lands must be saved. Orphan asylums, hospitals, and schools must be founded. So, like Abraham, Daniel was prepared to sacrifice his own son to the Lord, as if Isaac and John had no rights in the matter. God intervened to save Isaac. John had to work his own way out.

The Twa Davies, lifting him from his dark isolation, had given him new goals. So he formed a resolve that when he was of age, he would leave home and seek them. Meanwhile he labored harder than ever, clearing the new tract, cutting woodlands, making fences, and helping to build a house and barn — all this at a distance of six miles from the home base. Keeping the old farm going depended largely upon Margaret and Sarah. Even Danny and the twins had no more time for play. Only Joanna, the child born in America, and always her father's favorite, escaped servitude.

Fortunately for Sarah, David Galloway came back in the spring of 1856, bringing his parents, seven sisters, and the families of those who were married. Staying overnight at Fountain Lake, David was appalled at Sarah's thinness and pallor. When he heard about the new tract, he knew the reason.

David's mother, Jean Millar Galloway, and John Muir at once struck up a friendship. This old Gaelic woman, seemingly endowed with what the Scotch call "second sight," sensed the unique quality of the boy and predicted he would "go far." Throughout his life Muir paid tribute to this wise woman who fostered him in his youth.

David at once made plans to marry Sarah. Persuading Daniel to sell him the "home eighty," he arranged to farm for him the adjacent tract, now amounting to 240 acres. And Daniel acquired David's "eighty" adjoining Hickory Hill, thereby increasing his new farm to 400 acres. Sarah and David Galloway were married in December 1856, thus making Sarah once more mistress of Fountain Lake Farm. But from her wedding day on she worked no more in the fields.

Meanwhile the Muirs had moved to the new farm. High on a ridge topped with oak and hickory trees, the house was approached from the highway by a long sloping road. The L-shaped building preserved by the present owners [18] within a veneer of brick is today substantial and sightly. The Muirs did everything with a pride of craftsmanship. The fine white plaster in the rooms, put on nearly ninety years ago, is still unflawed.

The higher portion had two stories and an attic. Below stairs were a parlor, a buttery, and a small bedroom. Here Daniel slept and studied. Directly beneath his room was a stone-walled cellar, approached by an outside storm door. In this cold, cavelike place, by candlelight, among the potato and apple bins, John Muir, working at night, hilariously filled his "wisdom bins" with book knowledge, and carved out of hickory the inventions that first made him known to the outside world.

Life was austere at Hickory Hill, especially in winter. Except on special occasions the kitchen, in the lower angle of the house, was the only warmed room. The boys, sleeping upstairs, had to get up before dawn, thrust swollen, chilblained feet into frozen boots, and work all day in the frosty air. David Muir, in a letter written long afterward, gives a glimpse of their hardships: "John, do you remember our bedroom at Hickory Hill on the north side — never smelt fire or sun, window none too tight, three in a bed, Dan in the middle, and quilts frozen about our faces in the morning, and how awful cold it was to get up . . . and dress and go down to the kitchen barefooted? OO-oo-ooo, it makes me shiver to think of it, and going to Portage with loads of corn, running behind the wagon to keep warm and having to eat frozen bread for lunch. . . ."

So far as adornment and creature comforts were concerned, the house, according to Muir, was "a barren empty shell." Perhaps it was that bareness that gave him his lifelong delight in framed pictures, rich rugs, fine linen, and delicate embroideries. Wherever he came upon them in his travels, he praised them in letters and journals. Indeed, the whole family crowded their walls with pictures after Father left home. But let no one imagine the Muirs were an unhappy household, even in the barren period. That family of robust, lively youngsters knew how "to catch fun on the fly." When Father was there, laughter was suppressed beneath a surface solemnity. Meals continued to be sacramental, but John and David, unbeknown to the autocrat at the head of the table, vied with each other in making horrible faces, and looking cross-eyed. It is said that as a result of this David's eyes never got over a slight squint.

But when Father went down the road, bent on a soul-saving expedition, life flowed back to normal. Mother, tranquilly knitting by the stove, never rebuked their hilarity. John, his nose wrinkling in puckish drollery, was usually master of the revels. He couldn't resist breaking out into jigs or the mad Highland fling. His lithe, slender body, attuned to rhythm, seemed made for dancing. An excellent mimic, too, he put on a grand pantomime of playing bagpipes.[19] As he strutted and blew out his cheeks, humming a high, insistent note, you could almost see the waggle of his kilt and hear the skirling of the pipes.

These exhibitions were varied by songs they all sang together, and by humorous doggerel in which Dan and John were the champions. All the Muir children manifested briefly some talent in this direction, but John in his pixy moods throughout his life made up poems on the spur of the moment. Some of them he wrote down — all in the stilted forms of Scotch folk-balladry. It was only in prose that he was the true poet. In maturity he made frequent attempts at free verse, taking some passage he had written in his journals and rearranging it on a slip of paper.

There were also quieter sessions at Hickory Hill when the girls brought out their bits of lace-making and embroidery — Ann, unbeknown to her husband, taught all her daughters these feminine arts. Then John would read to them from a smuggled book while they listened raptly.

They had comforts too, thanks to Mother. After Grandfather Gilrye's death in 1852, she received a quarterly allowance of twenty-five pounds. Her bank was a black bag always carried on her arm, and out of it came funds to buy scarfs, shawls, an occasional new dress or ribbon for the girls, or linen to make finely tucked shirts for the boys.

John had a faculty for making friends who helped him on his way. Simple, humble people they were, but full of native wisdom.

Such a friend was William Duncan.[20] He lived on a farm two miles to the west, and was one Scot who had built his house by the side of the road — a symbol of his kindliness.

Soon after the Muirs moved to Hickory Hill, they began to dig a well back of the house. Duncan, a stonemason and miner in Scotland, advised blasting out the rock with dynamite; but Daniel ordered John to go down in a bucket and chisel through the hard sandstone. So the boy hacked away day after day, by the light of a candle lantern, at the bottom of the three-foot bore.

One morning, when the well was nearly eighty feet deep, a death-like faintness seized him. He called feebly for help. His father, leaning over the top, heard him and sharply commanded him to get back into the bucket. John, slumping into it, was hauled up and carried into the house, unconscious.

Already it was being said among the neighbors: "Old Man Muir works his children like cattle." On this day when they heard the news, there was great excitement. William Duncan hurried over to tell Daniel he must test the air each time before he sent John down. "Put down a burning bush or candle," said he, "an' if there's choke-damp there, it will dowse the glim."

The next day the boy was in the well again. When he had chiseled out ten additional feet, he struck the nether springs with an abundance of pure water.[21]

Soon after this the three Muir boys were down by the highway, cutting saplings to make fences, when Farmer Duncan came driving his old red oxen up the road. Seeing John, he stopped to talk:

"I hear ye like to read buiks, my lad."

"I do that, sir," John replied. "I read every guid buik I can get my hands on."

"Weel, maybe ye'll be coomin' ben the hoos the nicht, an' I'll hae a buik or twa for ye."

That night after supper John fairly leaped down the road to the Duncan farmhouse. Once there in the warm kitchen, his host brought out to him from the bedroom three huge leather-bound volumes of Scott's Waverley Novels. He went home with Volume I stuffed under his coat. It contained five novels packed into close, fine print.

At an early hour in the morning he was down cellar, reading by a guttering candle *The Bride of Lammermoor.* This carried him back to the heather-and-whin-clad hills of his boyhood. But it was not easy to hide so bulky a tome, and Daniel, searching one day for a tool — they all seemed to gravitate to the cellar — discovered it. A novel, he said, was "the spawn of Satan, the Deevil's ain buik o' lies!" Henceforth John had to be extra canny about hiding his books, for his father was an expert detective. In this the boy was abetted by his mother and sisters. Many a sly little plot was hatched and carried out in that household, with Daniel none the wiser.

About this time John borrowed from someone the writings of Humboldt and Mungo Park. One day he read aloud to his mother passages from Park's *Travels in Africa.* When he had finished, she said: "Weel, John, maybe you will travel like Park and Humboldt some day." Father, supposed to be miles away, had slipped in and overheard this. "Oh, Ann!" said he, "dinna put sic notions in the laddie's heed."

Nature wisely endows her children of genius with a wit and a will to forge their way through barriers. Daniel often had reason in those days to groan: "The verra Deevil's in that boy!" For, not satisfied with getting up at an unconscionable hour in the morning and making a great racket with hammer and saw right under the parental bedroom, now in the winter of 1857 he wanted to go to school. And, by some strategy not recorded, he got his way.

By this time John Muir was reaching out for social contacts. He had found a friend of his own age in Bradford Brown, who lived on the southern boundary of Marquette County near the Alexander Gray farm. Brown had two brothers, Daniel and William, and a stepfather named Eddy. Within a few rods of their farmhouse stood a log cabin known as "the Eddy School." In the summer of 1858 Brown wrote to John: "I should like first rate to meet over at the schoolhouse and speak pieces and sing our old 'Press Onward' song as we used to last winter. I wonder where our teacher has gone. . . ."

Fountain Lake from the west. Farm buildings stood directly across the lake.

The rear of Hickory Hill farmhouse, showing the storm-door entrance to the cellar where John Muir worked on his inventions

University of Wisconsin in 1860. *From an old catalogue. Left to right: South Hall, Main Hall (now Bascom Hall), and North Hall*

Fair Grounds, taken over in 1861 *and made into Camp Randall. The Temple of Art, where Muir exhibited his inventions, is the most distant building to the left*

In letters exchanged by the boys in later years the teacher's name is given as George Branch. Mrs. Daniel Brown, who declares her husband was also a mate of John Muir's in the Eddy School, recalls a stanza of the song mentioned above:

Press onward, 'tis wiser than sitting aside,
And dreaming and sighing and waiting the tide,
In Life's earnest battle they only prevail
Who daily march onward and never say fail.

Miss Jessie Duncan, William Duncan's daughter, states that John attended the Eddy School along with her two brothers, the three of them going south each morning by way of an Indian trail. These evidences plus Muir's published statement [22] that he attended school for but two months between the migration from Scotland and his entrance into the university, seems to dispose of the legend that he was once a pupil at the Red Schoolhouse near Fountain Lake.

Henceforth John Muir lived a more normal existence. He even joined the young people of the community in evening "bees" held in the schoolhouse. One of his pals on these excursions was John Cairns, brother of Katie Cairns, the champion speller of the neighborhood.

Delayed one night by chores, the two Johns arrived late for a spell-down.[23] The log cabin was jammed almost to bursting, and the door had been locked to keep out the tardy. Ever resourceful, however, the two wags cut a large thick square of sod with jackknives, climbed to the roof, and clamped it down over the chimney. The soft hum of voices within, soon grew into a strident roar. Someone opened the stove door, thus releasing more smoke, which billowed through the room in black clouds. Panic ensued, in which somebody yelled: "Fire!" The door was finally unlocked, and the frantic spellers spilled out, coughing, gasping, tumbling over one another to reach the fresh night air.

The practical jokers, having jumped down from the roof, innocently mingled with the blinded crowd, and nobody knew they hadn't been inside. They even joined in looking for the fire and along with others clambered up on the low roof and helped "discover" the sod on the chimney.

When the smoke was cleared out, they all went in and spelling was resumed. Sides were chosen and tricky words were fired like bullets by the teacher, sending many casualties to their seats. Finally Katie Cairns and John Muir stood alone, facing each other with the light of battle in their eyes. Back and forth for a long time Schoolmaster Branch hurled "hard dictionary words" at them. The audience was tense.

At last John went down. This was Katie's greatest triumph — to have spelled down John Muir! When the bee broke up, John met his rival at the door. "Katie," said he, "ye'll never spell me doon again!" And according to Katie's nephew, Chauncey Cairns, "she never did. John studied so hard after that, nobody could spell him down."

Many a courtship began in the old schoolhouse. Most of the young folks "were in a tease to get married." Romance was in the air. John Reid, the big, red-haired, ruddy-faced young Scotch farmer from over the hill north of the Muirs, was wooing Margaret. And David fell in love with Katie Cairns. So desperately smitten was he that he sighed like a furnace, and, when out in the fields, was known to sit down on a stump to write poetry to his beloved.

John Muir, in spite of his cellar-born sublimation, may have had a little brush with Cupid. The animated correspondence he carried on at this time with Charles Reid, filled with their ideals of maidenly charm and saying much about "the disease of falling in love," revealed him as not wholly unsusceptible. Charles hinted there was in John's life "a young female of eighteen with blue eyes and fair hair flowing." Outside of this teasing suggestion, however, there is no evidence of any early passion.

Certainly he showed none of the usual symptoms. When David lost his head over Katie, he began to preen himself into a spic-and-span neatness. John, on the other hand, was wholly unmindful of his unkempt appearance. He looked "as wild as a loon," his sisters said. His silken mop of hair was a sore trial to them. When they urged him to cut his "stack of hay" shorter or at least keep it combed, they found him "gey ill to persuade." They tried to civilize his manners too, for he was as full of barbs as a Scotch thistle, especially toward those he didn't like. But whenever he sensed a lecture in the offing, he would cry: "Get a pulpit, girls, get a pulpit!" and be off out of hearing. "John winna budge," they said in despair. It took years of rubbing up against people "like a pebble in a pothole" before some of his angularities wore off.

John was known in the family as "a lang-tongued chiel," and his wranglings with his father often filled the household with anything but harmony. More adroit than Daniel in argument, he usually came out on top. How the old man must have rued the fact that he made the boy learn almost the whole Bible by heart! For his own patriarchal preachments couched in Scriptural idiom, were too often refuted by his nimbler-witted son with contradictory quotations from the sacred Word. Unable to explain the conflicts, he called John "a contumacious quibbler."

When the graham-bread-and-porridge fad hit the neighborhood, Daniel announced they would all adopt the vegetarian diet. Moreover, he decreed a one-meal-a-day regime. The hired men grumbled, and the news got out. Rumor had it that Mrs. Muir and the girls were sick most of the time for lack of good food. As for John, he had been desperately ill with pneumonia caught the night his father sent him out in a storm to look for a lost sheep. It was a wonder he survived at all since Daniel, believing in the power of prayer to cure sickness, wouldn't send for a doctor. As soon as the boy was up, he had to begin plowing, though he was so thin and feeble he could hardly lift the share at the furrow's end.

While things were at this pass, William Duncan one day, with his wife beside him on the high wagon seat, met Daniel on the road. Bringing his oxen to a full stop, Duncan accosted his neighbor:

"A braw day tae ye, Mr. Muir. It's to Portage ye're gan the morn?"

"I am that," Daniel answered curtly.

"Weel, may I make bold to say, Mr. Muir, if John were my boy, I'd tak' him along to see Doctor Meacher. The lad isna weel."

"Our blessed Lord is my Guide, Mr. Duncan," said Daniel in his most pontifical manner, "and the Scriptures tell me: 'He healeth all our diseases. . . . Whatsoever ye shall ask in My name . . .' "

Whereupon Mrs. Duncan piped up: "Maybe ye hanna been askin' verra hard then. If ye waurna sae blind, ye'd see the boy's sick. Weel, an ye winna tak' him to a doctor, then see that he gets three guid meals a day. He works hard enough for twa men, an' he needs beef, an' plenty o' it!"

This conversation rankled, but Daniel was not convinced until an argument occurred that John later recorded in *The Story of My Boyhood and Youth.* The family had been talking over the everlasting food question, and Daniel was descanting upon "the foolishness of eating flesh." John then called his father's attention to the Biblical story of Elijah fed by the ravens. Daniel, who accepted the Scriptures as his sole rule of life, acknowledged his mistake. Surely the Lord would not have sent flesh to his Prophet if graham bread had been better.

According to Miss Duncan, Daniel began at once, on his marketing trips to Portage, to bring home "good beef, and plenty o' it." The health of the family improved, and Daniel, now convicted of his error, became quite humble. The next time he saw the gudewife, he said to her: "Ye were perfectly right, Mrs. Duncan. My family did need meat to eat. John and the girls have never been in such guid health as since I got the beef for them."

Duncan's suggestion that John be taken to see Dr. Meacher, was an error in diplomacy. Known as a student of Voltaire and "a free thinker," the pioneer physician was a thorn in the flesh to Daniel Muir. Already they had locked horns in a way most embarrassing to the latter. The plain-spoken doctor loved trees, and wherever he went he tried to save them from being chopped down, especially along the highway and on Government land. In at least one instance he bought the plot they stood on, to preserve them.

One night while in the Muir neighborhood he approached a schoolhouse where a prayer meeting was in full swing.[24] Knowing Daniel would be there, he went in and heard that gentleman address a long supplication to the Lord. In the pause that followed, he rose and denounced Muir before the whole congregation as a man who spent his time praising God while he was sending his boys and hired men to cut down trees on Government land adjacent to his farm.

Doubtless the charge was well founded, although it might have been made against almost any other farmer in the region. Neither here nor anywhere else in America had the social conscience been aroused to the evils of forest destruction on the public domain.

John, hearing this accusation, probably agreed in his heart with Dr. Meacher. Not long after this he and the physician established a lifelong friendship based upon their mutual passion for preserving wild nature. We do not know how much the boy protested against the felling of trees on the two farms. Sam Ennis recalled that John's expert axe cut down most of the virgin timber on the Fountain Lake land. But he was so deeply enslaved in those early years that all protests would have been futile.

In 1858 Charles Reid wrote to John about a great oak he and his brother had just cut down. John replied with a poem grieving over the noble old giant. The poem has not survived, but Charles commented upon it: "Your elegy on the tree was very fine. You seem to mourn its death."

By the late fifties John Muir was spreading his wings for flight. There was in him a quenchless thirst for knowledge, an insatiable eagerness to work out his own pattern. What that would be he had no means of knowing. Only one step ahead seemed clear. He would go out into the world and get a job in a machine shop.

The machine age had dawned for Wisconsin and other Midwestern states. Agriculture had struck a new low. The slump in trade after the Crimean War, the Panic of 1857, the failure of fraudulent railroad schemes resulting in widespread bankruptcy among the farmers, the exhaustion of the soil — all these had hastened the change by which the basis of economic life was being shifted to industry, from the country to the cities. In the South and beyond the Mississippi markets were opening up for machines, tools, and woodwares. To supply these the lower Fox was now lined with factories battening upon the harnessed water-power. Towns all over the southern part of the state were turning to manufacture. Industrial cities such as Buffalo, Detroit, Indianapolis, and Chicago had become centers for great foundries and machine shops. The opportunities opening up to young men of inventive ability were limitless.

So far as John Muir then knew, he was a one-talent man. Invention seemed to be his forte. During his final years on the farm he worked constantly to develop himself in this direction by studying algebra, geometry, and trigonometry. And he learned mechanical laws by whittling his ideas into wood supplemented by waste scraps of metal.

His inventive activities began while he was yet at Fountain Lake. His first tools were a vise, a few files, a hammer, and a coarse-toothed saw — all clumsy implements brought from Scotland. Needing a fine saw, he made one out of a corset steel. After this he contrived out of bits of cast-off iron to make his own bradawls, punches, and a pair of compasses. With these he fashioned water-wheels and windmills which he tried out in the meadow below the house. Many of them were found in later years by the neighbors, along with little dams where he had harnessed his water-power. James Whitehead has said: "I remember how some of the things he made from wood were marvels to me and filled my boyish mind with delight." His first invention of importance appears to have been a small self-setting sawmill. Damming up a little creek in the meadow, he tested it and he declares it was "proved and found perfect."

During his boyhood the main tool of lumber production had evolved from the primitive axe into the man-propelled ripsaw, and then into the muley-saw, a stiff, long implement motivated by steam. In the fifties the circular buzz-saw was installed in the larger mills. This thin steel disk with forward-set hooked teeth was revolved upon a spindle. It increased production tenfold. The double-rotary saw was perhaps being talked of, but was not put into use until the sixties, resulting then in a far swifter destruction of the American forests than any tool previously devised.

Nevertheless, John Muir in the early or middle fifties invented for his tiny mill a double rotary saw that worked with efficiency. His mechanical ideas always tended toward the creation of automatic labor-saving devices and mass production. Had he allowed this bent to be developed to its fullest possibilities, he would have defeated the principles for which he stood in after life. The time came when he had to disown his mechanical genius and adhere to his ideals.

After moving to Hickory Hill, since, as he says, "it seemed impossible to stop whittling and inventing," he began to evolve some remarkable clocks. With nothing but the initial help of a book that taught him the laws of the pendulum, he first formed in his mind the complete pattern of an elaborate horologe. Then carrying bits of hickory about with him in his pockets, he worked at the small parts "with many a weary, whittling nibble," in moments stolen from his field labors. These, finally put together, formed a gadget that looked more like a sawmill than a clock. But it would strike, register hours and dates, light fires and a lamp, and by means of a set of levers and cogwheels would tip a rudely constructed bed up on end at any desired hour. This he called his "early-rising machine."

His father, discovering it in the attic, told him he would be the better for it if he were "only half as zealous in his study of religion." However, he allowed it to be set up temporarily in the parlor, outside his own bedroom door. Maggie, tiptoeing one day about the house, spied him on his knees before it, peering cautiously into its works.

John's next clock was shaped like a scythe. Each part in it was shaped like an arrow or a scythe, the pendulum itself being a sheaf of arrows. And this clock would perform all the feats of the first one. Riveted to a mossy oak snag, it was carved with the Biblical phrase: "All Flesh is Grass." Daniel was so pleased with it he allowed it to be used in the household. Fifty years later it was still keeping good time in John's California home.

The next clock, made in 1857, was an ambitious affair probably inspired by the town clock of Dunbar, in that it had four huge dials and was designed to function from the top of the barn gable, where it could be seen from fields, highroad, and neighboring farms. Its size may be estimated from the fact that the main hand on each dial was fourteen feet long. John planned to house the works in a stout box beneath the gable and attach them to the dials through a hole in the roof. On one of his visits to the farm Bradford Brown saw this clock all ready to be hoisted to its place. John was aflame with enthusiasm over it — his masterpiece thus far — and Brown in a letter [25] speaks of "the great disappointment of the boy" when his father nipped the whole scheme in the bud because it would "bring bothersome trampling crowds about the farm." John suggested a compromise plan by which it would be placed high in a black oak near the house with the works contained in a watertight "cabin" among the leaves. But this too was condemned.

In fact, John's machines were becoming a nuisance to Daniel Muir. Everybody was talking about them, even as far away as Portage. Too many curiosity-seekers were dropping in at the farm, interfering with the work.

Up to 1860 the boy had no clock models to work from since he was not allowed to tamper with the one small family timepiece that stood on a bracket in the kitchen. But in that year Sarah helped him to buy one for himself. Taking this apart and putting it together again, he learned several new tricks by which he improved his former mechanisms.

Along with clocks he was inventing at this time an assortment of thermometers, pyrometers, hygrometers, and a barometer. The outstanding gadget of this class was a "field thermometer," also to be read from the outlying hills and meadows. It was built around an iron wagon-box rod, three feet long and five eighths of an inch in diameter. The pressure of this rod, expanding and contracting to variations in heat and cold, upon a set of levers made out of hoop-iron strips, and so multiplied 32,000 times, caused the big black hand upon a white dial to make many revolutions. These revolutions were registered on a small dial marked upon the larger one. John fastened this thermometer high up on the side of the house, where it recorded even the slight variations in temperature caused by the approach of a person within four or five feet. Everybody marveled at its sensitivity, and even Daniel conceded it to be quite a wonder.

Later John perfected a smaller thermometer out of an old washboard, much on the same principles, and with the same sensitivity. This one he took to Madison with him in 1860.

William Duncan was responsible for much of John's growing local fame. He was wont to come along about chore time in the evening; then he and the boy would duck down cellar to inspect some new contrivance. There they would talk in whispers so as not to disturb Daniel studying in the room above. Duncan was so proud of John he couldn't keep from telling folks about the latest clock that would "work like a man with a brain." "Mark my words," he boasted, "Johnnie Moor will mak' a name for himself some day."

Neighborhood comment was not all favorable. Like the boy Edison, John Muir had his detractors, who called him "queer" and his inventions "freaks." Some of them opined he would "come to no good." Impetus was given the dour prophets one September day when the threshers were at Hickory Hill.[26] John had made some combination door locks out of odds and ends of iron and copper wire. One morning he went off to Portage with a load of grain, leaving the stable doors locked with these. In the afternoon a cloudburst of rain and hail came down upon the men in the fields. Wet to the skin, they scurried for the barn, only to find all doors barred. David and Danny struggled to unlock them, and the much-tried Daniel, Sr., came charging out of the house, exclaiming: "The verra Deevil's in that boy!" He too wrestled with the locks. But not one of them had taken enough interest to learn the combinations. Needless to say, "the parental thrashing weather was very stormy" when John, ignorant of the trouble he had caused, came home in the autumn twilight.

As the months went swiftly by before he would be of age and free to follow his own will, we know from the few intimate records he has left that John Muir suffered great mental anguish. Often he faced the fact that machines could never satisfy his hungers. He would only be exchanging one kind of slavery for another. There were nights when he couldn't sleep for the conflicts that tortured him. While David slumbered peacefully beside him, dreaming perhaps of his Katie, he lay there in wide-eyed silence, torn with wild, insurgent longings. Many a time the old urge to find refuge in the heart of nature drove him out into the night to walk the roads until dawn. Toward the west he often went, down past the swamp and its crawling mists, and beyond that toward the grove near the Duncan farmhouse, where the whippoorwills sang in the dark.

At other times he would stop under "a certain noble old oak" that stood in the meadow below the house. There in contemplation of the universe he found peace. "I used to spend hours with my head up in the sky," he said. "I soared among the planets and thought!" [27]

And there were nights when he wandered west from the house along the ridge, his mother's old collie faithfully padding at his heels. When he reached the end, he would go down into a ravine and up the farther side to the white pine woods that bounded the farm on the north. Here in this "best place" he would lose himself and the doubts that harassed him, among the brooding, friendly trees.

The spring of 1859 brought his twenty-first birthday. But he still lingered on at the farm. How hard it was to leave his mother, his brothers, and Maggie, his closest companion in these latter years! In their work together in field and garden, and in their long stolen walks, they had "talked about everything in heaven and earth."

Throughout his life John Muir's need for human affection was the enemy of his freedom. His personal tragedy — if a man who knew so much joy could be said to have one — stemmed from the duality of his nature, from the devastating gulf between his passion for wandering and his intense devotion to his family. Now at the very threshold of that larger life he longed for, he delayed more than a year.

Late one summer's evening in the year 1860 William Duncan came along all on fire with a new idea. The State Agricultural Fair would open in Madison near the end of September. John had only to exhibit his inventions there, and every machine shop in the country would be open to him. When John expressed doubt that folks would care to look at machines made of wood, Duncan impatiently exclaimed:

"Made of wood! Made of wood! What does it matter what they're made of when they're so out-and-out original. There's nothing else like them in the world. That is what will attract attention, and besides they're mighty handsome things anyway to come from the backwoods."

So John Muir, accepting his friend's plan, prepared to leave home.

PART II

1860–1863

SEEDTIME AND GROWTH

HE DAY of farewell was filled with poignant experiences, and John went away with a troubled heart. He would never forget that last silent meal, his father's final denunciation and refusal to say good-by, the parting at the gate, where David waited with horses and wagon to take him to Pardeeville to catch the train, the girls crying, and — hardest of all to bear — his mother's unspoken grief as she pulled a gold coin from the black bag on her arm and slipped it into his hand.[1]

But at Pardeeville, where he had never been before although it was only nine miles from home, the adventure began to assume a more cheerful aspect. The inhabitants gathering about him to admire his machines gave him a foretaste of success. They thought he must be "a down-east Yankee" to be so clever. Best of all was the glorious trip to Madison aboard the cowcatcher platform, with his wild hair and beard streaming in the wind as the engine went "rushing through the landscapes as if glorying in its strength like a living creature."

As the train pulled into the capital, John, shouldering his bulky, bristling pack of inventions, leaped from his front seat to the earth, eager to try his fortunes. As he approached the Fair Grounds on foot, a fine view spread out before him under sunny autumn skies. A high oak-wooded ridge to the rear, and College Hill, crowned with university buildings, looming on the right, gave the fence-enclosed forty-acre plot the appearance of a spacious amphitheater.

In the last-moment bustle and din he found someone who directed him to the Temple of Art on a knoll as the most likely place to install his machines. Here he was welcomed by the superintendent of the building, Professor J. C. Pickard of the university, who found space for him and assigned him to Division C of the Catalogue as "John Muir, Midland, Marquette Co., 2 clocks, 1 thermometer."

The fair opened with a blare of military bands. Twenty thousand people from all over the state surged in at the gates that first day, milled about among the concessions, then made their way up to the Temple of Art. Everybody was in holiday attire — tall-hatted gentlemen, carrying canes; ladies in vast hoop skirts and Zouave bonnets; country folks awkward in their best bib and tucker.

John Muir, bashful in his rough home-made clothes, had probably never seen such a throng. Yet with the help of two small boys — sons of Professors Carr and Butler — who had offered their services, he was soon demonstrating his early-rising machine. With tight-shut eyes they lay down on the improvised bed while John, setting the clock to operate two or three minutes ahead, explained to the crowd in rich brogue and pawky humor just what would happen. And it did happen right on the second. The trick bed, with a creaking of wheels and levers, reared up at the head to an angle of forty-five degrees, projecting the sleepers violently out upon their feet, to great laughter and applause. After that the young wizard displayed his washboard thermometer, so sensitive that as someone chosen from the audience approached or receded, the dial registered changes in temperature.

Roving reporters scouting about for sensational exhibits soon spotted this one. John awoke the next day to find himself catapulted into fame. One newspaper [2] gave him first-page publicity under the caption: "An Ingenious Whittler." It went on to say: "The wooden clocks of our Marquette Co. friends were among the objects most surrounded by crowds." Another [3] reported that his inventions were "surprising, and could only have been executed by genuine genius."

This started a stampede. On the second day the space around the Temple of Art, according to one newspaper, was "so densely crowded together as to resemble a swarm of bees." On the third day the building was "so thronged that a passage could only be gained by strong pushing." John G. Taylor, a university student, later recalled John's exhibit as "the attraction of the Fair. I can even now see the crowd wending its way to see the wonderful creations of the Scotch boy."[4]

Buffalo Township visitors were dumfounded when they saw the neighbor boy they had dubbed "queer" and a maker of "freaks" suddenly acclaimed "a genius" and honored by the whole state. Agog with excitement, they took the newspapers home with them and passed them around the community. By the time they reached the Muir household, Mother and the girls were already bursting with pride. For William Duncan, one of the first to hear the news, had come romping up the road, shouting as soon as he got into the house: "I told ye that lad was a genius. Maybe folks will believe it noo!"

But Daniel Muir shook his head dourly and that night wrote his son a long homily upon the sin of vanity. John, receiving it along with his sisters' jubilations, made haste to allay his father's fears by saying he had refrained from reading the newspaper praise lest it go to his head. To Sarah he wrote whimsically of his bewilderment now that he was "adrift on this big sinny world. . . . Jumping out of the woods I was at once led and pushed and whirled and tossed about by new everythings, everywhere. For three or four days my eyes at least were pleased and teased and wearied with pictures and sewing machines and squashes and reapers and quilts and cheeses and apples and flowers and soldiers and firemen and thousands of all kinds of faces, all of them strange."

But among all the "new everythings" the one object that drew him like a powerful magnet was the university on the hill. Coming to the Fair Grounds in the morning, he gazed at the big dome of Main Hall — now known as Bascom Hall — flashing in the sunlight. And going out from the gates late at night, his steps turned in that direction. For hours he strolled along campus paths and stood hungrily outside the silent buildings.

The only exhibit rivaling John's clocks in popularity was the famous ice boat, the *Lady Franklin,* being shown by her inventor, Norman Wiard, "the Wizard of New Jersey." In due course John went to see this "greatest invention of the age," whose calliope dominated all other noises on the grounds. As he went in, Wiard was expounding to a rapt throng that his invention would ultimately solve winter traffic problems along all the rivers of the North. The flat-bottomed boat, designed to carry both passengers and freight, would run by steam on ice.

When he saw John, he greeted him affably as a fellow inventor, took pains to explain the mechanism to him, and ended by asking him to go with him to Prairie du Chien, from which port the boat was to make its trial trip on the Mississippi.

John, being an innocent at this time, rejected several more substantial offers to accept this one. But it must be remembered that the ice boat had bluffed leading engineers in the East and had taken prizes at scientific institutes. No money compensation was mentioned in their arrangement. John hoped, however, to gain valuable knowledge from working under a man said to be "greater than Fulton, Stephenson, and Morse." In return for his work in caring for the *Lady Franklin,* Wiard promised to give him lessons in mechanical drawing, the use of technical books, and training in his foundry.

The fair closed with the giving of prizes. Mrs. Ezra Slocum Carr, wife of the professor, was one of a special committee to judge irregular exhibits, and this group bestowed upon John an honorarium of fifteen dollars. In making a report the chairman of the committee said: "The clocks presented by J. Muir exhibited great ingenuity. The Committee regard him as a genius in the best sense, and think the state should feel a pride in encouraging him."

A few days later John boarded the two flat railroad cars that were to take him, his employer, and the ice boat to Prairie du Chien. Arriving in the afternoon, they were welcomed by the town band and most of the populace. During the weeks that followed, the *Lady Franklin* held the public spotlight against all contenders. The premonitory rumblings of Civil War, voiced in the recent Lincoln-Douglas debates and the Presidential campaign, were all but drowned.

To support himself John found two jobs. He took care of a cow and horse for an Irishman named Grogan; and he did chores for the Mondell House, a popular hotel at the corner of Bluff and Minnesota Streets.

The Pelton family, who owned and operated this hostelry, consisted of Edward Pelton, his wife, two children — Fannie and Willie — and his niece, Emily Pelton. Among the boarders were the school principal and several teachers. All together they formed an intelligent and vivacious circle of young people, and John, although a servant, was treated as a friend and equal. "How you must laugh at the memories of my odd appearance," he wrote Emily Pelton later on when he recalled how uncouth he was at the time.

With glee he told the home folks about the "city life" of which he was now a part, and the grandeur of the Mondell House. They even had a piano! The family was duly impressed. Mother urged upon Father that since John was "out in the world," he should have a suit of "boughten clothes." Father decided she was right, and on his next trip to Portage bought a very good suit for his son, and also a trunk to send it in.

Something happened to Daniel Muir when his eldest son left home. He would still do many harsh and even cruel things to his children, but a more loving and generous impulse manifested itself in fitful gleams. In a letter to Sarah and David written several years later he confessed that up to this period ". . . the deceitfulness of riches checked my spiritual growth."

The Mondell House formed the center of the town's social life. The young folks danced, and even indulged in kissing games. John was terribly shocked at first. Walking in one evening upon a riotous scene, he sternly rebuked the whole merry crowd for their "worldliness and silly talk," quoting Scripture to condemn their wickedness. Old Mr. Newton, father of Mrs. Pelton, trying by some jest to check his sermonizing, drew John's ire upon his own head and was denounced for "irreverence."

Our young John the Baptist was so stirred that he poured out his troubled mind in a letter to David and Sarah Galloway. David, with fine tolerance and a better understanding of the world, replied that all this was merely the harmless fun of normal, pleasure-loving young people. David did more than that. He took time off from his late harvesting to go to Prairie du Chien and talk things over with John.

A few years later Muir was ashamed to recall what an insufferable prig he had been. From the Yosemite he wrote to Emily Pelton: "Something or other jostled a bunch of the old Mondell memories. I thought of the days when I came in fresh verdure from the Wisconsin woods, and when I used to hurl very orthodox denunciations at all things morally or religiously amiss in old or young. It appears strange to me that you should all have been so patient with me." [5]

Mrs. Pelton, always understanding, became his closest confidante then and during the storm-tossed years of his university life. And the fragile little Fannie — not destined to live long — was as dear to him as if she had been of his own flesh. When he entered the room, she would stop her fretful crying and wave her tiny hands for him to pick her up. "Let me hold her," he would say to Mrs. Pelton, and in his strong arms she was soon cooing with delight at his songs and endearing Scotch phrases.

Emily Pelton was his companion on many a walk. Indeed, their friendship had advanced so far by late October when David Galloway visited him that he returned home to tell the family about "John's girl." For several years he and Sarah hoped this would be a match.

Meanwhile, as the winter came on, things didn't go well with the ice boat. When the Mississippi froze over, the townspeople clamored for the trial trip. Upon various pretexts Wiard put off the fatal day. Finally, however, amid a throng of onlookers, the *Lady Franklin* was launched, only to break down immediately in some vital part. At the next trial, and the next, other things broke. Wiard's fame as "one of the immortals" sharply declined. By January the newspapers were calling his invention "a humbug," and him "the notorious Mr. Wiard."

Although he had soon become dubious of the boat, John labored faithfully to the end to help make it successful. This in spite of the fact that he had received only one drawing lesson from his employer.

Through these months the memory of the university on the hill had haunted him day and night. One day late in January he boarded the train for the capital. "I was desperately hungry and thirsty for knowledge," he said, "and willing to endure anything to get it."

In Madison John found brief employment with an insurance man named Hastings, addressing circulars and serving the family as coachman. Ordered about as a servant and eating his meals in the kitchen, he found little pleasure in this work. The beribboned ladies of the household had their minds fixed upon millinery, fine dresses, and scaling the social acclivities. He was constantly obliged to drive them out in their fine carriage to make calls, even when they could have walked the distance in five minutes. Elaborate dinners were given, although betweenwhiles the fare was meager. John's letters to Mrs. Pelton during this period reveal his disgust with the artificialities and chitchat of "society."

In his spare time he walked on College Hill, gazing enviously at the students. To join them, he thought, would be the greatest joy of life. One day he talked with a young man who had seen him at the fair. And when he learned that he, too, could attend without much money, by boarding himself and living on bread and milk, he immediately called upon Dean John Sterling, the Acting Chancellor. It was "with fear and trembling, overladen with ignorance," that he approached him. But "Professor John" smoothed out all the obstacles and welcomed him to the university, "next, it seemed to me, to the Kingdom of Heaven."

John Muir lost no time in giving up his job and moving into North Hall, the men's dormitory. His rooms, on the second floor — properly speaking, on the first story above the ground floor — faced Lake Mendota on the north and the city on the east. From one window he could look down State Street and see the tin-domed Capitol looming at the other end. He preferred, however, the view over the broad, clean expanse of the lake, a piece of wild nature no man could mar.

After some preparatory work he was listed as a first-year student. To please himself he entered chemistry and geology classes taught by Dr. Ezra Slocum Carr. Then to please his mother — for every good Scotch matron longed to see her most brilliant son "wag his heed in the pulpit" — he enrolled under Dr. James Davie Butler for Latin and Greek. Since this combination did not lead to graduation, he was classed in the catalogue among the "Irregular Gents."

From the day the young rustic breezed into the university he was an outstanding personage. His fame as an inventor helped to smooth the way. Everybody looked indulgently upon his gaucheries because he was "a genius." His rooms became a show place to which students proudly brought their parents and even some of the legislators from home districts.

Soon after the trick bed was installed, fellows in the dormitory began to complain of the racket it made at five a.m. So John tied a stout cord about his big toe and hung the other end out of the window for Pat, the janitor, to pull each morning on his early rounds. All went well until another student saw it and, guessing its purpose, yanked it so effectively that John was not only hauled out of bed, but nearly out of the window as well. This is the only case on record of his being on the receiving end of a joke.

His ingenuity was boundless. As a variation of clock control for his bed, he used sun motivation on clear days. A reading glass in the east window focused the early rays upon a thread fastened to the sill. This burned through and released the bed mechanism.

Then there was the "Loafer's Chair." It was innocent enough to look at, but beneath the board seat lurked a spring attached to an old pistol loaded with a blank cartridge. The loafer who sat down in it was speedily hurtled out of his ease. Milton Griswold and I. N. Stewart, living in adjacent rooms, early became John's friends, and he fixed up a wire signal system whereby when a verdant-looking chair victim hove in sight, he gave them a tip to hurry in and see the fun.[6]

His climactic invention was a study desk.[7] It stood nine feet high on slender legs carved to represent small books. The slanting top consisted of a central bisected wheel co-ordinated with smaller cogwheels and pivot pegs. At the required time each morning the clock attached to the desk gave a warning burr-r-r, and things began to happen. The halves of the central wheel flopped up, dumping whatever book might be lying upon it into a car below. Then a knocker arrangement like a hand pushed the next book up to take its place. Charles Vroman, once his roommate, said it was "amusing" to see John sitting there "as if chained, working like a beaver against the clock and desk." [8]

This desk made a great sensation. One day Mrs. Sterling, the much-loved "Mother of the University," who was blessed with a sense of humor, called to see it. Pleased by her interest, John put the mechanism through its paces, explaining how he allowed himself fifteen minutes for each subject. When he had finished, she said quietly: "John, I see only one thing lacking in your desk." "And what is that, ma'am?" he eagerly inquired. "It ought to have a paddle that would rise up and slap you when you don't get your lessons," said she.[9]

"A course in starvation it would seem is a tremendous necessity in the training of Heaven's favorites," John Muir once said in an essay on Linnæus.[10] For like the Swedish botanist he knew what it was to have a stomach "achingly empty." Often on less than fifty cents a week he "cooked himself," having little else to eat than graham crackers. Too poor to belong to the Sorghum Club, a group who could afford molasses (but not butter) with their crackers, he ate his with water. His digestion soon balked and he came near collapse. Somehow his family found it out, and letters reveal that his father, stricken in conscience, sent him fifty dollars. A month later, in June, he sent forty dollars. Beneath all his harshness, he was, as John said, "foundationally kind."

The only gymnastic apparatus the university possessed was a rope dangling from a pole on the campus. But games, wrestling, racing, boating, and swimming made up for the lack. Often in the early morning John raced up the lake shore to the west end, to plunge into the chill waters. In warmer weather other boys went with him; but when the ice had to be broken, he went alone.

Since boyhood he had been the stern master of his body. Well known is the story of his bout with himself in Fountain Lake when

Dr. Ezra Slocum Carr

William Duncan

Dr. James Davie Butler

David Taylor

Muir's "student desk," invented by him in 1861 *On permanent exhibit a the Wisconsin State Historical Society Museum Madison*

he became faint while swimming and began to sink. Down, down into the soft vegetable ooze he drifted helplessly. Then that "other self" — ever watchful as in the dangers of later years — came to his rescue. "Kick out your feet!" it commanded. And kicking them frogwise, he rose to the surface. The next day he went back to the lake, swam out to a boat in the middle, and dove and dove, each time yelling: "Take that! Take that!! Take that!!!"

Mumble-the-peg was often played on the green that first spring. Some of the fellows were expert in twirling their jackknives to land point-down in the earth. Those who couldn't imitate the challengers' throws had to pull the blades out with their teeth. One day they challenged John. He was badly beaten and got his mouth full of dirt. But being too canny to let it happen again, he spent some hours alone in the hills, throwing his knife in all sorts of new ways. Then walking innocently up to a huddle on the lawn, and being challenged, he introduced so many new wrinkles that he soon had all his rivals eating dirt.[11]

But John found his greatest recreation in long Sunday rambles about the Four Lakes, as far as he could get away from Madison with its stately limestone mansions, and brick churches — chill, dark fortresses of orthodoxy.

There is no reason to believe John's exterior became any more sophisticated at the university. He still wore his drab, home-made clothes except on special occasions. His eager, twinkling blue eyes still looked out from a tangle of wild hair and beard. The men students who could wore beards, following the fashion set by the man in the White House. But their whiskers were dandified in comparison with John's. The twins wrote him that now he was out in the world, they hoped he would give more attention to his appearance. But he hastened to dash their hopes on that score, by repeating what one of the fellows said to him: "If I had a beard like yours, I would set fire to it!"

His unshorn locks did not detract from his popularity, however. A letter from David Muir, written some years afterward, gives a hint of his status: "Did I tell you that Viebahn called upon me last fall? He spoke of you as the hero of the University. He said they spoke of you there just as we were wont to do of Samson, Xerxes, Alexander, Jack Robinson, etc. They have traditions about you."

As an immigrant boy in a backwoods community, John Muir knew little of national problems. Upon arriving at the university he was thrown at once into a maelstrom of events soon to culminate in the Civil War. Lincoln's policies, slavery and tariff disputes, and the right of Southern states to secede, he heard discussed on every hand. As he listened, the quarrel between North and South seemed to him no more a justification for war than the old sectional rivalries in Scotland. On April 12, 1861 Fort Sumter was fired upon. Two days later it surrendered. President Lincoln called for 75,000 volunteers, and the nation was ablaze. "My country, right or wrong," had become the universal sentiment. Eight upperclassmen enlisted on the first day, and the stampede was on. The bearded and beardless alike rushed to the recruiting stations.

The university was from the start in full focus of the soul-stirring excitement prevailing in the state capital. The Fair Grounds, just over the hill's edge, became Camp Randall. On May 1 the Zouaves arrived in full force. Their brilliant uniforms and flashing swords, the grace and precision of their drills, took the city by storm. The Legislature adjourned to see them, and the classrooms on the hill were emptied.

John Muir alone remained silent and unresponsive. In his letters home he hardly mentioned the turmoil. He spoke of the "common and uncommon noises" heard from his room, "but the thrushes in that fine grove don't seem to care. They whistle just as they do on the black and burr oaks at Hickory. I always keep my window open so I can hear them fine."

After commencement John walked home for his first vacation. Before he arrived at Hickory Hill, he changed into his best clothes and slicked up his appearance generally; so much so that when the family saw him coming up the meadow road, they thought him a stranger. But the old dog, his mother's collie, recognizing him from afar, bounded to meet him. He was deeply touched by that doggish welcome. Fifty years later he wrote a little essay entitled "My

Dogs," in which he placed this collie first in the list of his great canine friends.

It was good to be at home again. He had wearied for the sight of them all, even to the point of illness. But Margaret was not there. She had married John Reid in December and had gone over the hill to live in her new log-cabin home.

His father, strangely gentle these days, agreed to pay him seventy-five cents a day for his summer's work. As they labored in the fields, John persuaded David to go back with him in the fall. Daniel consented to pay him the same amount toward his expenses. Since John had blazed his own way out into freedom, his brothers were consumed with restlessness. Eighteen-year-old Danny thirsted for science. So John taught him during the summer how to make a battery and work with chemicals.

When John returned to college in the autumn with David in tow, he found Madison had changed in those few weeks from a bedraggled, overgrown village to a large and bustling city. New stores, theaters, dance-halls, and saloons had sprung up everywhere, especially along the route leading to Camp Randall.

Some time that fall John Muir began to make frequent visits to the cantonment, a place he had avoided in the spring. The arrival of boys he knew got him started. When they were off duty, he took them on long walks into the country. Then they began to come to his rooms, bringing comrades to see his machines and hear him talk. James Whitehead, the neighbor boy from home, was one who came under his influence.

"During twenty years or more of public life," Whitehead said later, "I do not recall a single person that could compare with John Muir as a conversationalist. Easy, fluent and free from all display of superior knowledge, he told what he had in mind in simple, pure Anglo-Saxon. He possessed a poet's fervid fancy, and without intent or seeming knowledge his language was richly embellished." [12]

John, seeing the conditions surrounding these young boys snatched from farms and small towns, felt on their behalf something akin to his father's crusading zeal. One couldn't walk down the street without realizing that a horde of undesirables had flocked into Madison to prey upon them. Nearly every other house between the camp and the Capitol sold beer and whisky, while brothels crowded the by-streets. So he worked among the men, reaching as many as he could, striving to fortify them against present evils and the bloody ordeal ahead. According to James Whitehead, he talked to them like a father, appealing to them to look ahead to the years beyond the war. Success in the future, he told them, would depend upon their having lived a morally clean and wholesome life. He urged upon them "the necessity of having character formed, and being possessed of tightly-clinched principles before being put to such a trial as a three-year soaking in so horrible a mixture."

One October day the Seventh Wisconsin Regiment left for the front. John went to the station to see them off. That afternoon he wrote Mrs. Pelton his impressions and thoughts. As he helped B. strap on his knapsack, he noted how gleeful D. was "in his great blue coat . . . blowing his fife . . . amid chattering drums." Eager for slaughter, they were going away "on a half-dance, with a smile on their faces, and . . . a loud laugh." He alone, not blinded by martial pomp, saw clearly what lay ahead of them: ". . . the gallant charge, the well-directed grape-shot, the exploded mine rending hundreds limb from limb in a moment, the dreadful shell thrown precisely into the thickest crowd, sending righteous and wicked to shreds perhaps while asleep. If the whole abominable business is necessary," he mused, "if we must . . . cut the throats of the Secessionists, let it be done solemnly, as when a Judge sheds tears on pronouncing the doom of the atrocious murderer."

For a long time John sat at his window that afternoon, looking out upon the ineffable blue peace of Lake Mendota. And meditating upon the brevity of human life, he added to his letter: "As the leaf on the ripples of the Lake, generation follows generation. We are passing away. How great the need for energy to spend our little while to purpose."

John and David, harried by lack of money, decided to teach school during the winter of '61 and '62. David found employment in a near-by Dutch community, while John was hired by the McKeebey District,[13] ten miles south of Madison.

Having brought no clock, he devised a temporary one out of a tin pail and a coin. "It cost about two hours work and kept time by water passing in a fine jet through a three-cent piece." Later he made two others. One was a wheel-shaped instrument hung above the blackboard, operating a series of shingles. As each period came to an end, the shingle calling the next class dropped to a horizontal position.

But his masterpiece was a contraption to build fires. Each night he cleaned out the stove and replenished it. At the inner edge of the hearth beneath the shavings he placed a teaspoonful of sugar mixed with chlorate of potash. Above this by a wire attached to a clock he suspended an uncorked vial containing two drops of sulphuric acid. At the hour desired the slight strain on the wire caused the vial to pour out the acid upon the sugar and potash below. Instant combustion set the shavings on fire, and when he arrived on a cold winter morning, the stove would be roaring finely.

During his teaching term John gained local fame as a science lecturer. Soon he was being invited to speak in adjacent districts. The teacher in the village of Oregon, having heard him, asked him to speak at his school. To his students he said: "You are going to have a visitor next Saturday. I want all of you to give him your attention . . . as he is a very bright young man. He can teach more in a minute than I can in a day. I only wish I knew half he does."[14]

The school was agog when John arrived. One of the pupils, John Dreher, was still telling about him when an old man: "He had chestnut-brown hair hanging to his shoulders, and a long unkempt beard, and a rough ungroomed look even for that day when most folks didn't dress very well."

John Dreher was a bit hazy about the substance of the lecture, but he was so charmed that on the following Saturday he went with his schoolmates in a body, wading through three miles of deep snow, to visit the McKeebey school. Muir welcomed them heartily, put his clocks through their tricks, and performed chemical experiments for their entertainment. He also demonstrated how the fire was started in the morning.

Letters following him after he left this region and long afterward reveal the lasting impression he made upon both parents and pupils. Some of the boys went to the university because he had persuaded them.

In March 1862 John was again at North Hall — alone this time, for David, finding university work difficult, had gone home; not to submit again to his father's yoke, but to look for another way of escape. This he soon found, clerking in a Portage dry-goods store.

Soon after this startling changes took place at home, precipitated by Danny. His father had refused to let him go to school, saying he needed him on the farm. A few days later the young rebel informed his parent he *would* go to school even if he had to run away from home. Daniel Muir did not burst into a rage as expected, but asked for a little time to think things over. Three weeks later he told the family he was going to rent the farm to John Reid. They would move to Portage, where the children could all go to school.

Soon after their arrival Ann subscribed for a Madison newspaper. In a letter to John she said: "I think it is time we knew what is going on in the world." Since her eldest son had shown them the way, there was an urge in them all for a freer mode of life.

But Dan, still restless, announced one day that he was going to Canada, get a job, and earn money for college. When his father refused to give him his train fare, his mother supplied it. Although grieved when her sons left home, she encouraged them in going.

Conditions at Camp Randall were bad when John returned to Madison that second spring. The war had become a grim and awful specter, darkening the whole land. The boys who had danced away with smiles and boastings, had met the stern reality in the Battle of Falling Waters, at Bull Run, and in the Shenandoah Valley. Some were dead. Many more were in hospitals.

Camp Randall, filled with the sick and dying, was seething with revolt. The men were fed on stinking sowbelly and hardtack crawling with weevils. Hungry rats infested the tents and barracks. Smallpox and typhoid were rampant. As early as the fall of '61 the soldiers were dying off at the rate of one a day. That winter pneumonia took a deadly toll. The living buried the dead on the hill west of the camp. As the students sat in their classes in Main Hall, the muffled funeral drums and the crack of musketry came to their ears with ominous frequency.

Then in May 1862 came a consignment of 139 sick Confederate prisoners. There were not enough beds for them, or doctors and nurses to care for them. They died in their bunks — sometimes ten in a day.

Agonizing in his room as he listened to the death knells, or walking alone by the lake to get away from the sound of them, John Muir tried to think of some way he could save life, not destroy it. At last he decided he would study to be a doctor. The war would be over, perhaps, before he was ready; but so long as organized society was based on competition and greed, there would be other wars, and other wounds and sicknesses to heal. "How great the need for energy to spend our little while to purpose!"

He talked with Dr. Carr, who encouraged him in his plan. With another year of chemistry he would be ready for the University of Michigan Medical School at Ann Arbor. So at last he had a definite goal. He did not choose it because of any particular liking for that branch of science, but because he wanted to serve his fellow man.

John Muir attended the University of Wisconsin only two years and a half, yet in science he found that "glimpse of the cosmos" that determined his future career. With money earned doing chores he equipped a laboratory in his own rooms, and went far beyond the prescribed course in his experiments with chemicals and electricity. Before the end of his first term he was known as "the best chemistry student in the University."

Geology became to him a still more important revelation of nature's plan. Having access to the small but good university library and Dr. Carr's own larger, up-to-date collection of scientific books, he became acquainted with the advance of geologic knowledge up to that period.

Study of earth structure was in its infancy when John Muir came to America. Most geologists belonged to the various "learned professions" and had taken up geology merely as a hobby or side interest. Edward Hitchcock, whose textbook was still used in the university in Muir's time, was a clergyman. Benjamin Silliman, a lawyer, began to study geology only after his appointment to the chair of chemistry and natural science at Yale. Dr. Carr, John's teacher, was a medical man to begin with. Josiah Dwight Whitney, future State Geologist of California, was a chemist and mineralogist. Not until after the discovery of gold in 1848 had created a nation-wide clamor for economic surveys did geology become a recognized science.

In Europe, however, it was somewhat more advanced. The travel writings of Humboldt had done much to stimulate earth study. Darwin, by his explorations in the *Beagle,* added immeasurably to this. The students of Linnæus, making floral surveys in many lands, increased general knowledge. Hugh Miller, working among the old red sandstone quarries of Scotland, had given to the world a glimpse of the earth's great age. This he was at pains to reconcile with the Genesis story, reasoning that the "six days" of creation indicated æons of time.

One of the problems puzzling early American geologists, was the origin of the Drift — that vast layer of soil, sand, gravel, pebbles, and boulders derived from the far north, overlying eastern Canada and much of the United States down to the 40th parallel.

Postulating the Bible story of the Flood — for all were fundamentalists in those days — they accounted for the Drift by wild and fantastic theories. Some said the Noachian Deluge was caused by "the jar of earthquakes" that had broken the polar ice cap and sent floods of water carrying rocks and soil hurtling southward. Others believed the earth's crust had collapsed in places, releasing water from the interior. Still others said intense heat had melted the polar ice, causing freshets of cosmic proportions to pour south. Planetary collisions were even trumped up to explain the hypothetical Flood. All these theorists assumed a catastrophic First Cause and asserted the Drift had been transported by the torrential action of water and floating ice.

While American geologists were still floundering in the Deluge hypothesis, Louis Agassiz, son of a Swiss pastor, advanced in Europe in the late thirties and early forties his theory of glaciation to account for all Drift phenomena, as well as the polish and grooving of rocks and the excavations of canyons and lake beds. Basing his conclusions upon his researches among the glaciers of the Jura Mountains and the Alps, he declared the earth had passed through an Ice Age, during which "a universal ice sheet" had flowed southward from the North Pole, covering the hemisphere to a depth of five or six thousand feet, down as far as central Europe and Asia, destroying the vegetation of the preceding epoch. The glaciers of Switzerland, he said, were but dying remnants of this vast shroud.

Agassiz's earlier writings upon this theory, and especially his *Études sur les glaciers,* published in 1840, upset about as many applecarts as did Darwin's *Origin of Species* a few years later. They precipitated world-wide controversy. Out of the babel of tongues in America a few voices began to emerge in favor of this theory. Asa Gray, Professor Charles Dewey, and James Dwight Dana turned in the forties toward the new conception. Even the clerical Hitchcock, working always with one eye on Genesis, advanced sufficiently to include glaciers along with icebergs, landslips, and "waves of translation" as carriers of Drift.

Other scientists, loath to give up their ideas of a catastrophic cause, came to concede grudgingly the former existence of glaciers, but denied to them any significant eroding power. They were but brooms, they said, to sweep away the debris created by other, more potent agencies. J. D. Whitney was among these. He continued to maintain in the face of all evidence to the contrary that the Drift was "probably due to floating ice."

In the midst of this debate, in 1846, the dynamic Agassiz came to America and the next year joined the faculty of Harvard University. This vivid, eager man, who "never had time to make money" and who "was possessed by something so much greater than himself that pain, hunger, loneliness did not matter," was a great teacher. Young men flocked from all over the nation to study under him. Other teachers of science crowded his classes and warmed themselves as at a flame. So the glacial theory and Agassiz's methods of teaching began to spread like yeast throughout the country. Dr. Carr, then a college professor in the East, became imbued with them and, coming west in 1856 to the University of Wisconsin, put them into practical application.

Agassiz walked the hills with his pupils. He sat by the sea with them. In 1848 he traveled with a group of them to the Lake Superior region and there pointed out to them the evidences of glacial action. Using textbooks and scientific nomenclature sparingly, he taught his students to make the hills and woods their laboratories, to develop "the seeing eye." "No one," he declared, "can warp her [Nature] to suit his own views." "A physical fact is as sacred as a moral principle."

Dr. Carr, following his example, carried his classes out among the hills and along the lake shores around Madison. "Earth knowledge," said he, "has more spiritual value for the youth of America than erudition concerning the amours of Jupiter and Venus. . . . When I walk with students in green fields and forests, and show them Nature's basement rooms, how the foundations of the earth were laid, I see in them tokens of mental animation which are the strongest stimulants to my own exertions." [15]

The professor was well fitted to be a leader of youth. He was a large, clean-shaven, fine-looking man with an impressive manner of speaking. "His spirited lectures thrilled his hearers and filled his students with interest and animation," said one of his pupils. Another wrote home: "I was carried away with the subject and the Professor." John Muir said: "I shall not forget the Doctor, who first laid before me the great book of Nature." [16]

Thanks to Dr. Carr and the special reading privileges he extended, John soon became absorbed in the subject of glaciation. And, thanks to his early grounding in French, he was able to read Agassiz's writings in the original. He mastered the technique of glacial exploration set forth in *Études sur les glaciers* and *Système glaciare*. He made an intensive study of the methods of Agassiz, Guyot, and James Forbes in measuring the flow of Alpine ice rivers with stakes and boulders, to such good effect that when he found his first living glaciers in the Sierra, he was able to put them into instant practice.

Muir little dreamed in those days that he would be the one to discover the large part glacial action had played in sculpturing the mountains of the Pacific coast. Modern scientists have refuted the "universal ice sheet" idea of Agassiz, while accepting in essence his theory of the erosive power of glaciers. Muir, going west in 1868, premised his early investigations upon Agassiz's polar ice sheet theory. However, as will be revealed later by an extract from his Nevada journal, he came to doubt its universality.

Agassiz, being a pioneer investigator, did not in his lifetime arrive at the conclusion held by later geologists, that there has been a succession of glacial winters rather than one. Muir in his writings of the mid-seventies appears to have approached in some degree the present-day conception.

But apart from his doubts and questionings he remained essentially a disciple of the Swiss glacialist. "The glacier was God's great plow," said Agassiz, "and when it vanished from the surface of the land, it left it prepared for the hand of the husbandman. . . . I think we may believe that God did not shroud the world He made in snow and ice without purpose, and that this, like many other operations of His Providence, seemingly destructive and chaotic in its first effect, is nevertheless a work of beneficence and order."[17]

Muir might have said that, so perfectly does it express his own philosophy, told in a thousand ways in his own words. The meaning behind the fact, the evidences denoting law, order, creative intelligence, loving design, Muir sought and found in nature's processes.

Dr. James Davie Butler, viewing with alarm the trend away from the classics, did not wholly approve of Dr. Carr's innovations. It is said he even considered them "dangerous." For, being an eminent Greek and Latin scholar, he was an ardent champion of the older forms of education.

Although John Muir, in his devotion to science, never became more than an average student of the classics, he learned from Dr. Butler things vital to him as a potential writer. The professor, a devout disciple of Emerson, hammered into his pupils the necessity of keeping "a Commonplace Book," as the Concord sage had done "Be a snapper-up of trifles," he urged. "Seize ideas by the forelock," and put them down "stamped in Nature's mint of ecstasy." Thus his own speech was crowded with homely metaphors and similes, fairly tumbling over one another.

Discerning in John thoughts and phrases of power and quaint originality, the little bearded, gnomelike doctor fairly gloated over them, repeating them in his booming voice for other students to strive after. Being the first to discover literary genius in him, he taught him to prize "the native livery" in which his thoughts clothed themselves. "Do not throw away Nature's sweet blush," he insisted, "to buy rouge in Paris." Calling attention to the earth-and-farm-toil metaphors John used so effectively, he said: "They light up your meaning like windows. You've heard the stories Father Abraham tells. He picked those up in log cabins. But they're good enough for the Cabinet in the White House!" [18]

As a result of Dr. Butler's teachings John Muir, from the beginning of his wanderings, kept notebooks that would have delighted the professor's heart. In them and in his later writings he used freely the earth metaphors native to his speech, which give his style its unique charm and pungency.

Before John had been long at the university, Mrs. Carr brought her young sons to call upon him at North Hall. Already his desk stood against the wall, and other wondrous contraptions littered the place. "But to me the most captivating piece of mechanism," says Mrs. Carr, "was an apparatus for registering the growth of an ascending plant stem during each of the twenty-four hours. . . . A fine needle, threaded with the long hair of a fellow studentess, when attached to the plant, made the record faithfully upon a paper disk marked to indicate minute spaces with great exactness, while the rustic clock ticked the minutes and hours away." [19]

Mrs. Jeanne C. (Smith) Carr, at this time in her middle thirties, was looked upon as one of the social and intellectual leaders of Madison. One who knew her well,[20] describes her as "a young, pretty woman with tawny hair, a sweet expression and a charming voice. Plainly dressed, she was always going about botanizing,

DAVID GILRYE MUIR
in maturity

"I did look kind of innocent."
JOHN MUIR'S *first photo, taken at Madison in* 1863

DR. DANIEL MUIR
in maturity

Annie Muir (1863)

Mary Muir Hand (1863)

Sarah Muir Galloway (1863)

Margaret Muir Reid

Joanna Muir Brown

skipping like a girl." She was an artist and musician as well and, being a true lover of nature, was especially gifted in landscape gardening.[21] All together she was a person of wisdom and understanding. More than anyone else who came into John Muir's early life she became his teacher in the humanities. She formed the bridge between the crabbed isolation of his boyhood and the world of men he would have to live in. By her unfailing tact and faith in his genius she directed his aims and helped fit him for leadership.

He first entered her home as a chore-boy hired to stay on Saturdays with her boys and young Henry Butler. Soon the bashful country youth was invited to remain for dinner, and that led to a long series of happy evenings with her and Dr. Carr.

The Carr house, at 114 West Gilman Street, is still one of the fine old residences of Madison. Built of cream-colored sandstone and set far back on a wide, oak-shaded lawn, it embodies the best of the Midwest tradition in architecture. "Filled with books, peace, kindliness, patiënce," as John described it, it was to him a revelation of gracious living. The large high-ceilinged library he called "the kernel of the house." Tall bookshelves lined the walls, and above them hung the portraits of scientists and men of letters. It was here, as well as in his classes and in the library of Dr. Butler, that he came under the influence of Agassiz, Wordsworth, Thoreau, and Emerson.

Emerson's name and philosophy were in the very air one breathed at Madison. Here as throughout Eastern and Midwestern America the intellectuals banded into lyceums and literary societies, parroted his wise sayings, unconscious for the most part that in the phrases they so glibly mouthed lurked dynamite enough to blast into oblivion their pleasant little worlds of commerce and convention.

Only to a few did Emerson belong by right of understanding. Dr. and Mrs. Carr, disciples and personal friends of the great seer, came west intent upon ending in the University of Wisconsin what Emerson called "our long apprenticeship to learning in other lands." Through them John Muir was led to read "The American Scholar," and the essay on "Nature," both clarion calls of emancipation to young men dreaming dreams and groping for the light.

Muir was himself an original. He was never warped out of his own orbit or made a satellite to any man or system of thinking. But he was hospitable to Emerson's ideas because like cleavage planes in rocks, awaiting development, they were indigenous within himself. When Emerson said: "Every rational creature has in Nature a dowry and estate. It is his if he will," the words struck fire in Muir's mind. Remembering them, in due time he went out to claim his dowry and to reject all compromises. The gentle Emerson, happy in his Concord meadows, never wholly took possession of his estate. Like Moses, he only pointed the way. Thoreau and Muir alone of all his followers fully *lived* his Nature gospel.

Among the influences of John's university years that shaped his destiny, one of the most important was ushered in by his fellow student Milton S. Griswold.

On a morning in early June 1862, the two friends stopped to chat under a locust tree — still standing after more than eighty years — near the northwest corner of North Hall. Griswold, whose penchant for sharing his botanical enthusiasms with all and sundry was a joke among the fellows, pulled down a blossom and began to expound its close relationship to the pea, the bean, and the vetch. As he talked, John suddenly became deeply interested — so much so that on the following Sunday when Milton brought out a mass of plants for classifying and pressing, he joined him on the green. "I called his attention . . . to all parts of the plant," relates Griswold, "to the arrangement of its leaves and of the different organs . . . and then went step by step through the tables . . . until I located the name . . . and full description. . . . 'Why, Griswold,' John exclaimed, 'that's perfectly wonderful! I'll get me a botany right off, and we'll go botanizing together.' "[22]

In less than a week he had a Wood's *Botany*, and from that time on, the two friends explored together the creeks, bays, bogs, and woods about the Four Lakes of Madison. John had ferret eyes for the smallest blossom. "He would plunge out of a thicket with a new flower in his hand, shouting, 'Oh, Griswold, see here. Isn't this a beauty? How tiny it is. But see how wonderful!' "

Late in June he went home to work for David Galloway. All summer he labored in the wheat and barley fields. But in the early mornings, while the moon still hung low in the west, he was abroad gathering plants for the night's work ahead. Then when the first stars pricked the evening sky, and the whippoorwill called from the oak trees, he went to his task of sorting and classifying, toiling until midnight. He had always been "gey daft" about flowers, but hitherto it had been their individual beauty that delighted him. Now that he had the key to their myriad co-ordinations, he felt new vistas of understanding opening before him — glimpses of a universal pattern.

During the final year at the university John Muir opened himself in a greater degree to the social life of the campus and the currents of political thought surging about him. In January 1863 he allowed Griswold to propose his name for membership in the Athenæan Society. He had previously attended many of its debates, but always sat in the background. Once he had joined, however, he took a lively part. He even plunged into his first two debates as a volunteer. Soon he was ranked as one of the best speakers in the society.

Political science and economics were not then the orthodox subjects they now are for classroom study, but the fresh winds of democracy were by this time blowing strong on College Hill, and the quickening interest was finding free expression in the two debating clubs.[23] Here the germ of democracy brought to this country by the freedom-loving immigrants began to ferment and grow in the minds of their sons, eager to have a part in governing themselves. Frederick Jackson Turner, a student on the hill only a few years later, saw arising out of these racial components of the frontier "a new product which holds the promise of world brotherhood." The "Wisconsin Idea" was being born, an idea that was to make government responsive to the will of the people, to suppress the "old squatter ideal" of unbridled individualism and exploitation, to conserve and share for the good of the greatest number the earth and the natural resources that belonged to it.

No doubt the struggle of the university for survival against the lumber barons and other entrenched interests in the Legislature helped bring to birth the Wisconsin Idea. Carl Schurz, the great German-American, and Increase A. Lapham as Regents were among the leaders in that long fight. And nourished by the new spirit of democracy thus implanted in the university, there were to arise to leadership in the nation such men as La Follette, Van Hise, Turner, Commons, Ely, Ross, and John Muir.

The list of those men and women of Wisconsin who influenced John Muir's future work, may well include the name of Increase A. Lapham, the foremost conservationist of the state in that period. Early in his career at the university John met him, and in the thin, nervous little man of Quakerish habits and appearance he found a great student of nature. By sheer power of observation he had educated himself in geology, meteorology, botany, and scientific agriculture. Agassiz and Gray recognized his scholarship, and he collaborated with them. The Federal Bureau organizing the storm-signal service on the Great Lakes was inspired by him.

But the greatest battle of his life was to save the natural resources of the state. Ever since 1855, when he issued his first pamphlet upon the evils of tree-destruction, he had gone up and down Wisconsin warning the population of the coming exhaustion of the forests. And by every means at his command he appealed to the Legislature and the Federal Government to make laws for their protection.

John Muir was profoundly impressed by Lapham's teachings. A dozen years later he was using the same arguments, buttressed by his own extensive observations, in his appeals for the preservation of forests on the Pacific coast.

Certain books, too, had a large share in shaping Muir's career. Pre-eminent among them were the travel writings of Alexander von Humboldt. It can also be said that, even more than Agassiz, Humboldt influenced his convictions as a naturalist. An analysis of Muir's philosophy of nature in its grasp of cosmic unity amid the complexity of phenomena reveals a close affinity with that of Humboldt.

Just how many of Humboldt's thirty volumes on his travels in Spanish America [24] Muir may have read we do not know; but we do know he carried one to Canada in 1864 and was still poring over some of them five years later in the Yosemite. They inspired his lifelong desire to explore South America to such an extent that in his old age he felt he could not die until he had carried out that desire at least in part.

Humboldt in his travels became an ardent conservationist. In all his writings he pointed out the evils of tree-destruction. Of the laying waste of watershed forests, he found this to be universally true: "In felling the trees which covered the crowns and slopes of the mountains, men in all climates seem to be bringing upon future generations two calamities at once — a want of fuel, and a scarcity of water."

It is not too much to say that through John Muir Humboldt exercised a powerful influence in awakening America to the need of conserving watershed forests as well as other wild vegetation.

Among the pioneer writers upon conservation from whom Muir drew inspiration and knowledge should be mentioned George P. Marsh. This native of Vermont campaigned in the East, as Lapham did in Wisconsin, to save the trees. Lapham often quoted from him in his reports and other writings. In his *Man and Nature,* first published in 1864, Marsh was the first American to lay down in a book of general circulation the broad principles of conservation and to demonstrate by the deplorable examples of Asiatic and European countries what America was heading toward in the wanton waste of her forests. That John Muir made a careful study of it, is evidenced by his own copiously marked copy.

In the spring of 1863 Muir was consumed with restlessness. A fellow student once described him as "a storage battery of energy, encased in flexible, elastic steel." But his splendid vitality had been depleted by overwork. Moreover, he was depressed about the war and the mounting toll of death. In a letter to the Galloways he said: "This war seems farther from a close than ever. How strange that a country with so many schools and churches should be desolated by so unsightly a monster. 'Leaves have their time to fall!' . . . But may the same be said of the slaughtered upon a battle field?"[25]

His future was uncertain. The probability of being drafted into the Army lay like a blight across his plans to go to medical college. Meanwhile the old nostalgia for the wilderness gave him no peace. So he outlined a summer's "wander" down the Wisconsin to the Mississippi, thence up to the Falls of St. Anthony, across the river, and south through Minnesota and Iowa.

One day in April he cut his hair and beard, donned his "boughten clothes," and had his first photograph taken. In view of Daniel's ban upon "graven images," no Muir had ever appeared before a camera. Yet John dared to send one home. Commenting upon this picture in later years, he said: "I did look kind of innocent."

Arriving at the Portage home, it created a commotion. Father, sensing a suppressed excitement among his womenfolk, sleuthed about and found it. Ann and the girls waited in silence for the bolt to strike. But Daniel, saying nothing, walked to the window and studied it for a long time. Then, with a glint of whimsey in his voice, he remarked: "Yes, that's John all right. See thae big feet! "[26]

The whole family, relieved at his mild acceptance of his son's disobedience, set out upon a regular spree of having their pictures taken. Sarah and David Galloway, Margaret and John Reid, Annie, Mary, Joanna, and finally Ann herself visited the photographer.

John had planned to go alone on his summer's "geological and botanical ramble," but two of his college mates, Rice and Blake, begged to share the big adventure. The day after commencement they started out, tramping northwestward to Sauk City, crossing the Wisconsin, and proceeding west along the great gorge. Spread before them in what John called "rock scriptures," they could read the whole history of land building and degradation. The gorge, over four miles wide to begin with at Prairie du Sac, above Sauk City, had been torn and gouged out of the yielding sandstone at the time the river, flowing down from receding glaciers, had covered the floor of the chasm with fine sand and gravel and still later had trenched these deposits, leaving remnants in the form of terraces. Day after day as they walked westward they saw the abyss narrow toward its half-mile span at Bridgeport, because the advancing river had met the more resistant sandstones and limestones of the lower valley. It was a grand land for young Titans to clamber over. They zigzagged back and forth between bank and trench bottom, now climbing high bluffs, now scrambling among taluses, searching the limestone blocks for ferns. Seeing a tiny sedge perched in a rock cleavage far above them, John would ascend to it swiftly, finding footholds and handholds as if by instinct. As a mountaineering companion once said of him, he fairly seemed to slide up "like a human spider."

When they reached Prairie du Chien after two weeks of tramping, Rice, the youngest boy, was so crippled with a sprained ankle and sore muscles that John and Blake sent him home on the train.

While Blake rested, John called at the Mondell House. There was sorrow in his heart, for little Fannie had died in the preceding year, and within a few months her mother had followed her. Emily was now acting as her uncle's housekeeper. But for her, as for John, the place was bereft of all that had made it a home. As they strolled down the river valley, finding comfort — even joy — in each other's companionship, it would have been easy for him to speak words to the lonely girl that would have joined their lives henceforth. That would have pleased his family. But other voices — a blind, unconquerable urge toward freedom, potencies within himself not yet realized — were calling him on toward some unknown goal.

James Whitehead has described John Muir at this period as "a cheerful, optimistic, splendid man, six feet in height, straight as an arrow, with light hair, full beard, clear blue eyes and a skin smooth and transparent. . . ." It is not surprising that women found him attractive, then and later. But in this case as in others he succeeded in turning the relationship into a selfless and lasting friendship.

Giving up the plan to go north to the Falls of St. Anthony, John and young Blake crossed the Mississippi and headed south from MacGregor along the Iowa bluffs. From the heights where they camped the first night, they looked down upon the river in the morning. Across the great Mississippi gorge the bluffs of the eastern shore loomed black and near, as if one might leap over. White billowing fog filled the abyss between. As the sun rose, the fog thinned to diaphanous, irised streamers midway between the bluffs. Then the gleaming, full-bosomed river came into full view with its countless barges and white side-wheel steamers chugging ahead between long, narrow log rafts and drifting "strings."

As John gazed at the scene he got some idea of the magnitude of the lumber industry. Millions of feet of logs — slain white pine giants that only last winter stood lordly upon the hills of northern Wisconsin, logs that had come crashing end over end down the wild Chippewa, the Black, or the St. Croix, were chained now and floating to the sawmills below, destined to build houses, barns, fences, and bridges on the treeless prairies of the West. Maine and Michigan were already stripped in large part of their vast forests. Wisconsin was approaching the peak of lumber production. Minnesota was just at the beginning. Would it end only when there were no more trees to cut?

Finally breaking the spell that held them, the boys tobogganed down the steep slope and, after exploring a fossil glen, found their way in the torrid heat to the low shore where the glen's brawling stream died in the river.

Reluctant to resume their weary trek on foot, they thought it would be great fun to sail up the Wisconsin. They bought a regular little fairy of a boat and were soon rowing blissfully up the broad bosom of the Mississippi. The bliss lasted until they reached the mouth of the Wisconsin with its turbulent, outpouring waters. Then, "gloomy as a winter's day,"[27] they paddled mightily with their one pair of fragile oars, making about ten rods in two hours. Pausing in sheer exhaustion, they were swept once more down the stream. After several attempts they landed on the east shore, appropriated some boards, and set about hewing out four large oars. Then they camped for the night.

In the morning they embarked northward, their "hearts again trimmed with fresh hopes." But at the confluence the powerful current once more tossed the boat — "small and light as a baby's cradle" — on the boiling, tumbling waters. They all but capsized several times. Drenched with sweat and spray, they pulled up on a low sandy Ararat to rest and scold the little craft for being "as obstinate and unsteerable as Noah's ark." At last they tacked a card to the prow, addressed to a friend in Dubuque, Iowa, and watched it dance away on the river. The next morning Blake took the stage home from Bridgeport, fed up with adventure.

John, left alone, returned to Prairie du Chien, intending to go on to the Falls of St. Anthony. That night and again in the morning he called at the Mondell House to see Emily. Both times he was met by her uncle, who told him rather curtly that she was not at home. Later he found she *was* at home. For some reason Mr. Pelton wished to discourage their friendship.

John was puzzled by this rebuff in a family where he had known so much kindness. Suddenly he felt desperately alone and friendless. Deciding to return home, he set out on foot to retrace the rambling journey along the Wisconsin River gorge.

Later in July he arrived at Madison to get some of his belongings. The Carrs were away, but he called upon Dr. Butler. The story is told that the good professor, wanting to do something very special for his former pupil, offered him his own cherished copy of Virgil's bucolic poems to carry with him on future wanderings. John refused it, saying he wanted to see nature through his own eyes, not through Virgil's.

Leaving Madison by the north shore of Lake Mendota on his way to Portage, he climbed an eminence from which he looked back upon the city. "I gained a last wistful lingering view of the beautiful University grounds and buildings where I had spent so many hungry and happy and hopeful days. There with streaming eyes I bade my blessed Alma Mater farewell. But I was only leaving one University for another, the Wisconsin University for the University of the Wilderness."

And so after his first extended foray into wild nature he arrived at Fountain Lake Farm about the 1st of August, "heavy-laden with new plants, while all the pains of the excursion vanished."

When John came home, he fully intended to go to medical college at the University of Michigan in the autumn. Just why his plans were changed he never explained, except to say they had been "interrupted" or "delayed." Failure to collect certain money due him may have been the cause. In the fall of 1862 Daniel Muir had deeded him eighty acres of Hickory Hill land, the compensation according to court records being "loving kindness." John sold this tract, taking in exchange a note for $650. Small payments on this debt had helped him through his last year at Madison. There is reason to believe he depended upon the remainder for expenses at Ann Arbor.

The war draft just then in the offing was doubtless another reason. So few young men were left in the township that he could hardly hope to escape having his number drawn this time. Many had gone to Canada to avoid being drafted, but he had no intention of running away.

The war had taken a turn with the victories at Gettysburg and Vicksburg and the breaking of the Mississippi blockade. The North was frantic with joy. The approaching draft, it was believed, would be the last.

But at this time John Muir was passing through mental stresses that lay deeper than money disappointments and uncertainty about the draft. In the seventies he scribbled down in a hand-sewed notebook a fragmentary record of his inner struggles beginning when he left the university and extending over an eight-year period. Recently discovered among his papers, it provides a basis for understanding the turmoil of indecision through which he labored and his final triumphant resolution.

"I was tormented with soul hunger," he says. "I began to doubt whether I was fully born. . . . I was on the world. But was I in it? . . . This was the time when all the world is said to lie before us, when armed with the small bits of lessons from school and church, we are to . . . build our existences as a carpenter a house, hack and hew, add this and that by dint of sheer ignorant will. . . . A few friends kindly watched my choice of the half-dozen old ways in which all good boys are supposed to walk. 'Young man,' they said, 'Choose your profession — Doctor, lawyer, minister. . . . You must do your work as a part of society.' . . . 'No, not just yet,' said I. . . ."

So the debate went on between his "vague unrest and longings" on the one hand and, on the other, the duties society pressed upon him. He was twenty-five. People were beginning to look askance at him. He was the family "sport," and a sore riddle to his relatives. Those who loved him most feared he was going to be a misfit. Sarah gently prodded him: "You know, John, we expect great things of you." But even she expected him to achieve "great things" along time-honored grooves. David Galloway said: "Invent! Invent machines to lighten toil. You can help mankind that way." David Muir, married now to Katie Cairns, working his way up in Forbes's store in Portage and already "a pillar in the church," urged him to "forget those confounded weeds, marry, and go into business." "Marry," they all said. They did not know how much one side of his nature wanted a home and bairns of his own. But other instincts, striving for dominance, pulled at him to leave "the doleful chambers of civilization, the beaten charts" of human living. Tramping along the great rivers in those summer weeks, he had glimpsed the life he wanted — the life of freedom to wander and study the earth and the plants and to think his own thoughts.

"Civilization," he said, "has not much to brag about. It drives its victims in flocks, repressing the growth of individuality." Civilization had stifled him, confused his thinking, wounded his spirit, and failed utterly to answer his deepest needs. He demanded something beyond the endless treadmill of toiling that he might eat, and eating that he might toil. Surely human existence could not be so devoid of meaning in a universe where design and loving purpose are manifest in every flower, where the stars in their courses proclaim order!

And now a powerful compulsion was upon him to go out into the untouched wilderness, "not as a mere sport or plaything excursion, but to find the Law that governs the relations subsisting between human beings and Nature." Intuitively he postulated "an essential Love, overlying, underlying, pervading all things." Unity, co-operation, were fundamental. And yet he had not found love, unity, or co-operation regnant anywhere in competitive society. Physically man was an integral part of the universe. Spiritually he was an alien. He went forth over the earth as a conqueror, a destroyer, an enemy of nature and his fellow man. Somewhere he had gone down a blind alley, away from the true path of evolution.

During that fall, while he worked for his brother-in-law, John Muir decided that if his number was not picked in the draft, he would wander for a while in the Canadian wilderness. For his own peace of mind he must think these things out in solitude and find an answer.

The months dragged on into winter. The draft came, but John Muir's number was not drawn.

Now he waited for the first sign of spring. An anemone thrusting its silken hood above the black earth was to be the signal for his leaving. Meanwhile he spent those last evenings with Sarah and David and their two children, Anna and George, looking hungrily in upon their happy family life as if he would not see its like again.

In February the south wind was blowing. The wild geese were flying north along the sky lanes. On the 28th he found the first anemone blooming at the edge of a melting snowbank on a hillside. His preparations were all made, and on March 1, after bidding farewell to the family at Portage, he wrote to Emily Pelton: "I am to take the cars in about half an hour. I really do not know where I shall halt. I feel like Milton's Adam and Eve—'The world was all before them where to choose their place of rest.'"[28]

PART III

1864–1870

CALL OF THE WILDERNESS

FROM the day John Muir took the train at Portage until late October no letter survives to reveal his route. Only a few labeled plants and a hint in a subsequent letter indicate that he tramped through a portion of Michigan to Lake Superior and thence crossed into Canada.

"I quietly wandered away . . . happy and free, poor and rich," he says. "I traveled free as a bird, independent alike of roads and people. I entered at once into harmonious relations with Nature like young bees making their first excursion to a flower garden. Faculties were set in motion, fed and filled. The vague unrest and longings . . . vanished. . . . I felt a plain, simple relationship to the Cosmos."[1]

His locomotion carried him far without weariness. He walked with a long loping stride like an Indian, with toes pointing straight ahead and close to the ground. He seldom ran. His long legs moved in a steady rhythm, and his powerful lungs never brought him to a pause for breath.

His food — as in later years — consisted of bread when he could get it, or oatmeal flakes parched on the hot stones of his campfire, and tea. Often in too much haste to brew the tea, he would chew a mouthful of strong leaves, then wash them down with cold water. "It answers very well," said he, "if one has the mind to think so."

In March he was exploring the larger islands that span the straits between Lake Huron and Georgian Bay like stepping-stones. He collected plants on St. Joseph's and Manitoulin.[2] Early in April he was walking east along the northern shore of Georgian Bay, among the lakes and muskegs left in the wake of retreating glaciers. By

April 20 — the earliest date in the extant portion of his herbarium — he had come as far south as Simcoe County, Ontario. Late in May his "planless route" took him through a half-dozen townships in southeastern County Grey. Then partially doubling on his own track he came in June to the Holland River swamps. "By crooked, unanticipated paths, fast or slow," he traveled, "zigzagging like a butterfly," camping wherever night overtook him. Bog juices ran in his veins, so hearing of a new swamp, he went to it "as straight as a bee to a flower." Not then or ever in his life would he follow willingly a planned itinerary. He chose "to whirl . . . like a leaf in every eddy, dance compliance to any wind."

On a June day bread-hunger led him to a farmhouse near the town of Bradford. The kindly gudewife, Mrs. Campbell, opened the door, and as soon as they heard each other speak, they were friends. In spite of his beard she saw he was young — not much older than her own stalwart sons, William and Alexander. He looked gaunt and half-starved in his torn shirt and trousers, caked to the waist with brown swamp mud. Instead of letting him go with the loaf he asked to buy, she fairly pulled him into the house and set him down at the table where her boys were busily stowing away a hearty supper.

So began a month's sojourn with the hospitable Campbells. John learned with indignation that this family had been driven from the Highlands at the time of the Sutherland Clearances in 1840. This was another step in England's policy of turning northern Scotland into vast sheep farms. Evicted from their glens and hillside crofts, the starving men and women fled to the moors and barren coast, while the flames of their burning homes lighted ships far out at sea. Fortunate were those who could muster the price of passage to the New World.

"The Eternal events pile up," John Muir used to say as he contemplated the course of human history. Disturb the balance in nature's economy or in society, and you reap droughts, floods, wars, class struggles, revolutions. These will continue until man shall have learned the universal law of co-operation.

John did chores for his board, and a day's labor now and then in the fields. But most of his days he was abroad in the marshlands. In the eyes of other people the spirit of death seemed to brood over these swamps, but to him they were reservoirs of life. It was natural, he said, for his Highland blood to flow bogward. Not that he enjoyed wading in the dank, coffee-colored water with its treacherous footing, but the sphagnums and lilies floating above the sinister depths were worth any amount of discomfort.

Late one afternoon he was wearily trudging through a tangled mass of underbrush and fallen trees, looking for a tree where like a monkey he could make his nest for the night. Suddenly he saw ahead of him on a mossy bank of a stream the beautiful orchid calypso. Long he had sought in vain for the shy and lovely "hider of the north," which retreated as fast as human settlement advanced. Now in the midst of this dismal swamp, rising white from a bed of yellow mosses, she bloomed for him alone. "Hunger and weariness vanished, and only after the sun was low in the west I plashed on through the swamp, strong and exhilarated as if never more to feel any mortal care." [3]

In late July he said good-by to his friends and drifted south toward Niagara Falls. On August 1 he camped on a mountainside overlooking Burlington Bay. The next morning he was wading in the tamarack swamp bordering Lake Ontario. On a small mounded island he gathered the fragrant twinflower, *Linnæa borealis,* loved by and named for Linnæus. "Heaven itself would not answer without Calypso and Linnæa," he once told Mrs. Carr.

Gerardia purpurea, pressed among his pages, recorded his arrival on September 2 at Niagara Falls. Danny, who had been working in a sawmill in County Grey, joined him there. They camped together in a juniper forest on the heights above the stupendous white tumult of waters and for a week explored the precipitous river banks up and down.

Some time during those autumn weeks — perhaps while they were at Niagara — they received a letter from their mother. She told them another draft was approaching. Using her parental authority and that of her husband, she ordered Dan, as a minor child, to remain in Canada. Then she pled with John to remain with him. William Trout says: "While John's feelings did not at all coincide with their wish, yet especially for his mother and Dan's sake he complied."[4]

With summer almost gone, the early northern winter was not far behind. Being nearly out of money, both boys had to "den in" and work for their board. Dan told about the sawmill and rake factory in County Grey where he had worked for a jolly group of young Scotsmen who owned and ran the concern. Trout & Jay was the firm name, and the location a canyon near Meaford, on Owen Sound. They might find winter jobs there if they were content with good food and small wages.

On a Saturday night they arrived, hungry and tired, at the canyon cabin of the Trouts, to be welcomed into a big room made cheerful by candles and a fire blazing in the wide stone fireplace. Having wandered now for eight months, John was willing to work for almost nothing to have a home with these friendly Scots. There were William Trout, head of the firm; Peter, his brother; Charles Jay, his partner; and Mary, his sister and housekeeper.

Supper over, the men went into a huddle to discuss jobs. They had liked "the frank, fresh-faced, fun-loving Danny" on his previous stay with them and were glad to have him back again. As for John, they needed a first-class mechanic to help enlarge the factory. The job was his at a wage of ten dollars a month and board.

The first nine months of his sojourn in Trout Hollow were a happy period. All about were forests covering the hills and filling the glen with "an enclosing wall of verdure." And there were muskegs within a day's tramp. In the combined mill and factory, built over the Big Head River meandering down the canyon, the burr of saws was pleasant to his ears. The hours of work were not too long, and William was always willing to give him holidays for botanizing.

As the winter came on, blanketing the ground with snow and locking the whole land in an icy enchantment, they spent jolly evenings by the fireside. Sometimes John brought out his herbarium, showing his plants and relating his adventures in getting them. After a lapse of years both William and Peter wrote down their memories of John's life among them. These furnish the few clues we have of his first weeks in Canada.

In the spring, when the south wind breathed up the canyon, melting the snow from the hillsides, the birds came thronging back in long lines like webs in the sky — loons, horned grebes, snow buntings, blue herons, crows, mallard ducks, geese — all the winged host calling as they flew. In the woods and meadows were born the first shy trilliums and hepaticas. After that, life rose in a crescendo to high tide in June. John was content to "work and study and dream in this retirement, happy in being so comfortably separated from the world's noisy dust." [5] He would "hardly accept of a free ticket to the moon or to Venus, or any other world," and deplored such "miserable hymns" as

"This world is all a fleeting show
For man's delusion given."

Indeed, since coming into the wilderness he had shed the last remnants of orthodox belief. "I never tried to abandon creeds or code of civilization; they went away of their own accord, melting and evaporating noiselessly without any effort and without leaving any consciousness of loss." [6]

Soon after he came to the hollow, the Trouts, who were Disciples, asked him to teach a class of boys in Sunday school. He consented on condition he might do it in his own way. Hence the group became an elementary science class, and the woods their laboratory.

John Muir was a master teacher. On week-ends Harriet Trout, another sister, brought her teacher friends from Meaford to join the cabin family. Soon he had them all studying botany and keeping herbariums. According to William Trout, some of their most delightful evenings were spent sitting on a big log in the front yard, listening to John as he told them something of the planets in the star-strewn strip of heavens above them. If a log, a student, and a teacher constitute a university, they had one. Muir was often tempted to follow this or that branch of science to its far reaches — to become a specialist instead of a generalist. Astronomy was one of his temptations. He longed to become what he called "a hunter of the sky."

Dan left the hollow in May 1865. Restless and ambitious to go to college, he wanted to earn more money. By midsummer he had a job in a Buffalo machine shop.

After his departure John was "touched with melancholy and loneliness." But a deeper trouble than loneliness afflicted him — "the pressure of Time upon Life." He was now twenty-seven. The months were eating away his "handful of hasty years." A week's botanizing in July around the shores of Owen Sound only increased his unrest.

"I would like to go to college, but then I have to say to myself, 'You will die ere you can do anything else.' I should like to invent useful machinery, but it comes, 'You do not wish to spend your lifetime among machines. . . .' I should like to study medicine that I might do my part in lessening human misery, but again it comes, 'You will die ere you are ready.' "[7]

Then in a burst of longing he brought out the nub of the whole matter: "How intensely I desire to be a Humboldt!"

Yet because he needed money to follow the Humboldt trail, in September he signed a contract with his employers to improve the machinery by inventing gadgets to speed up the output. For a specified 30,000 broom handles and 12,000 rakes he was to receive half the profits.

William Trout, four years older than John, was a master mechanic and millwright with several patents to his credit. During the early months he had taught the younger man everything he knew, "but I felt," says he, "that I could by no means take rank with him."

All that fall and winter of 1865, John says: "I was haunted with inventions that tortured me sleeping or waking until I worked them into visible forms." He sat up late at night covering unused sheets of his herbarium with drawings. Often he was unable to solve a certain problem. But while he slept, his "other self" organized and formulated his ideas, supplying the missing link in his reasoning. Then rising in the dark of a frosty morning, he leaped down to the mill-race with a chisel on a long pole, to cut the iron wheel free from ice, that he might begin making models and patterns for castings. "My mind seems to bury itself in the work that I am fit for little else," he wrote to Mrs. Carr.

By November he was "busy almost to craziness . . . inventing machinery twenty-four hours a day. . . . It seems as though I should be dragged into machinery whether I would or no." His first completed invention was a self-feeding gadget to take the place of the old hand-feeding machine. This turned out eight broom, rake, or fork handles per minute, with a total of 2,500 a day, thus doubling the former output. Then he set to work on automatic devices to make rake teeth, bore and drive them, here again doubling production. Says William Trout: "He was a real live inventive, designing mechanic, systematic, practical; and it was a delight to see those machines at work."

By February 1866 John had completed the 30,000 hardwood broom handles, and had them stored about the factory for final seasoning. After this he turned out 6,000 finished rakes. He had 6,000 yet to make, and then with money in his pocket he would be free once more to wander.

On the night of March 1, while they slept, a terrible blizzard roared over the hills and down into the hollow. A spark from the cabin chimney settled on the factory roof, was fanned into flame, and before they discovered it, the whole plant was a raging furnace. Not even John's notebooks and the greater part of his herbarium could be saved. There was no insurance on the property. Outstanding accounts just about balanced the debts. Trout asked John to help rebuild the plant and share as a partner in the profits. "No," he replied, "I love nature too well to spend my life in a work that involves the destruction of God's forests!"

They gave him a note for three hundred dollars, which he cut down to two hundred. Then with what cash they could raise among them — enough to pay his fare back to the United States — he said good-by to his friends and took the train for Indianapolis.

Upon arriving in Indianapolis John Muir found work at once with the firm of Osgood, Smith & Co., manufacturers of hubs, spokes, felloes, and other carriage parts. The business of this firm, established in 1847, was one of the largest of its kind in the country. Its most distinctive product was the Sarven patent wheel.

John's advancement was rapid. He was put in charge of a circular saw at a wage of ten dollars a week, and his skill and speed were evident at once. At the end of the first week he was given charge of all the circular saws, with a raise to eighteen dollars. A few days later he was ordered to supervise the installation of new equipment. Soon after that he suggested to the firm a labor-saving device by which parts of the Sarven wheel could be produced automatically, and also certain improvements in the wheel itself. The results were a free hand and a boost to twenty-five dollars per week.

"John Muir, Sawyer," as he was listed in the city directory, found a congenial home in the house of Levi Sutherland, a Scotsman and fellow sawyer. His Sundays were spent in the woods. He had chosen Indianapolis among the industrial cities of the West because outside of it stood one of the finest deciduous forests in America.

One spring afternoon he might have been seen walking up and down past the home of the distinguished Merrill family at the southwest corner of Alabama and Merrill Streets, trying to muster courage to present himself at the door. He had a letter to deliver from Dr. Butler, introducing himself to Miss Catharine Merrill,[8] a letter that said among other things: "If you walk the fields with him, you will find that Solomon could not speak more wisely about plants."

Fortunately for the bashful caller, a small boy opened the door. That boy, Merrill Moores, the ten-year-old nephew of Miss Merrill, later recorded their first meeting:

"One beautiful evening . . . a tall, sturdy man with blue eyes and a clear ruddy complexion as well as handsome hair and beard . . . approached and asked if Mrs. Moores and Miss Merrill lived there. He had a marked Scotch accent and was obviously a working man, but was plainly and neatly dressed; and he at once impressed me as the handsomest man I had ever met."[9]

Within a few minutes John was seated in the parlor, enthralling the two sisters and the big-eyed boy with the story of his Canadian rambles. He told them also of his work in the broom and rake factory and the inventions he had made. In reply to the question: "Did you take out patents on your devices?" he stated: "No. I believe all improvements and inventions should be the property of the human race. No inventor has the right to profit by an invention for which he deserves no credit. The idea of it was really inspired by the Almighty."

Finally he told them of the machine he had already invented for Osgood, Smith & Co., which would "automatically make wooden hubs, spokes and felloes and assemble them into a fully completed wheel, lacking only the metal tire to be attached by hand."

Merrill Moores, later an eminent lawyer, and for ten years a Congressman from Indiana, well acquainted over a long period of years with Muir's employers, had this to say in mature years: "This machine was a success, and I am told that all wooden wheels to this day are made by machines following the plan on which Muir's unpatented wheel-making machine was designed."

Miss Merrill lost no time in gathering up a flock of grown-ups and children, including her own nephews and nieces of the Graydon, Moores, and Ketchems families, to follow this wonderful new Pied Piper out to the woods. They were fascinated by him, and Miss Ellen Graydon, still living, says: "Mr. Muir had the twinklingest blue eyes I have ever seen in my life."

Among those who shared those walks was Miss Eliza Hendricks, a vivacious, intelligent girl obviously much attracted by the young laborer. He called at her home several times, but, as later revealed in his letters, the real magnet was a "lily grandmother" in the family. For Muir loved serene, beautiful old people as much as he did children. Miss Eliza, who never married, remained his steadfast friend throughout life. Her letters, punctuating the years until they were both old, disclose her unselfish, happy devotion to his career.

Eager to have other friends meet this remarkable diamond-in-the-rough, Miss Merrill planned to bring them together at her home. But his orbit was the woods and open fields, his proper audience those who could become as little children. As soon as he realized he was the guest of honor of the occasion, he became clamlike in his taciturnity and soon left. When the guests had gone, Merrill heard his aunt say: "It's too bad. They will never realize how wonderful he is."

He consented, however, to teach a class of boys at a mission Sunday school sponsored by her for the children of workingmen. This was anything but a solemn indoor affair. Forming his boys into a club, on Sunday mornings he vanished with them into the woods. On other occasions they met in his room to experiment with his trick bed and other machines and to learn elementary chemistry.

Muir's intentions when he went to Indianapolis were to earn a few hundred dollars, and then go on with his studies in wild nature. But as the months passed, the temptations increased to make machines his career. He liked "the rush and roar and whirl of the factory," and the hearty approval of the heads of the firm added to the congeniality of his labors. Moreover, the men in the shops liked him and came to look upon him as their leader and champion. More than once he protested boldly against their ten-hour work day. Long before the Russell Sage Foundation made its surveys, he saw that as men labored beyond the fatigue point, their efficiency decreased.

He became interested in a young fellow sawyer, Henry Riley, who wanted to earn his living on the land. John lent him money to make the experiment. Failing at it, John got his job back for him and taught him skill. A letter from Riley, a successful mechanic in after years, paid tribute: "You taught me all I know about machinery."

But before long the old conflict arose in John's mind between machines and the call of the wilderness. It was even a greater one this time, for his ambition had been temporarily aroused. "I was in great danger," he says, "of becoming so successful that my botanical and geographical studies might be interrupted." [10]

Loyalty to his clan was a powerful link in the chain that bade fair to bind him. Knowing his father's centrifugal tendencies, he was ever on the watch for some emergency that would throw the burden of family support upon his shoulders. Finding his land a white elephant, Daniel Muir was trying to sell it. Foot-loose once more, his fanatical missionary zeal might take him to the other side of the world. Meanwhile John's sisters were chafing at the home environment. Mary, at least, who was gifted in art, should have a university training. Dan had his heart set upon a medical career, and John felt an obligation to help him as a proxy for himself. So his conscience bedeviled him in the name of love and duty.

In the fall of 1866 the firm's heads appointed him to make a detailed survey of the factory and suggest means of eliminating leakage and of increasing production. True to his Scotch instinct he abhorred waste, so he set about this task with enthusiasm. Industry in America had developed faster than the science of management. Therefore, without any models to work upon, John Muir became one of the first, if not the very first, of the efficiency experts in the country.

After checking conditions in the plant, he presented in December his criticisms and recommendations in the form of two charts.[11] The smaller one, entitled "Beltology," dealt with the devitalizing effects of day-and-night variations of temperature upon leather held at tension. Worn belt joinings also caused loss of energy. All this waste brought him to an indignant climax: "It seems preposterous to me, Gentlemen, that in every department . . . you cast your big greenbacks in bundles to the moles and bats!"

"The Chart of One Day's Labor" was the caption of his reorganization plan built upon co-operation as the basic theme. "The grand central difficulty . . . of this factory is lack of *unity*. . . . In all good communities 'no man liveth to himself,' and in the departments of good factories no man or machine worketh to itself. The effects of but few delays and jars terminate where they begin, but are transmitted from . . . department to department, which . . . are dependent on each other like the series of events connected with 'the house that Jack built.'"

He went on to explain the evils of a ten-hour day. Making a graph of the "work-line" through the hours, he demonstrated that the peak of efficiency was reached in the forenoon. Falling off before lunch, it revived later, only to drop precipitously after five o'clock. "Lamp-lighted labor is not worth more than two-thirds day-light labor," he asserted. Truly a revolutionary idea in 1866!

Under the heading: "Plans of Sawyers and Shop," he detailed leaks due to fumbling and waste motion by workmen. He suggested rearrangement of stock and equipment for easier and quicker handling, and a method by which refuse wood could be converted into fuel. And having learned his economics on a Scotch farm, he declared the area of loss could be diminished and profit increased "by the exercise of half the forecast of a harvest mouse!"

Whether or not his employers appreciated his quaint allusions, they did grasp the fact that he had exceptional talent for technical administration. In the large extension about to be built they proposed to put his ideas into effect and to reorganize along these lines.

Reduction of the working time, however, was not so simple. Only a short while before, factories had been run on a twelve- to sixteen-hour basis, and the ten-hour day was considered a large concession to labor — not then spelled with a capital letter. The theory was that firms cutting the work-period below the accepted minimum could not compete with other firms.

Although he had made no formal study of economics at the university, John had read widely and had an intelligent grasp of the trend of events in his own day. Now that the war was over and the industrial North triumphant, he saw unbridled competition, implemented by mass production, abroad in the nation. The opening up of the West to settlement and exploitation offered unlimited sources of raw materials for Eastern factories, and markets for their products. America was running amuck with dreams of prosperity.

The Adam Smith economic philosophy endorsed competition as the law of the universe. *"Laissez faire"* had become the slogan of all business. "The gobble gobble school of economics," John Muir called it.[12]

Even the science of that day gave its blessing to competition, demonstrating that the struggle for existence and the survival of the strongest were the universal law of life. Muir, although an evolutionist, denounced this mechanistic doctrine as "damnable." As early as his Canadian sojourn, according to William Trout, he condemned "the dark chilly reasoning that chance and the survival of the fittest accounted for all things."

It is evident from numerous hints in his writings that he leaned toward the theories of Lamarck, Buffon, and others, that organisms evolve by intelligent need and impulse implanted within the organisms themselves. Such was the theory of Samuel Butler, a critic of Darwin in the late nineteenth century, who maintained that "All body is more or less ensouled." In Muir's belief God was ensouled as a Principle in all forms of matter. "Now all of the individual 'things,' or 'beings,'" he said, "into which the world is wrought are sparks of the Divine Soul variously clothed upon with flesh, leaves, or that harder tissue called rock, water, etc. . . ." [13]

Postulating, therefore, this innate, unifying God Principle, he saw natural forms evolving not by competition, but by co-operation. Man as an integral part of the universe could progress only by following the same law.

John Muir believed in machines as means of releasing man from drudgery, setting human energies free for higher development. They "should be the property of the human race." But if he was so naïve in 1866 as to believe he could share his creative gifts with all mankind, he was speedily disillusioned. His own genius lay in the creation of labor-saving, automatic machines. These, by substituting machine-power for man-power, would throw men out of employment. The wan, pinched faces of the children of Dunbar, which he could never dismiss from his thoughts, were the results of just such labor-saving, life-destroying machines.

One day in early March, 1867, Fate took a hand and brought to an end John Muir's long inner conflict. He had stayed late at the factory to readjust a new belt. Riley, his faithful shadow, was alone with him at the time. John was unlacing the joining, using a slender, sharp file. Suddenly this slipped, flew up, and pierced his right eye on the edge of the cornea. Without saying a word he walked to a window, his hand cupped over his eye. There facing the dim light he drew away his hand, and as he did so, the milk-white aqueous humor dropped out upon it. Utter darkness followed. In that moment of horror, he has declared: "I would gladly have died where I stood."

Riley, hovering close behind, heard him say wonderingly: "My right eye gone! Closed forever on all God's beauty!"

For nearly a week he lay in his room utterly shattered. "My days were terrible beyond what I can tell, and my nights were if possible more terrible. Frightful dreams exhausted and terrified me." In his despair he reached out to his friends. "The sunshine and the winds are working in all the gardens of God, but I — I am lost!" was the burden of his cry, scribbled on scraps of paper to Mrs. Carr, Dr. Butler, the Merrills. The cry went also to David Muir, telling him to soften the blow for Mother.

At this dark hour Catharine Merrill came into his room "like an angel of light." Although the Sutherland family doctor had said the eye was gone, she insisted upon calling a specialist. After a careful examination he assured John the sight had not been lost. The aqueous humor would be restored, and although the vision would always be imperfect, in time the other eye would take on its functions. He would be able to see about as well as ever.

So the world and its beauty were to be his once more. The sudden revulsion from sick despair was like a resurrection. "Now had I arisen from the grave," he chanted. "The cup is removed, and I am alive!"

Four weeks he had to remain in the darkened room. His left eye, blinded through nerve shock and sympathy, gradually recovered, and he spent much time whittling, making toys for the Sutherland children.

Letters poured in upon him from the Muir clan, the Butlers, Carrs, and Trouts, all urging him to spend his convalescence with them. Even before Mrs. Carr received the better news, her faith in his destiny did not waver. She wrote: "I have often in my heart wondered what God was training you for. He gave you the eye within the eye, to see in all natural objects the realized ideas of His mind. He gave you pure tastes, and the sturdy preference of whatsoever is most lovely and excellent. He has made you a more individualized existence than is common, and by your very nature, removed you from common temptations. . . . He will surely place you where your work is."

An inch at a time the window blinds were raised, and his club of boys arrived in relays to read to him. His keen ears learned to know the step of each one in the hallway. Merrill Moores was his most constant reader, and with his brother, sister, and cousins brought him flowers. Muir wanted "God's posies, the wild flowers," he told them. At this period of his life all cultivated flowers were to him "distortions." So they scoured the woods for the first-born of spring. Miss Katharine Graydon, one of the children who visited him, has related that often he told them stories of the things he had seen and heard, and that throughout life they "cherished the memory of that dark room and of those beautiful stories."

Judson Osgood and Samuel Smith were among his daily visitors. The new shops were finished, they told him, and he had only to go in and take command as foreman, with a substantial raise in salary and shorter hours for himself. They also discussed with him a plan whereby in the not distant future he would become a partner. He was on the highroad to big things, they assured him.

But John, who had never liked highroads, was dreaming of wildernesses in those days. Someone had given him an illustrated folder about the Yosemite Valley. Up to this time his greatest desire had been to explore the Amazon. Now he had a second goal, to see the deep Sierra valley with its sun-crowned bastions, and study its flowers. "From many a weed's plain heart," he told himself, he would learn secrets of life.

On an April day, one month after the accident, when soft gray clouds filtered the sunlight, he headed south for the woods, on his first walk. When he returned a few hours later, he had made his final decision. Two reasons motivated him — "that I might be true to myself,"[14] and the knowledge that he could find no joy apart from wild nature. "This affliction has driven me to the sweet fields," said he. And having driven him, it left no hesitancy in his mind. "God has to nearly kill us sometimes, to teach us lessons," he commented.

Burning his bridges behind him, he resigned his position and, taking Merrill Moores with him, traveled home for a brief visit. They went immediately to Mound Hill, the new home of David and Sarah Galloway, a few miles north of Portage. Finding in this home "a cordial Scotch welcome," they made it their headquarters while they roamed the vicinity. Along with Anna and George and two-year-old Cecelia they made many picnic trips about the farm. In the course of these John discovered a tiny gem of a lake "shaded and sheltered by a dense growth of small oaks." He named it Fern Lake, for encircling it he found "a perfect brotherhood of the three Osmundas — regalis, Claytoniana and cinnamomea." Cecelia Galloway, who well remembers Fern Lake on Mound Hill Farm, zealously guarded by her father from trampling cattle for Uncle John's sake, says of it:

"In the dark heart of the oak woods . . . was a cold little pool that had no inlet and no outlet, but was always full of water. Around its edge were reeds and cat-tails and blackberry vines, and on the steep sides sloping down to the pool were tall royal osmundii ferns almost as high as my head, tier above tier looking down at the little pool like people sitting in a theatre. . . . My uncle said that if one could go down deep enough they would find glacial ice still remaining there, the slow melting of which formed the spring and the pool."

The memory of this lakelet was to haunt John Muir as he went south and west. Somewhere on the way he began to think of how to preserve both it and Fountain Lake. As soon as he got his first job in California, he wrote to David Galloway asking him to guard Fern Lake from all harm, and to sound out Sam Ennis, the current owner of Fountain Lake Farm, about his buying the land around the larger lake. Then and there the National Park idea had its first small beginnings in his thoughts. Letters reveal that Galloway protected Fern Lake as long as he owned Mound Hill. But Sam Ennis asked too great a price for the Fountain Lake acreage. In view of John's contributions to family finances at that time, he could not afford to buy it.

One day John, with Merrill, started out to tour the farming region where he had lived as a boy. They spent their nights at Hickory Hill, where the Muir family was once more residing. When they arrived, Merrill tells us, they found Daniel Muir sitting in the shade of trees outside the house, copying a huge quarto tome of Foxe's *Book of Martyrs*. "Looking over his copy . . . I asked him the reasons for frequent omissions of words; and he answered: 'Aboot a half of the book is in Layton, an' I dinna ken Layton, an' the words would be of sma' use to me.'"

Merrill's sharp ears picked up some things in that home he didn't like, and he marveled at John's patience in enduring them. His father found fault with him and "made no secret of his belief that the study of geology was blasphemous and was accustomed to rebuke John unceasingly. . . . And I regretted to discover that he regarded botany as almost as wicked as geology."

That last visit home was not a happy one. According to a well-authenticated story,[15] John, one day becoming exasperated by constant nagging to the effect that in his wanderings and studies he had been "walking in the paths of the Deevil," flared up and said: "I'll tell you this, Father, I've been spending my time a lot nearer the Almighty than you have!"

Another scene occurred on the day they left Hickory Hill. While John was saying good-bye to his mother and sisters, Daniel broke in with this:

"My son, hae ye na forgotten something?"

"What have I forgotten, Father?"

"Hae ye no forgotten to pay for your board and lodging?"

John pulled his wallet out of his pocket, handed over a gold piece, then said: "Father, you asked me to come home for a visit. I thought I was welcome. You may be very sure it will be a long time before I come again."

He kept his word. Father and son were to meet but once again in this life.

For years John had been searching in vain for the fern *Aspidium fragrans*. While he was at Portage, Dr. Lapham sent word to him through Mrs. Carr that he would find it among the ravines at Wisconsin Dells. So he and Merrill took the next train for Kilburn, where the river thunders and boils through a deep post-glacial limestone gorge. They found the fern in at least one of the ravines opening into the gorge and, according to Merrill, they "pronounced its odor most entrancing."

After staying over night in Kilburn, they built a raft and floated down the Wisconsin thirty miles to Portage. This voyage had its vicissitudes. In order to pole the raft efficiently John took off his shoes and stood in his bare feet on the wet logs. At one point, when a steamer passed them, plowing a wide swath through the water, the waves swept over the raft and carried away the shoes. "Never mind," John shouted above the chugging engines, "I'll buy a new pair at my brother's store."

A few hours later they cut an odd figure as John, barefooted and looking his wildest, and trailed by his small companion, entered the general-merchandise store of Parry & Muir on Cook Street. David, now a leading merchant and careful of appearances, hustled his brother to the back of the store while he looked for shoes big enough to fit him. They had none. David thought he might have a pair at home, and hinted they should stay there while he went to get them, "for fear of what people might think."

"Think," chuckled John. "Let them think! Feet were made before shoes, weren't they?"

So the three of them traipsed up the busy main street en route to David's cottage. He was deeply embarrassed, but John, wholly unconscious of his looks, talked all the while about their wonderful adventures. That the townsfolk were agog over the incident is shown by the fact that the story is still current.[16]

Another shoe story is related by Zona Gale,[17] who loved the salty folklore of "Friendship Village."

They tell . . . that once, after a brief visit to his family, he [John Muir] was leaving again, coming up the sluggish Fox in a canoe which grounded. Wading ashore he lost one shoe, and in Portage entered a shoe shop to repair the loss. He went to the store of James Brodie, another Scotchman, was fitted to a shoe for the shoeless foot, paid, and moved towards the door.

"Hey, mon," said Mr. Brodie, "take out your other new shoe."

"No need of it," said John Muir, departing, "I've two shoes now."

Getting back to the former narrative, John and Merrill were invited to stay the night with David and Katie. And David, truly proud of his brilliant brother, asked a local cleric named Collins to meet him at supper. The talk drifted to natural science, John upholding the theory of evolution by telling how plants, through variation, evolve new species. Fundamentalist Collins, drawing himself up in his best ministerial manner, delivered himself of this profundity: "Mr. Muir, I have never yet seen a chair develop into a chairman."

John cast one contemptuous glance in his direction, then deliberately turned his back and spoke not another word.

When the indignant preacher had departed, fully convinced John was an atheist and a lost soul, David took his brother to task for his downright rudeness.

"I wouldn't waste my breath talking to a fool!" said John.

Although he seemed determined to go out into the wilderness, he had taken careful stock of the family situation. His father, he felt, would be safely tethered for some time to the farm and Foxe's *Book of Martyrs*. As for the girls, Mary and Anna were launching forth as teachers, and Joanna would follow them in due time. At present no one needed his help. Meanwhile he thought "it would be a fine thing to make and take one more grand sabbath day three years long during which I would go botanizing in tropic lands and woods, thus accumulating a stock of wild beauty . . . sufficient to lighten and brighten my after life in the gloom and hunger of civilization's defrauding duties."

Leaving Merrill at Sarah's home, John went to Packwaukee to see Mrs. Galloway, "that old Scotch lady . . . as motherly almost as my own mother . . . watching my career as far as it had gone. . . . I told her about the walk I had in visiting her. I said, 'Just a mile or so back here, just as the sun had set, I heard a little . . . song sparrow that seemed to be saying, 'the day is done, the day is done. . . .' "

She said, 'Well, John, your day will never be done. There is no end to the kind of studies you are engaged in, and you are sure to go on and on. . . .' "[18]

With her prophetic words still ringing in his ears, he returned with Merrill to Indianapolis. On September 1 John Muir, "all drawbacks overcome . . . joyful and free," took the train southward bound. "I might have become a millionaire," he once said, "but I chose to become a tramp!"

With the cosmic address: *"John Muir, Earth-Planet, Universe,"* inscribed and encircled with ecstatic curlicues on the flyleaf of his first extant journal, John Muir set forth on his wanderings.

Dreams brooded over for years seemed about to find fulfillment when he stepped off the train at Jeffersonville, Indiana. He would walk down to the Gulf and take a ship for the northern coast of South America. Thence like "another Humboldt" he would tramp southward until he found one of the tributaries of the Orinoco, follow it to the main river, and explore that basin. From there he would cross the divide to the basin of the Amazon. Finally he would build a raft to float down that mightiest of rivers all the way to the Atlantic.

"Doomed to be carried of the spirit into the wilderness," he went obeying at last the inner compulsion which Mrs. Carr called his "Dæmon." Among the first pages of his journal [19] he wrote: "In some persons the impulse, being slight, is easily obeyed or overcome. But in others it is constant and cumulative in action until its power is sufficient to overmaster all impediments, and to accomplish the full measure of its demands. . . . Many influences have tended to blunt or bury this constant longing, but it has outlived and overpowered them all."

He was twenty-nine years old, already past the uncertainties of youth. His growth had been slow, like that of the oak or sequoia, but a growth to endure. Nature takes time with her chosen men.

In the dawn he crossed the Ohio into Kentucky. With compass in hand he threaded his way through the streets of Louisville to the suburbs beyond. Here he paused in a grove of oaks that "spread their arms in welcome." Against a brown bole he leaned his map and rough-hewed his route southward "by the wildest, leafiest, and least trodden way" he could find. Then shouldering his pack, he struck off over the flowing, oak-clad hills, "not, however, without a few cold shadows of loneliness."

Live oak draped with tillandsia in Bonaventura Cemetery, Savannah, Ga. Drawing by Muir in his journal of his thousand-mile walk to the Gulf, 1867

48 in their dwellings of leaf & flower. Myriads of the most gorgeous butterflies too, all kinds of happy insects seem to be in a perfect fever of joy & sportive gladness. The whole place seems like a centre of life. The dead do not "reign there alone."

It was in October [19th] that I first beheld Bonaventure, to me ~~by~~ far the most impressive assemblage of [animal &] plant creatures I ever met. I was fresh from the green oceans of western prairies, the garden like openings of Wisconsin oaks, the ~~beech~~ [beech] & maple [& oak] woods of Indiana, ~~the constant verdure of Kentucky,~~ the ~~tangled~~ [dark] mysterious [swampy?] ~~[illegible]~~ [cypress] forests of ~~the~~ alluvial bottoms ~~above~~ Savannah & multitudes of strange tropic plants glowing in splendor unspeakable, but never since I was allowed to walk ~~the~~ woods have I found so overwhelmingly impressive a company of trees as the ~~avenued~~ [Illinois?] mossdraped

Page of Muir's journal of his thousand-mile walk to the Gulf, 1867

In the early light of the sixth day he reached the great caves of Kentucky, which opened black Avernian mouths in many a glen. Among the ferns growing about their lips he "lingered . . . a long happy while," feeling the cold, strong wind issuing from their gargantuan throats as from a nether, sunless world. Near Horse Cave he sought information from a villager, but found him too "practical" to waste his time with weeds, caves, fossils, or anything else that could not be eaten.

Content to be one of God's fools, he answered his own questions henceforth. But there was no sullen hanging back in his manner. He met every man with a cheerful "Howdy." Nor was there a trace of racial snobbery in his make-up. At many a shanty table he ate corn pone with Negro hosts, grateful for kindness wherever he found it.

On the ninth day, bearing away southward, he ascended the Cumberland Mountains in Tennessee: "the first real mountains that my foot ever touched or eyes beheld . . . the most sublime . . . picture that ever entered my eyes."

Everywhere he found the people desperately poor, many farms deserted, orchards and fences in ruins, the owners having been "killed or driven away during the War"; singly or in roving guerrilla bands, men preyed upon one another like wild beasts; the few inhabitants distilled moonshine or sold ginseng for a living; every stranger was hated as a Yankee peddler or Government spy.

In the Tennessee Valley he stopped long enough to send his plants back to David and thus lighten his pack. It was well that he did so, for he was weak from hunger and thirst, and a slow fever was beginning to burn in his veins. Here, too, the land was prostrate under the effects of war. Roads wandered as if lost, and the towns were mere huddles of filthy shacks. The clay soil, overcultivated by the pioneers and eroded by mining, "yielded no roastin' ears now" to feed the wretched families eking out a Tobacco Road kind of existence.

Some days later he was in Georgia, walking along the bottom land of the Savannah River. Vast swamps lay in his way. Ghosts, according to the Negroes he talked with, as well as alligators lurked in their somber depths. Even the winds had an uncanny moan. Fever was giving him fancies as it burned him with a thirst not to be quenched by the water in the black and silent pools.

Arriving at Savannah, he learned that the draft he had asked David to send him there had not come. He spent the night at a cheap lodging-house. Still no draft came. Hungry and almost penniless, he wandered four miles out from the city and late in the afternoon found himself in an old, neglected cemetery, "so beautiful that almost any sensible person would choose to dwell here with the dead, rather than with the lazy, disorderly living." In the midst of this graveyard, known as the Bonaventure Cemetery, stood a white pillared mansion in ruins, once the home of a wealthy planter. Nature had done her best to reclaim the grounds from man's "labored art blunders." An avenue of noble live-oaks embowered the ancient driveway, draped from their crowns to the earth with long shining skeins of tillandsia.

Knowing that in a graveyard he would be safe from prowling Negroes, he made camp. With a dollar and a quarter — all the cash he had left — he went back to town to invest in crackers. He returned under the moon. Just before entering the cemetery, thirst compelled him to drink from a dull, sluggish, coffee-colored stream that ran by the road.

Faint with weariness, he lay down, his head pillowed upon a grave. Mosquitoes and "large prickly-footed beetles" creeping across his face caused his slumber to be "not quite so sound as that of the person below."

The next day he prepared to "hole in" until the draft came, by making a little bower of sparkleberry bushes tied together to support a roof of rushes, and spreading over the floor a mattress of tillandsia. Here he sat some hours each day writing up his notes. The peace of his surroundings, where "graves are powerless in such a depth of life," inspired one of his most notable utterances upon Death:

"On no subject are our ideas more warped and pitiable than on death . . . we are taught that death is an accident, a deplorable punishment . . . the arch enemy of life, etc. Town children, especially, are steeped in this death orthodoxy. . . .

"But let children walk with Nature, let them see the beautiful

blendings and communions of death and life, their joyous inseparable unity . . . and they will learn that death is stingless indeed, and as beautiful as life, and that the grave has no victory, for it never fights. All is divine harmony."

Each morning he staggered into the city, "dangerously hungry" and gaunt on his diet of crackers and stagnant brown water. On the fifth or sixth day the money arrived. Out on the street with silver in his pocket once more, he bumped into a vast black mammy carrying a tray of gingerbread. He bought the whole trayful and went down the walk greedily munching it. Still hungry when the last crumb was gone, he headed for a restaurant and had "a large regular meal on top of gingerbread! Thus," said he, "my 'marching through Georgia' terminated handsomely in a jubilee of bread."

With a full stomach he took the next boat bound for Fernandina on the northern coast of Florida. Arriving before breakfast, he bought a loaf of bread and made for "the shady, gloomy groves sunk to the shoulders in sedges and rushes." Shadows of loneliness and incipient illness lay heavy upon him as he reclined on his elbow, eating bread. Suddenly a noise from the rear startled him. His sick fancy instantly conjured up an alligator with "big jaws and rows of teeth, closing with a springy snap" upon his anatomy. But when he turned, his "man-eating alligator became a tall, white crane, handsome as a minister from spirit land."

A bit ashamed of his nervous fears, he started across the state on a railroad embankment, the only dry place he could find in this "watery, vine-tied" land of flowers. But soon he was plunging off through brown swamps in pursuit of tall grasses, gorgeous blooms and strange trees.

"The grandest discovery of this great wild day was the palmetto. . . . They tell us that plants are perishable, soulless creatures, that only man is immortal, etc.; but this, I think, is something that we know very nearly nothing about. Anyhow, this palm . . . told me grander things than I ever got from human priest."

One day in a desolate stretch of woods his path was blocked by a gigantic Negro who rolled the whites of his eyes at him in a fearsome manner. Where did he come from? the black man asked.

Where was he going? Why was he there where he might be robbed and killed? And finally in a quavering voice he asked: "Do you carry shootin' irons?"

That gave John an idea. Thrusting his hand back toward his pistol pocket — although he had nothing there — he advanced threateningly. "I allow people to find out if I'm armed or not!" The ex-slave, long imbued with fear of the master race, again showing the whites of his eyes, this time in terror, stepped aside, and John went on.

Everywhere as in Tennessee he saw the effects of war, "not only on the broken fields, burnt fences, mills, and woods ruthlessly slaughtered, but also on the countenances of the people . . . the ineffacable marks of the farthest-reaching and most infernal of all civilized calamities."

Arriving on the Gulf coast near the town of Cedar Keys, he stopped at a sawmill to inquire about passage to Cuba on a lumber schooner. Since none would leave for two weeks, he asked Mr. Hodgson, the mill-owner, for a job and got it. His employer, a kindly man, soon introduced him to his home near by, where he was welcomed with true Southern hospitality.

Shortly thereafter he began to feel "a strange dullness and headache . . . an inexorable numbness" that he couldn't shake off. Then the fever broke upon him "like a storm." Carried unconscious from his bunk at the mill to the Hodgson home, he was nursed through weeks of desperate and well-nigh fatal illness. Some granite hardihood, planted deep in the substructure of his being, fought for his life, and at long last he emerged from the Valley of the Shadow to wander feebly along the seashore or lie for hours under a mossy live-oak, or float in a boat among the keys idly studying the strange birds that screamed "with a foreign accent." As he gained strength, he wrote a few letters. He asked David to send him a hundred and fifty dollars at New Orleans, for he had by no means given up his plan to enjoy "the glorious mountains and flower fields of South America." To the Merrills and Moores he wrote of his liking for the South, where human life was "in reverse"; ". . . choirs do not sing, lecturers do not come and none mar their comfort by mending that of others, nor do merchants seek each other's blood."

Often he climbed to the flat roof of the Hodgson house to view the sunset over the sea and the keys "in their bath of purple and gold." Sitting there in the Southern twilight, pencil in hand, he meditated upon man and the cosmos and the democracy of nature. Never before had he expressed so fully his emancipation from orthodox forms of belief: "The world, we are told, was made especially for man — a presumption not supported by all the facts. A numerous class of men . . . have precise dogmatic insight of the intentions of the Creator, and it is hardly possible to be guilty of irreverence in speaking of *their* God any more than of heathen idols. He is . . . as purely a manufactured article as any puppet of a half-penny theater."

After going on to consider at some length the beliefs and taboos of "this modern patchwork of civilization," with "its ecclesiastical fires and blunders," he ended by saying: "I joyfully return to the immortal truth and immortal beauty of Nature."

On a calm, cloudless evening in January 1868, as he stood on the roof, he saw off shore the white sails of a Yankee schooner. Instantly he decided to seek passage on her. "The pretty white moth" proved to be the *Island Belle*, bound for Havana. Within a few hours he had said good-by to his friends, who protested he was not well enough to go, and arrived on shipboard just as the wind they were waiting for began to fill the languid sails.

The wind soon increased to fury. The captain urged him to go below, saying no landsman could endure such a storm. But although weak and ill, he stayed on deck, clinging to a rope, exulting in the first sea storm he had experienced since boyhood.

All too soon the wild voyage ended when they sailed into Havana Harbor to anchor in the lee of the castle walls. For nearly a month he remained in the environs, spending his nights on deck and his days "on the flower side of the Harbor," zigzagging up the coast, exploring swamps and thickets of cactus and matted vines, or running down into the cool sea to be buffeted by the great waves that rolled in from the Gulf. He was reluctant to forgo "the unseen and unwalked" mountain ranges of the interior, where Humboldt had gone; but having had five or six relapses into fever and night sweats while in the harbor, he dared not take the risk. For the same reason he was compelled to give up, for the time being, the trip to South America. Only the cold cathartic winds of the northern mountains could purge away the entrenched malarial germs. So he decided to go to California.

About mid-February he was on an orange steamer en route for New York, clinging to a mast on deck while the storms that raged off Cape Hatteras beat upon him and cooled his blood. On March 10 he sailed for Aspinwall and the Isthmus on his way to "California's weeds and flowers." His steerage accommodations in a ship jammed to the gunwales with humanity did not afford him a pleasant voyage. Loath always to dwell upon hardships, he could never be induced to talk about it. His journal dismisses it with the single comment: "Never had I seen such a barbarous mob, especially at meals."

On the morning of March 28, 1868 John Muir landed on the San Francisco wharf. With him was a globe-trotting cockney named Chilwell, who had agreed to go with him to the mountains. As they walked up Market Street, Muir saw nothing but the ugliness of commercialism. Stopping a carpenter with a kit of tools, he asked where he could find the quickest way out of the city. "But where do you want to go?" asked the man. "Anywhere that is wild," said Muir. "He seemed to fear that I might be crazy, and that . . . the sooner I got out of town the better, so he directed me to the Oakland ferry."

Exultant at being now "on the wild side of the continent," Muir with his companion was soon tramping southward from Oakland among the green, rounded, oak-clothed hills toward the Santa Clara Valley. The air was "throbbing with lark song" as they struck off eastward from Gilroy toward Pacheco Pass. From this height Muir looked down upon "the floweriest piece of world" he had ever seen. Descending into it, he followed his own erratic pattern up and down the broad Central Valley as the flowers in their

April glory led him. Finally, directed by his compass, he and the impatient Chilwell reached Hill's Ferry, by which they crossed the San Joaquin River; then they began the ascent of the Merced toward the Yosemite Valley.

Muir has left little record of his first impressions of that "most holy mansion of the mountains." Doubtless he found it too vast, too overpowering to be put into words. Some time after he returned to the plains he wrote to Mrs. Carr that "the magnitudes of the mountains are so great that unless seen and submitted to a good long time they are not seen or felt at all."

After ten days' stay in the valley they came back to the vicinity of Snelling, where they found work in the harvest fields of Thomas Eagleson. His fever "cooled with mountain winds and delicious crystal water," Muir now enjoyed such health as he had seldom known in his life. Since he needed money, he was content to remain here for a time. The wide Central Valley stretched far to the north and south between the Coast Range on the west and the sharp, snow-clad Sierra on the east. "They form together with the purple plains and pure sky, a source of exhaustless and unmeasurable happiness from all the fields where I work," he wrote to David. "Farming was a grim, material, debasing pursuit under Father's generalship. But I think much more favorably of it now."

The harvest over, Chilwell went his way. But sheep-shearing was just beginning, and John hired out at good wages with a gang of thirty men — "a mixed, mongrel, unanalyzable" assortment of Spaniards, Indians, Irish, English, and Scotsmen.

Wild horses, Arabian in origin, brought to California by the Spanish dons, roamed the plains. In intervals between sheep-shearing jobs, he "gentled" some of these bucking broncos for Mr. Eagleson. He was an expert horseman. Incredibly quick and agile, he was as hard to throw as a *caballero* who had spent his life in the saddle.

In the fall he worked on the ranch of Pat Delaney, near La Grange. In his employer he found a kindred spirit. The tall Irishman, whom he dubbed Don Quixote, had been educated for the priesthood, joined in the gold rush, mined for a time, and then became a rancher. From the day he hired John, he treated him as a friend and fellow intellectual and did everything possible to further his purposes.

Late in the fall John was hired to herd sheep for John Connel, alias Smoky Jack. His first California journal [20] relates his herding adventures from the night he walked out two miles from Snelling to take charge of the flock of eighteen hundred starving animals.

"Worse than a Hottentot's hut," was his comment as he surveyed his living-quarters. Generations of shepherds had left the cabin in a state of inconceivable filth. Outdoors things were even worse. Not a square foot of ground remained unencumbered with "ashes, old shoes, sheep skeletons . . . old jaws and craniums, and rams' horns. . . . And besides these dead evils, a good many wild hogs prowled about. . . ." So going within he chose the least dirty spot on the floor, wrapped himself "doubtfully" in his blankets, and "drifted off into merciful sleep."

In the morning after a breakfast of flour-and-water pancakes and tea, he went out to let down the corral bars, and the famishing flock "came crowding out, gushing and squeezing like water escaping from a broken flume, crossed Dry Creek, and scattered over a dozen hills and rocky banks. . . ."

Two trained sheep dogs had been left with him, and with their help he galloped up hill and down dale, heading off the leading "secessionists" in an effort to confine them within a square mile or so. About noon, to his surprise, the whole flock became drowsily quiet and lay down to enjoy a siesta.

In this lonely spot he lived for five months. Yet seldom in his life did he know more contentment. Every day was illuminated by the processes of nature. After long drought came torrential rains. As the season advanced, he observed and wove into his journal the crescendo of life as it returned to the plains in plant, bird, and insect form. His daily jottings have the quality of a musical tone-poem. At the beginning translucent silver mist broods over mountain and plain. Deep thunder growls in the distance or crashes overhead. Soon living waters come brawling down every gully. Then come brief interims when harp tones of gladness well up above the dark diapason. A fern unrolls its tiny bundles among the rocks. Mosses, liverworts, cresses, and purple mushrooms come to life among the boulders in the creek bed. Insects try their new-born wings. A meadowlark pours forth the mounting joy-theme in liquid melody.

In the spring John found his sheep-tending duties complicated by the arrival of many "little, thick-legged, wrinkled duplicates — unhappy lambs born to wretchedness and unmitigated degradation." Then came freezing weather, and in driving sleet he spent his days striding over the hills in search of them, carrying them in his arms to the cabin. At one time he had more than two hundred woolly babies sprawled on his floor, thawing them out by a roaring fire, feeding them milk from a bottle. Most of them he saved. Some died. Nor did death take a holiday among the grown sheep. One morning he found a hundred dead where they had huddled together in pitiful groups against the searing cold. Mingled among the sheep were dead hogs. One pair of little pigs lay side by side in a sand bed they had burrowed into. "Poor unfriended creatures! Man has injured every animal he has touched."

But life and warmth flowed back, and nature's own wild children, the flowers, birds, and insects, unweakened by man's commercialism, multiplied and bloomed and sang in the sun. The lambs salvaged from death "feel skippy and gay, and they run in bands around the clay bank, dancing as if they were daft!"

One day John was tramping the range singing at the top of his voice Burns's *Highland Mary*. "Ah, there was a mon to warm the heart, as bonnie a chiel as ever trod yird." He was always wishing the twain of them might roam the earth together. "And indeed he was always with me, for I had him by heart." Just as he reached the hilltop with the words:

> *There simmer first unfaulds her robes,*
> *And there they longest tarry,*

he chanced to look down into Twenty Hill hollow, a shallow oval bowl, sunk in "a fairy-land of hills." And there h
patches of the golden summer robe of the plains

Nature was not leisurely here. All forms of

to fruition, packing bulb and seed with the life principle, as if knowing the brevity of their cycle. Early in April the season reached its climax, its high note of beauty. Two weeks later "the plains are dim and brown already. . . . The glory has departed." By mid-May all plant life was as dead as if burned in an oven. The sheep were again famishing for the high green summer pastures of the Sierra.

After completing his contract with Smoky Jack, John worked once more for Pat Delaney, and that generous Irishman offered him a summer job with good pay, taking his sheep band to the Tuolumne Meadows for pasturage. Billy, an under-shepherd, would do the work, while he furnished the brains of the expedition, with time to botanize and explore the peaks and canyons.

During those months of his isolation, life had been eventful for his friends and family. Dr. Carr had resigned from the faculty of the University of Wisconsin and with his wife had arrived in Oakland to make their home and "plant" their children in California. John's sister Mary had reached the parting of the ways with her father. Following her brother's advice, she had gone on with her sketching, studying as best she could without a teacher. This had to be done in Daniel's absence. One day he returned unexpectedly, to find a box of her drawings on the table. In pious fury he took them outdoors, threw them into a puddle, and stamped on them, shouting that he did it to save her soul. The gentle Mary fled from home to take refuge with her married sisters. John, hearing about it from Sarah, wrote at once, telling Mary she was to go to the university in the fall to study art, music, and botany. Then on June 1, just before leaving for the mountains, he sent to David a Wells Fargo draft for $200 to be held in trust for her expenses. He told David he had still $500 subject to his call if needed for either himself, Dan, or the girls. From this time on until her marriage he made himself responsible for Mary's support. In fairness to Daniel Muir, however, it must be told that he later relented toward his daughter and contributed some money toward her expenses at Madison.

On June 3 the sheep caravan set out for the Sierra. Muir's journal[21] of the next three months interweaves many themes, sublime and commonplace. Although its narrative is objective, it is most of all a revelation of nature's own prophet, coming home at last to the mountains. For this event he had been born into the world, and all his wanderings thus far had been but preparations. With "the old bondage days" left behind, he reached heights of joy such as he had not known before and would seldom surpass in later years.

On the night of July 10 they camped on Tamarack Creek on the Tuolumne Divide just above the Merced Canyon. The next morning John, sauntering away out of sight and sound of the camp, examined the granite pavements glistening in the sun, peering through his lens at the parallel striæ upon them. Then he turned his attention to the composition and color of the boulders and soon saw they were erratics, borne from a distance. "And with what tool were they quarried and carried?" he asked. Swiftly, as by intuition, the big truth came to birth in his mind — the region had been overswept by a glacier flowing from the northeast, "grinding down the general mass of the mountains. . . . A FINE DISCOVERY THIS!"

A day or two later they camped in the Yosemite Creek Basin on the Tuolumne Divide overlooking the Yosemite Valley. Under the spell of the sublime scene John took off shoes and stockings and crept to the edge of the mighty brow over which the great fall plunges into the green gorge below. But he wanted to see still more directly down into the torrent of snowy waters. When he had gone as far as reason told him it was safe to go, he saw yet below on the sheer rock a tiny ledge, just wide enough for his heels. "With all sense of fear smothered," he slipped his body down the face of the cliff until his feet came to rest on the narrow shelf. Then shuffling along twenty or thirty feet, he looked directly "down into the heart of the snowy, chanting throng of comet-like streamers" of the fall. He did not know how long he stayed, or how he scr[illegible]bled back to the rock's top. He knew only that this had b[illegible] most memorable day of days," with "enjoyment enoug[illegible] that were possible!"

This was his first adventure into extreme danger. Many times after that he was to take similar hazards without fear because he recognized clearly the reality of his "other self." In the duality of man's nature he saw that an ancient inherited wisdom, stored in the subconscious, was ever ready to be called into action. This always told him if a feat was practicable, and he trusted it despite the protestations of reason.

Many a day he sat or stood on the summit of North Dome, overlooking the valley. Here on the rock's massive head he entered into complete kinship with the cosmos: "No pain here . . . no fear of the past, no fear of the future . . . no petty personal hope or experience has room to be." Space and time ceased to exist. His mother, his friends in the East, seemed "within voice, reach or touch."

One afternoon as he sat sketching on the Dome, he was seized with the certainty that Professor Butler was below in the valley. He jumped up and started to run down to find him. Then self-consciousness swept over him as he looked at his ragged, soiled clothing. Forcing himself to climb back to camp although "never for a moment wavering in my determination," he postponed his visit until the following day. In the morning, clad in clean overalls, a cashmere shirt, and "a sort of jacket," he started down by way of Indian Canyon. Bashfully he entered the Hutchings Hotel, among tourists who stared at him as if he were "some strange unclassible [sic] wilderness creature."

Seeing "Professor J. D. Butler, Madison, Wis.," written in the register, and learning that the party had gone to see Vernal and Nevada Falls, he ran the four-mile distance, "heart-hungry . . . in glad pursuit," and found him "as a compass-needle finds the pole." [22]

This was Muir's first recorded experience in telepathy. He was to have at least two remarkable ones later on. Having no superstition in his make-up, he did not regard them as miracles, but rather as phenomena produced by natural forces not yet understood.

Early in August the caravan crawled eastward along the Mono Trail, Muir scouring the adjacent region, as they advanced, for glacial evidences. On the night of the 8th, being near Lake Tenaya, he took off his shoes and "climbed the magnificent mountain rock at the east end of the Lake. . . . Almost every yard . . . shows the scoring and polishing action of a great glacier that enveloped it and swept heavily over its summit. . . . This majestic, ancient ice-flood came from the eastward. . . ."

The next day, scaling the divide, he discovered the ice river had risen five hundred feet from the Tuolumne side to cross it before descending into Tenaya Canyon. He concluded: "This entire region must have been overswept by ice." That same day he made another important discovery: namely, that canyon lakes of large size and depth existed only at the foot of steep declivities "where the down thrust of the glaciers was heaviest."

In the vanguard of the sheep he arrived at the Tuolumne Meadows — a series of "flowery lawns" embowered in forests and encompassed by mountains. Dana "in red velvet" and Gibbs towered to the east; Cathedral and Unicorn to the south. On the west arose Hoffmann's "battlemented summit," while on the north a multitude of lofty unnamed peaks formed a long, continuous wall. They made camp near the Soda Springs on the north bank of the Tuolumne River. The next day, "unweariable and well-nigh immortal," he wandered "from meadow to meadow, every one beautiful beyond telling." All the way up he had deplored the swath of devastation created by the sheep. "The harm they do goes to the heart," he said. Now in these surpassing meadows of the Tuolumne he indignantly exclaimed: "To let sheep trample so divinely fine a place seems barbarous!"

During the month they remained there, Muir climbed Mount Dana, Lyell, and other peaks and tramped down Bloody Canyon, finding in that abysmal gorge a wealth of evidence that a great glacier had plowed its way down the eastern Sierra wall to the Mono plain.

During those weeks, in addition to formulating the main outline of his glacial theory, he learned the supreme lesson that nature is one living, pulsing organism. Theoretically he had believed in this unity before. Now he saw it demonstrated beyond all doubt. In various ways he stated his ultimate certainty that "when we try to pick out anything by itself, we find it hitched to everything else in the universe. . . . The whole wilderness in unity and interrelation is alive and familiar . . . the very stones seem talkative, sympathetic, brotherly. . . . No particle is ever wasted or worn out but eternally flowing from use to use." [23]

On September 9 they broke camp and took the trail for the lowlands. Gazing back regretfully as he followed the sheep, he exulted: "I have crossed the Range of Light, surely the brightest and best of all the Lord has built; and rejoicing in its glory, I gladly, gratefully, hopefully pray I may see it again."

After working for some weeks on the Delaney ranch, Muir returned to the Yosemite. This time he was accompanied by Harry Randall, a young Philadelphia tenderfoot working on the ranch, in whom he had taken an interest. Before going he wrote to his brother David, enclosing $290 for the university expenses of Mary and Dan. After reminding him of the reserve fund of $500 he was holding for the needs of any other members of the family, he said:

"I start tomorrow for the mountains — the Yosemite. . . . I know that looking from the business standpoint you now occupy you will say that I am silly and imprudent, and that I value my time at too cheap a rate. Well, ahem, I have not time to make a long defense. The winter storms of the Sierra are not easily borne, but I am bewitched, enchanted, and must go. . . ."

A few days later he and Harry, calling themselves "partners," arrived at the Hutchings Hotel in the valley, and applied for jobs. They had come just at the right time. James M. Hutchings, the landlord, a tall, spare Englishman with a white beard and brilliant eyes, said he needed two men, one to milk the cow, drive oxen, and haul logs. Harry, about to say he didn't know how to milk cows and drive oxen, was nudged by John to keep quiet. Then when Hutchings's back was turned, he said: "You can do it all right. I'll show you how." [24] Muir himself was hired as a sawyer.

The Yosemite Valley as a white man's habitat was still in the pioneering state in 1869. No roads had been built, and the only transportation was by mule and mustang down steep, zigzag cliff-side trails. During the winter, mail was brought in once a month by Indian Tom on snowshoes.

In 1855 Hutchings, then living in San Francisco, began to publicize the valley in the *California Magazine,* which he edited. As a result of his articles republished in the East, tourists soon began to trickle down the granite walls. Two rude hostelries were built — the Lower Hotel, near the foot of the present Glacier Point Trail, and the Upper Hotel, on the banks of the Merced, facing Yosemite Fall. In 1859 Hutchings bought the Upper Hotel and took up a claim of 160 acres adjacent to it. About the same time James Lamon, a Virginian, took up land in the upper end of the valley and planted an orchard.

As a result of its growing fame as one of the earth's wonders, a movement arose to preserve the Yosemite as a park. Foremost among the advocates was Josiah D. Whitney, who in 1860 as head of the California Geological Survey began his task of exploring and mapping the Coast Range and the Sierra. Accordingly a bill was passed by Congress, and signed on June 30, 1864 by Abraham Lincoln, setting aside as a grant to the state of California the valley itself and the Mariposa Big Tree Grove.

The California Legislature accepting the grant in 1866, entered into "solemn compact" with the Federal Government to hold this area "for public use, resort and recreation." Thus the first wilderness park in the United States was created.[25]

As provided by the Act the Governor, with eight other commissioners appointed by himself, was placed in charge of the area, and Galen Clark, a pioneer living in Wawona, was made Guardian to enforce the rules against trespass, settling, and the cutting of timber.

Since the Act had made no reservations in favor of the claimants within the valley, Hutchings began a ten-year litigation in Sacramento and Washington to retain his land. He was on the point of leaving for the East to carry on this battle when John Muir arrived in November. In view of the rapidly increasing tourist trade, Hutchings was in a sore quandary to provide accommodations. Lumber must be provided; cottages, porches, and additions must be built. Moreover, the muslin partitions between bedrooms in the main hotel must be replaced by wooden walls. So before leaving on his journey, the landlord outlined for his new sawyer an appalling mass of work to be completed during the winter and spring.

The day after they had been hired, John and Harry set to work building for themselves a cabin of sugar-pine shakes. They chose a site near Yosemite Fall on the sunny north side of the valley, not far from the winter cottage of the Hutchings family, where they were to board. Carrying flat stones up from the creek bed, they first paved the floor and made a fireplace. Ferns had covered the ground here, so John spaced the slabs to permit the tiny bundles of fronds to unroll in the spring. In one corner he made a channel for a little singing brook. His one window faced the fall. Beneath it he made a rude desk, and trained plants to form a green arch above. The hammock beds were suspended at the right angle to afford a view of the fall in the night. A stout table, a bookcase, a bench, and two chairs upholstered with sheepskin completed the furniture of the little hut, which Muir called "the handsomest building in the valley."

John had come into the Yosemite expecting to pass a solitary winter. He was therefore surprised to find here in the heart of the mountains so charming a group as the Hutchings family. Mrs. Elvira Hutchings, many years younger than her husband, was a frail, Madonna-like woman with a passionate love of beauty in flowers and art. Unequal to the rigors of pioneering, she had rallied but slowly from the birth of her third child, Charlie, an ailing, crippled boy born in August 1869. John found in her a fine spiritual philosophy and a comradely interest in botany. One thing that troubled him, however, was her addiction to diet fads. Having suffered from those in his own boyhood, he was distressed to see her children undernourished.[26]

Florence, or "Floy" as she was called, born in 1864, and now a girl of five, had been the first white child born in the Yosemite. She was a strange little elf, as wild as the rock-walled valley she lived in. Because of her lightning-quick movements John nicknamed her "Squirrel," and referred to her in letters as "that tameless one" and "a little black-eyed witch of a girl." She often visited John and Harry in their cabin and would beg for food. With John's connivance Harry would take her down to the barn when he milked Buttercup and give her a nourishing drink, warm and fresh from the cow.

Gertrude, or "Cosie" as she was known, born in 1867, was a cuddlesome, blonde baby of two, affectionate and sunny. At once she became John's favorite among the children. Still living, Cosie — now Mrs. Gertrude Hutchings Mills — recalls her "small child's memories of a patient gentle man holding my sister or myself upon his knee while he showed us the composite parts of flowers . . . or of our trotting after him in the meadows looking for blossoms and their insect visitors.

"I have a mental picture of my brother when a year old, sitting in a large dishpan . . . and John Muir talking to him. That was typical of his kindly understanding for helpless things that endeared him to everyone."

An important person in the family was Mrs. Florantha Sproat, Mrs. Hutchings's mother, also nurse, cook, and domestic manager of hotel and home. She early won favor with John and Harry by her "memorable muffins," of which they both ate large quantities. She and her daughter took a profound interest in the Indians, and Mrs. Sproat, having absorbed their nature lore, knew all the weather signs.

In mid-December came deep snow, heralded by Mrs. Sproat, "our weather-prophetess." Looking up at the low-flying mists smothering all but the shoulders and crown of Half Dome, which the Indians called Tissiack, she said to John: "I do not like these clouds hanging about the rocks so far down." But what she didn't like made his heart leap with joy. All that night the snow fell and he was up at dawn, running along the meadow to see the rocks in their sublime white robes.

"Tissiack stood like a god . . . awful, incomprehensible. . . . Never have I beheld so great and so gentle and so divine a piece of ornamental work as this grand gray dome in its first winter mantle woven and jeweled in a night."

From that time on through the changing seasons he kept a daily chronicle,[27] recording each new bit of life as it unfolded in bird, beast, insect, and flower.

When John Muir contracted with James M. Hutchings to operate his sawmill, he did it with the certainty that no living trees would have to be felled. In their love of trees these two men, so at variance in other ways, were in accord. More than a hundred great pines had been uprooted in the storm of 1867, and these would supply an abundance of lumber for years to come. As soon as they had completed their cabin, they went to work, John rebuilding the sawmill and installing the machinery, while Harry helped James Lamon saw and haul the logs.[28] As soon as enough lumber was piled up, building began. In this John had the help of two carpenters, but being more deft with hammer and saw, he was largely responsible for the improvements. He not only did much of the partition work in the hotel itself, but planned and built in large part the artistic River and Rock cottages, and the "Big Tree Room," unique in that it was constructed around the bole of an enormous cedar.

By mid-April the vanguard of the tourist host began to straggle down the trails, to alight at the hotel veranda, stiff-legged and swathed in veils and linen dusters. In Hutchings's absence John was pressed into service as a guide. Any notions he had as to man's innate love of nature received a severe set-back. Piloting the visitors about the valley floor — for only the most daring ventured higher — he watched in vain the "blank fleshly apathy" of their faces as they stolidly gazed at the fall and the great rocks. Not a gleam of awe or wonder disturbed them — "finished and finite clods, untroubled by a spark."

Worst of all were the featherheaded young ladies just out of boarding schools — and some not so young — who chattered as they teetered along on paper-soled, high-heeled shoes, carrying frothy red parasols. John fairly seethed within when they responded to some piece of magnificent scenery with a chorus of "cheap adjectives," such as "pretty," or "charming." Frequently these Victorian maidens played the age-old game of appealing to his chivalry by squeals of affected timidity and threatened swooning at sight of a harmless little snake. He could be quite unfeeling on such occasions. An older woman friend, observing his conduct toward a certain young lady of a Boston Brahmin family, chided him for not improving his opportunities. But he had a sterner purpose in life than squiring ladies or flirting with them. Harry thought him almost a woman-hater, certainly a confirmed bachelor. Hearing of his marriage some years later, he wrote: "I did not think you would ever get married. But it seems you did have one weak spot, and I am glad to hear it, for that completes you as a man."

Hutchings returned about May 10 and, much to his sawyer's delight, said he would take over all the guiding from that time on. John could confine himself to the mill, with Sundays off for his own rambles. "I am very, very blessed," he wrote to Mrs. Carr. "The Valley is full of people, but they do not annoy me. I revolve in pathless places and in higher rocks than *the world* and his ribbony wife can reach."

But this didn't last long. It was somewhat disconcerting to Hutchings when a steady stream of important people — scientists, professors, writers, artists — came bearing notes from Mrs. Carr, committing them to John Muir's special guidance. Dr. Carr was now a professor in the University of California, and already they had a large circle of eminent California friends in addition to those of the East who came pouring west on the new transcontinental railroad. Mrs. Carr had been in the valley the summer before and had formed a warm friendship with Mrs. Hutchings, and Hutchings himself knew she was not a person to be lightly put aside. So John was summoned from his mill duties to convoy the notables.

Mrs. Carr had a deep purpose in sending these people to him. As she said in a letter, she coveted for him more than all else "kinship with kindred minds." This, she hoped, would mellow him toward society in the mass. And John himself, in the process of being mellowed, said gratefully: "You have sent me all my best friends!"

The first of these was J. B. McChesney, Superintendent of Schools in Oakland. Muir, finding him to be a true nature-lover and "all gold," as Mrs. Carr said he was, led him at once to his holy of holies, Sunnyside Bench,[29] to spend a night with the Upper Yosemite Fall. There, baptized in the moon-irised spray, the two men formed a lasting friendship.

Judge Gilbert Winslow Colby[30] of Benicia, arriving with a party of friends in June, was another brought in contact with Muir by Mrs. Carr. It being a Saturday night when they came, he proposed an overnight trip. So after climbing to Glacier Point they made camp in a fir grove skirting Sentinel Dome. In the gray dawn they went to the top to see the sun rise from behind the fretted summit peaks of the Sierra, suffusing all the granite wilderness beneath with glory.

To every intelligent listener these days John Muir was telling his impassioned story of the glaciers, and doubtless Judge Colby heard it that morning on the summit of Sentinel Dome. For using that as an observatory, John had already worked out for himself the whole majestic saga of the Glacial Period from its prime when ice filled the valley, down through the slow centuries as the ice mantle shallowed and retreated toward the shadowed amphitheaters beneath the highest peaks, followed by the ascent of the life zones up the burnished pathways it had wrought.[31]

With the arrival in the Yosemite of John Muir, ex-sheepherder, sawyer, carpenter, and, as he called himself, "an unknown nobody in the woods," the stage was set for one of the most acrimonious scientific controversies that ever rocked America. Unbeknown to himself, he was to be one of the chief actors in this drama. The other was Josiah D. Whitney, Professor of Geology at Harvard University and State Geologist of California.

Whitney had been appointed to the latter post in 1860 by a Legislature that cared nothing about geology as such. They employed him to find in the shortest possible time just where the gold-bearing rocks lay. But Whitney had carried on the survey in a scientific spirit, devoting the early volumes of his report[32] to the state's geology and paleontology. For that he had won the enmity of the mining-land speculators and the politicians. Through years of conflict he had gone on with the work, often at great personal sacrifice. When the legislators, whom he called "the jackasses at Sacramento," had voted inadequate appropriations or refused them altogether, he had used his own money, or borrowed at interest. Moreover, being a lover of nature, he had fostered the creation of the Yosemite Park.

Muir, who hated the frenzied exploitation of raw resources rampant in the state, had applauded his integrity. Writing from the plains to Mrs. Carr, he said: "Conspicuous, energetic, unmixed materialism rules supreme in all classes. Prof. Whitney . . . was accused of heresy . . . because in his reports he devoted some space to fossils and other equally dead and un-Californian objects instead of columns of discovered and measured mines."

But soon after coming to the Yosemite he read Volume I of the *Geology* and Whitney's *The Yosemite Guide-Book,*[33] and found himself violently at odds with the State Geologist's theory of the origin of the valley. The abundant evidences of glacial action he had seen on Glacier Point, on the rock walls, and in the fir-clad moraines on the floor of the gorge had convinced him that a great ice river, filling the chasm to its brim, had quarried and excavated it to its present depth.

On the other hand Whitney maintained that the Yosemite had been created by a primal cataclysm. In his own words: ". . . during the process of upheaval of the Sierra, or after, there was at the Yosemite a subsidence of a limited area, marked by lines of 'fault' or fissures. . . . In other and more simple language, the bottom of the Valley sank down to an unknown depth, owing to its support being withdrawn from underneath. . . ."

Elsewhere he said that in the process Half Dome had been "split asunder in the middle, the lost half having gone down in what may truly be said to have been 'the wreck of matter and the crash of worlds.' " Into this almost bottomless trough, Whitney had been forced to conclude, all the detritus of all the centuries had been falling, gradually filling it to its present level.

Being a bred-in-the-bone catastrophist, he denied that ice had any part in gouging out the chasm and sculpturing the walls. While admitting that glaciers had in some remote period existed in the Sierra, he refused to believe they had ever entered the valley itself.

Clarence King, a brilliant young member of the survey, possessing much of the swift, intuitive vision of John Muir, had in 1864 seen on the walls of the Yosemite "unmistakable ice striæ," and in the moraines on the floor other signs of glacial action.[34] These led him to believe that a glacier had once filled the gorge to a depth of at least one thousand feet. He stated that on his way from North Dome to Lake Tenaya he had "gathered ample evidence that a broad sheet of glacier . . . gathered and plowed down into the Yosemite. . . ." He submitted his observations to his chief, and they were included in Volume I of the *Geology,* published in 1865.

But when Whitney wrote *The Yosemite Guide-Book* some years later, he declared the King findings to be "an error," and went on to say: "There is no reason to suppose. or at least no proof, that glaciers have ever occupied the Valley or any portion of it . . . this theory, based on entire ignorance of the whole subject, may be dropped without wasting any more time upon it."

Muir's first written comment upon the Whitney theory was contained in a letter to Mrs. Carr of April 13, 1870: "Whitney says that the bottom has fallen out of the rocks here — which I most devoutly disbelieve."[35]

But at the same time, or soon thereafter, he was vocally expressing his disbelief to parties whom he led about the park. Whitney's *Yosemite Guide-Book* was snatched up eagerly by the traveling public, since with his long kite's tail of degrees and honors, he had enormous prestige. On the other hand, who was John Muir, a mere hireling of Hutchings, that he should contradict "the first geologist of the age"? And yet believing that "a physical fact is as sacred as a moral principle," he forgot his shyness, and did just that!

As he stood with a group of listeners perhaps on Glacier Point, looking at the abyss at their feet and Tissiack towering beyond, the inevitable "Whitney says . . ." in the mouth of a tourist was the red flag that set him going. Pointing eastward toward the clustering peaks of Lyell and sister summits along the range, he would trace for them on the living map the course of the two main tributary glaciers as they descended the giant stairways of Tenaya and Merced canyons to their convergence at the head of the Yosemite, into one grand trunk glacier that filled the gigantic gorge, and he would say: "Why, I can show the Professor where the mighty cavity has been grooved and wrought out for millions of years. A day and eternity are as one in His mighty workshop. I can take you where you can see for yourself how the glaciers have labored, and cut and carved, and elaborated, until they have wrought out this royal road."[36]

Some of those who listened were converted by the logic of his arguments, and before long the California newspapers were giving publicity to Muir's glacial ideas. Thus there came to be two conflicting theories in the public mind as to the origin of the Yosemite. (Still a third — perhaps not so well known — was advocated by certain scientists, to the effect that the valley was the result of water erosion.)

In due time Whitney, hearing of the Scotch upstart who dared to contradict his Olympian pronouncements, hurled contemptuous invectives at him, calling him "that shepherd," "a mere sheepherder," "an ignoramus," and the like.

Clarence King, who might have come to the support of Muir with his own observations, did not. Whitney was greatly liked and respected by the men who worked under him in the survey, and they stood in awe of his learning. This bond may have impelled King to silence. Moreover, it must be remembered that he subscribed to his chief's belief in a catastrophic origin for the valley, and thought glaciers had small eroding power. At any rate in his later writings he treated "Muir's vagaries" with a scorn second only to that of Whitney.

But support was destined to come soon to John Muir in his fight for the glacial theory.

Early in August 1870 Joseph Le Conte, Professor of Geology in the University of California, arrived in the valley with a party of nine students. Calling at the mill, they found Muir working in the dust and din of the saws, and Le Conte described him in his journal[37] as "a man in rough miller's garb, whose intelligent face and earnest clear blue eyes excited my interest." This was the greater because Mrs. Carr had spoken enthusiastically of the young man, urging the professor to seek him out. Le Conte called repeatedly at the mill, amazed to find "a man of so much intelligence tending a sawmill — not for himself, but for Mr. Hutchings." Finally he invited him to join the party for a trip to Mono Lake, and as Muir said later: "I gladly left all — and followed him."

On August 10 they left the valley on horses by way of the Coulterville Trail to Gentry's Station, thence to travel eastward toward the summits.

Muir was amused to see that this expedition — made up mostly of scientists in the bud — was the last word in military equipment and discipline. He felt like a rookie as they zigzagged up the trail under the command of "Captain" Frank Soulé, once of West Point, now a student instructor at the university. Soulé, tall, hawk-faced, was every inch a captain as he bestrode his high-stepping dapple-gray, leading his smart little company as if on parade. Each youth, wearing a spanking new uniform, bristled with pistols, cartridges, a hunting knife, and a rifle slung over his shoulder. The formidable nine were followed by the commissariat loaded upon Old Pack, a sure-footed veteran mule of many a mountain trail, tintinnabulating with enough long-handled pans, pots, and kettles — to say nothing of provisions — to supply a regiment.

Trailing at some distance in the rear rode a very unmilitary pair, the professor and John Muir, both lean and cadaverous, looking like Don Quixote and John the Baptist. Their nags went as fast or as slow as they liked, for the reins dangled loosely on their necks, while their riders, leaning forward or turning to look back, earnestly discussed rock cleavages or compared the granite of the Appalachians with that of the Sierra.

Early that afternoon the party camped in a fir grove near the top of Three Brothers. Relaxing from discipline on spruce-bough beds, the boys slept or loafed as they looked up through tall trees at the blue sky and floating white clouds. Le Conte, sitting against a tree, wrote in his journal:

"Mr. Muir gazes and gazes, and cannot get his fill. He is the most passionate lover of Nature. Plants and flowers and forests . . . haunt his imagination. He seems to revel in the freedom of this life. I think he would pine away in a city or in conventional life of any kind."

After an hour or two of rest the two scientists strolled over to Eagle Peak to gain an all-inclusive view of the Yosemite and its hinterland. Before them to the east sprawled the granite pathways down which the sinuous, viscous ice rivers had once crawled, gathering mass and power from tributaries, forced by pressure to flow uphill to surmount resistant barriers, then plunging down Niagara-like precipices to gouge out lake basins, converging at last with cosmic deliberation to form the master glacier filling the Yosemite.

As Le Conte, a pupil of Agassiz, stood listening to Muir's exposition of the whole stupendous system, he was profoundly impressed with the reasonableness of his "discovery." Commenting that night in his journal, he declared: "I strongly incline to the belief that a glacier once filled the Yosemite." As they journeyed on up the axis slopes, further investigation confirmed his inclination. They also saw eye to eye as to the importance of rock cleavages in determining present forms. Muir had already analyzed these forms as vertical, diagonal, horizontal, and concentric — the last named being responsible for the domelike rocks. The quarrying glaciers disinterring and sweeping away the fragments and boulders along lines determined by their developed planes had brought into relief the El Capitans, Cathedral roofs and spires, obelisks, and round domes we know today.

The only detail upon which they differed was the amount of preglacial denudation, and therein present-day geologists differ with Muir. Le Conte, while agreeing with Muir that glaciers had been the main eroding agencies, contended that the Sierra canyons such as the Yosemite had undergone considerable water erosion before the glaciers came, while Muir maintained that weathering and water had only a slight influence upon the gently undulating surface of the range. Streams of ice, he said, explained all the phenomena. "Constant and inseparable relations of trend, size and form of the Sierra valleys to their fountains as well as their grooved and broken sides, proclaim ice."

Sunset and the alpenglow came on while their talk continued. It ended only when "the boys" arrived, whooping like Indians and dragging pitch-pine logs for a bonfire on the rim of the canyon. When they lighted it after supper, the vast pyramid of flame fairly blotted out the stars. Soon three fires blossomed out of the black depths below. Guns were fired from above, and answering shots came from the valley. The professor, gauging the time between flashes and reports, estimated they were three thousand feet above the floor.

The second night's camp at the western end of Lake Tenaya was also memorable. After supper Muir and the professor strolled down to the lake's edge and either by wading or by jumping reached a sofa-shaped rock islet a little way out in the shallow water. Muir in writing his memories of that "camp meeting" on the rock exclaimed: "I doubt if John in Patmos saw grander visions than we!"

The third night they camped at the Soda Springs in the Tuolumne Meadows, and the next afternoon they arrived at the foot of Mount Dana. From this point on the following morning they climbed to the red-brown summit, Muir and one of the students dubbed "the Poet" being first to reach the top. The professor, plodding steadily like a tortoise, came in third, ahead of most of his hare-brained-and-footed boys. From this height the two scientists viewed the whole Merced-Tuolumne system, thus confirming to Le Conte's mind the essential truth of what he called "Muir's discovery."

Another day they descended through the Dantean depths of Bloody Canyon, Muir demonstrating to his companion from the evidences on every hand that a glacial plow had gouged its pathway down the eastern flank of the range. Among the volcanic cones and craters that stand about Lake Mono on the plains, like relics of a dead Inferno, Muir left the party to return to the Yosemite, while Le Conte and his boys, with military formation somewhat restored, journeyed north to explore Lake Tahoe and the American River, to find glacial evidences there.

Among all the celebrities who have visited the Yosemite, none ever created a bigger sensation at the time or left behind so many romantic tales and legends as the Honorable Mrs. Thérèse Yelverton, who arrived in the valley in July 1870.

Everyone knew the tragic story of this brilliant, warm-hearted woman, told for more than a decade in newspapers, novels, plays, and ballads.[38] The beautiful daughter of a Manchester silk-manufacturer she had seen both the heights and the depths of life as a lady-in-waiting to the Empress Eugénie, and as a nurse in the Crimean War. In the mid-fifties she had been married, first in a common-law ceremony in Scotland and later by a Catholic priest in Ireland, to Captain William Charles Yelverton, son and heir of the impecunious Irish Viscount Avonmore. After a few months her husband left her to marry another woman of greater wealth. Then, to protect himself from charges of bigamy, he dragged his first wife's name through the courts of Scotland, Ireland, and England, besmirching her reputation in an effort to prove their marriage invalid. The nine-year litigation culminated in a trial before the House of Lords, at which time the much-persecuted woman ably defended her own case, but lost it because of a feeling of class loyalty among the noble Lords who sat in judgment. Her small means exhausted, she set out on a world tour to earn her living by writing travel articles and books, the latter entitled *Teresina Peregrina,* and *Teresina in America.*[39]

When she went to the Yosemite, she at once sought out John Muir as her guide. Her charm had so won over Hutchings, her host, that whether he liked it or not, he delegated his sawyer to accompany her. The young naturalist, so completely out of "the commonplace jog-trot of people, the like of whom I have never met in all my travels," piqued her interest and her desire to attract him. Sympathetic accounts portray her as a tiny woman with "red-brown hair," "a small heart-shaped face," "exquisite hands," and "a magical voice." But beauty of the sophisticated sort held no lure for him, although he had keen sympathy for her as a human being cruelly wronged. Moreover, at this period and for some years to come his all-consuming passion for the wilderness lay like a sword between himself and love for any woman.

Soon after meeting him she decided to write a novel [40] about the Yosemite, with Floy Hutchings [41] as the heroine, and John Muir as the hero. With this in view, on their rides and walks she drew him out upon every conceivable topic. When she got back to her cabin, she put down the marrow of his opinions, approximating his unique form of expression. Because she had a real gift for reporting, her book contains an authentic portrayal of Muir at this time.

Always craving for herself a status of respectability, Mrs. Yelverton put herself into her story as "Mrs. Brown," the wife of a university professor. As such she went to the Yosemite and met "Kenmuir" (Muir) for the first time: ". . . the lithe figure approached, skipping over the rough boulders, poising with the balance of an athlete, or skirting a shelf of rock with the cautious activity of a goat, never losing for a moment the rhythmic motion of his flexile form. . . ." Upon nearer view she was impressed by his "bright intelligent face . . . his open blue eyes of honest questioning, and glorious auburn hair. . . ." Indeed, his face, "shining with a pure and holy enthusiasm," reminded her of a painting of Christ she had seen in Italy.

After this introduction Mrs. Yelverton proceeded to acquaint her readers with her hero's convictions upon art, music, religion, and Man himself. In matters of art Kenmuir was a Pre-Raphaelite. He faithfully "drew and painted every flower and blade of grass and every feathery sedge just as it was in nature." He had little use for the artists who squatted about the meadows with their easels or perched on trails in a vain attempt to put down the glories of the Yosemite. Hating all artifice, elimination, or substitution so far as nature was concerned, he vehemently resented the liberties they took in the name of "composition." "Then do you think you can COMPOSE better than the Almighty?" he demanded of one brush-wielder. Not waiting for a reply, he declared: "Man is the most arrogant biped that ever walked the earth!"

On one occasion Kenmuir was descanting upon the water-music of Yosemite Fall: "O, I love to climb up into that top chamber,—the great Concert Hall,—and hear the liquid roll of music all night long!" When Mrs. Brown questioned the use of the word "music" as applied to the inorganic roar of water, he cried out: ". . . why do you set up artificial before natural music? Man's trumpery inventions before God's great works!"

Irreverent he was toward most of the shibboleths of religion. Commenting upon the orthodox heaven, he said: ". . . the Paradise which our preachers are always locating here and there out of reach, and furnishing with harps, and fountains, and jewels, and gold, is often in our very midst, ringing in our ears, flashing under our eyes, if we were not so stupidly deaf and confoundedly blind as not to perceive it."

As to "Lord Man" and his vaunted "civilization," Kenmuir was deeply pessimistic. Out of his high preoccupation with mountains he "seemed to come down to humanity with considerable pain. 'Man,' he said, 'is the only mistake, it seems to me, in the works of the Creator, and there does appear to be something radically wrong about him.'" And again he said: "Man has got astray out of his orbit, or away from the ends for which he was created."

As the weeks went on John Muir found his popularity with Thérèse Yelverton becoming a nuisance. Convoying the famous "Countess" — as she was often called — along with an ever increasing horde of chattering sycophants and co-celebrities about the valley and near-by trails was absorbing even his free time when he wanted to be away in the "Beyond," following the channels of dead glaciers. Things reached a climax when she asked him to travel with her to the Orient as her secretary.[42] With this new complication he felt the time had come to extricate himself from a situation daily becoming more melodramatic. The chance came late in the fall when Harry Randall, grown tired of chores and mill work, decided to leave the valley. Muir threw up his job, declaring he would go with him and work for Pat Delaney. He left in haste, not even collecting the notebooks lent to Mrs. Yelverton with permission to copy his nature descriptions.

They left the Yosemite by way of Merced Canyon, being probably the first white men to traverse the entire length of that boulder-choked gorge.[43] Somewhere en route they made a detour to an unnamed sequoia grove. Possibly they went up Moss Creek Canyon to the Merced group of Big Trees. No longer in a desperate hurry, they camped several days and John Muir wrote to Mrs. Carr one of those utterly hilarious letters that always marked his "escapes" from the deadly perils of "civilization":

Do behold the King in his glory, King Sequoia! Behold! Be-

hold! seems all I can say. . . . I'm in the woods, woods, woods, and they are in me-ee-ee. The King tree and I have sworn eternal love . . . and I've taken the sacrament with Douglas squirrel, drunk Sequoia wine, Sequoia blood, and with its rosy purple drops I am writing this woody gospel letter.

. . . I was talking the other day with a duchess and was struck with the grand bow with which she bade me goodbye . . . but this forenoon King Sequoia bowed to me down in the grove . . . and the highbred gestures of the lady seemed rude by contrast.

There goes Squirrel Douglas, the master-spirit of the tree-top. It has just occurred to me how his belly is buffy brown and his back silver gray. . . .[44]

Several letters from the Viscountess — now called that by courtesy since the death of the old Viscount Avonmore in October [45] — followed Muir to the Delaney ranch, begging him to return to guide her out of the valley. But adamant to all pleas, he continued to gang-plow the fields of the Don.

Restless, despairing of his return, she decided to leave the Yosemite. It was late November, the time of storms that might any day block the trails. What followed was quite in line with the whole stranger-than-fiction life of this woman. She set out under sullen skies with a party of Englishmen to ride to Clark's Station. Not finding her saddle comfortable, she turned back to exchange it, arranging with her escorts to overtake them at Inspiration Point.

Having made the change, she started out a second time. Black ominous clouds had settled low like a ceiling over the valley. Thunder crashed in the mountains. A chill wind moaned through the trees. As she went up the trail, darkness descended and thick, blinding snow swirled about her. But with her stout little mustang she struggled on to Inspiration Point, only to find her escorts gone.

Now she was lost indeed. In the bitter cold gale she took refuge in a hollow pine for the night. In the morning she discovered her horse had wandered away, and the trail was completely obliterated. Stumbling about, half-frozen, her mind dazed with terror and fatigue, she fell over a twenty-foot precipice into blessed oblivion.

Her story would doubtless have ended there had not Leidig, the hotel man, traveling that way, seen her small shoe-prints in the snow and traced them to the spot where she lay unconscious.

When John Muir received her next letter, telling of her awful experience, he was most contrite. He told Mrs. Carr it seemed strange he did not sense her anguish in that terrible night, and he felt almost guilty for not having gone back to guide her out.[46]

The Viscountess remained in the Bay region until the following autumn, finishing her novel and arranging for its publication. The plot fairly drips with Victorian sentimentality and melodrama. Its only merit lies in her portrayal of John Muir, and in scenic descriptions, many of which were copied from his journals.

Before sailing for the Orient she wrote to Muir, sending back the notebooks she had borrowed. It was a frightened, lonely, but still gallant Teresina who scribbled this note:

Dear Kenmuir: — I am just starting for China — and wish very much you were going with me. You ought to have been ready to wander away with me and see all the beautiful places. Don't forget me as I never shall you. . . . I want to keep up a correspondence with you more than all other people. . . .

Keep to your good old life. Nature is the best friend. The happiness of fortune is a fable.

It is blowing great guns and I have to start tonight. Think of me tossing on a little schooner on the west ocean with no one but a Dutch captain to speak to. . . .

In January 1872 she wrote to him from Hong Kong, revealing resentment at some of the criticisms leveled at her book:

My dear Kenmuir, How I have wished for you, and sometimes longed for you avails me not to say. It is sufficient to make you comprehend that I never see a beautiful flower or a fine combination in nature without thinking of you and wishing you were there to appreciate it with me. . . .

. . . Even that so-called "Pacific Churchman" can't leave me alone. . . . He is one of the criticizers of Zanita — have you read any of them? . . . One says that your character is all "bosh" and exists in my imagination. I should like to tell him that you had an existence in my heart as well! Only fancy the Pacific Churchman hearing that!

I can see you sitting reading this as calm and still as your own heart. I used to envy you that, for mine will not be still, but is restless and unquiet. . . .

Your sincere friend,
Therese Yelverton.

PART IV

1871–1875

SURRENDER AND DEDICATION

HILE he plowed Pat Delaney's land that fall, John Muir was waging for the last time the old battle over his future. The three-year lease he had taken out of his life-span for his own purposes had expired some months before. His ultimate decision could no longer be postponed. He was still wrestling with it in December when a note came from Hutchings, asking him to return.

From the beginning there had been mutual dislike between Muir and his employer. In Muir's opinion Hutchings was shallow, vain, and not quite fair in his dealings with him. On Hutchings's part resentment inflamed by jealousy of his sawyer's popularity with the tourists soon mounted into a fanatical hatred, fraught with fantastic suspicions. Gertrude Hutchings Mills, knowing all the circumstances of this one-sided feud, has this to say: "my father had a violent and unreasoning dislike for him — unwarranted and most regrettable." [1]

On one score, however, Hutchings had real ground for complaint. Muir was called away too often from the mill to guide celebrities. Hutchings grumbled that he "just wouldn't attend to business, but wandered about studying wild flowers." [2] Unable to find another sawyer of equal skill, however, he asked him to come back, notifying him he would need for his sister the little cottage John and Harry had built. So when Muir returned to the valley in January 1871, he built for himself "a hang-bird's hang-nest" [3] beneath the gable at the north end of the mill, facing the fall.

By March the snow had melted from the valley floor and spring was returning with its myriad forms of life. Absorbing it through every pore of his body, he experienced a new birth of freedom.

Emerson had said: "If a single man plant himself indomitably on his instincts, and there abide, the huge world will come round to him." Muir's instincts told him to remain in the wilderness, and upon them he would stand, no matter what the outcome. In the intimate records of his autobiographical notebook he summed up the process of his thinking, and his new resolve:

There are eight members in our family. . . . All are useful members of society — save me. One is a healer of the sick. Another a merchant, and a deacon in good standing. The rest school teachers and farmers' wives — all exemplary, stable, anti-revolutionary. Surely then, thought I, one may be spared for so fine an experiment.

With this argument, he declared:

. . . the remnants of compunction — the struggle concerning that serious business of settling down — gradually wasted and melted, and at length left me wholly free — born again!

I will follow my instincts, be myself for good or ill, and see what will be the upshot. As long as I live, I'll hear waterfalls and birds and winds sing. I'll interpret the rocks, learn the language of flood, storm, and the avalanche. I'll acquaint myself with the glaciers and wild gardens, and get as near the heart of the world as I can.

Hunger and cold, getting a living, hard work, poverty, loneliness, need of remuneration, giving up all thought of being known, getting married, etc., made no difference.

And so as John Muir that spring followed the upward-moving zones of life after the annual death of winter, he became intuitively convinced that the glacial winter had not ended. Somewhere among the shadowed amphitheaters high up in the lee of serrated peaks, living glaciers yet lingered. Beginning with the near-at-hand beds of vanished ice rivers, he joyously, yet painstakingly, investigated the boulders and moraines, measuring heights, widths, and trends and sketching his evidences into his notebooks and upon hundreds of sheets of paper. Looking at the striæ on a boulder, he touched the stars. "Religion is on all the rocks," he said. Ice dominated his every thought and action. "Waking or sleeping I have no rest."

"And then came Emerson. . . ." If anything had been needed to heighten and buttress his dedication to wild nature, it was supplied in those brief hours of communion between this Wise Man of the East and his young disciple.

Before leaving for the Yosemite, Emerson had spent a few days in San Francisco. Mrs. Carr, tied up with commencement affairs at the San Mateo School, where she was a botany instructor, had been unable to call upon her old and revered friend. But she wrote him a letter, telling him of John Muir as one of his spiritual sons, who had carried his own ideals to an ultimate realization. She besought Emerson to receive and talk with him. To Muir she also wrote: "Mr. Emerson will be in the Valley in a few days, and in your hands, I hope and trust, the dear old singer in the places where we have sung his songs."

The party, arriving early in May, stayed at Leidig's Hotel. Sentinel Rock towered above them at the rear, with a thread of waterfall slipping down the naked granite front. Resting on the veranda, they could gaze across the valley at the great fall with its "long deliberate waters" swaying from side to side, blown by the wind.

Emerson at this time was in the late Indian summer of his years. With mind still undimmed, but quiescent, he was content to sit and watch the ebb and flow of life about him, finding it good. Always handicapped by bodily languor which had made him physically timid, and easily untuned by argument or opposition of any kind, he found it wiser now to submit to the smothering care of his friends and so husband his frail strength to remain free and poised within. As Walt Whitman said of him at this period of his life: "Emerson only lost the outward, the superficial — the rest of him remained unharmed!" While his friends chattered, he sat for the most part silent and absorbed, speaking occasionally in words of minted wisdom.

The morning after their arrival they began their jaunts about the valley. As they passed the Royal Arches, Emerson, mounted on a pied mustang, looking up at them and at sunlit Half Dome beyond, remarked: "This Valley is the only place that comes up to the brag about it, and exceeds it." [4]

On the third day they rode and climbed to the Casa Nevada, a small hotel perched on the rocks below Nevada Fall. After eating one of Mrs. Snow's famed chicken dinners, they sat on the porch overlooking the Giant Stairway and the grand valley beyond. But little of the stupendous scene did that very bookish party take in, for according to James Thayer, self-appointed Boswell to Emerson and historian of the trip, they disported themselves discussing Dante, Michelangelo, Vittoria Colonna, Ruppini, Manzoni, and Machiavelli. Like Plato's cave-dwellers, they had so long lived in a world of shadows and reflected objects that they had no power to face primary realities in the sunlight. Emerson, too, from old habit, had brought along his purple bag filled with books. But there is no record that he read them in the Yosemite.

In the late afternoon Emerson "rode home with quiet happiness." And when the sun sank in the west and the purple shadows gathered in the valley, leaving only the grand face of Half Dome shining above them like the very sun itself, he sat with his friends on the veranda as they talked earnestly of Greville and Boccaccio's *Decameron*. Also of metaphysics and metaphysicians, while the mighty organ tones of the great fall rang unheeded in their ears.

On one of those evenings a note was handed to Emerson. Since he had been in the valley, men and women had gone about speaking of him in awed voices, as of a divine presence in their midst. Now as he sat in the twilight, a hushed crowd gathered about in the shadows to gaze at the saintly old man. A few even went up to shake his hand. But not so a tall, bewhiskered, roughly clad young workman hovering on the outskirts. So far he had been too bashful to put in an appearance, although he knew Mrs. Carr had prepared the way. Even now failing to muster courage, he sent a note instead. Thayer relates that it was "an admiring, enthusiastic letter written by a young Scotchman named Muir," asking to be allowed to call.

The following morning the royal Emerson, not waiting for his humble suppliant to come to him, called for his mustang and, accompanied by Thayer, rode to the mill, where he found the young sawyer at work.

Many years later Muir recalled the two supreme moments of his life. One was when he found Calypso blooming alone in a Canadian swamp. The other was this meeting with Emerson. All his shyness fell away in that shining presence. He was conscious only of one desire — to give all he had to this man, to lay all his treasures at his feet. Drawing him up the ladder into his hang-nest, he there spread out before him his rocks, dried plant specimens, and dozens of pencil sketches of peaks, glaciers, and forest giants, begging him to accept them. Emerson smilingly declined, softening his refusal by saying he would like to bring his friends to see them.

But Muir's enthusiasm was unquenchable. With what Thayer condescendingly terms "amusing zeal," he besought the great nature prophet to remain in the valley for a while and go away alone with him to camp among the mountains. Muir, relating the same incident, says: "I proposed an immeasurable camping trip back in the heart of the mountains. . . . 'We'll go up a cañon singing your own song, "Good-by, proud world! I'm going home," in divine earnest.' . . . But alas, it was too late, — too near the sundown of his life. The shadows were growing long, and he leaned on his friends. His party, full of indoor philosophy, failed to see the natural beauty . . . of my wild plan, and laughed at it. . . . Anyhow, they would have none of it, and held Mr. Emerson to the hotels and trails." [5]

In the days that followed, Emerson slipped away alone more than once and came to the mill, where the two of them sat in the hang-nest and talked — the Elijah and Elisha of nature transcendentalism. The old man listened with Olympian composure, now and then asking a question in "his thrilling voice" to draw Muir out. And so the disciple poured out to his master his long-pent-up, most intimate thoughts, knowing that in this man who "inhabited eternity," [6] he had at last found perfect understanding.

Without any doubt Emerson, too, found a deep joy in these conversations. For here in the wilderness, doing common labor in a sawmill, he had found the living embodiment of his own Man Thinking, his Poet, who, looking upon Nature with unveiled eyes, could integrate the Parts into a mighty Whole.

When the Bostonians left the valley, Emerson, loath to part with his friend, asked him to ride with him as far as Clark's Station.

Muir, eagerly accepting, suggested they should camp for the night among the Big Trees. Emerson, unflanked for the moment by his party, said: "Yes, yes, we will camp out." [7] So Muir counted on "at least one good wild memorable night around a sequoia campfire." Uninhibited by Thayers, Forbeses, and Hathaways, what talk they might have! And what silences!

The next day as the party made its chattering way through the majestic forest, Muir, keeping close to Emerson, interrupted now and then to call attention to individual trees. Thayer, also riding as near to Emerson as the trail would allow, to take down his every word, became a bit impatient. "We grew learned and were able to tell a sugar pine from a yellow pine, and to name a silver-fir, and the 'libocedrus' . . . second cousin to the Sequoia."

At least once, according to Muir's notes, he succeeded in drawing Emerson aside by quoting a line from his own "Woodnotes": "Come listen what the pine tree sayeth." It was on a ridge high in a forest where lordly sugar pines dominated. Muir, loving the sugar pine above all other trees, remarked how they spread "their arms with majestic gestures, addressing the surrounding trees like very priests of the woods." [8] Emerson gazed long and in silence, then said that surely no other forest had "so fine a preacher or so well-dressed and well-behaved and devout a congregation." [9] Some time later he exclaimed: "Oh, you Gentlemen Pines!"

Yes, Muir seemed to know all about trees. But when it came to book knowledge — ah, there they had him! "It was pleasant," Thayer exultantly records, "as we rode along to hear him [Emerson] sound M. on his literary points. M. was not strong there. . . . Upon these matters Mr. E. talked to him . . . a good deal."

At noon they lunched among the pines, and when they had eaten, some of them lay on the ground resting. Others discussed Sir Walter Scott, competing in the number of passages they could quote. John Muir, who doubtless could have matched them ten to one with these quotations, reclined against a tree in silence, contemplating the green spires above. Perhaps he recalled something Emerson had written: "Man Thinking must not be subdued by his instruments. When he can read God directly, the hour is too precious to be wasted in other men's transcripts of their readings."

Could this be the same Emerson, old and weary and smothered in cotton-wool by friends, who worshipped literary culture as a fetish?

In the late afternoon as they approached Clark's Tavern, Muir mentioned what he supposed was a settled arrangement, that Emerson and he would camp that night among the sequoias. Had he thrown a bomb into their midst, it could hardly have wrought a bigger commotion. The women, especially, with their erstwhile soft Boston voices almost shrill, protested: "No; it would never do to lie out in the night air. Mr. Emerson might take cold. . . ." So preferring for him "carpet dust and unknowable reeks," they carried him off in triumph to Galen Clark's hostelry, where they were vastly relieved to find in their host what Thayer called "a solid, sensible man from New Hampshire." Muir trailed along to the hotel, reporting that Emerson "hardly spoke a word all the evening, yet it was a great pleasure simply to be near him warming in the light of his face as at a fire."

In the morning the party rode on to the Mariposa Grove, and while the others amused themselves measuring lengths and diameters of great logs and riding gleefully through a hole like a barn door in a standing tree, Emerson and John Muir walked apart, "sauntering about as if under a spell." Spending their last precious moments in silent communion, they paused beneath a fine group of trees. And Emerson, looking up with bared head and reverent face, said in a hushed voice: "There were giants in those days!"

While they sat eating lunch on the forest floor, Muir made an impassioned plea: "You must not go away so soon. It is as if a photographer should remove his plate before the impression was fully made." [10]

But all in vain. After the honored guest, at Clark's request, had named a sequoia after the New England Indian sachem Samoset, the horses were led up. When Emerson had been helped to mount, Muir stood for one final moment beside him. "You are yourself a Sequoia," he said. "Stop and get acquainted with your big brethren."

The old man sadly shook his head, and then, taking one more look upward at the grand domes of verdure, commented in his slow, hesitant way: "The wonder is that we can see these trees and not wonder more!"[11]

Muir stood for a while gazing at the spot where Emerson, riding in the rear, had turned about and waved a last good-by and then vanished from his sight. ". . . He was past his prime, and was now as a child in the hands of his affectionate but sadly civilized friends. . . . It was the afternoon of the day and the afternoon of his life, and his course was now westward down all the mountains into the sunset."

Meanwhile Emerson, going down the western slope of the Sierra, thinking of the man he had left behind, turned to his companions with these words: "There is a young man from whom we shall hear."[12] That Emerson went away with sorrow in his heart was reported later to Muir by Dr. Butler, who called on Emerson upon his return to Concord. "Emerson told me how regretfully he was taken away by the Bostonians from camping with you under the Big Trees."

Muir, left standing alone on the edge of the forest, experienced that day such loneliness as he had never known — the desolation of a dream unfulfilled. But now that the deluge of literary verbiage had ebbed into silence, the birds came out of their hiding-places and "made cheer" for him. In the light of his campfire that night the grand brown boles of the trees — friends of all his years — stood round about, reminding him they had not gone to Boston. Nor had the flowers. As he sat in the glow, he "quickly took heart," and out of his reverie added these words to his notes: "His mountaineering is done, yet we can still go on with him — a clear-souled guide — upon the high ranges of Truth."

Still thinking of Muir, and troubled with regrets, Emerson stopped in Oakland on his way to San Francisco and, leaving his party, went alone in a dense fog to seek Mrs. Carr and pour out to her the joy he had found in those few brief days of their companionship. And Mrs. Carr, writing the next day to Muir, told of that visit:

Coming in last night from a hard day's work . . . who should I find but Mr. Emerson, and of course you know the rest. How weariness fled and my delight was full you do not need to be told.

But if there is any joy of angels to be had in the flesh, it is that of finding your soul confirmed in its faith through the soul of another.

And so dear friend, my joy in you was full. And I laugh to think how they go up to the mountains — the beautiful ones — to find YOU in the confessional, the only soul I know whom the mountains fully own and bless!

I have laid up in my heart so much that he told me. . . . I wait to talk with you about it. . . .

While life lasted, neither Muir nor Emerson forgot their hours of radiant communion, so much not put into words had passed between them. Several years after Emerson's death John Burroughs, browsing through his journals, found a short list of great names entitled "My Men." The last name, added in old age, was that of John Muir. And Muir in old age wrote this: "Emerson was the most serene, majestic, sequoia-like soul I ever met. His smile was as sweet and calm as morning light on mountains. . . . A tremendous sincerity was his. He was as sincere as the trees, his eyes sincere as the sun." [13]

Having resolved to remain in the mountains, Muir found his desires crystallizing into a stern new purpose. The scarred peaks and mystic canyons were calling him to explore the secrets of their origins. First of all, Whitney's catastrophic theory must be refuted by facts. Muir had no ambition to make himself famous as the originator of the glacial theory — only to make the truth known.

Early in the year 1871 he had set about hunting down on the top of the Tuolumne Divide a dead glacier that had once had its center in the Yosemite Creek Basin and had flowed down over the north wall into the valley. All his Sundays were spent on the trail of it. As soon as Emerson's party had gone, he was back on the scent with renewed determination.

By June he began to get fragmentary results. Intuitively he felt that a certain canyon had been wrought by this glacier, but the evidences, dimmed or obliterated by water and weather, had so far eluded him. One Sunday morning he had a premonition he would find them. As if led, and "full of faith," he ran northward toward the head of the basin. And before he had gone four miles, he found the evidence he had been seeking, in a narrow hollow where the ice had wedged through between resistant rocks, "thus deeply grooving and hardening the granite and making it less susceptible of decomposition." [14]

After finding this missing link, it was as though veils had been swept from his eyes as he followed Yosemite Creek to its source among the snows of Hoffmann, everywhere discovering in strips of moraine matter and boulders evidences of the glacier that had once followed that course. In that one day of clarified vision he determined the length and width of the ice river and mapped out its general route.

Before he estimated the height, he was interrupted by visitors. Arriving in July was Dr. Clinton L. Merriam [15] of the Smithsonian Institution. Profoundly impressed with Muir's findings thus far, Merriam asked him to write him the final results of his lost-glacier sleuthing.

One thing still trammeled him—his bondage to the sawmill. So on or about July 10 he sawed his last log and severed all relations with Hutchings. Exulting in his emancipation from "cold enslaving musts," he vanished into the "Beyond," to spend six weeks exploring summit peaks and canyons. Returning in August just long enough to replenish his bread sack, he left again. "I expect to be entirely alone in these mountain walks," he wrote to Mrs. Carr; ". . . the gloamin' will be very lonely, but I will cheerfully pay this price of friendship, hunger and *all* besides." [16]

One of the problems he had to solve had to do with shadows. From Sunnyside Bench he had noted that the shadows on the floor of the gorge coincided with the grove-clad moraines; also that the shadowed south wall of this southwestward trending valley was quarried and eroded to a far greater extent than the sunny north wall. Out of these facts he had evolved a working hypothesis that glaciers were mothered by shadows, and their existence and effective eroding power prolonged in the protecting coolness.

Now free at last for intensive study, he carried his observations back toward the axis, and again down the canyons of the Merced system, to find the same principle working universally. Peaks, spurs, and high canyon walls were comparatively unscarred on the sunny sides where the ice had melted earlier, while on the opposite walls where shadows lingered they were shattered and deeply eroded. The deep névés where the glaciers had their birth were always on the shadowed sides of peaks and ridges.

Aside from scientific problems another urgent question now faced John Muir. Should he write down his theories and discoveries for publication? Hitherto he had sternly rejected the idea of writing, arguing with some bitterness: "What I have nobody wants. Why should I take the trouble to coin my gold? Some will say it is Fool's Gold. It cannot be weighed on commercial scales. There is no market. . . . A tree takes sunshine and grows; our souls take Beauty, strive and grow. But neither may be used to warm and fructify others who keep away in shadow. Only a few may be persuaded to come and see." [17]

Now, however, several people were urging him to write — Mrs. Carr, Le Conte, Merriam, and Emerson. But the mere thought of shaping his ideas into articles acceptable to wise men in laboratories made him self-conscious. The very nerves and muscles of his hand became rigid when he tried.

Upon his second return from the axis he found awaiting him John Daniel Runkle, president of the Massachusetts Institute of Technology. He had come to learn at first hand of Muir's glacial findings. After a five-day trip with him through the canyons to the névés beneath the summits, Runkle was convinced of the truth of Muir's theory and begged him to write it out for the Boston Academy of Sciences.[18] He also tried to induce him to go to Boston to teach, offering him a choice of departments under his charge. But Muir was deaf to all such lures. Runkle's urging him to write, however, probably helped to tip the scales in that direction. A few days later Muir announced to Mrs. Carr his decision to write a book about glaciation. He said also that he was "tempted to try" writing for the magazines.

In the same letter to Mrs. Carr he protested against her distress over his lack of polish. An artist named King, returning from the had given her a sorry picture of Muir's wild state. But hould he or she bother about anything so petty when he was ng a cause incomparably greater than self? "I feel sure that if u were here to see how happy I am . . . you would say, 'Keep your mind untrammeled and pure. Go unfrictioned, unmeasured, and God give you the true meaning and interpretation of his mountains.' "[19] And Mrs. Carr, catching his vision, wisely yielded, sending back these words: "I do say from my heart, 'God bless thee and keep thee in thy chosen work.' "

Merging himself with the elemental that he might be "like a flake of glass through which light passes," he was forgetful of personal concerns and doubtless often uncouth in appearance. When after a season of rapt communion among the peaks, his slim body, lithe and powerful as a rapier, came dancing down the mountainside, his little friend Cosie Hutchings was often frightened by his wild aspect — that fey look in his eyes, his clothes in tatters, and his face smeared with soot to keep away the snow-burn.

But certain older people had a quite different impression of him on such occasions. When Mrs. Yelverton said of him in her book that his face reminded her of a painting of Christ she had seen in Italy, one put it down to her over-fervid imagination. But it seems others thought likewise. The artist William Keith, who met Muir in the valley in 1872, told William Colby in later years that when Muir came down out of the mountains, "We almost thought he was Jesus Christ. We fairly worshipped him!" Keith was reminded also of the painting of Jeremiah in Sargent's *Prophets*,[20] and often nicknamed his friend, "the Prophet Jeremiah."

In September Muir was again on the trail of his "Lost Glacier," exploring its fringes and tributary basins for final details. Then, returning to the valley, he began a series of letters to Dr. C. L. Merriam and President Runkle, descriptive of his hunt. These he revamped into a single article entitled "The Death of a Glacier" and sent it off to the *New York Tribune*.[21] To his astonishment, it was accepted and paid for, and he was urged to write further communications.

In the yellow days of October he tramped up the Upper Merced

Basin, exploring on the south side the high flanking spurs that festoon the long, straggling Merced Range. On the morning of the 6th, while advancing up the largest and last of the névés that yawn between Red and Black Mountains, he was amazed to discover in a little whispering stream a substratum of fine gray silt. "*Glacial mud! A living glacier!*" he shouted as he got down on his knees and panned it in his hands. It *was* freshly ground *glacial meal!*

Hot on the trail now, he leaped up the steep shank of the moraine above and soon beheld sweeping down from beneath the precipices of Black Mountain, to end at his feet, his first *living glacier.*[22]

Whitney stubbornly reiterated to the end of his life that there were no living glaciers in the Sierra. Clarence King used all his weapons of brilliant satire to do likewise. But John Muir went his patient way, penetrating fastnesses untrodden by either of them, and in the course of the next two years discovered no fewer than sixty-five authentic small living glaciers.

While on this same October journey, he found his second "High Altar" — Sunnyside Bench had been the first — in a little lake hidden away among battlemented walls in the heart of the mountains, which he chose to call Lake Nevada, or Shadow Lake — now known as Lake Washburn. Tramping up the Upper Merced Canyon through the chain of four little yosemites, he found it in the highest of the series. Caught in a storm on Mount Lyell, he retreated to it and that night lay warm and safe in the lee of a boulder by the lakeside while the winds roared and the snow whirled down in a blinding mist. Three days he lingered in this enchanted canyon. Then came a still, shining morning when he "felt like a horse brought out to run." He made bark snowshoes and set out to traverse the white wilderness, sure-footed and swift as he skimmed over the newly packed snow down to the valley.

In the roughly scribbled notes [23] of this sojourn appears the first recorded foreshadowing of the humanitarian crusade to which he would give the later years of his life:

"Heaven knows that John Baptist was not more eager to get all his fellow sinners into the Jordan than I to baptize all of mine in the beauty of God's mountains."

Determined to make a "last raid of the season," Muir a few days later mounted once more to the domed Yosemite Creek Basin and, striking off over the high divide to the northeast, came abruptly to the brow of a gorge whence he looked down more than 4,000 feet into the grand Tuolumne Canyon. He camped there that night, and was up in the morning at the first bird call, "loose-limbed and ready to plumb the Gorge." Shouting in sheer ecstasy, he went bounding over the beveled rim of the wall, sure-footed as a mountain goat. Finally he reached the shimmering river below and followed it down into the Hetch Hetchy Valley itself — "one of Nature's rarest and most precious mountain temples."

Advancing in a kind of enchantment into the lush floor meadows, he looked about him at the high encompassing walls, seeing features so alike in form and position, as to leave no doubt that this valley and the Yosemite had been sculptured by the same tools and processes. And yet each of the sister valleys was distinctive — the Yosemite the more austere, Hetch Hetchy the more intimate, gracious, and charming.

Just as the first shadows purpled the floor, he turned toward his bedroom on the heights. With the strength of ten he climbed exultant, without pausing to take breath. Only the last thousand feet, which he had run over in his descent, slowed him down, and he looked back "in quiet joy to see the setting sun blessing the mountains."

John Muir was snugly cabined at Black's Hotel for the winter. A. G. Black and his wife had become his warm friends, and when he left Hutchings's employ, they urged him to make their hotel his headquarters. In the winter he served as caretaker and as such had the whole domain to himself.

In the solitude and comfort of his cabin he set about the serious business of writing. His success with the *New York Tribune* taught him he might earn his living, for a while at least, narrating the daily happenings on nature's grand stage, along with the homespun concerns of the few pygmy humans in the foreground. So he wove together vivid and humorous word pictures of the Yosemite and the community "night life with its seven whiskey soirees a week."

To tell so graphic a story one suspects he must have attended some of them when the bibulous gathered to drink deadly varieties of the whisky genus, and tell "bar-stories" and yarns of mining-camp shooting scrapes. Another choice bit was his description of a bachelors' Christmas banquet concocted in "ladyless kitchens." Not even Mark Twain or Bret Harte could turn out a more convincing glimpse of life in the raw West.

But as if for his benefit, Nature herself staged two stupendous spectacles during those months. The first was a storm in mid-December. For two days and nights "the jubilee of waters" lasted. He was abroad every hour in the thick of it, reveling in the wild elemental mingling of winds, waters, and rocks. On New Year's Day he gathered his notes into an article.[24] In view of his future career as a conservationist, perhaps the most important thing in it was his first written criticism of the State Park Commission and the destruction of natural beauty in the Yosemite in the name of "vulgar, mercenary 'improvement.'" He found his only comfort in the thought that the walls at least were "unimprovable" by "the money changers." And the domes and falls, thank heaven, were everlasting!

Nature's second grand show was an earthquake.[25] Sleeping in his cabin on the night of March 26, he was awakened by "a strange wild thrilling motion and rumbling." Disregarding the hard fist of fear in the pit of his stomach, he ran out into the moonlit meadows. But for once he couldn't run far. The earth twisted and jerked under his feet. There was an infernal rumbling like the pounding of giant hammers from beneath.

Then after a moment of calm came the climax. Eagle Rock, high on the south wall of the valley, was toppling, then falling like a fiery comet out of the sky. All fear forgotten, he bounded toward the descending mass, and before the huge heated rocks had settled, groaning, into their places on the valley floor, he leaped upon them in a shower of dust and falling fragments, shouting: "A noble earthquake, a noble earthquake!"

In the restored calm that followed, he sauntered about the meadows, joining a cluster of men jittery and pale in the waning starlight. They were all converted that night to Whitney's cataclysms, and in their panic they blamed Muir for his absurd theory that ice had ground out the valley. He tried to allay their fears. "Cheer up, cheer up," said he. "Smile a little and clap your hands. Mother Earth is only trotting us on her knee to amuse us and make us good!" [26]

But they were not amused. Angry words were spoken. In their hysteria they called his ideas "crazy" and him "a fool," [27] as if theories mattered in the face of impending doom!

Then with what sense they had left, they commandeered every mule and mustang in the valley and got out with the utmost speed. A storekeeper among them, by some strange quirk of caution, put his keys into John's hands to hold for him, should he return this side of eternity. "Crazy" he may have thought him, but at least he trusted him.

As Muir walked home in the dawn, he stopped by the Merced. All was quiet as if the turbulence had never been. The River of Mercy on her way to the sea sang her deathless song. And a brave owl — his calm and steadfast friend on many a night — called from the tall pine at the corner of the hotel: "Too-hoo, too-hoo." [28]

By the summer of 1872 Muir had good reason to believe he could make his living by writing. In February Dr. Carr had taken his letter about "The Jubilee of Waters" [29] to Editor Benjamin Avery of the *Overland Monthly,* who received it enthusiastically. Two months later his "Twenty Hill Hollow" [30] had been accepted by the same magazine. Moreover, his first *Tribune* article on the death of a glacier had been republished in *Silliman's Journal* of January 1872 — a notable recognition from the scientific world.

But having written one glacial article, Muir decided to "hold my wheesht" for a while. He felt it would be presumptuous for him to contend with more experienced geologists, since he knew only the Sierra. He needed to study other countries at first hand. Thus he found himself faced with two alternatives. Should he be a naturalist or a geologist? His scientist supporters were clamoring for glacier articles. The lay readers wanted his interpretations of nature as a whole. Events of the year 1872 helped him decide.

In July Merrill Moores — now a sixteen-year-old boy — arrived to spend the summer with him. Merrill recorded that he found Muir "looking as young and really handsomer than . . . on our Wisconsin ramble."

That spring Muir had built a cabin up the valley near the home of James Lamon. Almost hidden in a clump of cornus bushes, it stood on the river bank opposite the Royal Arches. He had built it in anticipation of Merrill's visit, and also because he thought his sister Mary might come west to live with him.

One of their earliest trips together was to Mount Lyell, to plant stakes across the glacier near the top of the mountain and thus measure its flow. Muir's method was modeled after the technique of Agassiz, Forbes, and Tyndall in their Alpine investigations.

Many scientists of world repute were converging upon California that summer of 1872 to attend a convention or give lectures. Mrs. Carr saw to it that several of them sought out John Muir in the Yosemite. He rejoiced when he heard that both Agassiz and Professor John Tyndall, the English scientist, were expected. Having read several of Tyndall's books, he agreed with his theory as to the viscous composition of glacial ice. Muir knew, too, that he was no mere dry-as-dust laboratory pundit, but climbed the mountains with an ecstasy akin to his own and a will to search into the spiritual meaning behind physical phenomena.

Unfortunately Muir has left no record of their meeting. But Merrill tells us that on the Lyell trip John taught him how to use "an aneroid barometer presented to him by Professor Tyndall." Moreover, a few months later a box arrived containing a hundred dollars' worth of delicate instruments for his mountain work. Muir, writing home, said they had been sent him by "a friend in England." It seems almost certain that Tyndall must have been that friend.

Asa Gray, the Harvard botanist, was the next scientist he met. They had already been in correspondence, and Muir had sent him floral specimens. The two flower-lovers spent a week tramping together. Merrill, who went along to care for the horses, was deeply impressed by the tall, kindly professor. Gray had his "traveling legs," and Muir found him more nearly a match in walking than any other man he had climbed with except Galen Clark.

Gray, too, as had Emerson and Runkle, urged him to go east to teach, telling him to come to Harvard, where "good and able and enthusiastic friends" would gladly push him ahead.[31] But, like Emerson, Gray found the young mountaineer no "mush of concession." Summing up his reaction to all such offers, Muir said: "I 'can't see it.' . . . I have been too long wild, too befogged to burn well in their patent, high-heated, educational furnaces." [32]

Upon his return east Gray sent him copies of his own various works on botany, saying: "So you can set to studying botany again." He kept Muir busy sending specimens packed in moss. In every letter he urged him to continue botanizing in the Sierra, searching for new and curious things. One of the new things he named *Ivesia Muirii* in honor of its discoverer. Then egging him on, he said: "Get a new Alpine genus, that I may make a Muiria glacialis!"

Later in the summer John Torrey, Gray's former teacher and sponsor, came to the valley. Muir spent several happy days with the old botanist, and it may well be surmised that the combined influence of Gray and Torrey at this time helped to wean him away from making geology his specialty.

During August Agassiz arrived in San Francisco after his long sea trip along the coast of South America. But he was too ill to go to the Yosemite. Muir sent him "a long icy letter," telling him of glaciers living and dead, and urging him to come to the Sierra. Elizabeth Agassiz, answering for her sick and aged husband, said that when he read the letter, he exclaimed: "Here is the first man who has any adequate conception of glacial action." [33] He hoped, he said, to return next year and spend a whole summer with Muir on the mountains. But death intervened between him and the fulfillment of this plan.

Le Conte also reported that while conversing with his old teacher he had mentioned Muir as perhaps knowing "more about the glaciation of the Sierra than anyone else." Whereupon Agassiz responded heatedly. "He knows *all* about it!" [34]

Both Mrs. Carr and Le Conte tried to persuade Muir to come to the city to meet the great teacher. But no hunter ever watched his traps more sharply than John Muir his stakes. He was measuring the flow of several glaciers at this time, and the season was growing late. To Mrs. Carr he wrote: "My horse and bread . . . are ready for upward. . . . Ink cannot tell the glow that lights me at this moment in turning to the mountains. I feel strong to leap Yosemite walls at a bound. . . . I will fuse in spirit skies. I will touch naked God." [35]

So master and disciple never met. It is tempting to speculate upon the effect such a meeting might have had upon Muir's career. Few men could resist the persuasive power and charm of Agassiz — his "transmitted touch." Would he have thrown his mantle upon the younger man, commanding him to carry on in the Andes and on all the continents the cause of glacial investigation?

In October Muir was abroad on a ten-day trip in the summit region. On the final day as he rounded a headland among the headwaters of the Tuolumne, he came suddenly upon a sublime view of a cluster of wild, snow-laden peaks. Lyell and Maclure clothed with white glaciers, towering against a cobalt sky, dominated the eye. In the foreground a valley aflame with red, purple, and gold, with a young river cascading down the meadows. Here was a landscape made to order for an artist's brush. He lingered for hours gazing at it, and wrote into his journal a wish that he could put down on canvas the beauty he saw.

Late the following day he descended to his cabin below the Royal Arches. Soon came little Floy Hutchings leading three men, who introduced themselves as William Keith, Benoni Irwin, and Thomas Ross — all artists. Keith, a stocky, shaggy-haired Scot with deep-set luminous eyes, pulled out a letter from Mrs. Carr.

It was a great day for both of them when John Muir met William Keith. That first night they began to call each other Johnnie and Willie. Born in Scotland of Highland blood, in the same year, seven months apart to a day, they inherited the love of nature implicit in the Gaelic temperament. They were like two axis peaks with the same granite base. But Keith, living in cities most of his life, had never broken his way through into that elemental passion that was Muir's. And then as if Destiny was taking a hand in his affairs, he met Mrs. Carr, and that wise woman, understanding what these two Scots might mean to each other, brought them together.

Keith explained to Muir just what he wanted. For the artist's purposes the Sierras were too vast, too massive, diffused, and all-inclusive. "Do you know any piece of Alps that would make a picture?" he said. "Yes," exulted Muir. "I saw it only yesterday. The crown of the Sierra is a picture hung on the sky, and mind you, it needs none of your selection, or 'composition.' I'll take you there tomorrow." [36]

Two days later the four men, with Merrill, were traveling along the upper Tuolumne River toward its head. It was a joy for Muir to guide such a party as this. "There's naebody like a Scotchman to see beauty," he maintained, and these artists were all Scotch. Keith and Irwin were already established. Ross was only a plumber, yet he had talent.

Late in the afternoon, just as the mountains were transfigured in carmine and gold, they rounded the headland and faced the wild cluster of peaks. Without saying a word, Muir reined his horse aside and waited to see the scene reflected in the faces of the others. In silence they dismounted and stood as if stunned. Then Keith, his shaggy mane bared, "dashed forward, shouting and gesticulating and waving his arms like a madman."

The next morning, leaving his friends happily sketching, Muir set off in the dawn to climb Mount Ritter — something he had long wanted to do. Ritter, which he called "the King of the mid-Sierras," was, he felt, a textbook for the study of all other mountains. Clarence King had attempted to climb it, but failed. So far as known, no one had yet scaled the summit.

Crossing the axis on foot, he proceeded south along the eastern flank of the range. After camping that night in a valley by a glacial lake and waterfall, he went on in the morning, and a few hours later was climbing a long spur of the mountain that thrust itself eastward between the headwaters of Rush Creek and the tributaries of the San Joaquin. As he climbed, he faced the frowning mass of Ritter, bristling with black crags above him.

Descending to a glacier at his left, he crossed it diagonally upward; then picking his steps with intense caution, scanning the rock for every seam and fissure, he began to zigzag up the sheer, ice-covered, sunless precipice that towered at the head of the glacier. But footholds became fewer and farther between, and when little more than halfway to the top he was all at once brought to a dead stop with arms outstretched, clinging to the face of the rock. Unable to move hand or foot, he could see in the granite cliff ahead no more seams or fissures.

"Suddenly," he relates, "my danger broke upon me. Faith and hope failed, suffered eclipse. Cold sweat broke out. My senses filled as with smoke. I was alone, cut off from all affinity. Would I fall to the glacier below? Well, no matter. . . . Then as if my body, finding the ordinary dominion of mind insufficient, pushed it aside, I became possessed of a new sense. My quivering nerves, taken over by my other self, instinct, or guardian angel—call it what you will, became inflexible. My eyes became preternaturally clear, and every rift, flaw, niche, and tablet in the cliff ahead, were seen as through a microscope. At any rate the danger was safely passed, I scarce know how, and shortly after noon I leaped with wild freedom, into the sunlight upon the highest crag of the summit. Had I been borne aloft upon wings, my deliverance could not have been more complete." [37]

While "this strange influx of strength" and magnified vision persisted, he climbed on without conscious effort among the beetling, shattered crags of Ritter. All about him towered "thickets of noble peaks," and as far as he could see north and south along the axis of the Range stretched a weird, inhuman pathway of jagged summits. To the east lay the ashen desolation of the desert, while westward the Gothic mountains flowed away in a sea of gray granite domes and ridges toward the far-off plains of the San Joaquin.

The sun was low in the west when he left the summit and scrambled down the shadowy east side. The wild, cosmic upsurge of energy, lasting for about six hours, faded with the light. Bearing away to the north, guiding his course by canyon trends and the marching black peaks above him, he finally reached his last night's camp by the lake, where the white waterfall chanted its song in the dark.

The next day he "sauntered" back to his friends. When he appeared, they whooped in welcome. Needlessly worried, they had conjured up all sorts of "civilized fears." Keith, the epicure, hankered after sugar in his coffee, and other good things to eat. "Muir was always a poor provider," said he in later years. He took along the needfuls, but left out the trimmings.

While the artists sojourned in the valley, working up their sketches, Muir made two more trips to the mountains. On one of them he observed his stakes on Mount Lyell. Planted in a straight line across the widest part of the glacier, they now described an enormous arc. Thus he was able to measure the rate of flow per day near the lateral moraines and the greater speed in the center.

On his second return in late November he found the artists had formed a plot to take him home with them. Perhaps because he had known so much loneliness and because Keith already seemed like "a verra brither," he consented.

Arrived in the Bay cities, he was subjected to an overdose of civilization. The Carrs, McChesneys, Le Contes, and Keiths all wanted to entertain him and introduce him to their friends. He was rushed back and forth across the Bay on ferries, and up and down hills on clanging street cars to art galleries, libraries, museums, and editorial offices. He walked so much on hard pavements that his feet ached. Mrs. Carr had a group of choice spirits eager to meet him, such as Edward Rowland Sill, Ina Coolbrith, and Charles Warren Stoddard, the highest names in California's Golden Age of Poetry. Stoddard at once dubbed him "the Faun," and ever afterward called him that. When he got over his bashfulness at meeting so many celebrities, he formed lasting friendships among them.

Keith took him to visit his friend Benjamin P. Avery, a gentle, frail man and worthy successor to Bret Harte on the *Overland*. Avery took an immediate interest in John Muir and begged him to send all his literary output to him.

"The Faun" was soon worn out with the hurly-burly. One day his well-meaning friends hustled him into a photograph gallery to have his picture taken. With a groan he submitted. But he wasn't pleased with the result. In a letter to Sarah he said: "My friends compelled me to sit for my picture in town last month. I was terribly dazed and confused with the dust and din and heavy sticky air of that low region. . . ." To David, who said the eyes did not look natural, he wrote: "I was so frightened out of more than half of each of my senses by the blaze and glare of everything about me."

"After two weary homesick municipal weeks" he escaped the vigilance of his friends, boarded a train, and, when he reached Turlock, literally fled toward the mountains. Over the stubble fields he raced as if devils were at his heels, conscious only that the town was behind him, and the mountains above and before him.

Ecstatic upon his return to the valley, "to feel the living electric granite" once more beneath his feet, he went on a regular orgy of wild winter excursions, to clear away the blur and benumbing effects of walking on "dead pavements" and breathing "dead city air." But his feet and limbs had in those few days lost something of "the tone and tune of the rocks," and on one of the trips he had his narrowest escape from death. On a late December day he started out to explore the full length of Tenaya Canyon — a feat never before accomplished. In crawling around the glacier-polished shoulder of Mount Watkins, a thousand feet above a sheer-walled gorge, he suddenly fell backwards, his head striking the granite. Returning to consciousness some time later, he found he had plummeted down to the very brink of the gorge. Here his plunge toward certain death had been blocked by a few frail spiræa and live-oak bushes that feathered the edge of the abyss.

At first violent trembling, then anger and shame swept over him. His body had failed him. He felt "degraded and worthless." He owed his life to some poor little bushes. Determined and firm-muscled, he ran back to the spot where he had fallen, rounded the shoulder successfully, and then continued to punish his rebel body by forcing it to master feats he would ordinarily have avoided. With all the sternness of his father haranguing two little boys, he scolded his feet: "There, that is what you get by intercourse with stupid town stairs and dead pavements!" Like a saint donning a hair shirt to chastise himself, he made his "ill-behaved bones" repose that night on a bare boulder, without benefit of pine boughs. Even his bumped head had no pillow of grass or flowers!

"I find this literary business very irksome," said Muir in the spring of 1873, "yet I will try to learn it." Like Emerson he had begun his writing by the notebook method, putting down his impressions at the time into flashing sentences or brief paragraphs. Emerson's sentences in his essays remained like a multitude of precious jewels put together without a clear thread of continuity. Muir, on the other hand, after much labor, achieved a flowing, unified style. He early sensed, too, that lengthy descriptions were tiring to the reader, and so learned to subordinate description to narrative. On his pages the wilderness sparkles with action, drama, and human interest. He strove for words and incidents to light up his meaning "like a fire on a hill." He studied also to keep himself and his mystical interpretations of nature in the background. The "unutterable things" he had experienced on mountain peaks found small place in his articles. Such "trances of thought and mountings of the mind," he believed, went beyond the frontiers of lowland thinking and were "incommunicable." For this reason his journals and fragmentary notes, written in the very presence of the immensities for no eye but his own, remain the truest index to Muir at his wildest and best.

By April he had fifteen articles in preparation. Meanwhile Mrs. Carr took to Editor Avery Muir's letter to her about the Tenaya Canyon jaunt. This was published in the April *Overland*.[38] Soon thereafter came a Hetch Hetchy article,[39] and another on the Grand Tuolumne Canyon.[40] By this time Muir had taken rank with the *Overland* as "our leading contributor."

About this time the family emergency he had long foreseen came to a head. Daniel Muir, having sold his land, was planning to leave for Bristol, England, to join with George Müller in operating his famous orphan asylums, reputedly supported by prayer and faith. As soon as John heard the news, he wrote at once to David Muir, urging him and David Galloway to break up the scheme. At the same time he asked him to tell his mother and sisters that "whether this side of the sea or that, they need take no uneasiness concerning bread."[41]

The firm stand taken by John brought about a compromise. Daniel decided to join a group of Disciples working at Hamilton, Canada, with Salvation Army methods. He wanted to take his wife and daughters with him, but Ann said no and remained in Portage. It wasn't a separation in the modern sense. He could always come home to her, but she would not go with him.

In the Canadian city his restless spirit found peace. Preaching on the streets, visiting the sick and dying in the hospitals, he was to know the happiest eight or nine years of his life. "I am renewing my youth as the eagles. . . . Oh, it is good that I broke away from you all and came to Canada. . . . I have had truly an apostolic experience, and I cannot be pleased with anything else."[42]

"The Mountains are calling me and I must go," John Muir wrote in September, just before starting out with Galen Clark, Dr. Albert Kellogg, the botanist, and Billy Simms, a stripling artist, to explore for the first time the whole length of the Sierra.

On this journey a new John Muir began to emerge. As a geologist he was bringing to a climax his studies in mountain structure. But that phase of his life was about to be submerged in Muir the naturalist, the crusader for conservation. A prophetic note was struck in the opening entry of his journal.[43] At their first night's camp in Clark's Meadows, he observed the universal devastation produced by sheep: "The grass is eaten close and trodden until it resembles a corral. . . . Nine tenths of the whole surface of the Sierra has been swept by the scourge. It demands legislative interference."

Bearing off to the south, they reached the South Fork of the San Joaquin. Leaving his companions in camp, Muir ascended the yosemites of that river basin. Although making glacial observations his main purpose, he was gleaning a harvest as varied as life itself. A heightened sense of his relationship to all nature pervaded him, giving him a new orientation toward his fellow man as a part of the Wholeness.

In the highest of the yosemites he met the king beast of the wilderness, the mountain sheep, living "in the boundless sufficiency of wild nature." How mean, how ignoble in comparison, were the stupid domesticated sheep — each one but "a fraction of an animal." Warped by scientific breeding from their elemental instincts, they had been degraded into "mongrel victims of civilization." Man appropriates for his sordid commercial purposes the noblest creatures — even his fellow humans, Muir reflected.

Along the way he climbed mountains. According to his notes, he found the summit of Mount Millar the finest vantage point for viewing the whole range. From here he could see the colossal topography as a harmonious unit in which glacial denudation was the key that unlocked every secret, brought every form and trend into relationship. All had been sculptured by the same razing, dismantling, beauty-creating agency of ice!

But all the way down the Sierra the trees vied with glacial evidences for his attention. Mutely they seemed to be calling him to tell their story to the world. Camping near the confluence of the North Fork of the Kings with the main river, he wrote: "A noble company of pines reared their brown columns and spread their curving boughs above us in impressive majesty. . . . Beyond was another circle . . . a black, sharp-angled line of tree-writing along the base of the sky. Who shall read it for us?"

The next day they looked forth upon the grand Kings River Canyon of the South Fork, which John Muir declared contained "all that is most sublime in the mountain scenery of America." Seven years later Muir was to make his first attempt to embody this great yosemite within a national park, the beginning of a fight of nearly sixty years to preserve from exploitation its wild beauty for the whole American people.

He spent nearly a week wandering in ecstasy among the vast sequoia forests that reach their maximum on the high divide south of the Kings. While camping at Thomas' Mill, he had his first view of the wholesale destruction being carried on. He didn't say much about it at that time in his journal, but the profound impression it made upon him was to bear fruit later on.

One day he entered the group of trees that two years later he named "the Giant Forest." "The General Grant," he found, had been "barbarously destroyed by visitors hacking off chips and engraving their names in all styles."

The climax of his journey in point of altitude was the ascent of Mount Whitney. On October 15, with no equipment but a spirit level, climbing by way of the Hockett Trail, he gained the top of a mountain now known as Mount Langley. This, according to Clarence King's report published in the *Geological Survey of California,* was Mount Whitney, the highest mountain in the range. But as soon as Muir got there, he saw a few miles to the north a still higher peak. Using his spirit level, he found it to be about 500 feet higher. Without wishing to upset anybody's applecart, he knew a mistake had been made.

He set off at once to reach the real Mount Whitney. Night came on, and with it a freezing gale. With food gone and no wood to make a fire, he went on climbing. Pain and fever from an ulcerated tooth made him less careful of his safety than he ordinarily was. About eleven o'clock he reached the crest of a mountain — now known as Mount Muir — still several hundred feet below his goal. It was 22 degrees below zero, and he had neither coat nor blanket. Recklessly he tried to scale the needlelike-appearing projections that still lay in his way. But when an intense drowsiness overwhelmed him, he decided to wait until morning.

Doubtless this was one of the most terrible nights of his life. Drifting into unconsciousness, he would jerk himself awake with the knowledge that sleep meant death. Then he started to dance the Highland fling, leaping high in the air, swinging his arms like flails, and clapping his benumbed hands. Soon he fell exhausted, to swoon away into slumber. Then by sheer power of the will to live he would force himself up once more.

In the dawn he set out again for the summit. Half out of his mind with cold, hunger, and the blazing pain in his jaw, he struggled on. Suddenly he stopped and clung to the rocks, with everything swimming about him. Then, as in previous emergencies, the other self took control. "I felt," he has related, "as if Someone caught me by the shoulders and turned me around forcibly, saying 'Go back' in an audible voice." [44] So he went resignedly down the mountainside.

Muir made no secret of his faith in guidance by the not yet understood forces of nature either within or without ourselves. In a published article he has said: ". . . we are governed more than we know, and most when we are wildest." Among his notes he wrote: "If a magnetic needle, a strip or particle of iron be shown its way, shall the soul of a free man be left unguided?"

Two days later, after making a careful study of the topography, he set out once more for Whitney, this time ascending from the eastern side and pushing up a canyon past the north shoulder. The Survey people had said it couldn't be climbed from this side, and a mountaineer he met said it couldn't. But he went on, camped at the timberline, and on the morning of October 21 stood on the helmeted summit of Whitney, the first man to have made the ascent directly from the eastern side.

Wandering about on the granite top of this highest mountain within the United States, he found in a yeast-powder can records left by those who had so recently preceded him, they having climbed from the south. In his little tan leather notebook he copied them down:

Sept. 19, 1873. This peak, Mt. Whitney, was this day climbed by Clarence King, U. S. Geologist, and Frank P. Knowles, of Tule River. On Sept. 1st. in New York, I first learned that the high peak south of here, which I climbed in 1871, was not Mt. Whitney,[45] *and I immediately came here. Clouds and storms prevented me from recognizing this in 1871, or I should have come here then.*

All honor to those who came here before me.

C. King.

Notice. Gentlemen, the loky finder of this half dollar is wellkome to it.

Carl Rabe,

Sept. 6th, 1873.

Muir replaced the records as well as the half dollar, and went away without adding his own name. That night he wrote in his journal this brief statement: "I climb to the summit by 8 a.m., sketch and gain glorious views, and descend to the foot of the Range."

John Muir returned to the Yosemite after "a simple saunter" northward along the eastern base of the Sierra and by way of Lake Tahoe. He began immediate preparations to go to Oakland for the winter. In view of the speed with which he had fled from the Bay cities less than a year before, this was about the last thing we should expect of him. It was by no means what he preferred:

"I would rather go back in some undiscoverable corner beneath the rafters of an old garret with my notes and books and listen to the winter rapping and blowing on the roof."

But he had writing to do. A series of articles on mountain structure for the *Overland* was his first objective. Also he had several naturalist articles half-finished. He needed contact with editors and an occasional reference book. Perhaps, too, he longed for association with kindred minds.

All these years he had told himself and his friends that he didn't "mould in with the rest of mankind"; and that he knew little about men, having seen them "only afar off and in the lump." But Mrs. Carr's emissaries had mellowed him. And her counsel began to get under his skin: "You must be social, John, you must make friends . . . lest your highest pleasures, taken selfishly, become impure."[46]

December found him installed for the winter at the home of J. B. McChesney in Oakland. He set about his writing at once with his usual driving zest. But to select — ah, there was the rub! "I can't do it quick," he cried. "Can't get a reasonably likely picture off my hands. Everything is so inseparably united. As soon as one begins to describe a flower or a tree or a storm or an Indian or a chipmunk, up jumps the whole heavens and earth and God Himself in one inseparable glory!"

He groaned over the inadequacy of language to express his meaning. "The dead bony words rattle in one's teeth." However skillfully put together, they were but "mist rags," pale ghosts of thought, mere hints that might lead "some living souls" to the august realities of nature.

It is safe to say that his "Studies in the Sierra," in which he set forth his glacial theories, gave him greater anguish than anything else he ever attempted. Mrs. Carr had warned him that he must curtail his poetic exuberance in them to gain the attention of scientists, and he found it a valuable discipline, teaching him to prune the lavishness of his native fancy. Through doing this he came to appreciate the strength of the unadorned phrase. But with all his restraint he had to write in his own way. He never played the sedulous ape to any man in form or diction. He followed the quaint folkways of his speech, using pithy phrases and metaphors of pregnant earth wisdom with the freshness of the morning upon them. Although these "Studies" may fall short in details of modern geologic doctrines, they are, and will remain, literature.

With equal determination he set about exploring humanity. Reveling in old friendships and deepening them, he formed many new ones. With the Le Contes — those "twin stars," Professors Joseph and John — he spent many an evening at their Oakland home, discussing glaciers, their velocities and other physical laws. Then there was Ina Coolbrith, librarian at the Oakland Public Library, and while he went there often to read, he usually remained to talk.

Social affairs where folks had to dress up were anathema to him. He refused to be "dinnered," and he was skittish about parties and teas. If he was inveigled into one, he was quite capable of shocking everybody by his bull-in-a-china-shop behavior, as when he found himself present at a seance.

Everybody was dabbling in spiritualism in the seventies. Seances were being held in the homes of the eminently respectable, even the learned. The Le Conte brothers, it is said, were keen investigators. One of Muir's friends, meeting him on the street one day, invited him to his home for a social evening. "Are ye sure it's nae table rapping ye're askin' me to see?" queried Muir. "Oh, no, no, just a friendly gathering," the man assured him. "We'll probably spend the evening just talking. You'll meet a lot of your friends there." With this understanding Muir went to the party.

"After the common greetings were over," says Muir, "there came an awkward pause that seemed to betoken ghost weather. Pretty soon as if by prearrangement, everybody got up and went into another room and sat down at a big round table." [47]

But Muir refused to sit and at once became unmanageable. They tried to smooth him down, saying that as he was a scientist, they wanted him to observe and see if he could explain the phenomena. A violin beneath the table would be played without touch of human hands. "Just sit down, Mr. Muir, and we'll put out the lights, so our spirit friends can get to work."

"All right," said he, veering off and peering under the table. "If you want me to observe, I'll stand off here and watch the violin. And I don't want the lights put out. I have to see the thing I study."

"But, Mr. Muir," they cried, "can't you understand there may be forces in nature so delicate and refined that even the glance of an eye would at once arrest and spoil all their wonderful manifestations?"

"No, I don't understand anything of the sort," snorted Muir. "A mechanical force strong enough to jingle the fiddle strings, couldn't be hurt by a mere glance of an eye. I've been praying all my life, 'Open mine eyes that I may see.' Now you tell me to close my eyes, or sit in the dark while something goes on under the table I'm supposed to pass judgement upon. . . . Why, mon, if I'd make such a fool of myself, I'd never be able to look a pine tree in the face again! . . . But I don't want to spoil your pleasure, or research, as you call it. I'll go back in the other room, and read while you enjoy your ghostly music."

Retiring to the parlor, he had hardly seated himself before a sharp, clear tapping began on the footboard beside him. He got up and tapped back with his shoe. Then ensued a long silence. No music sounded from the seance room. After a while his friends trailed back into the parlor, "displeased and out of sorts. It seems the spirits had informed them they were offended by my skepticism, and refused to perform."

The party soon broke up, and everybody went home in high dudgeon.

Foremost among Muir's new friends was John Swett. Before meeting him he had heard much from the Carrs and others about the doughty little schoolmaster of San Francisco who as teacher, principal, and State Superintendent of Schools had fought corruption in politics and had built up a school system throughout

California that was regarded as a model for the whole country. And he had heard, too, about Mary Tracy Swett, whose family had opposed her marriage to a mere schoolmaster. She had married him anyway, and took in boarders to help meet expenses. Among them at various times were struggling young artists and writers who were kept on whether or not they could pay their board.

Soon after the two Johns met, Swett and Keith began to make weekly trips over to Oakland to visit Muir and listen critically to his articles in progress. Keith gave most of his attention to the illustrations, urging his friend to adopt a more impressionistic style of drawing, with less detail. Swett tried to pry him out of the rigidities that Muir in those early days put into everything he tried to write for public consumption. "Write as you talk," he would say. "Stop revising so much. You make your style so slippery a man can't stand on it."

Then there was "the Strentzel Trinity." Dr. John Theophile Strentzel, one-time political exile from Poland,[48] educated in Europe in medicine and horticulture, now a large landowner and fruit-raiser of Contra Costa County, happened to call one day with his wife[49] and daughter, Louie Wanda, at the Carr home when John Muir was there. Had he known of their coming, wild horses could not have drawn Muir thither. Having scented out that Mrs. Carr had some match-making plans for him and this young lady, he was correspondingly offish, fleeing to the hills whenever she tried to bring them together. Two years before this meeting she had expressed herself quite frankly in a letter to Louie Strentzel: "I want you to know my John Muir. I wish I could give him to some noble young woman 'for keeps' and so take him out of the wilderness into the society of his peers."

And what of Louie herself? By deliberate choice this dark-haired girl with the quiet, steadfast gray eyes had remained a countrywoman. A graduate of Miss Atkins' Young Ladies' Seminary at Benicia — later Mills College at Oakland — she had developed outstanding talent as a pianist. Offers had been made to induce her to go on the concert stage. But loving home more than any possible fame, she refused. "The world's prizes" meant no more

Upper end of Yosemite and Half Dome

"But what rock is so caressed and fondled by clouds as Tissiack?"

JOHN OF THE MOUNTAINS (page 137)

"I was so frightened out of more than half of each of my senses by the blaze and glare of everything about me." Muir *on his visit to San Francisco in the winter of* 1872

to her than to the young naturalist she met that July day at Mrs. Carr's.

Her father was one of the earliest scientific horticulturists of California, and she had gained from him a knowledge of botany and the technique of fruit-growing and ranch management. She had a shrewd business sense, and because of the doctor's frail health she had for years shared with him the work of supervision, keeping accounts, and hiring and paying "hands." On a ranch that produced and shipped hundreds of tons of fruit annually, this was no sinecure.

Many suitors from the city and neighboring towns and ranches, had sought the hand of this eligible young heiress, but she had remained single. Why should she marry unless the right man came along? She was twenty-seven that summer of 1874 when she met John Muir.

The doctor and his wife had been eager to meet the young scientist. His articles, appearing almost monthly in the *Overland*, were creating much public interest. When Mrs. Strentzel read in the May issue the first of his series on mountain structure, she sighed and confided to her diary: "How I should love to become acquainted with a person who writes as he does. What is wealth compared to a mind like his! And yet I shall probably never see him."

We have no record of the first conversation between John Muir and the Strentzels Three except that, upon leaving, the white-haired little doctor with his gentle, Old World courtesy, begged him to visit them in the Alhambra Valley. In this he was cordially seconded by Mrs. Strentzel, the very image of comfortable, matronly kindness. To this invitation Muir — longing for further wanderings as soon as he could escape from writing — made some vague response, promising to come, but setting no time. More than three years were to elapse before a sudden impulse prompted him to avail himself of their hospitality.

In September John Muir completed his seven "Studies in the Sierra" and, taking the last of them to the *Overland* office, washed his hands, for the time being, of all things glacial.

Then, walking "in a dreamy, exhausted daze" one afternoon, he came upon a goldenrod beside the pavement, dying in the summer's heat, withering like himself in this alien town atmosphere. But the poor flower still had power to call to him: "Away for your life, be fleet! Go to the mountains where you belong!" He turned about, hurried home, pounced upon the few possessions he needed to take with him, said good-by to the McChesneys, and shouting: "I'm wild once more!" ran for the railroad station.[50]

Glutted with society and its small, smooth, creamy talk during those weary months in the lowland bogs of culture, the rough, ribald speech of mountaineers was music in his ears. Their hearty welcomes warmed his heart. He felt he had indeed come home.

Once more in the Yosemite, sitting beneath the great pine in the yard of Black's Hotel, he wrote to Mrs. Carr the longest, most eloquent of all his letters, relating as a kind of memorandum, the events of his hegira mountainward. And yet it was a letter of farewell — farewell to old scenes and old labors. "No one of the rocks seems to call me now, nor any of the distant mountains. Surely this Merced and Tuolumne chapter of my life is done. . . . I feel that I am a stranger here. . . . I will go out in a day or so." [51]

But he lingered on into the month of October, exploring former haunts. By Lake Nevada he camped four nights. Face to face with the calls of destiny, he was dedicating himself to new tasks.

Returning from that retreat, he wrote to Mrs. Carr a most significant letter:

"I have ouzel tales to tell. . . . I am hopelessly and forever a mountaineer. . . . Civilization and fever and all the morbidness that has been hooted at me have not dimmed my glacial eye, and I care to live only to entice people to look at Nature's loveliness. My own special self is nothing." [52]

By October 15 Muir was on his way to Mount Shasta by way of Lake Tahoe. He noted that the pines and firs about the lake's edge had been sadly decimated, and great trees were crashing down the skid roads on every mountainside. At Lake Donner, a few miles away, he found the whole fringe of the forest "hacked and smashed."

Always interested in the fate of the Donner Party as a supreme example of what happens to city-dwellers alienated from wild nature, he said: "They were not good mountaineers. . . . The whole winter could have been spent delightfully in so beautiful a spot." [53]

From Redding he set out on foot for Shasta along the old California-Oregon stage road, taking notes, as he advanced, for a series of letters he had promised to write for the *San Francisco Bulletin*. Further series of *Bulletin* articles were to record his wanderings for years to come. Trudging along one morning on the hot dusty highway, he came face to face with the mountain: "When I first caught sight of it over the braided folds of the Sacramento Valley, I was fifty miles away and afoot, alone and weary. Yet all my blood turned to wine, and I have not been weary since." [54]

On November 1, high on the mountain's flank, he left Sisson's Hotel for the summit. With him on the first lap of the journey was the guide, Jerome Fay. Camping that night on the upper edge of the timberline, they rose at half past one in the morning, Fay to return to the hotel, Muir to ascend alone. By ten he reached "the utmost summit," where he spent two hours tracing the lava channels down to the plain, and the pathways of glaciers, still filled with flowing ice.

A storm was fast approaching when he descended to his camp. His plunging barometer told him it would be no light affair; but, knowing how to live in compliance with the elements, he hollowed out a snug lair to fit his body in the lee of a great lava block, built up a wall of resiny pine chunks, and made a cheerful little campfire. In the white misty twilight he snuggled beneath his warm wool blankets, anticipating a grand holiday. With food enough for a week, by rationing he could make it last three weeks.

Then "the storm came grandly on." The clouds were a black ceiling. Snow crystals, beaten into fine dust, drove past him on the roaring blast. On the third day he wrote in his journal:

"Wild wind and snow. Drifts changing the outlines of mountains—pulsing outlines. Three inches of snow on my blankets. Sifted into my hair. Glorious storm! A fine Clark crow visits me, sits on cones of P. flexilis, and pecks them open. . . . The cone sometimes breaks off; he follows, diving like a hawk, picks up and carries to a limb."

Clarence King, with a party of four, had climbed Shasta in 1870. As in his Sierra articles, he did full justice to the perils he met, in the brilliant account he wrote for the *Atlantic Monthly*.[55] As usual he described the scenery with great crashing chords of Æschylean terror.

Muir, playing with a lighter touch, introduced into his journal and elsewhere [56] many grace notes, such as mountain sheep huddled under a pine near by, squirrels frisking over his blankets, a bird eating pine nuts — thus humanizing the bleak wilderness, making it friendly. Like King he reveled in the rush and thunder of storm and avalanche, but his fine ear was ever open to the music of insect wings.

On the fourth day, to Muir's disgust, Jerome Fay hove in sight through the trees below him, riding one horse and leading another. Sent by the anxious Sisson, he had come to "rescue" Muir. Reluctantly he broke camp and rode down the mountainside.

Leaving Shasta at the end of December, Muir went to Brownsville — also known as Knoxville — to visit Emily Pelton, now living in California with relatives named Knox. From this town high on the divide between the Yuba and Feather river basins, he explored adjacent forests. The morning after his arrival he donned his host's old coat and pushed out into the woods to see how the trees behaved in a wild gale. The storm was holding high carnival when he climbed to the top of a Douglas spruce towering above the surrounding forest. The tree beneath him rocked and swirled, forward, backward, around and around. No bucking mustang ever gave him so mad a ride. But with iron spikes in his shoes and steel muscles in hands and arms, he clung to his wild steed as lightly as "a bobolink on a reed." [57] He had often said: "The power of imagination makes us infinite." So from his high perch he heard in the winds the roar of the seas they had passed over, and breathed a thousand fragrances released from deep pine forests and blooming meadows.

On another day when earth and sky were mingling in one vast

tempest, and the melting snows in high fastnesses were pouring down over the lower levels in tidal waves, he wrote to his "Dear Mrs. Mother Carr": "The pines are in ecstasy, and I feel it and must go out to them." When he returned that night, wet as a musk-rat and dripping puddles, Emily and his hosts bestirred themselves for his comfort, pitying him for having been out in such frightful weather. But with face glowing as if he had just come down from Mount Sinai, he exclaimed: "Don't pity me. Pity yourselves. You stay here at home, dry and defrauded of all the glory I have seen. Your souls starve in the midst of abundance!" [58]

Back in Oakland after his outing, Muir toiled with dogged fury at his writing, whipping his new harvest of experiences into articles. Bees, wild sheep, and storms buzzed, bounded, and roared through his thoughts. "The world, as well as the mountains, is good to me," he wrote to Sarah, "and my studies flow on in a wider and wilder current by the incoming of many a noble tributary."

In April he returned to Shasta, this time to make barometric observations for the Coast and Geodetic Survey and find a suitable position on the summit for a geodetic monument. Accompanied by Jerome Fay, he was caught in a sudden storm [59] on the top of the mountain. Thunder crashed as they hurried down to take refuge in a hollow at one side, where hot springs and gas-jets spat sulphurous fumes. All that night they wallowed in the blistering mud, freezing on top and parboiling beneath. Yet Muir with one arm inert with cold, and beard congealed into icicles, contemplated the heavens:

"The mysterious star-clouds of the milky way seemed near and beautiful and shone with tranquil radiance. . . . Serene and tranquil, far removed from the wild winds that roared about our turbulent speck of a planet, and the far smaller specks of men who suffered." [60]

After an eternity of fourteen hours, day began to dawn. Breakfasting on the whisky Fay had left in his flask, they arose and staggered down to their timberline camp. "We rolled, slid and shuffled down, our feebleness accelerating rather than retarding our speed."

While they were rubbing their benumbed feet with snow, they heard Sisson, far down among the firs, calling to them. Muir this time was quite willing to be rescued. But when he stood up, he couldn't walk. Sisson hauled him on a canvas sheet to the waiting horses.[61] He had to be hoisted to his saddle, more helpless than he had ever been.

Down through the tall firs they rode and out into the grassy meadows where violets bloomed in the warm sun. "Now, we're coming to God's country," shouted Sisson in vast relief. But unshaken in his loyalty to nature's wholeness, Muir replied: "Yes, this is God's country — all these grand forests, and the sunny fields where the mountain apples grow, and the strawberries and the violets. But they all depend upon the benefactions of the mountain itself that you call desolate and God-forsaken!"[62]

When they arrived at the hotel, Sisson put the two men to bed. Then Mrs. Sisson, followed by the Chinese cook, bustled in with trays of coffee, eggs, and toast dripping with butter. Soon the five children — Norman, whom Muir called "My Boy," and his little sisters — came bringing spruce boughs for his pillow, and "lavish handfuls of lilies" to scatter upon his coverlet. The sun streamed in at the windows through young poplar leaves. How sweet life appeared, as if he was seeing it anew!

When Muir reached the Bay region once more, with feet still lame and stumbling — he was to suffer from the results of the freezing for the rest of his life — he transferred his luggage to the Swett home in San Francisco. The big, three-storied house at 1419 Taylor Street, was to be his town home for five years, and it was here in this joyous, busy household that "the hooks of civilization" were fastened into John Muir for good and all. He would return often like Antæus to gain strength from contact with the wilderness, but henceforth he lived no ivory-tower existence apart from his fellow men.

John Swett, who had a genius for fostering prophets, saw that with his abilities channeled, Muir was capable of great achievement. He proposed, therefore, to take him in hand, as he had already taken Henry George. The young man walked into the trap with eyes open. "Here I am safe in the arms of Daddy Swett," he gleefully announced to Mrs. Carr.

The Swett family consisted of John and his wife Mary, two old grandmothers, and three children — Emily, Frank, and John. In June a new baby was born whom Muir had a share in naming Helen, since that was the unanimous choice of Father, Mother, and "Uncle John."

The Keith family, too, lived near by on Clay Street and spent many evenings in the Swett home. On such occasions the three men often ascended to Muir's room on the third floor, to discuss his articles. Muir had so far mellowed in his habits by this time that he smoked a pipe along with his friends, and the room became a blue haze. Keith urged him to send his writings to Eastern magazines and so gain a wider audience. Still dubious about his ability, Muir needed this practical prodding. As a result he sent his "Living Glaciers" in revised form to *Harper's,* where it met with instant acceptance.[63]

But when he went to Keith's studio in the Mercantile Library Building, he was the mentor. According to Brother Cornelius, the official biographer of Keith, "the Muir ideals of the truth, character, and grandeur of nature, especially of the mountains, were now Keith's artistic aim." [64] Soon after their second outing together in the Sierra in the summer of 1873, Keith's paintings began to take on "Muir realism." Brother Cornelius speaks of the canvases of this period as "Muir-Keiths."

So highly did Muir think of his friend's landscapes at this time that he became their foremost interpreter and "greatly enhanced Keith's fame." His reviews of several of them, copied far and wide over the country, started the great buying rush that made the artist wealthy. In earlier years Keith had been overshadowed by two rivals, Albert Bierstadt and Thomas Hill, both deservedly famous for their Sierra landscapes. Muir undoubtedly did more than any other man to raise his friend to first rank in public esteem.

One could not live long in California in the seventies without hearing of the revolutionary doctrines of Henry George, known as "the Prophet of San Francisco." Certainly one could not live in the Swett home without gaining an intimate knowledge of them, for John Swett, perhaps more than anyone else, was the midwife who was bringing them to birth. Along with a group of other men, he was meeting on Sunday nights at the George home to discuss land-taxation and other methods of curbing monopoly. John Muir may have joined this group occasionally. Certainly he must have read George's momentous pamphlet, *Our Land and Land Policy,* because in his writings of the summer of 1875 certain phrases and ideas of George became evident.

Henry George like John Muir, was a man of intuitive perception. His flashes of insight summed up to this:

The earth as our common mother should belong to all the people of the planet. Land with the inherent raw resources, is the source of all wealth. Poverty, ignorance, sickness, and crime stem from Land Monopoly. "Man is a land animal," and, dispossessed of land, is reduced to serfdom. "Each for all and all for each" is the Law of the Universe. But man has revised that to read: "All for a few."

California, the greatest of the land states, had suffered most from land speculation and monopoly. Much of the best timberland in the Sierra had been seized, and the fertile farming land in the valleys had already been blocked out for private ownership and was held at prohibitive prices. Single landlords owned from 20,000 to 100,000 acres. Certain companies owned as much as 400,000 acres. Railroad grants sprawled all over the Central Valley and invaded the forest-clad mountains. The water sources in the High Sierra streams, and the natural reservoirs had also been seized as private property. One corporation alone controlled the water supply of a large part of the state. Small ranchers in the valleys and foothills were being starved out for lack of irrigation, and their land grabbed up by the monopolists.

Meanwhile San Francisco in the decade following the completion of the railroads was far from realizing its dreams of prosperity. Landless and unemployed men and their families swarmed into the city, where they were huddled into squalid tenements and shacks along the waterfront. Mobs rioted in the streets, led by Dennis Kearney, shouting: "Hang the capitalists!" Smoldering hatred was rampant against the millionaires who lived in gingerbread palaces on Nob Hill, only a few minutes' walk from the festering, disease-vice-and-crime-begetting Tar Flat slums on the waterfront. The Swett home on Taylor Street lay between these concentrations of wealth and poverty, and John Swett's son Frank recalls how the bad boys of the neighborhood used to gang up on young Willie Hearst whenever he ventured forth alone from his father's mansion, arrayed like Little Lord Fauntleroy.

Henry George, in pamphlet and lectures ascribing these human inequalities to land monopoly, proposed as a remedy the single tax. Speculation, he believed, would come to an end if the unimproved land were taxed its ground-rent value. This, with all other taxes abolished, would support government and give back to the community the values it had created. Moreover, he would have government carefully conserve the public domain in trust for the people, allotting it in small tracts of not more than eighty acres to a buyer.

In their Sunday-night talks George was clarifying in his own mind the theories he would a little later put into his book *Progress and Poverty*. But although John Swett edited the manuscript for his friend, and advised him to go to New York to get a wider hearing, he was never himself converted to the single-tax idea. He argued for a progressive land tax to prevent monopoly. Moreover, he favored progressive income taxes to limit the accumulations of great wealth.[65]

Nor is there any evidence that John Muir accepted George's remedy. He had little patience with economic panaceas. But he was profoundly stirred by George's revelations of the nation-wide advance of land monopoly. He had seen it in its pioneer beginnings in Wisconsin, but having lived apart in the wilderness in recent years, he had much to learn of its present encroachments. Now he was awakened to the monstrous evils that would have to be subdued if the forests and the water resources were to be conserved. He began that summer of 1875 to investigate them for himself.

In July Muir traveled down the Sierra to Mount Whitney, guiding George Bayley of San Francisco and Charles Washburn, a university student. His outstanding experience was their sojourn in the Kings River Yosemite on the South Fork. The great rock forms of the Merced Yosemite he found here in like relationships, not individually so spectacular, but "from no position of the Yosemite walls could a section five miles in length be selected equal in downright beauty and grandeur to five miles of the middle portion of the south wall of the new Valley."

However, the primeval paradise was already being invaded by "land grabbers." Nailed to a pine tree he found the following notice:

We the undersigned claim this valley for the purpose of raising stock, etc.

Mr. Thomas
Mr. Richard
Mr. Harvey & Co.

This sign seemed to him the seal of doom. In grief and anger he sent forth in his next *Bulletin* letter[66] an appeal to all nature-lovers, urging them to "visit the valley at once, while it remains in primeval order. Some twenty-five years ago the Tuolumne Yosemite was made into a hog pasture, and later into a sheep pasture. The Merced Yosemite has all its wild gardens trampled by cows and horses . . . all the destructible beauty of this remote Yosemite is doomed to perish like that of its neighbor. . . ."

In solitude save for the companionship of "a small tough brown mule" he named Brownie, Muir in September made his final trip for the season down the Sierra. A momentous journey in enjoyment, it was far-reaching in results.

He never wrote anything finer than the sunset and dawn scenes and the nocturnes of those leisured weeks, minted in white-hot ecstasy and confided to his journals.[67] Never had he entered more fully into the elemental, open to "the mysterious impressions of every sight and sound. The sinking of the so-called busy world, the vital sympathy of the very God-world."

In the rambling, faded, water-soaked notes of those inspired days — many of them blurred beyond recall — is the essence of Muir's philosophy of man and his relationship to nature. Henry George was wont to descant upon the theme: "Man is a land animal." But here in the deeps of the wilderness with all his racial memories crowding about him, Muir expressed his oft repeated conviction that "Man is a forest animal. . . . Let an imprisoned man see the grand woods for the first time . . . he will enjoy their beauty and feel their fineness as if he had learned them from childhood."

In due course he arrived on the Kings-Kaweah Divide south of the Kings River, to find Hyde's sawmill "moaning like a bad ghost." Up on the mountainside the lordly sequoias were being felled, dragged to a chute, and sent hurtling down to the mill, where the largest were "blasted into manageable dimensions for the saws. And as the timber is very brash, by this blasting and careless felling on uneven ground, half or three-fourths of the timber was wasted." [68]

On the way down the forest zone he had seen the splendid Fresno Grove of Big Trees being destroyed. It would soon be gone. Now in this region where the grandest of all the sequoias grew, he learned that other mill companies in addition to the Hyde concern were soon each to set up its "sore, sad center of destruction."

It was while in this vicinity that he camped one night in the great grove which he then named "the Giant Forest." Until a late hour he walked "through the deep shadowy aisles, wholly dissolved in the strange beauty, as if new arrived from the other world."

Pushing on southward to the Tule Basin, he found yet another grand forest that he wanted to explore. But Brownie was starving. All the mountain meadows had been swept clean by sheep. One night like Balaam's ass the poor beast rebelled. Muir was making his fire when the long-suffering mule stole up behind him and, "in a pitiful mixture of bray and neigh, begged for help. It was a mighty touching prayer." His remorseful master gave him half of the unleavened cake he had saved for his own supper. The next day he led him down to the foothills, where they found food for man and beast. Returning with a sack of barley for Brownie, Muir explored briefly the southern end of the 270-mile sequoia belt, and the Kern Basin beyond.

Throughout the whole trip he had been interviewing mountaineers, mill workers, and farmers and had learned that most of the best land as well as the water sources in the high mountains had already been pre-empted by rich speculators, mill companies, and public-utility corporations. Farmers were forced to pay dearly for water. Many had been starved out. Those who remained were organizing into Granger groups to fight for their rights. A few of these findings Muir put into a *Bulletin* letter.[69]

From this autumn journey stemmed two important results: a first-hand knowledge of land-and-water monopoly, and a greatly strengthened resolve to lead men back to the healing powers of nature. Muir's thoughts went out to "the thousands needing rest — the weary in soul and limb, toilers in town and plain, dying for what these grand old woods can give."

November brought Muir down to the Swett household to go on with his writing. He was fairly launched now as a naturalist, having done his duty by geology when he published his glaciation thesis in the *Overland*.[70] Had it appeared in a scientific journal in the East, it would doubtless have made a deeper impression upon the geologists of that day. Most of the scientists continued to spurn his theories, while adhering to the old ideas that the U-shaped valleys of the Sierra were produced either by cataclysm or water erosion, with little or no ice action.

As the years passed, however, certain geologists of the more liberal school began to discover facts that supported Muir's main claims. Israel C. Russell of the University of Michigan in the early eighties found evidences of glacial action in the Mono region,[71] although still holding to the Whitney theory as to the Yosemite. Grove Karl Gilbert of the U. S. Geological Survey, in the nineties rediscovered the effect of shadows in conserving glaciers on the sides of Sierra canyons, peaks, and ridges.[72] And Henry Gannett, Chief Geographer of the U. S. Geological Survey, in 1901 set forth the theory that "hanging side valleys," such as that occupied by Yosemite Creek and culminating in the great fall, are characteristic of deeply glaciated canyons. The Yosemite Valley, he declared, therefore, was "quite an ordinary product of glacial erosion." [73]

But on the whole it has remained for present-day scientists to recognize the essential rightness of Muir. François E. Matthes,[74] of the U. S. Geological Survey, eminent among living authorities upon glaciation in the Sierra, has this to say of the pioneer theories of Muir, Whitney, and other geologists involved in the long controversy:

In neither the Yosemite nor in any other valley of its type is there evidence of any dislocation of the earth's crust . . . on the other hand, there is abundant proof of powerful glacial action such as Muir had recognized. To be sure, the glaciers did not reach down to the foothills, nor did they excavate the canyons in their entirety, as Muir supposed. The ice age, it is now clear, was preceded in the Sierra Nevada by long periods of canyon cutting by the streams. . . . But let no one cite these recently determined facts to Muir's discredit, for geologic science in the sixties and seventies . . . had not advanced to the point where any man, however expert, could have detected and proved them. Whatever shortcomings may be found today in Muir's geologic interpretations, they are to be attributed primarily to the limitations of the science of his day. To one thoroughly at home in the geologic problems of the Yosemite region it is now certain, upon reading Muir's letters and other writings, that he was more intimately familiar with the facts on the ground and more nearly right in their interpretation, than any professional geologist of his time.[75]

And as Mr. Matthes elsewhere declares: "It was John Muir . . . who first saw clearly that the glaciers themselves had done most of the excavating."[76]

PART V

1875–1887

NEW GOALS

JOHN MUIR came down from the mountains that fall of 1875 with the firm resolve to make all the wilderness better known and loved, that it might be cherished for future generations. To conserve the watershed forests was an economic necessity. Else there would be no water supply and hence no agriculture in the valleys. The lowlands would become a desert.

But holding consistently throughout his career to the higher as well as the lower pragmatism, he said: ". . . wildness is a necessity . . . mountain parks and reservations are useful not only as fountains of timber and irrigating rivers, but as fountains of life." [1] And again he said: "Everybody needs beauty as well as bread, places to play in and pray in, where Nature may heal and cheer and give strength to body and soul alike." [2]

His remedy for human miseries was more radical than that of George. It was as radical as Christ's formula: "Ye must be born again!" Man must be made conscious of his origin as a child of Nature. Brought into right relationship with the wilderness, he would see that he was not a separate entity endowed with a divine right to subdue his fellow creatures and destroy the common heritage, but rather an integral part of a harmonious whole. He would see that his appropriation of earth's resources beyond his personal needs would only bring unbalance and beget ultimate loss and poverty for all.

That winter as he sat in his room, he was thinking along these lines. Often he went out to walk. Turning his back on the bizarre splendor of Nob Hill, he would climb to the top of Russian Hill. Here he looked abroad upon a scene of cobalt waters and dreaming hills and mountains as beautiful as the Bay of Naples. But always below him on the waterfront of San Francisco sprawled Tar Flat with its concentrated squalor — the wretchedness that had started Henry George on his crusade. Here was a challenge that gave John Muir no peace.

Sometimes he crossed on the ferry to ramble in Marin or Contra Costa County. On the way home he would walk through Tar Flat, his arms laden with the day's harvest of flowers and leafy twigs, "and it was most touching to see the quick natural enthusiasm in the hearts of the ragged, neglected, defrauded, dirty little wretches of the Tar Flat waterfront. . . . As soon as they caught sight of my wild bouquet, they quit their pitiful attempts at amusement in the miserable dirty streets and ran after me begging a flower. 'Please, Mister, give me a flower — give me a flower, Mister,' in a humble begging tone as if expecting to be refused. And when I stopped and distributed the treasures . . . the dirty faces fairly glowed. . . . It was a hopeful sign, and made me say: 'No matter into what depths of degradation humanity may sink, I will never dispair while the lowest love the pure and the beautiful and know it when they see it.' "[3]

On other days he sat in his room, supposedly writing, but in reality watching from the window a little human drama enacted daily in the porch and back yard of the Dumkroeger family next door. The family consisted of a hard-working father and several boys, all mothered and toiled for by a young daughter, hardly more than a child. "But on a little shelf of the back porch she had a row of plants in cans and damaged crockery — geranium, tulip, a small rose bush. This was her garden, which she carefully and lovingly tended though working so hard, stopping in the hurry of housekeeping duties to touch tenderly and look into the faces of her humble plant friends. A fine study — nature in a human heart, in which the scenery surpassed that of mountains."[4]

He never tired of this bit of human scenery, and the girl, if she saw that bronzed and bearded face looking down upon her, was unconscious that by tending her poor plants she was making history. For along with the dirty, defrauded little wretches of Tar Flat she was nerving him for the great battle ahead and helping to lay the foundations for the National Park system of America.

The nature prophet had begun to find honor in his own country. Invitations to lecture were coming in. At first he refused. But being asked by the Literary Institute of Sacramento to address them on January 25, he accepted. When he groaned, saying he wished he were still "an unknown nobody in the mountains," Keith offered to let him take along one of his finest alpine canvases. "You can look at that, Johnnie," he said, "and imagine you are in the mountains." Swett cannily suggested that some of the legislators might hear him. He had been asked to speak on glaciers. But couldn't he slip in something about trees? He could — and did.

It was a stormy winter night in Sacramento. He had gone early to the Congregational Church to place the large framed Keith where the light would shine upon its white mountain splendor. Then he went for a walk to brace himself for the ordeal, hoping the storm would keep people away. Coming back, he was appalled to find a big audience. Stumbling up to the platform, he started to speak to that blur of faces. Beginning inauspiciously, he said it was his first public talk, that he had no skill as a lecturer, that he feared he would fail. All this, according to the next day's *Daily Record,* "fell dismally upon the audience." They, too, feared he would fail.

Then something prompted him to turn and gaze at the painting. "Look at the picture," Keith had said, "and you will forget your bashfulness." Suddenly all fear left him. He was away on the mountain peaks, running wild once more. According to the same newspaper account:

He forgot himself and his audience, only remembering that he was to make clear some wondrous mysteries. . . . His manner was so easy and so social, his style so severely plain and so homely . . . as often to provoke a smile, while the judgement gave hearty approval to the points. Indeed, Mr. Muir was at once the most unartistic and refreshing, the most unconventional and positive lecturer we have yet had in Sacramento.

After this initial success he was fairly besieged to lecture. He spoke in several surrounding cities, and again in Sacramento. But only the fact that he was terribly in earnest, caused him to subject himself to the nausea and nervous chills that he always suffered. As his friend Charlotte Kellogg once said: "He preferred a wilderness of wild beasts to a formal audience." [5]

One January day Muir wrote his first article urging Government control of the forests. Then he mailed it to the *Record-Union* in Sacramento in the hope it would be read by legislators. It appeared in the February 5 issue under this caption:

GOD'S FIRST TEMPLES
How Shall We Preserve Our Forests?
The Question Considered by John Muir, the California Geologist — the views of a Practical Man and a Scientific Observer — A Profoundly Interesting Article.

In this exposition Muir appealed to "practical men" by stressing the economic results of forest destruction in floods, droughts, and river channels choked with silt overspreading lowland fields with detritus. Waste and destruction due to sawmills, fires set by stockmen, and sheep hordes annually invading the Sierra, were proceeding at a terrific rate. Within a few years the forests would be gone. Then bringing his argument to a climax, he cited European countries where forestry economics had been studied by governments with most beneficial results. "Whether our loose-limbed Government is really able or willing to do anything . . . remains to be seen." Nevertheless, he urged legislative action to that end.

John Burroughs once said of John Muir: "He could not sit in a corner of the landscape, as Thoreau did. He must have a continent for his playground." [6]

"My life-work is over all the world," Muir had said during that last winter in the Yosemite. And by the summer and fall of 1877 he had hit his full stride as a wanderer. Had he been shod with seven-league boots, he could hardly have covered more territory in the span of seven months.

May found him in Utah, scaling the canyon cliffs and peaks of the Wasatch Range, tracing ancient glacial rivers down deep, maze-like valleys, and reveling in the flowers that carpeted the terraced foothills about the Great Salt Lake. But Mormon humanity piqued his interest even more than did nature, and the journals of that trip are the most delightfully "folksy" he ever wrote. The people he found were wholesome, normal, happy, and "as rich in human kindness as any . . . in all our broad land." He was bewildered when he tried to reconcile them with "the dark and bloody history of Mormonism." Striving to find the key to the mystery, he went to the Tabernacle and heard Brigham Young exhort his people to be industrious and virtuous. . . . Still searching, he went to a mothers' meeting addressed by Mrs. Eliza Snow (Smith) Young, one-time wife of the Prophet, now a wife of Brigham Young. She spoke to the women upon silk culture, thrift, and the virtues of motherhood. He was so impressed by this revered woman's sincerity and fine spirit that he went up to talk with her. She told him about the Mormons' long hegira westward and their pioneer hardships; of the time they were all near starvation, when they shared the little they had and taught their children to share.

Yet he found a darker side to the picture — women with weary, repressed faces, worn out by too much child-bearing. He noted that they gathered in groups, instinctively drawing together because of common burdens borne in the name of their religion. (How sorely he had seen his own mother and sisters burdened in the name of religion!) Polygamy, he decided, was more degrading to men than to women. Mother love had a spiritualizing influence, raising them above sensuality. "The production of babies is the darling pursuit and industry of Mormons, and their reckless overbearing enthusiasm with which they throw themselves into the business is truly admirable . . . every woman a factory, yielding herself far beyond her strength."

Staying one night at a farmhouse, he discovered to his embarrassment that they pitied him for his childlessness:

Coming down from mountains to men, I always feel a man out of place; as from sunlight to mere gas and dust, and am always glad to touch the living rock again and dip my head in high mountain sky. In Mormon baby thickets I feel more than ever insignificant. One compassionate woman looked me in the eye with wonder. I say I've not had baby opportunities. . . . Water birds and squirrels and wild sheep are my only children. A Mormon woman tells you at once . . . : "I've nine, ten, fifteen," and then asks: "How many have your wives yielded? What of your fruit?" My companion gladly sings out, "I've eight!" "Well, that's not bad." And then she turns full on me. I look out of the door to the mountain instinctively, and fortunately there are mountains before every Utah door, and say: "I've not got any!"

One day, becoming a bit surfeited with man and his strange creeds, he went swimming in the Great Salt Lake. "It was the finest water baptism I ever experienced. . . . Salted, braced, I ran bounding along the beach with blood tingling as if I had discovered a new glacier." [7]

Then, looking south, he beheld the white snow-clad Oquirrh Mountains, "dipping in smooth curves . . . toward the Lake." He lifted up his arms to salute them while the god within him chanted:

> *"Now I shall have another baptism,*
> *I shall dip my soul in the high sky.*
> *I shall go up through the pines and firs,*
> *Among the wind waves on the mountains."* [8]

After ascending the Oquirrhs in quest of golden lilies, he returned to the lowlands and spent two weeks in and about the town of Gunnison, south of Lake Utah, lodging in the home of Joseph Angell Young, son of Brigham. In this family he found "a human lily . . . the prettiest lily-lass in Utah" — a child just blooming into womanhood, and so fair that her beauty is even today a legend. Charmed by her, he wrote a tribute to her in a *Bulletin* article entitled: "Mormon Lilies." [9] "Among my memories of this strange land — will ever rise in clear relief . . . the Mormon lily of San Pitch."

Nor did the Lily of San Pitch ever forget John Muir. In her scrapbook she kept the tribute he had written to her. The Lily herself died a few years ago, but in the family cherished memories still persist of the tall, blue-eyed stranger who came their way so long ago.[10]

After pausing at Lake Tahoe and the Yosemite on his return from Utah, John Muir, bestriding the landscape like a Colossus, went on to southern California, to spend "five shaggy days in the San Gabriel Mountains." Sauntering up the coast he visited the *Sequoia sempervirens* groves in the Santa Cruz Mountains, and lectured "without too much scare" at the San Jose Normal School.[11] Taking all these events in his swift and competent stride, he planned to explore the Oregon forests before winter.

But arriving in San Francisco, he learned that Asa Gray, his wife, and Sir Joseph Hooker, the English botanist, were in the city, waiting for him to guide them to Mount Shasta.

Early in September the party, including Muir, stopped briefly at the Rancho Chico on the Sacramento River, where the pioneer, General John Bidwell, his wife, and her sister Miss Sallie Kennedy, joined them with horses and a camp outfit.

From their main camp on the timberline the three scientists explored the adjacent region in search of plants. One night while sitting by the fire, Gray said: "Muir, how comes it that you have never found Linnæa in California? . . . The blessed fellow must be living hereabouts no great distance off."

The next morning while Sir Joseph and John Muir were exploring a canyon, the Englishman spied a little green vinelike plant on the bank of a creek. "What's that?" he cried, dismounting. "Isn't that Linnæa? It's awfully like it." Then finding a few faded flower stalks, he shouted: "It IS Linnæa!"

Mrs. Bidwell in her manuscript reminiscences recounts several humorous anecdotes of the trip in which Muir figured: ". . . at night Mr. Muir would make immense fires to display the beauties of the silver fir, which in the glow . . . assumed the appearance of enormous pagodas of filigree silver. Mr. Muir would wave his arms and shout: 'Look at the glory! Look at the glory!' "

The two older scientists would gaze calmly and appraisingly at the "glory," but say nothing. All his ecstasy seemed to fall on empty air. Mrs. Bidwell, becoming indignant, said: "Why do you tease Mr. Muir? Don't you think it is beautiful?" "Of course it is," they responded. "But Muir is so eternally enthusiastic, we like to tease him."

After Sir Joseph and the Grays had left the party, the others took a trip to Mount Lassen and Cinder Cone. Their pathless route lay through a forest where many trees had fallen in a recent storm. Although Muir had never been here before, his woodcraft saved them on one occasion from being lost. It was night, and he, tying a white kerchief about his head to serve as a guide, went ahead. Suddenly something big and black loomed in the moonlight, and the women screamed: "It's a bear, Mr. Muir, it's a bear!" But he, never slackening his pace, shouted back: "Dinna ye ken a rock when ye see one?"

One day they were footing it over a barren volcanic plain when Muir discovered glacial striæ upon the lava. "Hurry, run, see this wonderful thing!" he yelled at them. Mrs. Bidwell, panting along in the rear, breathing red dust, gasped out: "I can't hurry any faster than I am. I'm spitting blood now." But Muir had no mercy. "Oh, never mind that. Hurry. This is worth dying to see!"

Upon their return Muir remained with the Bidwells at Rancho Chico for a week. Standing at the river landing one day with his host, he remarked that he would like to float down to Stockton in a skiff. Whereupon the General ordered his carpenter to make one for him. When finished it was christened the *Spoonbill*. Bidwell, however, thought it a wretched job. "It's a poor thing," said he with a frown. "A poor thing, but mine own!" tallied Touchstone Muir.

When it had been loaded with a roll of warm blankets and more food than he wanted, he rowed out into the current, with the Stars and Stripes gaily fluttering from bow and stern, as he shouted good-by to his friends on the bank.

In view of its climactic ending, this voyage [12] was perhaps the most momentous of his whole life. But all unconscious that Fate had him in leading, he lay back in his little boat, floating as in a dream, merging himself in the color, sound, and life of the populous river world, gazing at white clouds high in the sky, and at birds weaving wing patterns in the air.

Snags — embedded, up-ended logs — and hidden sandbars abounded in the treacherous river. But the boat under the skillful hand of her pilot soon developed so much prowess in avoiding these that he rechristened her *Snagjumper*. One day the *Snag* sprang a leak. He hauled her out on shore, whittled down a swollen board with his jackknife, and hammered it back with a stone. After that she was sounder than in the beginning.

But the journey, idyllic as it was, was not sufficiently muscle-stretching. He had to get up into the mountains once more that season. So leaving the *Snag* tied up at the Sacramento waterfront, he took the train for Visalia.

The Yosemite of the Middle Fork of the Kings River — one of Clarence King's "inaccessibles" — had long challenged Muir. No white man had gone all the way down the abysmal gorge to the confluence. But picking up a young fellow named John Rigby who begged to go with him, he accomplished that feat, although they nearly starved in the process, and Muir had to support, almost carry his companion over the latter stages.

Two days after they emerged, he was camping beside the Merced River at Hopeton. With a package of nails, a stone hammer, and some old sun-twisted fence rails, he fashioned another boat — *Snagjumper II* — and was soon adrift on the river, his one remaining flag flying from the prow.

Comparatively free from incident was his long float of 250 miles down the Merced and the San Joaquin. And so destiny brought him in the fullness of a late November day into the broad-bosomed current of the San Joaquin and Sacramento conjoined, safely to dock off the town of Martinez. There bidding farewell to the *Snag*, he strode two miles across the hills to the Alhambra Valley where "the Strentzel Trinity" welcomed him as an honored and long-awaited guest.

A few days later Muir turned up at the Swett home in the city. In response to Mary's questions he disclosed he had been visiting the Strentzels. He made haste to say he considered the doctor a thoroughly scientific man, and that the two of them sat up half the night talking. Mary archly inquired: "Did you by any chance observe a young lady about the house?" "Well, yes," he admitted, "there was a young lady there."

Mrs. Swett along with Mrs. Carr, had done some wishful thinking about these two. But now as she looked ruefully at him, she wisely held her tongue. "After his long trip he stood there . . . in a faded greenish-hued coat rather out at the elbows and wrist, his beautiful hair hanging down almost to his shoulders, and I wondered how his appearance had impressed Louie Strentzel. It worried me . . . that he had made his acquaintance with this girl in such a plight." [13]

Muir soon settled down to his old routine. Aside from lecturing upon trees, glaciers, and Utah's Mormons, he spent several hours a day writing. Helen, now a chubby child of more than two years, was his constant companion. He told her mother he could write better with her there.

During those winters Muir had much exercise for his gift of telling animal stories. Sometimes they were couched in doggerel rhyme that bubbled to his lips as spontaneously as prose. But always they were true interpretations of the wild life he had seen. The children went unwillingly to bed unless "Uncle John" first gathered them about the fireplace and told them a story of the water ouzel, the Douglas squirrel, the packrat that stole his barometer, or the mother grouse leading the hunters away from her nest.

It is no mere coincidence that Muir wrote some of his best bird and beast and other nature studies during this period. Mary and John Swett had a share in the credit too. Often when he had agonized all day over his writing, trying to make the fountains flow, he would come downstairs and regale them with delightful, impromptu narratives of his wanderings. Mary, being a wily woman, would egg him on with questions. Then when he was fairly launched, and the genius within him in fine fettle, either she or her husband would say: "Now, John, go upstairs and write that down just as you have told it to us." [14] He would meekly go, and the winged words he had sought all day in vain came in flocks and droves, faster than he could put them down.

One after another those great nature stories came pouring from the nib of his quill pen — "Snow Banners," "Snow-storm on Mount Shasta," "The Humming Bird of the California Waterfalls,"

"Wind-storm in the Forests of the Yuba," "New Sequoia Forests of California," and "The Douglas Squirrel of California."

His first *Scribner* article, "The Humming Bird of the California Waterfalls," [15] had far-reaching results. The editors begged him to submit to them everything he should write henceforth. Robert Underwood Johnson, one of the staff, and an ardent nature-lover and poet, was profoundly roused by Muir's descriptions of the Western wilderness. The foundations were then laid between master and disciple for an association that in future years was to mean much to the cause of conservation.

It was this same version of the ouzel story that attracted the attention of David Starr Jordan, then teaching science in an Indiana university. Enthusiastically he read it to his classes at the time, and long afterwards in writing a tribute to Muir he declared it to be "the finest bird biography in existence." [16] His admiration for its author, thus kindled, led to their friendship and their close collaboration in saving the Calaveras Big Tree groves and other forest areas.

During the spring of 1878 Muir made many visits to the Alhambra Valley. And judging from Mrs. Strentzel's diary, his time was not all spent holding scientific discussions with the doctor. There were walks on the hills, and in the blooming orchards, when Louie was his sole companion.

But as summer approached, he declared his intention of going to the wilderness once more. June found him on his way to Nevada with a Coast and Geodetic Survey party under Captain A. F. Rodgers. After making their way up through the "scalped hills" of the placer-mining region, where man's greed had left little to delight the eye, they came to Hangtown, now Placerville, where they stopped overnight. In this hollow there was still much beauty. The main street, flanked by pretty cottages, wound along the valley's trend between high hills clothed in dark forests.

Strolling alone in the gloaming, Muir paused in an old cemetery where desperado and saint alike had found rest after the fever of the Gold Rush. As he climbed the hill above, he caught the sound of a sweet voice singing.[17] Approaching in the darkness, he saw a woman in white, sitting by an open lighted window of a cottage. Careful to keep out of sight, he listened hungrily. She was singing "the plaintive and reassuring 'Mary to the Savior's Tomb.'" The flowers freshly laid on the graves down there, and the lovely song borne out upon the summer night, spoke to him of "the enduring quality of human love, and of immortality no matter what our surest science may say."

Human love was coming to mean a great deal to John Muir in these days. Frequent hints such as this, of loneliness and a longing for a home of his own, crept into his letters and random notes. Would he like Ulysses, be "always roaming with a hungry heart"? He was forty, and too long had he stood out in the darkness, looking in at the light and warmth of other men's lives. The wise Emerson had warned him that "Solitude is a sublime mistress, but an intolerable wife." To Sarah John had written: "Little did I think when I used to be, and am now, fonder of home and still domestic life than any of the boys, that I only should be a bachelor, and doomed to roam always outside the family circle."

The next day the Survey party rode up the Truckee River, flanked by hills from which all the forest glory had been chopped and burned away. The eastern slopes of the Washoe Range were also denuded. Only blackened stumps remained, mute witnesses of the ruin wrought by man. "Every pine and fir within reach of the locomotive's scream will eventually be called on literally to help push the car of Progress. . . ."

Over the Carson Range they rode, down into the Walker River Valley, and up again to the crest of the Pine-nut Range. The topography of the state, Muir observed, was "like a farmer's field with furrows all trending north and south." But he found little at first in the blurred landscape to indicate glacial action. Not until he reached Mount Jefferson[18] of the Toquima Mountains did he find U-shaped canyons, moutonnéed rocks, and glacial meadows. But after noting these in his journal he went on to say: "Strange to say, on the same range immediately north of this mountain and adjacent, the range presents no plain trace . . . but on the contrary, every feature . . . seems to be strictly due to atmospheric erosion. It is sun-beaten and at least, during the last glacial period, seems to have been wholly free from ice."

He had come to Nevada still believing in the main in Agassiz's theory of the polar ice sheet flowing south, but the evidences he found caused him to surmise that the Swiss scientist had gone too far in his assumption. In his journal Muir says: "There possibly was a period of general glaciation of the whole continent by a general flow from the north southward, sweeping like a mighty wind over this and all the other plateaus, *but of this action I have as yet found no monuments that I am capable of reading.*"

One thing to be noted in his published observations [19] on Nevada glaciation is his frequent reference to more than one glacial winter. Apparently he had come to take that for granted. Unfortunately his journal, packed full with lead-pencil writing, is badly faded. But passages still decipherable — such as the two above — seem to hint that he was on the brink of important discoveries that, if followed up, would have led him to the modern conception that glaciation in the Great Basin was purely local.

Soon after entering the state, from their camp on the Walker River — a lovely brier-rose oasis on the edge of the desert — Muir had written the first of several letters back to the Strentzels. In these letters as in their conversations, he and the doctor waged a never ending debate on the merits of wild fruits versus tame. From a post office rejoicing in the name of Poison Switch, Muir had sent some wild prunes to the rancher, recommending them as having "a fine wild flavor" that would compete with any of his "pampered peaches" or even of his "boasted oranges." A few days later Dr. Strentzel replied, commenting sourly on the prunes, and offering to send Muir some grapes of high culture — Tokays and Alexandrines.

"Friend Muir" immediately dispatched a thirsty plea from the dusty, alkaline environs of Austin: "Try me, Doctor, on tame, tame Tokays!" Henceforth through days and nights of terrible heat and thirst, grapes became the object of their inmost longings. They talked grapes. They dreamed grapes — glorious red and purple clusters, their skins bursting with dark nectar. One desert experience on Lone Pine Mountain came near being a thirst to end all thirsts. It was only through Muir's greater endurance and presence of mind that they all came through alive.

From the time they heard the grapes had been shipped, they haunted the railroad stations. Muir had directed they be sent to Eureka. But they did not come. Reluctantly the party moved on to Hamilton, leaving instructions for forwarding. More delay. A telegram was sent out as a searcher. They had one more chance at Ward before going "out of grape range." One of them stood on guard at the station as train after train came in. Still no grapes!

Finally John Muir was down on his knees in their hotel room, thirstily sorting out his harvest of pine tails, tassels, and burs, when Captain Rodgers pranced in at the door, carrying aloft the richly laden box. With a shout they ripped the cover off.

"The fruit was in perfect condition, every individual spheroid . . . all fresh and bright and as tightly bent as drums with their stored-up juices. The big bunch is hung up for the benefit of eyes. Most of the others have vanished, causing as they fled, a series of the finest nerve-waves imaginable."

Thus Muir was converted to the merits of cultivated fruits.

April had always been a time of beginnings for John Muir. His life began in that month. In April he first climbed the Sierra, and beheld the wonders of the Yosemite.

On an April day in 1879 he wrote his first letter to Louie Strentzel. Addressing her formally, he was making stilted headway with it when a messenger arrived with a huge box from the ranch. The contents broke down his shyness: ". . . Boo!!! aren't they lovely!!! The bushel of bloom, I mean. Just came this moment. . . . An orchard in a bandbox!!! Who wad ha thocht it? A swarm of bees and fifty humming-birds would have made the thing complete."[20]

Six days later, making flowers an excuse for writing again, he said: "Alack, alack! Miss Strentzel, the big bouquet is dying, dying, dying, and so are the roses. We all do fade as a leaf, fade as a bouquet on a bachelor's table. . . ."

In spite of the lure calling him to the Alhambra Valley, however, he would probably have gone early in the spring to the forests of Washington and British Columbia had not a nation-wide Sunday-school convention been scheduled for the Yosemite in June. Several speakers of great repute were to lecture, and Muir had been paid a hundred dollars in advance to give two addresses on glaciation. In addition he had agreed to conduct tours and make a campfire talk. He saw a chance here to preach his tree gospel.

On the evening of June 7 Guardian Clark formally opened the convention. The following morning two lectures were given: one upon Alaska by Dr. Sheldon Jackson, head of the Indian Missions in that territory; the other by John Muir upon "The Geological Records of the Yosemite Valley Glaciers." The *San Francisco Chronicle* relates: "The latter fairly electrified his audience, and over a hundred followed him up the Eagle Point Trail. . . . This was fun for him for he leaped over the crags like a goat. . . ."

That night one of the divines, Dr. Guard, fearful lest the convention turn into a scientific jaunt rather than a religious feast, preached upon "Modern Acclivities and the Bible." The essence of his speech was a solemn warning that "men go everywhere and know everything save the way to Heaven. Only the Bible can guide them thither."

The really big gun of the session was to be fired on Thursday when Joseph Cook, famed Boston orator, said to be "greater than Daniel Webster," was to give his first address. On his train trip west he had devoured Whitney's *Yosemite Guide-Book,* and standing upon that thesis as to the origin of the valley, he had prepared his discourse. At the hotel someone ventured to inform Dr. Cook of the glacial theory just then winning popular acceptance. But he, bending his Websterian brows upon the speaker, would have none of it. "I stand with Whitney!" he proclaimed.

On Thursday night the little chapel was packed to the doors. A large overflow listened outside at open windows, cupping their ears to hear the great orator, who "resembled Webster in height and general massiveness," as he stamped ponderously across the platform, pounded the pulpit, waved his arms, and thundered, thrilling his rapt audience with his majestic periods. Finally he sat down, mopping his empurpled face and feeling he had settled the matter for all time.

After the tempest of applause died down, a quiet, bearded man who looked like a farmer got up from his seat in the audience, took his place by the pulpit, and began to speak in a low, gentle voice. It was like the calm after a storm. He began by praising the preceding lecturer for the eloquence of his presentation, convinced, he said, of his own unfitness to follow so distinguished an orator.

Then he began to relate his years of wandering among the mountains. His charmed audience followed him as he threaded the main canyons to the high summit névés, then trailed him down as he described the glaciers that had once filled those canyons, deepening, molding, quarrying, polishing them, and finally converging "like the fingers of a hand" and breaking over "the dam of domes" into the great valley below. According to the newspapers, Dr. Cook sat there "amazed," and when Muir had finished, went out without a word.

In the early morning of Friday John Muir led a party up the Glacier Point Trail. More than two hundred followed him, Joseph Cook foremost among them! Standing on the point, Muir showed them the whole record written into the living landscape. In the face of the evidence, Dr. Cook, being a man of real intelligence, was, according to one newspaper, "obliged to abandon his armchair theories and accept the unanswerable demonstration."

Leaving the Yosemite, Cook went to Monterey to give a course of lectures. Here he presented a greatly revised version of his former speech, in which he accepted *in toto* the glacial theory and acclaimed John Muir as "the Hugh Miller of the Pacific Coast."

Having contributed his share to the program, Muir returned home to prepare for his northern journey. Since hearing Dr. Jackson speak on Alaska, he had decided to make that country his main objective.

But he had a more immediate purpose to carry out — one that took him to the Alhambra Valley. "The Trinity" had been reading with glee and pride the newspaper accounts of the convention, and when he appeared at their door, they hailed him with "Welcome home. You have covered yourself with glory!" [21]

That evening the elder pair, feeling the air charged with new portents, retired early, leaving the young people alone in the parlor. About midnight Mrs. Strentzel, unable to sleep, heard the door of her bedroom open softly, and a moment later Louie was kneeling beside her, whispering: "All's well, Mother. All's well, and I'm so happy." [22] The next morning they all met at the breakfast table. And Mrs. Strentzel, incurably romantic, confided in her diary: "I don't believe there were ever four happier people in the world."

Muir's first trip to Puget Sound and Alaska was one of the supreme travel adventures of his life. From the moment the *Dakota* sailed into the Straits of Juan de Fuca he was in a world of enchantment. Before him were tree-clad islands gracious in the sunlight. On the right as they moved along the strait, and later from Victoria Harbor, he viewed with rapture the magnificent Olympics,[23] towering in massive grandeur 8,000 feet and crowned with sculptured white glacial summits, their long slopes darkly clad with spruce and fir, plunging down to the Sound — "the arm and many-fingered hand of the Sea." New vistas unfolded with every mile, of sky, land, and water blended in unimaginable harmonies. He could never get enough of this ineffable beauty. His friend Thomas Magee of San Francisco had come with him, and together they sailed up and down the Sound three times, past the long chain of snowy fire-mountains on the mainland, stretching north into British Columbia and south into Oregon. After a side trip up the Frazer River, they went to Portland, whence Magee sailed home "to his business and his wife."

Muir, unencumbered by either, went north on the steamship *California,* bound for the trees and ice of Alaska, sailing in a trance of enjoyment up the archipelago.

The only flaw was the presence on board of a party of Presbyterians with their wives — Dr. Sheldon Jackson, Dr. Henry Kendall, and Dr. A. L. Lindsley, all high officials of the Board of Missions. The relations between him and the clerics remained mutually stand-offish. Early in the voyage they dubbed him "that wild Muir," and later events did not soften their judgment. His opinion of them and the sarcastic comments he made may not have been quite fair. A deeply ingrained prejudice against missions was a hang-over from his youth.

When they docked at Fort Wrangell, an Indian town sprawling in a bog, the young resident missionary, S. Hall Young, sprang up the gangplank to greet his clerical guests. But as he shook hands with them, he noticed, standing apart, a man dressed in a long, shabby gray overcoat and a Scotch cap. Oblivious of his surroundings, he was eagerly surveying the islands and distant mountains. Introduced to Young as "Professor Muir, a naturalist," he and the missionary clasped hands and at once coalesced into a lasting friendship. "I sat at his feet," wrote the ardent Young long afterward, "and at the feet of his spirit I still sit, a student, absorbed, surrendered." [24]

"The divines" departed with Young to his home in the old abandoned fort, while Muir a little later found lodging with John Vanderbilt, a merchant. In this hospitable home was a child of whom he wrote to Louie: "Little Annie Vanderbilt is the heart kernel of this house. She often makes me think of Helen — a dainty white dot of a lass, pink as a daisy, fair as any flower in the dew, our little Doctor of Divinity."

Muir wrote in his *Travels in Alaska* of the trips he took with the mission party at Young's invitation. Detailed space will not be given to them here except to present a few facts not so well known. They went first northward along the coast in the river steamer *Cassiar,* intending to convert the Chilcat Indians far up the Lynn Canal. Engine and boiler trouble soon beset them. In the course of it Muir came to know the young Irish engineer, Robert Moran, and spent much time below decks with him. When the boilers threatened to burst, the ship was stopped amid a good deal of picturesque profanity from Captain Lane. The divines hastily convened in the cabin to debate whether or not it was wise to incur the expense of the trip, which they would have to make slowly, if at all. Muir slipped out of hearing of this "economical conference," to walk on shore. Here among the rocks and trees he found that "Divinity abounded . . . plenty of natural religion in the new-born landscapes." The next morning the *Cassiar* was creeping cautiously southward, the doctors having decided to leave the Chilcats to live and die yet awhile unsaved.

A few days later the party was steaming up the Stickeen River, again in the *Cassiar*. Muir once more hobnobbed in the engine room with Robert Moran. Both of Celtic origin, they had an almost equal love of the wilderness. Moran, having run away from home in the East, had been earning his living in logging camps and by running river steamers. He was able to give Muir much first-hand knowledge of forest destruction in Oregon, Washington, and British Columbia, and the fraudulent methods by which the lumber companies seized vast tracts.

One afternoon the *Cassiar* dropped anchor at Glenora to await a favoring wind — an event memorable in the lives of John Muir and Hall Young. Secretly the two men plotted to climb the highest mountain in sight, Glenora Peak. Then to escape the solemn doctors, Young planned a bit of strategy. Sending out runners, he invited a village of Indians to a powwow on the beach. "The divines," armed with Bibles, notebooks, and an interpreter, "went gaily to the fray." Young stayed just long enough to see the speech-making get started, then slipped away. Muir, after wangling some hardtack from the cook, met him, and off they went as gleeful as two boys playing hooky.

After some hours of strenuous climbing through blooming alpine meadows and forests, they came to a glacier. Zigzagging across it through a maze of deadly crevasses, they were confronted by a sheer slate precipice perhaps a thousand feet high, leading to the summit. Had Young been alone, he would have thought it unscalable. But seeing Muir, his "control," slide up the cliff ahead of him, almost as if he were flying, he gritted his teeth and scrambled after him.

At last they reached a narrow ledge about fifty feet from the top. The sun was just setting, however, and Muir, not satisfied with less than the whole round radiant horizon, ran on along the ledge and was soon out of sight around a bulge in the rock. As he leaped over a gully, he called back a warning Young did not hear. When the latter came to the gully, he jumped, landed on a stone that

Daguerreotype of Mrs. Louie Strenzel Muir, *wife of John Muir*

Dr. Ezra Slocum Carr
in later life

Mrs. Jeanne C. Carr

"melted away," and was swept sprawling down to the edge of the precipice overhanging the glacier far below. Making a wild grab for rocks on either side, his weak shoulder joints took that moment to become dislocated.

Muir, hearing his scream, shouted reassurance, then worked his way down to a point below Young's projecting legs, seized him by the belt and the seat of his trousers, and drew him gently over the brink. Then holding him with his great steel-muscled hands, he lowered him from foothold to foothold, down the thousand feet to the glacier.

Reaching it, Muir, laying his friend down on the ice, succeeded in setting one shoulder, but not the other. The missionary, faint with shock and pain, could hardly walk. But advancing slowly through the night hours, with Muir supporting, half-carrying him, building fires now and then to warm him, they arrived in the morning at the gangplank. Dr. Kendall stood at the rail scowling down upon the truants. When they asked for help, he did not stir, but bending horrendous brows upon Young, began to scold him: "It's all very well for Mr. Muir to go on these wild goose chases, but you have a work to do. You have a family, and a church, and it is very wrong for you to jeopardize your life in foolhardy scrambling." [25]

Captain Lane, who had been fuming up and down the deck over the delay, now rushed forward and, rudely elbowing the old doctor away from the end of the plank, giving him a backward punch that almost knocked him down, yelled: "Oh, Hell!! This is no time for preaching. Don't you see the man's hurt?"

Another surprising thing happened a few minutes later. Mrs. Kendall, a tall, grim woman who in spite of her religion had not smiled since the death of her children, took charge. Sitting on the cabin floor with Young's head in her lap, she fed him coffee with a spoon. Dr. Kendall began again:

" 'Suppose you had fallen down that precipice, what would your poor wife have done? What would have become of your Indians and your new church?'

"Then Mrs. Kendall turned and thrust her spoon like a sword at him. 'Henry Kendall,' she blazed, 'shut right up and leave this room. Have you no sense? Go instantly, I say!' And the good Doctor went."[26]

Muir saved more than one life during his mountaineering years, but never except in this case did he write about it. Young, lecturing and writing, told the story many times in what Muir felt to be an exaggerated form, giving him too much praise. Others took up the theme, with less knowledge of the facts. Finally George Wharton James wrote for the *Craftsman*[27] a wildly distorted account. Then Muir, to put a stop to all this superman stuff, related the incident in his *Travels in Alaska,* toning it down to saner levels. But a comparison of the Muir and Young narratives reveals only slight factual differences.

The doctors having sailed for home, Young and Muir planned a canoe journey north. While Young was delayed by his wife's approaching confinement, Muir scoured the adjacent region. Going up the Stickeen on his way to the headwaters of the MacKenzie River, he found Moran tending the engines on the steamer *Gertrude.* Again they had long talks.

Muir "impressed his personality strongly and without effort upon others," David Starr Jordan once said. This was true in the case of Robert Moran. The humble engineer had a long road to travel before he became the builder of the battleship *Nebraska* and other famous ships, a man of wealth, and Mayor of Seattle. But when he arrived, he used his influence to conserve the forests. In later years he bought 10,000 acres of magnificent timberland on Orcas Island in Puget Sound and gave it to the state to be preserved as a park.[28] To the end of his life, in 1942, he attributed to Muir's influence, the fact that he became a conservationist.

October came, and plans for the canoe voyage matured. Certain difficulties arose. Chief Toyatte who was going as captain, ran into domestic storms. His wife wept, sulked, and prophesied he would be killed by hostile tribes. The mother of Chief Kadachan, their interpreter, threatened that if anything happened to her son, she would steal Young's new-born baby girl.

When Muir read the letters from his fiancée, he realized that Louie and these dark women of Alaska were sisters under the skin.

"So far, so far away," she wrote, "and still another month of wandering in that wild Northland. . . . I shiver with every thought of the dark cruel winter drifting down, down — and never a beam of sunshine on all that wide land of mists . . . what a blessed Thanksgiving if only you come home."

But she would have many weeks of waiting yet. On October 9 he wrote her he was just beginning to get down to work. "Surely you would not have me away from this work, dawdling in a weak-willed way on your lounge, dozing and drying like a castaway ship on the beach." Five days later he added a postscript: "Leave for the North in a few minutes. Indians waiting. Farewell."

In spite of a tearful send-off they were soon sailing over the shining waters of Sumner Strait, and thence northward along the western shore of Kupreanof Island. All emerged from "the doleful domestic dumps" and behaved "like a lot of truant boys on a lark." Captain Toyatte, with an infallible knowledge of winds, tides, and reefs, stood high in the stern, paddle in hand to steer the course. And when it came to camping, the others could reason and wrangle to their hearts' content over sites, but when the masterful old chief strode up, pointing out the best place with his paddle, they yielded — Muir, too, in most instances, for he recognized him as a master of woodcraft. To Muir himself Young pays tribute as "a man of steel. He knew just what to do and how to do it. . . . I have camped with many men, but have never found his equal as a man of the wilderness." [29]

In the long evenings, sitting by the campfire, Muir learned much of Indian humanity and found it good. The four natives, feeling that these white men were their friends, unfolded the saga of tribal life, their history, wars, heroic legends, and religion, with their belief in immortality for man and beast. Muir was deeply impressed with the fact that to the Indian mind all Nature was "instinct with deity." And although deity was personalized in spirits that inhabited mountains, rivers, and waterfalls, he with his own deep-seated paganism, felt these children of the wilderness came nearer to the truth of an immanent living Principle in all matter, than did the tutored, civilized exponents of Christianity.[30]

At Fort Wrangell and all the way up the island-fringed coast Muir had been hearing about an inland bay of snow and ice that the natives called Sitadaka. Vancouver's Chart, which they carried with them, made no mention of it, and up to this time no white man had seen it. To find it became Muir's main goal. In due time they set sail on Cross Sound, and that night, following directions given them by the Hoona Indians, they camped within an inlet on the north shore, near the southwest promontory of Sitadaka.

The next morning among drifting icebergs and a pelting rain they entered the bay on the west side, and camped that afternoon beyond the first glacier on their left, which Muir named the Geikie, after the Scotch geologist. The following day was Sunday, "and of course we remained in camp." This business of keeping the Sabbath holy by stagnating had been a sore trial to Muir. It seemed "weak and craven out here in the wilds where God himself works on Sunday. We should keep ourselves in right relations to Nature — come and go at her bidding." He set out alone, however, to the northward to observe. After being cramped in a canoe so many days, it was a relief to stretch his limbs with the most arduous climbing. From a ridge 1,500 feet high he "gained some noble views of five glaciers that pour their crystal floods directly into the salt water. . . . The clouds hung low, veiling the higher portions of the fountains, but every now and then I gained glimpses of a wide sea of ice in which the mountains rise like islands in the white expanse."

Thus he had his first general view of the region later to be named Glacier Bay,[31] the first explorer to gaze upon those vast, mysterious, dim white solitudes of ice and snow, stretching away toward their fountains among high mountain fastnesses.

When he got back to camp that night, "wet and weary and glad," he found the Indians on the point of mutiny. They were afraid of being devoured by monsters, of drowning among the bergs, of being shut in by winter storms and ice. Muir called them to the campfire, and with that quiet confidence which so often had put faith into the faint-hearted he told them that for ten years he had wandered alone in dangerous places, and God had always taken care of him. He said he had always been warned when it was time to go. Until then they were safe. "You will all have good luck while you travel with me." [32]

Then old Toyatte rose and declared his heart was strong once more. If the canoe turned over, he wanted to take the Ice Chief in his arms and sink with him. He would be a good companion to enter the next life with. Thus ended the mutiny. Young, too, recognized on this and other occasions that Muir had sources of strength that he himself, with all his theological training, knew not of.

During five days they explored the bay and its fiords. The second glacier on the west Muir named the Hugh Miller, for another Scotch geologist. Then after rounding the head of the bay, where they entered the fiord of "the Pacific," they sailed down along the eastern shore, and obtained "our first broad view of the great glacier afterwards named the Muir, the last of all the grand company to be seen. . . . I was strongly tempted to go and explore it at all hazards. But winter had come, and the freezing of its fiords was an insurmountable obstacle." [33]

Emerging from Sitadaka on the morning of October 31, they proceeded up Lynn Canal to visit the Chilcats. Delayed by adverse tides and winds and another Sunday bog-down, Muir explored on foot the glacial snouts along the route.

Nearing the village of this chief tribe of all the Thlinkets, they stopped on the canal bank for "a general slicking up." Young emerged from the process "all washed and combed and looking-glassed to a rather ridiculous extent." Muir, shying away from such vanity, says: "I found an eagle's tail feather which I stuck in my cap and found myself ready for the noble savages." [34]

"The Great Missionary Chief and the Great Ice Chief" were ceremoniously received by the Elder Chief arrayed in state in a calico shirt. Three days and nights they remained as his guests. Two palavers a day were held, all to packed houses. Those who couldn't get into the chief's lodge looked down through a smoke hole in the roof. Young made numerous speeches. Muir made five, in which he told them all men were brothers, regardless of color or race. They were so delighted with the Ice Chief that they begged him to come back and be their teacher. If he did, old and young would go to school. As an inducement they offered him a native wife.

The first night they were sorely disturbed by a baby's anguished crying. Muir got up to learn what was the matter. The Indian women told him the child's mother had died, and they had no milk to feed it. The new-born boy was starving to death. Muir at once woke up the crew's cook and ordered him to carry in all the cans of Eagle-brand milk they had brought along for their coffee. Eight cans were left, just enough to last them till they got back to further supplies. He opened one of these, mixed the contents with warm water, and, holding the baby in his arms, fed him. Then he walked the floor with him for several hours, soothing his cries and feeding him at regular intervals. Later he bathed him. When they set out on their return journey, they left with the women all that remained of the milk, along with Bachelor John's instructions on infant care. The baby lived.[35]

As they sailed down the coast, winter was closing in, and they had several narrow escapes. Muir's perennial eagerness to see the "Beyond" led to the only serious clashes they had on the entire trip. Confident of his own power to cope with every hazard, he could not understand their caution. One evening they ran into Sum Dum Bay — known also as Holkham Bay — where in the dim light they nearly wrecked the boat on a rock, thinking it the back of a whale. After that a sandbar almost capsized them — all because they hadn't camped outside as Toyatte advised. Daylight revealed the bay as a great two-branched fiord comparable in size with Sitadaka. At Muir's insistence they sailed up the west branch amid charging bergs. When he wanted to go as far as the front of the glacier itself, Toyatte lost all patience and told him he had no right to risk all their lives in such a wild attempt. Reluctantly Muir yielded, promising himself he would come back next season to find that "Lost Glacier."

As they proceeded southward, the crew's irritation reached a climax when near Cape Fanshawe they were all but dashed upon a reef in a storm — again because they hadn't camped where Toyatte said they should. At the height of the danger Muir shouted: "Go across, go across!"

"Very well, if we die, you die too,"[36] the old chief answered grimly, turning the boat toward the reef. Soon they were among jagged rocks and had to paddle for dear life. Just then a high wave lifted them, heaving them safely over the reef into clear water. Muir had foreseen this, but their escape did not lessen their exasperation. Toyatte gave vent to his feelings by telling the white man he was a fool to risk all their lives to carry out his own ideas.

Muir, too, with his hatred of slaughter, had been sorely tried. One morning Stickeen Johnny shot a buck. Young, jubilant at the prospect of fresh meat, went out with a butcher knife to help cut it up. Exultantly "he came in with the big knife in his coat pocket and the bloody head in his hands." Muir, sick with disgust, told him he looked "more butcher than minister follower of the Prince of Peace." [37]

Despite these frictions, white men and Indians remained firm friends. On November 22 they landed on an island within view of Fort Wrangell and built a signal fire. Soon a canoe of natives was racing to welcome the wanderers home. Young naturally was eager for news. Muir told him no news from towns could be important. "We find news only in the wilderness!" said he. He held a different point of view, however, in later years, when no man ever hungered more avidly for news of wife and babies than he.

Thanksgiving and Christmas had come and gone for Louie Strentzel without a word from her wanderer. Sitting by the dying firelight late one night while the wind moaned without, she wrote:

Do not be vexed because I am not so eager and jubilant as your own strong spirit. You must know that my heart is in all your work and that I rejoice over your gains. . . . But . . . you are more precious to me than any work, and it hurts me to feel so utterly powerless in aiding you and shielding you from pain. . . .

Yet . . . I would not have you come away . . . though I long to see your face more than words can tell. . . . Oh, John, though my weak fears so often dim all else . . . sometimes I think I comprehend the delight and precious value of your work to your own soul. Knowing this, I dare not call to lead you from the way that you feel best, wherever it may guide.

Early in January the clouds lifted. A letter came from John, written at Portland. He was on his way home, but "entangled in a snarl of lectures while trying to keep free. . . . No sooner had I landed than I was pounced upon and kuffed [*sic*] into the lecture business."

A nuisance it was, but he must earn what money he could. He had almost a thousand dollars in a San Francisco bank, but he had promised half of it to help pull the Vanderbilts out of a tight place. And his Scotch pride would not allow him to go to his bride empty-handed to live on her means.

In mid-February he came to the Alhambra Valley. The hills were ablaze with poppies and lupines. The blue herons were building their nests in the orchard. And all the air resounded with "the merriment of larks!"

John Muir and Louie Strentzel were married on the 14th of April 1880. In spite of lowering clouds and torrential waters pouring down the valley, the ranch house had been made into a bower of flowers. The walls were almost covered with blooming boughs of the red astrakan apple. Dr. Dwinell, a clergyman from Sacramento, delayed by floods, was met at the station by the bridegroom in a buggy, and rushed to the ranch. As he stood before the young couple and pronounced the solemn words, he was impressed with the fact that this was a marriage of more than ordinary fitness, of mutual dedication to a high purpose. When he arrived home, he wrote to Muir: "I shall not expect less from you, but more . . . from the influence of the fellow-worker who will be more than an admirer, a helper. . . . May each find inspiration and strength and faith for achievement from the other, and the blessing of God be on you both."

The marriage excited far more than the usual nine days' wonder. Letters and telegrams snowed down upon them. Muir's friends and relatives rejoiced that he had at last "come to earth" and was "now a member of the human family." Mrs. Carr, writing to Louie from her Pasadena home, Carmelita,[38] said of her former protégé: "Before fame, and far stronger than my wish to see his genius acknowledged by his peers, I have desired for him the completeness which can only come in living for others — in perfected home relations." She went on to say she felt they had "always been mated" and their union "foreordained." To Mrs. A. G. Black she wrote: "This is the only woman I ever knew who seemed a mate for John."

Apparently John thought so too, for he wrote to General Bidwell: "I am now the happiest man in the world!"

The day after the wedding John Muir went into the orchards and vineyards, and there he labored until late in July. Then came the pause while the sun did its ripening work. This interim before the main harvest in October, he and his wife had agreed, should be his each year for a trip to the wilderness. This time "the Lost Glacier" in the left arm of Sum Dum Bay was calling him — that river of ice behind the thundering bergs, stretching away northeastward to its high white fountains.

The last day of July saw him and his friend Thomas Magee once more on a steamer sailing north. He wrote almost daily to his wife, sharing his adventures with her by sketching the colorful scenes along the way, and the human beings he found picturesque or amusing. As he approached the wharf at Victoria, he saw a British warship — a symbol of imperialism.

Her Majesty's ironclad Triumph is lying close alongside. How huge she seems and impertinently strong and defiant, with a background of honest green woods! Jagged-toothed wolves and wildcats harmonize smoothly enough, but engines for the destruction of human beings are only devilish, though they carry preachers and prayers and open up views of sad, scant tears.[39]

On the wharf itself he saw "a typical John Bull, grand in size and style, carmine in countenance, abdominous and showing a fine tight curve from chin to knee, when seen in profile, yet benevolent withal and reliable, confidence-begetting."[40]

A few days later they arrived at "dirty, angling, wrangling Fort Wrangell." S. Hall Young, who had come down to greet the monthly mail, was amazed to see Muir on deck, dressed in the same old coat and cap. Leaping down the gangplank, he shouted: "When can you be ready?" Then seeing his friend was nonplussed over his sudden appearance, he cried: "'Man, have you forgotten? Don't you know we lost a glacier last fall? . . . Get your canoe and crew and let us be off!' "[41]

Returning from Sitka, whence Magee sailed for home, Muir found "the adventurous evangelist" had made all plans for their second voyage north. Lot Tyeen, an Indian owning a stout, swift boat, had been hired along with his son-in-law Joe and one Billy Smart.

Old Toyatte was dead, killed by his enemies in a whisky brawl. The chieftain, whom Muir called "the noblest old Roman of them all," had tried to make peace between the warring tribes by offering all his blanket-wealth, and when the shooting began, he stood in front of a blockhouse trying to call his men back. As Young stood beside him there, the old man fell dead at his feet, shot through the heart.

At the last moment, just as they were embarking, another passenger joined the party. It was Stickeen, the little black-white-and-tan dog, "smooth and glossy as a berry," belonging to the Youngs. Muir protested stoutly that he was nothing but "a helpless wisp of hair, a soft little lap-midget" — in short, "an infernal nuisance." But Stickeen settled matters for himself by walking down the plank and curling up with a sigh upon his master's coat in the bow.

This time it was Captain Lot Tyeen who stood high in the stern, "massive and capable," as they sped over the silver waters. Muir was bearing the whole expense this time, so they made few stops. He was also vaguely uneasy about his wife and wanted to return south by the next mail steamer. She was well when he left home, but he couldn't shake off a fear that something had gone wrong.

Before long they entered Sum Dum Bay. Muir first explored and mapped the eastern glacial fiord, now known as Endicott Arm, naming the glacier at the head of it Young Glacier.[42] Then on August 21 they crossed the main bay to invade the upper or western arm. For more than twenty miles they fought their way among rocking bergs and between stupendous walls into this "wild unfinished Yosemite." At length about nine o'clock, before dark, the shouting of the Indians told Muir that the "Lost Glacier," so long hidden, had been "hunted back to its benmost bore."[43]

Camping six miles down the channel, Muir was up at dawn with Stickeen, "unfussy as a tree," trotting soberly at his heels as they climbed to a point above the snout whence he could see the long sprawling tributaries of the glacier flowing down from their sources among the clustered peaks. Vancouver's Chart — made seventy years before — had given no hint of these two mighty arms of the bay explored by Muir. Doubtless the glaciers had not receded to form fiords when the English navigator made his maps.

On another day they sailed up Stephens Passage to the site of the present city of Juneau. Camping on Douglas Island beside a gravelly creek bed, Muir was convinced gold could be found there. The next day they met two prospectors named Joe Juneau and Joe Harris, and he told them of the camp site and its mining possibilities. They accepted his hint and camped there too. Before long they found rich quartz deposits. This led to the historic stampede to that region, and the founding of Harrisburg, later named Juneau.[44]

On their way westward over Cross Sound, Muir and Young landed on an island. Stickeen, bounding off the boat, ran wild into the woods. When they re-embarked, he was nowhere to be found. But being as much at home in the water as a seal or an otter, he soon came swimming after them. Muir ordered the boat back to pick him up. When the dog passed over all other legs to shake himself between Muir's knees, that soft-hearted Scot made a feint of kicking him away. But Young noted that as usual his kicks "failed of their pretended mark." Stickeen was not deceived by Muir's bristling, often harsh exterior, and nothing could shake his devotion. Young later wrote to Muir of that persistent wooing of the man by the dog:

You will recall the steps, your protests when he embarked . . . your constant animadversions on his usefulness, and the nuisance he was; your unfavorable comparisons with the brilliant dogs of your acquaintance; your sharp reproofs. And on his part a forgiving spirit that was far more than human — it was canine! How he followed you through thick and thin, asked your pardon for your own faults, curled up by your side at night, and patiently rose from his warm nest . . . at unearthly hours to toil over heart-

shaking mountains and foot-cutting glaciers, keeping close to your feet, and amply rewarded for his self-sacrifice by a very rare chirrup or pat. . . .

On the evening of August 29, as they neared the open Pacific, they camped in a driving rain on the north shore of the sound, within the entrance to Taylor Bay. In the distance they could see dimly the front of Taylor Glacier, "rounded like a snout." Muir got up at an early hour, ate a breakfast of "bread and rain," stored away a crust, and set off to explore the glacier. Just as he started, still under "the jet-black mantle of night," Stickeen stole out of the tent to follow. From within, Young heard Muir scolding, hissing at him, uttering dire threats to drive him back. But the stubborn little "muggins" never budged, only "begged with his tail and his eyes." "As well might the earth get rid of the moon," groaned Muir as he fished out for him the crust he had put into his belt for his own lunch. Then he set off up the glacier's left margin while the storm "moaned and roared," Stickeen following at his heels with his "sober fox-like gliding trot."

Through the morning hours they advanced up granite slopes, through forests of fallen trees undermined by the glacier, crossed the ice river itself to the eastern shore, and followed it north. Then recrossing through a maze of crevasses, they explored the western margin northward, penetrating a branch that led off steeply toward the sea and pursuing it to the end over "the wild, up-dashing, flame-shaped waves" of ice that filled the jagged rocky channel.

Although reveling in the tumultuous beauty, Muir was not too absorbed to notice that Stickeen's feet were soon cut and bleeding. Several times he stopped to wrap handkerchiefs about the sore little paws, tying them stoutly to form moccasins.

Back at the confluence later in the afternoon, they had still fifteen miles to go to reach camp, much of the distance over the ice itself. In the dusk they came to a maze of crevasses "of appalling depth and width." Tracing them up and down, Muir found places he could leap across, Stickeen "flying over like a bird" in his wake. But as the darkness thickened and snow began to fall, they made slow headway. Muir envisioned a night on "the gashed wilderness of ice," dancing to "the boding music of wind and stars."

Then came an end of the crevasses that could be leaped. Muir found himself and his four-footed companion on an island of ice, facing a grand crevasse forty or fifty feet wide, caught as in a death trap. But danger only whetted his wits and steeled his muscles. Kneeling at the edge of the terrible abyss in which "Death seemed to lie brooding," he saw, far below, a sliver bridge of ice "hung diagonally from side to side like a loose rope." Seeing in that their only slender hope of survival, he leaned over and began to cut steps down the blue wall. Then lowering himself from step to step, he cut others below. "Life and death lurked in a single glint of my hatchet," he said, as he worked on until he reached the sliver. Hitching his way across this, he shaved away in front of him the knife-edge of ice to make a path four inches wide for Stickeen to follow. After cutting his way up the opposite sheer wall to safety, he turned to reason with the terrified little dog, "overshadowed with darkness and the dread of death," until he too ventured slowly down into the chasm and across the bridge, to emerge with "a gush of canine hallelujahs!"

"How eloquent and telling he at once became in voice and gestures — a perfect foam and effervescence of joy. He fairly shrieked and wept for joy as if the concealed emotion of a lifetime had suddenly found vent, the veil rent asunder. I tried to catch him, fearing his heart would break with joy, but I might as well have tried to catch a whirlwind, as he shrieked and yelled as if saying, 'Saved, saved, saved!!!' "[45]

Young has given a moving account[46] of their arrival in camp. At ten o'clock, when he and the Indians had almost given up hope, Muir emerged from the darkness. Stickeen, who was wont to come bounding in, ready to wolf down his food, this time walked feebly like a little shadow at his chosen master's feet. Spurning the meat Joe held out to him, he crept away to his blanket in the tent. And Muir, who usually strolled in, a rapt fey look in his eyes as of an inner radiance shining out, bursting to relate the day's events, now staggered with weakness, his eyes dazed with exhaustion. They led him passive as a child to the fire, stripped off his soaked, tattered garments, and clothed him anew. Without a word he sat heavily down on a stone and began to eat mulligan stew and drink the hot coffee put into his hands. He ate as if forcing himself, that he might gain strength. Not until wild strawberries and a third cup of coffee were placed before him did he speak. Then, looking up out of his daze, he said: "Yon's a brave doggie."

Whereupon Stickeen, stretched on his bed in the tent, opened one eye and feebly pounded his tail. Finally, as Muir's strength returned, the floodgates opened. He talked until midnight, relating to the entranced Young the adventures and the terrible dangers they had encountered. Before he had ended, Stickeen walked slowly forward and lay down with his head on Muir's foot, "gazing into his face and murmuring soft canine words of adoration to his god."

One more great experience remained for Muir on this trip — a week upon and alongside the mighty glacier in Sitadaka that bears his name. Unable to persuade the Indians to venture farther than a camp on the lower east lateral moraine, he camped alone higher up. Stickeen, having won his spurs as a mountaineer, was his inseparable companion, "his clean little shanks twinkling along" in the wake of his adored man-god. One day they crossed the glacier diagonally, traveling about thirty miles, the dog's feet wrapped in handkerchiefs. Another day Muir and Young planted stakes in the ice river to measure its flow, and found it advanced fifty or sixty feet every twenty-four hours.

The objectives of the journey attained, the voyagers went scudding down Chatham Strait. Thence sailing by night they passed through Peril Strait and along the west side of Baranof Island to Sitka, where they learned the monthly mail steamer would sail within a few hours.

Letters from home told Muir his fears for Louie had been well founded. She was now happily restored, but within a week after his departure she had been taken desperately ill — possibly because of a fall on the stairs. Almost delirious with fever and pain, she yet refused to allow her father to send for John. Already she had become the Spartan wife. Two weeks later she wrote:

. . . *after many sleepless nights of strange shadows and wild wandering phantoms, the fever cooled . . . leaving me free from pain, hopeful and strong of heart. I shall not fail you when your heart has need of me.*

Now *I* know *that neither time nor space can ever separate us, and that wherever you be, here or there, I am with you truly so long as my soul is faithful to you.*

Farewells were said at the Sitka wharf. The saddest of all partings was that between Stickeen and his chosen master. Muir, sitting on a coil of rope with the dog between his knees, reasoned with him just as he had done that night on the ice, telling him to be a brave wee doggie. Stickeen wagged his tail to show he understood, but his whole despairing soul was in his eyes.

The final wrench came when he was carried crying and struggling down to the canoe, and the Indians rowed away. Until they passed out of sight around the curved shore of the sound, John Muir stood on the wharf, gazing after the small dark figure of the dog leaning over the stern of the boat, moaning for the friend he would never see again.[47]

Muir gained from his association with Stickeen "a deep look 'ben the heart' " of dogs and all our "horizontal brothers" of the animal world. He knew now past all doubt that they were endowed with the same passions and imbued with the power to reason, differing only in degree from that of "the vertical mammal," man. "He enlarged my life, extended its boundaries. . . . In all my wild walks, seldom have I ever had a more definite and useful message to bring back. Stickeen was the herald of a new gospel" [48] — a gospel Muir was to preach for the rest of his life. The little dog had a kind of immortality, for he went with him, living perennially in his thoughts. Muir filled a large notebook, and the flyleaves of many a book he read, with memories and comments upon him. Hundreds of children and grown-ups heard him tell of that day and night on the ice. And the reading world has taken *Stickeen* to its heart, as one of the greatest dog stories ever written.[49]

Freed for the time being from the pull of the wilderness, Muir spent a happy autumn and winter at home. In December he announced in a letter to his sister Mary: "We expect a long visit from a relative of the family that will no doubt claim a good deal of my time. . . . That exacting relative has no name as yet. I mean a baby who is to appear in a month or two!"

On March 25 the new relative arrived, and they named her Annie Wanda. To John and Mary Swett the ecstatic father wrote: "We are five now — four steadfast old lovers around one little love. Bloom-time has come and a bloom baby has come and never since the Glacial Period began on earth were happier people."

But that spring Muir's health was being sorely affected by the heavy ranch toil, and most of all by his exile from wild nature. Nervous indigestion and a racking bronchial cough beset him. He weighed only a little over a hundred pounds. Louie, deeply troubled, urged him in vain to go to the mountains.

One day in March he received an invitation to a formal dinner in Oakland in honor of Captain C. L. Hooper and other officers of the revenue cutter *Thomas Corwin,* about to sail for the Arctic in search of the lost steamer *Jeannette,* which had gone in 1879 on a polar expedition.[50] Muir went to the dinner, where he was given the seat of honor next to Captain Hooper, who urged him to accompany the expedition as his guest and cabin mate. He refused, saying he was needed at home. But the Captain told him to talk it over with his wife.

The next morning at breakfast he told the family about the invitation and said that he had declined it. Dr. Strentzel was pleased, remarking that no man with a wife and child had a right to go off on such a wild-goose chase. Louie said nothing at the time, but a few hours later in their own room she told her husband that he must accept. It was a rare chance. He needed the trip for his health and his writing. She was quite well now, and there never was a healthier, happier baby than Annie Wanda.

On the afternoon of May 4, when the *Thomas Corwin*[51] steamed out of the Bay to the booming of cannon and the dipping of flags in salute, John Muir was on board. On the way north they ran into storms, and he was seasick for the first time in his life. But as the stout ship plowed steadily on through gray, tumultuous waters, he got back his sea-legs and "a savage, all-engulfing appetite." His cough vanished, and he slept nine hours at night "in the best bed on the ship."

As they forced their way into the harbor of Unalaska in the Aleutian Islands, through mountain-high waves, he stood looking out from the pilot house in the bow. On either side he saw jagged, towering masses of black rock with still higher ice-sculptured white mountains beyond, looming into the dark sky. But even in the wild blended glory of storm, sea, and mountains his thoughts were divided. That day he wrote to his wife: "I was just thinking . . . of our warm, sunny home, and Annie in her soft blankets . . . and of the red cherries down the hill. . . . Oh, if I could touch my baby and thee."

When night came, he dreamed he heard the baby crying and bounced out of bed with such violence that he woke up Captain Hooper.

By the end of June they were crawling through the ice pack off the northeastern coast of Siberia. From the natives they learned that a whaler had sighted the *Jeannette* early in September 1879, locked in ice fifty miles off the south coast of Herald Island. This information plus the letters George Washington De Long, the *Jeannette's* commander, had written to his wife before he vanished into the Arctic in search of the North Pole furnished them the only clues they had as to the ship's course.

On their return they stopped at East Cape, and Muir climbed the high mountain spur that forms the cape itself. Alone he stood on the summit, 3,000 feet above the ice and water pouring through Bering Strait, speculating upon the fate of the thirty-three men of the *Jeannette's* crew. Could he have been a receiving station for thought-waves that day, he would have known they were still living, tragically clinging to the hope of survival, somewhere in that illimitable white realm stretching to the northwest. For their story thus far was as follows:

On September 6, 1879 the *Jeannette,* listing heavily to starboard, had been solidly frozen in by the polar pack off Herald Island. For nearly two years she lay locked in her cradle of ice, helplessly drifting to the north and west. Exactly three weeks before the day when John Muir stood on East Cape, she had been set free, only to sink beneath the waters with torn keel and crushed hull. But before she sank, De Long and his men had transported provisions, dogs, nine sledges, and three boats to the ice, whence they started out on a 500-mile trek over the floes and open water toward the Siberian coast, hoping to land at the delta of the Lena River.

Knowing nothing of this, the *Corwin* party sailed north into the Arctic, and late in July moored the vessel to an ice floe 1,000 feet southwest of Herald Island, where they knew De Long had intended to land and leave cairns. As soon as the Captain gave permission to form a landing party, there was a wild rush for the rail, each man wanting to be first to set foot on earth. They struck out regardless of the crevasses, pinnacles, and huge up-ended blocks of ice lying between them and the shore. Arriving there after several narrow escapes they tried to scale the sheer bluffs that bristled like ramparts against invasion.

From Captain Hooper's Government *Report* [52] we learn that during the whole zigzagging approach toward the island, Muir stood on deck, scanning the land through a spyglass, fixing in mind the heights, depths, and trends of the topography. After the main party left, he picked up his axe and skin boat and set off diagonally to the north with two or three followers, by a longer, but smoother route. Coming to the shore, he cut steps in the cliff and was on top before the larger group down the coast had mastered their bluffs. Then with a well-thought-out plan he followed a ridge in easy ascent to the summit of the granite island. The other party meanwhile, struggling up a ravine, were forced back by falling rocks. After a descent as dangerous as the climb, they got back to the shore, agreeing with Kellett [53] and other navigators that the island was "inaccessible."

Muir, traversing the whole backbone of Herald Island, found it moutonnée in form, with smooth parallel ridges and valleys trending north and south. In one of these he found a dying glacier. Searching in every direction for cairns, he found nothing to indicate that the *Jeannette* party had landed there. The midnight hour he spent on the highest point, 1,200 feet above the sea. Forty miles to the west he saw the hills and cliffs of Wrangel Land, blue in the clear Arctic twilight. But in "the deep inhuman silence," he tells us, he found himself ever turning to the far north where the ice met the sky, as if he vaguely knew of the struggle of doomed men against death, that lay beyond that dim white curtain.

He wished he might remain all that strange night on the granite height, but the Captain had asked him to make haste. Ten miles of shifting, treacherous ice stretched between shore and open sea.

One night soon after this, Muir dreamed they had discovered the wreck of the *Jeannette.* He must have talked in his sleep, for at six a.m. the Captain was shaking him wide awake, demanding: "Did it have rigging on it?" [54] Bounding out of bed, he learned the crew had picked up a ship's spar. Attached to the jackstay was a piece of hempen rope, apparently of English manufacture, but also used in U. S. Government navy yards. Attached also was a block of Oregon pine. (The *Jeannette,* originally a British vessel, had been repaired with Oregon pine at Mare Island just before sailing for the Arctic.)

During the ensuing days they bore in gradually from the south toward Wrangel Land. On the morning of August 12 they put on full steam and forced their way among the ice floes to within a cable's length of the shore. Then they landed and Captain Hooper took possession in the name of the United States. The land of mystery searched for in vain by the Russian Baron Wrangel, and sighted by Kellett in 1849, was now for the first time touched by human foot.

Here, too, they looked for cairns, since Commander De Long had said that if he had to take off from that point on sledges for Siberia, he would leave cairns to guide any possible rescue party. But none was found.

Could they have pierced the mists of the vast polar wastes to the west, they would have seen those thirty-three men, starving and hobbling upon frozen feet, still struggling on over ice floes and among the islands of the New Siberia group. Exactly one month later, on September 12, they reached open water, where they divided their company among the three boats, the heroic De Long and the ship's surgeon taking into their cutter the badly crippled members of the party and those made sick, blind, or insane by hardships. One boat immediately went down with all on board. The other two groups, including the Commander's, unable to save their comrades, fought their desperate way over the ninety-six miles of intervening water and ice toward the Siberian coast. Only a pitiful remnant reached the inland settlements. De Long, the doctor, and all of their party except one perished one by one on the bleak delta.[55]

While Muir and Captain Hooper were still exploring the coast of Wrangel Land, they were hastily summoned by the ship's whistles, for the ice pack was fast closing in. Before leaving, they built a cairn on a headland, enclosing records and marking the spot with the American flag.

John Muir, always longing for wild adventure, played for a moment with the idea of remaining behind. Navigators had theorized that Wrangel Land might be a continent extending to the North Pole. He wished he might explore and find out.[56] Had he been unmarried, it is possible he would have attempted it.

A few days later, after escaping the ice pack with difficulty, the *Corwin* anchored off Point Barrow, where they received letters. Muir was first at the rail to take them and hand them out to the homesick men crowding about. The last in the pile was from Louie. That night he wrote to her:

My Beloved Wife:—Heaven only knows my joy this night in hearing that you were well. Old as the letter is . . . it yet seems as if I had once more been upstairs and held you and Wanda in my arms. Ah, you little know the long icy days, so strangely nightless, that I have longed and longed for one word from you. The dangers, great as they were . . . would have seemed as nothing before I knew you . . . our work is nearly all done, and I am coming home by the middle of October.[57]

Captain Hooper still hoped to penetrate the rapidly congealing ice floes to search the eastern coast of Wrangel Land. But on the way their ice-breaker was damaged and had to be cut loose. Then the rudder chain gave way, making advance impossible. Two days later they were homeward bound.

At Unalaska were more letters from Louie. "So many messages have come that my heart goes singing all the day," said she. ". . . I will not doubt any longer. . . . From the first I have been comforted by your unwavering faith, and I know not anything of evil can overcome you!"

Drawing by Muir of Herald Island, in the Arctic Ocean, showing the Corwin landing party

Drawing by Muir of Unalaska, Aleutian Islands

Mount Shasta. First climbed by John Muir in December 1874

In the same packet was a letter, redirected to Muir, from Miss A. C. of Boston, one of the impressionable young ladies he had guided in the Yosemite, who long continued to write him doleful letters. With some asperity she said: "Your wife is too indulgent, I should say, if she consents to your wild life." Muir reading her querulous words, must have fervently thanked the destiny that had guided him aright among the shoals of womankind.

At home again in October, Muir was soon buried in the grape harvest. With a new supply of "wilderness health" he settled down to enjoy his little valley world. To add to his satisfaction, John Swett was now his neighbor, having bought the adjacent ranch above, which he named Hillgirt.

Dr. and Mrs. Strentzel were building their own big new home on the lower end of the ranch, the old house built in 1853, with the original acreage, having been turned over as a wedding gift to John and Louie. Thus Muir felt free to make changes, to create more warmth and sun within by dormer windows and two additional open brick fireplaces. Annie Wanda, the light of his eyes, was the center of all his planning. To Mary he wrote: "Our own little big girl makes the home, and the farm, and the vineyard, and the hills, and the whole landscape far or near, shine for us."

There were many other demands, too, upon his time, such as preparing his own Government reports on Arctic botany and glaciation,[58] helping Captain Hooper, with notes and sketches, to assemble his *Report,* and sending Arctic plants to Asa Gray.[59]

An outstanding task of that fall and winter of 1881 was Muir's co-operation in forming two bills to be introduced in Congress:

1. *A Bill to provide for the enlargement of the Yosemite Valley and Mariposa Big Tree Grove Grants.*
2. *A Bill to provide for setting apart a certain tract of land in the State of California as a public park.*

As to the Yosemite Grant Bill, it may be said that while Muir found much to criticize in the State Commission's management of the park, he thought an extension of its boundaries to include valuable timber and water sources was better than no protection at all. It would at least withdraw such land from private entry.

Bill number two,[60] introduced in Congress in December 1881 by Senator John F. Miller of California, was designed to create a great national park or reservation — the terms were used interchangeably then — in the southern Sierra. The boundaries as approved by Muir approximated those of the combined Kings Canyon and Sequoia National Parks established in later years. They would have included the great scenic canyons and also the sequoia groves south of the Kings River.

Both of these bills, recently discovered from clues in Muir's correspondence and unearthed from Congressional archives, reveal that he was working to set aside these tracts of the public domain nearly ten years earlier than has been known up to this time.

These measures never got past the Public Lands Committee of the Senate. The idea was too new. The people were not ready, or sufficiently informed, to resist exploitation of the national heritage. And the men elected to Congress — many of them wearing the collars of railroad and lumber kings — did not look kindly upon any plan to exclude portions of the public land from private encroachment.

The idea had long been germinating in Muir's mind. We have seen his early efforts to protect Fountain Lake and Fern Lake in Wisconsin. During his first years in California he made some attempt to buy and so preserve, a tract near the Tuolumne River — probably Twenty Hill Hollow. Still later he contemplated taking up a claim in the Sierra, to preserve certain forest land. But he gave up both plans because he would have been compelled to live upon the areas with a shotgun well loaded against rampant squatters.

Disheartened for the time being by the failure of the bills he had inspired, Muir turned to his own affairs. And in view of Dr. Strentzel's failing health and dependence upon him, he saw no immediate chance of going on with his public career. The next seven years were devoted to horticulture. Many of his admirers considered them lost years. But they were rich in human experience, and without doubt he emerged from them stronger, riper in wisdom, and better equipped for leadership.

At the beginning of his intensive ranching period he leased a large area from his father-in-law and set to work developing it. Money meant little to him personally—his habits remained as simple as those of a Tolstoy or a Thoreau—but he wanted to provide for the comfort of his family, both near and distant. Misfortunes had come to several of the Wisconsin members of the clan. His father, broken in health and unable to live longer in the harsh Canadian climate, had gone south to Arkansas to live with his favorite daughter, Joanna, and her husband, Walter Brown, then engaged in the sawmill business. But though feeble and crippled from a broken hip, he was restless and determined to go back to Canada and continue with his preaching. The whole Muir family, always keeping in close touch by letters, were much distressed. Ann Muir, who had long suffered her husband's aberrations in loyal silence, lost all patience with him. She wrote to John: "I am not surprised at your fretting about the news of Father. . . . But our fretting is of no avail."

John did worry over his father, however, and over the trouble he was causing the gentle Joanna and her husband, just then struggling to make their own start in life. But there was nothing he could do about it except to send money to help with expenses.

Then a miracle happened. Joanna's first baby, Ethel, was born, and immediately a change came over the battered but indomitable old man. Hamilton and its unsaved sinners vanished from his thoughts, and he became loving and considerate. Often he sat buried in thought, and when his daughter called him to his meals, he answered: "I haven't time. I have much thinking to do."

Finally out of his thinking he brought himself to talk humbly with Joanna about his past mistakes. Most of all he was burdened with the memory of his harshness to John. Over and over he charged Joanna to rule her children only by love. Hell-fire and the wrath of God ceased to be the theme of his speech. A little child had led him into the knowledge that love is the basic law of life.

Thus with the father problem solved for them all, John Muir strove to help the rest of the family. He tried to persuade his mother to make her home with him in California. But Ann, the "home-body," would not consider moving to a strange country. Then John, sending a generous check to pay all expenses, invited Sarah and Margaret to make him a long visit. The two weary, semi-invalid women found a new lease of life in the warm, friendly valley as they wandered about in a trance of delight, eating oranges off the trees, picking flowers in the winter, and inspecting the new Strentzel home with its sixteen beautiful, high-ceilinged rooms, built for hospitality, with wide brick and marble fireplaces everywhere. To them it seemed a palace. The whole experience was a revelation to them of gracious living, and when they went home, they wrote their gratitude for "the princely and tender kindness" they had received from John, Louie, and the Strentzels.

With the management of the combined ranches devolving largely upon John Muir's shoulders, he set out to bring every acre up to peak production. Land formerly given to hay and grain was planted to vines and fruit trees. He did most of the planting himself, and both trees and vines prospered and bore fruit as never before. As the Gaels say, he had the gift of "green fingers." Dr. Strentzel had been a dilettante in comparison. Through years of scientific experimenting with the best varieties of fruit obtainable in Europe, he had performed an inestimable service to California horticulture. But the practical Muir, believing the period of experiment was past, favored concentration upon the most successful varieties. Bartlett pears and Tokay grapes commanded the highest market price; therefore he set about grafting Dr. Strentzel's sixty-five varieties of pears to Bartletts, and the many kinds of grapes to Tokays.

Nobody ever got the better of him in a deal. His tilts with the fruit jobbers of San Francisco made history in the valley. Since the famous Strentzel products were demanded by both Eastern and Western markets, the commission merchants fairly haunted the ranch.

"I'll take five hundred crates on commission," an agent would say.

"You'll buy a thousand outright at fifty cents, or you'll not get any," answered the shrewd Scot.

"But if you don't let me have them at my price, they'll rot on your hands."

"Let them rot!"

On steamer days the ranch wagons streamed down the valley at dawn, loaded with fruit to be sold on the Strentzel wharf at Martinez. On one occasion the buyers formed a conspiracy against him. Not one of them made a bid for his grapes. When they thought they had him worn down, they offered a low price. "Too late," he snapped, and they went off empty-handed. The next day's steamer bought twice the amount, and at Muir's price.

So it came about during the eighties that a lean, brown-bearded man in a buggy, with his right foot dangling out at the side, was a familiar sight along the road leading to Martinez. Driving up to the bank, he would pull from the back a big white bag labeled "Laundry" and vanish within. In the ten years he gave to more or less intensive ranching, it is said he laid away in that local bank a savings account of $50,000 which he never touched in his lifetime. Moreover, several banks in San Francisco housed his growing wealth. He had a canny instinct about not putting all his eggs into one basket.

But with all this "money-grubbing" John Muir was living a full life as a family man. The well-being and education of Wanda were his first concern. Louie or Grandmother Strentzel, fearing John was working too long in the hot sun, would often take the baby down to the vineyard along the wine-scented rows until they found him. And he would put aside whatever he was doing and walk back to the house with the child in his arms.[61] Or he would take her for a stroll along the creek or up a cool canyon in the Briones Hills to see the wild gowans. All of the flower names he taught her as soon as she was able to lisp. "For how would you like it," he would ask, "if people didn't call you by your name?" Up in his study she would sit on his knee drawing flower or animal pictures in his choicest notebooks. One of her lifelong memories had to do with a bird's nest in an apple tree outside the study window, and the way he coaxed the feathered people up to the sill with morsels of bread on a string.

Most unorthodox were Muir's ideas on what a child should be taught: "More wild knowledge, less arithmetic and grammar, keeps alive the heart, nourishes youth's enthusiasms which in society die untimely. . . . Go to Nature's school — the one true University."

Brought up in an atmosphere of poetry and song, each of his children early acquired a rhythmical mode of expression. When Wanda was five years old, her mother took down from her speech a kind of nature chant with real poetic quality. Muir labeled it and kept it among his treasures. As Wanda and her younger sister Helen grew up, they vied with each other and with their father in writing humorous doggerel rhymes to celebrate important happenings. Some of these are still extant.

Very unorthodox he was also in their religious training. God was to be reverenced not as a person, but as a loving, intelligent spirit creating, permeating, and controlling the universe. They were not taught to pray, except that on one occasion Muir told his wife he wished they might know the Lord's Prayer. So they learned it along with the other great poetry of the Bible, and that of Milton, Burns, Wordsworth, and Shelley.[62]

Let no one think John Muir had dropped out of public life without causing a ripple. Among the many who protested were the botanists Charles C. Parry and Albert Kellogg of the California Academy of Sciences, who begged him to return to the great tasks he had once undertaken so ably. Robert Underwood Johnson was an eternal gadfly on his flank, trying to sting him into action. "Have you abandoned literature altogether? . . . Has the ink in your fountain entirely dried up? . . . Have you put your hand to the plow, and then turned back?"

Johnson despairing of getting any response out of Muir, appealed to Muir's wife, begging her to persuade her husband to take up writing once more. She needed no urging. No one was more troubled than she to see the ranch cares sapping his health and burdening his spirit with the consciousness of a cause forsaken. When the summer of 1884 came, he was looking extremely "shadowy," beset as he was with all his usual lowland ailments. She urged him to go to the wilderness, but when he refused, saying the ranch would go to ruin, she declared she needed a vacation herself. She wanted to see the Yosemite with John Muir as her guide. So in July Wanda was consigned to her grandmother's care, and off they went. The falls, the river, the towering rocks were a revelation to Louie's beauty-loving eyes. Her rapture matched that of her husband. But she was worried. "I am anxious about John," she wrote to her mother. "The journey was hard for him, and he looks thin and pale and tired. He must not leave the mountains until he is well and strong again."

They made brief forays about the valley and the nearer heights. She was no practiced mountain-climber, and he would not leave her. Moreover, neither of them was willing to stray from post and telegraph offices, lest Wanda or the old folks might become ill in their absence. Needless to say, they didn't stay long. Louie urged John to remain behind, but wild horses couldn't have kept him there. Soon he was back in the old treadmill, from which it seemed no human influence could extricate him. It must have been about this time that he wrote on the flyleaf of a book, these words: "Time partially reconciles us to anything. I gradually became content — doggedly contented, as wild animals in cages."

That fall, winter, and the following spring the shadows blackened over the Wisconsin family. David Galloway, as dear to John Muir as his blood brothers, died from grief over the drowning of his only son, George. Sarah was deeply stricken. Annie had consumption. Katie, David's wife, died in March. Muir felt he should go east to comfort his sorrowing relatives, but he and his wife knew a second child was on the way. He could not leave her to bear the brunt of the ranch cares.

On a late August day, however, as he was sitting in his study reading, there came to him the most powerful inner compulsion he had ever known. It was like a voiced command telling him he must go east if he would see his father alive. Joanna in her last letter had said Father was well and happy and had a good appetite; but John Muir knew — he could not tell how — that the old man was near the end.

Louie got him ready for the journey, stipulating that he stop to rest under a pine tree at Shasta, and in the Yellowstone. From Shasta he wrote to her:

How green are the meadows and cool and deep the streams, and how boundless the wealth of the woods. . . . Never while I live will this mountain love die. . . . I still feel a strong draw . . . impelling me to leave all and linger here. But I will not — putting away temptation as a drunkard would whisky, and I shall make all the haste I can, both away and back.

To this letter his wife replied:

Oh, my beloved husband, why do you strive against the guidance of your good angel that would lead you . . . where there is rest and peace. . . .

Even your mother and sisters would understand. My father and mother at last realize your need of the mountains! Then as for the old ranch, why it is here, and a few grapes more or less will not make much difference this year.

But it would make a difference . . . whether you come back shadowy and ghostly, or strong and well.

He arrived at the Yellowstone too ill to react at once to "the strange region of fire and water." But invited by two honeymooners, Mr. and Mrs. Frank Sellers of Chicago, to go on a 150-mile horseback and camping trip with them through the park, he accepted with alacrity. When Louie heard of the plan, she wrote:

Oh, if you could only feel unhurried and able to rest with no thought of tomorrow, next week, or next month. There must be the charm of healing in your own high wilderness.

Only one week in the Rocky Mountain wilderness for John Muir! Oh, my beloved, you are cruel to yourself.

In that week's journey he suffered several mishaps, such as being taken desperately ill at Old Faithful Geyser, and in his weakened state being thrown from a horse, and getting some thorough wettings from rain and hail. Nevertheless he gained strength.

Meanwhile no mishap could long dampen his sense of fun. Mr. Sellers recalled in a letter: "I can see . . . you sitting on the slippery edge of some geyser as the rain pelted down, serenely quoting Bobby Burns' remarks about the hot hereafter and 'the Deevil' as the mud balls puffed and choked and spluttered back at you."

On August 30 he arrived unannounced at Portage. Walking into his brother's store, he found him bent, gray, and older-looking than himself. Together they walked to David's house on Howard Street, where their mother was living with Annie, Sarah, and her girls. Sarah was crushed with grief; Annie thin and racked with coughing. Only Mother was her strong, serene, erect self, standing like a rock in a storm. As soon as John stepped into the house as head of the clan, he brought a measure of light and comfort to the distressed family. David was already "laughing with some of his old-time boyish light-heartedness," and Annie was fired with joy and hope when John told her she was to return with him to California and find health. Obediently she set about getting ready.[63]

He remained a week in and about Portage. Returning from a trip to Buffalo Township, where he visited with William Duncan and Davie Taylor, he found the whole populace eager to greet him as a celebrity. To save his mother and sisters from callers, he set up headquarters in David's store, where he sat "assiduously smoking" and talking to all and sundry.

"I have been regarded as a great curiosity here," he wrote to Louie, "and have been called on to recognize about a thousand people that I had never heard of but who disclosed they knew me passing well, etc."

The family were all proud of him, and when Sunday came, Sarah's Cecelia, now a young woman of twenty, wanted to take him to church to hear her and Uncle David sing in the choir. He had other ideas, and on that morning was sitting on the side porch listening to the birds in the mulberry tree. Cecelia, all dressed up and wearing a new hat trimmed with stuffed birds, came out to lay siege to him. Whimsically he told her he could praise God just as well hearing the birds sing; whereupon in her eagerness she danced around in front of him to make a stronger plea. But the words died on her lips when she saw his gaze fix itself sternly upon her hat. His eyes were like flashing points of steel. Taking his pipe from his mouth he ejaculated: "That's a *devil* of a hat you're wearing!" He said nothing more, but Cecelia crept away, and from that day on never again wore birds on her hat.[64]

On September 24 he arrived with David and Annie at Joanna's home, now in Kansas City. Mary — married to a lawyer, Willis Hand, and living in Kearney, Nebraska — having been summoned by a telegram from John, had already arrived. They found their father lying in bed, his silken white hair making a halo about his saintly old face. He had been failing rapidly, Joanna said, for a month. (It was a month since John had received the telepathic or premonitory message.) In a bewildered stupor he would ask: "Is this my dear John?" as his son bent over him talking broad Scotch to rally his memory. "Ye're a Scotchman, aren't you?" Then starting up and gazing fixedly upon him, he would say: "Oh, yes, my dear Wanderer." [65]

Having telegraphed money for Sarah to come, John took the train to bring back Dan and Maggie, now living in Nebraska. Maggie was ill at the time, but she and her husband, John Reid, promised to follow within a few days. Stopping at Lincoln, where Dan was practicing medicine, John picked him up. Arriving back in Kansas City, they found their father still alive, with "short-lived gleams of recognition like feeble rays of light from the moor. . . . He drew me down with a low moaning sound to kiss him and held my hand for a long time, and would not let me go."

On the night of October 6 John sat alone with his father, having sent the others to rest. Toward midnight he saw the change coming and called them. So as the old man sank into the sleep of death, seven of his eight children stood about him weeping, for, as John Muir said: "In all our devious ways and wanderings we have loved one another." [66]

On January 23, 1886 a second child was born to John and Louie Muir. Helen, as they named her, was frail and ailing from the start, and her life hung by a thread. For a year and a half her father hardly left the ranch, fearful lest she become ill. Even the shortest trips to the mountains were barred.

But he did not forget the trees. He was sorely troubled over the exploitation going on unchecked in Washington, Oregon, and the Sierra. Pleas were coming to him from all over the country to head the rising movement to save the forests. Was ever a man so beset with conflicting loyalties? In the welter of ranch cares, ill health, and family responsibilities, how could he find leisure or peace of mind to write articles appealing to the people at large? And yet the urge to do so was becoming almost irresistible.

In the spring of 1887 he was asked to contribute to and edit two large volumes of nature studies to be known as *Picturesque California,* to be published by J. Dewing & Co. of New York and San Francisco. His wife seized upon the opportunity with enthusiasm and persuaded him to accept. That winter he sent out pleas to John Reid, and then to David Muir, to come and act as foreman and take over all responsibility for the ranch. But both of them were deeply involved financially where they were and could not cut loose. So Muir went on for a while longer, carrying the double burden of ranch work and trying to write.

Louie by this time almost hated the ranch for what it had done to her husband. Nobody knew better than she that he had come to a parting of the ways. His labored, uninspired efforts on the first *Picturesque California* articles told her that whatever divine fire he had once possessed was all but gone. He must get out into the wilderness once more to recapture it. He could no longer serve two masters.

PART VI

1888–1900

A LEADER OF MEN

ONE day during cherry-picking time in May 1888, S. Hall Young appeared unheralded in the orchard. Muir, seeing him, dropped his basket and ran to meet him, crying: "Ah! my friend. . . . You have come to take me on a canoe trip . . . have you not? My weariness of this humdrum, work-a-day life has grown so heavy it is like to crush me. . . . I, who have breathed the mountain air . . . condemned to penal servitude with these miserable little bald-heads! . . . And for money! Man! I'm like to die of the shame of it."[1]

Young spent the night with him, the two of them sitting in the study, talking until the morning hours.

In June, with Louie's connivance, Charles Parry invited Muir to go with him to Lake Tahoe, to identify certain species of manzanita and ceanothus growing there. To everybody's surprise, he went without protest. Leaving the sulphuring undone, and the workmen without a responsible head, he fled from the ranch as if his life depended upon this respite from "the eternal grind, grind, grind." Moreover, he sent word to Keith that upon his return he would go north and hoped they might go together. Keith, along with other Western artists, had been engaged to illustrate *Picturesque California,* which was to contain material descriptive of the entire Pacific coast.

In July, off on their first mountain trip together since the seventies, Muir and Keith stopped for two days at Mount Shasta. Here, as at Lake Tahoe, commercialism had done its worst. Muir was appalled at "the destruction of the forest about Shasta. The axe and saw are heard here more often . . . and the glory is de-

Mount Rainier from Paradise Valley. Muir party camped in 1888 *to the left of Fairy Pool in the foreground*

JOHN MUIR *in* 1890

parting." As he turned from "the raw shingle town of Sisson, glaring in the Shasta meadows," and climbed among the lower forests, he faced the ugly fact that while he had been "money-grubbing," this devastation had been going on without protest. Soon all the divine, healing beauty would be lost. But it was not yet too late. In the chapter he was soon to write for *Picturesque California* on Mount Shasta, he would boldly urge that this region be made a national park [2] "for the welfare and benefit of all mankind, preserving its fountains and forests and all its glad life in primeval beauty."

When the two friends stopped at Portland, Keith was ill from "the villainous food on the train." But Muir, who was ill too, was all on fire to climb Mount Hood. A day on the summit, he told Keith, would cure his stomachache. But the artist said no and sent for a doctor. Muir, grumbling and looking "like Carlyle in a fit of dyspepsia," went off for a solitary ramble on the heights back of the city.

Mount Rainier was the supreme goal of the journey north. On August 8 Muir and Keith were joined at Seattle by six young men bent on climbing the mountain. They were E. S. Ingraham, Superintendent of Schools in Seattle; Daniel Waldo Bass, an attorney; Charles V. Piper, a botanist; N. O. Booth, a teen-age boy; Henry Loomis; and A. C. Warner, a photographer. At Yelm Prairie, Philemon Beecher Van Trump, local postmaster, consented to go with them as guide.[3] Muir took an instant liking to him, and henceforth called him "Peter Van Trump," or "My Van Trump."

On the morning of August 9 "the whole gypsy cavalcade" set out via the Yellowjacket Trail, along the Nisqually River, turgid with gray mud and boulders from the glacier above. Something they had eaten the night before made the whole party sick. Whatever it was, they took it with them and ate more of it. "There was poison and sickness in every pot," said Muir. With the godlike mountain ever before them as a shining goal, however, they forgot their pains and went on undaunted.[4] What with that rare pair of jokers and Scotch yarners, Muir and Keith, there was never a dull moment in camp or on trail. And at night the two of them sang folk ballads — Muir with his sweet tenor, and Keith with a rich baritone that could have made him famous.

They arrived at last to make camp in Paradise Valley, a short distance above the site of the present Paradise Lodge. Muir called it "the most extravagantly beautiful of all the Alpine gardens I ever beheld." Beside their "Camp of the Clouds," as they named it, was a clear blue lakelet — now known as Fairy Pool — reflecting the heavens, the towering pines, and the dazzling white mountain looming above, "wholly unveiled, awful in bulk and majesty, filling all the view like a separate, new-born world, yet withal so fine and so beautiful it might well fire the dullest observer to desperate enthusiasm." Nature's two interpreters, artist and poet, stood gazing, wholly rapt — Keith's grizzled mane tossed back, his eyes glowing like coals of fire; Muir's face lighted with the old flame of determination to feel the topmost stone under his feet.

Too bad that at this inspiring moment the cayuse carrying the provisions should have chosen to begin a series of volcanic cavortings that sent pots, pans, and food hurtling in all directions. Muir's special box of crackers whizzed through the air and landed in the lake. Having disgorged his load, the rebel beast stampeded off into the woods, with all the other horses galloping after him. But the loss of material things didn't divert John Muir from the mountain. He had told his wife he didn't expect to climb it, and Van Trump heard him say he didn't feel fit. But when the old mystic ecstasy ran rampant in his veins, all his weakness fell away. As he wrote later to his wife: "Did not mean to climb it, but got excited, and soon was on top."

Only the weariness of his companions held him back from starting out that day. He spent the afternoon walking about the lush meadows, "considering the lilies," and spying out routes for the climb. Young Warner went strolling with him. To this day he recalls Muir's method on a saunter: "He walked with bowed head, searching the ground for plants. When he found one he wanted to examine, he sat down and looked at it through a lens. He never stood up long, but sat to conserve his strength." [5]

Keith had no desire to feel the mountain beneath his feet, and he feared snow-blindness would interfere with his work. Just above the lake and adjacent to the camp stood a big sloping boulder just right to lean against and view the mountain. He was soon propped up against this rock, making sketches. If he got tired of that position, he had only to walk about fifty paces in the opposite direction to get a fine view of the Tatoosh Mountains, jagged and high in the sky.

Keith's art through the eighties had been emerging from Muir's influence. He no longer strove for realistic detail, but when in the presence of nature, gathered hints on paper and in his subconscious, of evanescent lights and glooms, to take home with him. The emotions he felt at the time would on some future day burst forth in white moments of inspiration, to blend themselves into an improvisation of the scene upon canvas.

Leaving blankets and all but iron rations behind them, seven of the party set out soon after noon on August 14 to scale the summit. From the south they followed the Nisqually Glacier for several miles, then struck off up the flank leading to the Cleaver or spur that divides the Nisqually from the Cowlitz Glacier basin. By nightfall, according to Mr. Warner, they reached the foot of the great rock, Gibraltar, at some distance above the site now known as Camp Muir. Here, Muir tells us, they scooped out a hole in the sand and built up a wall of rocks to shelter them from the wild, bitter gale blowing sand and volcanic ash into their eyes. "Camp Misery" the place was well named by later mountaineers camping on this spot.

"In the morning we were astir by four o'clock," relates Muir, "not boisterous after a sleepless night, but with cheery hearts. And the view of the mountain top, so grandly heaving itself into the sky, cheered us on and supplied strength." [6]

Their way now lay upward along a narrow, "desperately steep" seam in the precipice. Rocks came volleying down from the frowning, crumbling brow above them. Often they had to crawl on all fours, conscious that a slip in the sloping gravel would mean a fall to the glacier, 1,500 feet below, "cleft and tumbled into a chaos of blocks and crevasses."

Muir, reacting like a warhorse to the scent of danger, felt "warm and ambitious." "This is a good mountain to prove one's mettle," he told the others. With his own muscles and nerves in perfect attunement for rapid climbing, he yet slowed his own pace to guide them. Taking the young boy Booth under his special charge, he felt out footholds for him with his alpenstock and helped him over the worst places. He was equally considerate of Warner, staggering along under the weight of his camera. "We all loved him," says Warner, "for his thoughtfulness for others. With his cheering and encouraging words he urged the wearied climber to push on to the goal, he, Muir, meanwhile waiting for him."

At long last they emerged where the spur ended in the mountainside, and the ice-cap began that stretched upward and surrounded the summit. Hammering steel calks into their soles, they attacked it. "It was now all leather and muscle and steel pitted against deadly, desperate, nerve-shaking ice-slopes and crevasses." [7]

About a thousand feet below the top Booth fell down, gasping: "I can't go on." They left him there to await their return. At noon, after seven and a half hours of climbing, six of them stood on the summit, shouting triumphantly with what breath they had left. "How eerie strange it sounded," says Warner, "on that bleak and echoless height!" The wind blowing everlastingly makes no sound. Muir, whose keen senses left nothing unnoted, said: "You cannot hear it except as it flows past your clothing."

Arrived at the top, Warner, without pausing to rest, began taking pictures — the first ever made on that height. Fearing lest his glass negatives might be broken, he had brought along two sensitized films just received from the East. Thus for the first time in the Northwest films were used that day.

While his companions were variously occupied, Muir sat apart, silent, absorbed, drinking in the stupendous view that comprehended the Cascade Range reaching from the north far down into Oregon, its flanks clothed in "black interminable forests," and the white cones of its fire-mountains rising above them like beacons in the sky.

After nearly two hours on the summit Muir's weatherwise eyes saw signs of an approaching storm, and he warned them they must descend at once. Just as they started down the mound, Booth hove in sight, stumbling over the bulge in the ice-cap. They waited. Finally he, too, stood on the summit beside them, the seventh to make the successful sixth ascent.[8] With his last step he gave out a cry that was more of a groan than a shout. But the other six made up for its feebleness with a lusty cheer for "the indomitable lad."

While the blue-back angry snow-clouds massed overhead, Muir shepherded them down the icy dome. Blinded by the white glare, they could hardly see the crevasses that yawned in their path. After several narrow escapes they reached the Cleaver and passed it without mishap. Then they skidded and strode down the smooth lower slopes, "heart and limb exultant and free." Muir had found his release on that mountain top; he felt within himself all his old prowess of body and mind restored as by a miracle.

About seven in the evening they limped into camp "with swollen and blistered faces and weak and watery eyes." One man was blind for two days. But their nausea was gone, and Muir relates they "made heroic attacks on the canned stuff."

That night while his companions, swathed in blankets, slept by the campfire, Muir, longing for the old solitary communion with nature, strolled alone in the forest.

When one is alone at night in the depths of these woods, the stillness is at once awful and sublime. Every leaf seems to speak. One gets close to Nature, and the love of beauty grows as it cannot in the distractions of a camp. . . . Jubilant winds and waters sound in grand harmonious symphonies — wild music flowing on forever from a thousand thousand sources, winds in hollows of the glaciers glinting on crystal angles, winds on crags, in trees, among the elastic needles sweeping soft and low with silken rhythm, and winds murmuring through the grasses, ringing the bells of Bryanthus.[9]

Meanwhile at home on the ranch Louie Muir had reached a momentous decision. On August 9, while her husband was on his way up the lower slopes of Mount Rainier, she wrote to him:

A ranch that needs and takes the sacrifice of a noble life, or work, ought to be flung away beyond all reach and power for harm. . . .

The Alaska book and the Yosemite book, dear John, must be written, and you need to be your own self, well and strong, to make them worthy of you. There is nothing that has a right to be considered beside this except the welfare of our children.[10]

Upon his return to Seattle, Muir received this letter. And when he arrived back at the ranch a few days later, he found his wife firmly resolved upon a plan to unload his burdens by selling and leasing large portions of the land. This could not be achieved in a day, but it was progressively attained during the next three or four years. With her ardent co-operation Muir was never again to be wholly enslaved.

Since his rebaptism in the wilderness Muir was writing with his old-time power, now tempered by the judgment of maturity. To avoid interruptions he chose a hide-away in an obscure San Francisco hotel where for days at a time he would work at high tension, frequently sending his output to his wife for criticism.

His only recreation was an occasional stroll among the sand dunes where the Golden Gate Park was being created. One day observing a slender youth named Enos Mills bending over a fragrant ground-creeping plant, he fell into conversation with him. From that talk and later ones at the ranch and on the slopes of Mount Tamalpais, Enos Mills, one of the greatest of Muir's disciples, received his driving urge to write and work for the preservation of wild nature in the national parks.[11]

In early June 1889 Robert Underwood Johnson, now associate editor of the *Century,* formerly *Scribner's Monthly,* arrived in the city to get Gold Rush articles and to recapture Muir's inspired pen for that publication. The naturalist called upon him at the Palace Hotel, where in trying to find his room he got lost in "the confounded artificial canyons" of the hallways.[12] Upon meeting the editor he urged that they get out into the mountains to talk.

A few days later they were in the Yosemite. "Muir loved this region as a mother loves a child," said Johnson. But they found the valley a scene of progressive desolation under the management of the State Commission, operated largely for the profit of the "combine" that owned the hotels and stables and plowed up the meadows and cut down the trees to make hayfields for horses, mules, sheep, cows, and hogs.

Leaving the valley, the two friends rode to the Tuolumne Meadows to camp beside the Soda Springs. Here, too, they found widespread devastation: charred stumps where great trees had once towered; the forest floor "bare as the streets of San Francisco"; even the young firs and pines had been "trampled and eaten out of existence by hoofed locusts."

As they tramped by day or rested by night, "camping beneath large stars," Muir and his "very friend," Johnson, talked together. "None but the Baptist had so rapt a look," Johnson tells us in his poem [13] of tribute to Muir, "as he poured forth his innermost joy in Nature and her healing powers free to all mankind." Johnson came to regard him as "great Nature's priest."

A crumb of beauty was to him a feast.
He gave her sacrament to all who came,
Sight to the blind and vigor to the lame.

But looking about them upon the despoiled forests, meadows, streams, and waterfalls, there were "tears in his voice" as Muir deplored the havoc man's commercialism had wrought. Johnson, listening, was moved as seldom in his life, and he began to plan to do something about it.

On one of their final nights they sat long by their Tuolumne campfire, making history. The editor proposed that they work together to make this Yosemite hinterland into a national park. Muir, skeptical of success, said the people of California, blinded by money-making, were indifferent to the destruction of their natural resources. Senator Newton Booth had once introduced a bill in Congress to create such a project, but it failed, as had his own effort in 1881 to establish a reserve or park in the Kings-Kaweah region.

But Johnson, refusing to be daunted, urged Muir to write two articles for the *Century* portraying the primeval wonders of the region, outlining boundaries for the proposed park, and appealing to the whole American people to make it a reality. As for himself, he would enlist all possible aid in the East, and at the right time after the articles had appeared would have a bill introduced in Congress.

Muir, heartened by this unlooked-for support, agreed to write the articles. Upon his return home a few days later he fired the opening gun of the campaign in an article for the *San Francisco Bulletin*.[14] Although he had no hope that the valley itself would become a part of the projected park — at least for many years — yet he exposed the abuses and havoc wrought under state control. Of the damage done to the surrounding region he said: "Sheep have already swept most of the herbaceous vegetation of the Sierra out of existence. Not one garden accessible has been spared."

In other newspaper articles and interviews Muir depicted the rapid and ruthless destruction going on over the entire Sierra. To allow this to go on unchecked was "to kill the goose that lays the golden egg." He urged Federal management for the watershed forests as "a perennial fountain of wealth as well as of beauty."

America had not forgotten Muir's vibrant articles of the seventies. He was quoted far and wide by the Eastern press, and within a few weeks the drive for the conservation of California's forests and the Yosemite wonderland was launched on a nation-wide scale.

By the early summer of 1890 Muir had completed his two articles for the *Century*. But he was once more worn to a shadow with grippe and nervous indigestion. Against the advice of a physician he prescribed for himself a camping trip on Muir Glacier.

"If you go on this journey in your condition, you'll pay for it with your life," warned the doctor.

"If I don't go, I'll pay for it with my life," said Muir.

On June 14 he sailed for Seattle "like a Crusader bound for the Holy Land." Soon he was rid of his cough and sore throat and was eating "all kinds of compounds, even to codfish."

At Port Townsend, Henry Loomis of the Rainier party joined him with equipment and provisions. Arriving on the steamer *Queen* at Glacier Bay, they made camp on the east lateral moraine within a mile of the front of the Muir. He spent the next few days preparing for a sled-trip on the glacier. With a manual dexterity like that of Thoreau, he cobbled his shoes with thick new soles, and made a sleeping-bag out of a bearskin, some red wool, and a canvas sheet. "Like one of Wanda's caterpillars I can lie warm on the ice," he wrote to his wife.

The *Queen* on her next trip brought lumber from Sitka, with which they built a snug, sound cabin that survived for many years. With spruce boughs and scraps of lumber Muir then made a sled three feet long by eighteen inches wide, shoeing the runners with long steel strips. When loaded, it weighed about a hundred pounds.

One day the *George W. Elder* steamed up the inlet, and discharged from among its passengers, Harry Fielding Reid, the scientist, with a group of students. With their seven or eight tons of scientific paraphernalia and other freight, they pitched camp near by. "We have now quite a village!" exulted Muir.

On the morning of July 11 he set out to the north to explore the upper reaches of the glacier. The main events of each day he scribbled into a small notebook. But on scraps of paper — presumably carried for kindling — he wrote down his thoughts upon nature, his fellow man, beauty, and the meaning of life and death. Fortunately these, or a portion of them, have been preserved.[15]

Trees always set him pondering. Standing on the bleak top of Hemlock Mountain,[16] where the winds blow eternally, with the living and the dead all about him, he wrote: "The clearest way into the Universe is through a forest wilderness. . . . Nature takes fallen trees gently to her bosom — at rest from storms. They seem to have been called home out of the sky to sleep now."

As he went deeper into the white wilderness where no man had gone before, incidents were recounted humorously in his scrambled notes. One morning he was beset from afar by howling wolves, and he retreated to a mountainside boulder where he could fend off a frontal attack with his alpenstock. As soon as the wild cries died away, he resumed his journey on the glacier's broad back, after naming the place Howling Valley. Another day he pitched headlong down an icy slope of Snow Dome to a gravel talus below. Just then two ravens swooped out of the sky, uttering weird cries as if "impatiently waiting for bone-picking time." Shaking his fist at them he shouted: "Not yet, you black imps. Not yet! Wait awhile. I'm not carrion yet. Go back to your gray friends, the wolves, for your dinner. I was only sliding for fun. My body flesh is not yet cast away. I shall need it for a long time." [17]

Advancing from the right margin toward the middle of the glacier as it veered toward the northwest, his way became gorged with enormous blocks of ice, buckled at all angles into frozen chaos. To surmount these and cross the crevasses, encumbered by his heavy sled, was a feat few men could have accomplished. But he was all-powerful that day with exhilaration. When he sat down on his sled at noon to munch his crust, he wrote: "To dine with a glacier on a sunny day is a glorious thing and makes common feasts of meat and wine ridiculous. The glacier eats hills and eats sunbeams."

Camping that night on the glacier's wide expanse, miles from any firewood, he shaved splinters from beneath his sled, made a fire in one of his tin cups, and brewed his tea in the other over the flame. Then with feet wet and cold, for his shoes were wearing out, he snuggled down into his bag on the sled pieced out with stones, "cozy and comfortable . . . resting in the midst of the glorious scenery." But not to sleep. Oh dear, no. This was an experience to be enjoyed. At midnight he was scribbling with benumbed fingers: "Solemn loveliness of the night. Vast star-garden of the Universe. . . . In this silent, serene wilderness the weary gain a heart-bath in perfect peace."

With his cough completely gone — "no microbe could survive in this icy world" — he plodded on the next day. Late in the afternoon he reached the left-hand shore, exhausted, and with shoes cut to ribbons. But he climbed to the top of Quarry Mountain where he built a fire and spent the night meditating upon the cosmos and the unity of all created things. Stumbling down in the morning — for he was nearly blind now from the snow glare — he pursued his way along the margin, crossing the confluences of several tributaries. He tried to sketch, but everything looked double to him. Then came gray clouds stealing over the sky, and he lay down that night with face and burning eyes gratefully uplifted to the caress of snow crystals.

In the morning he made goggles (of what he does not tell), pulled the beak of his cap down to make shade, and set out down the glacier toward camp. Near the end of the day he suddenly dropped into a deep water-filled crevasse concealed beneath a thin crust of ice and snow. Down over his head he plunged; then rising, he struggled valiantly until he pulled himself out upon the farther edge. In the lee of an island cliff near by, he stripped off his soaked garments, crept into his bag, and "shivered the night away." He had a favorite Scotch expression with which he met most of the lesser ills of life, and he put it down now among his notes: "It micht hae been waur!" Yes, it could have been worse!

Toward nightfall on the 21st — the tenth day of his trip — he was just going to bed when he saw Professor Reid and young Loomis coming to ferry him across the inlet. Once more in camp after one of the greatest adventures of his life, he said: "I had a good rest and sleep and leisure to find out how rich I was in new facts and pictures and how tired and hungry I was." [18]

When Muir came home in September, the park campaign had reached the boiling-point. His two *Century* articles, "Treasures of the Yosemite," and "Features of the Proposed Yosemite National Park," [19] had precipitated the final stage of the conflict. Copied in part or in whole by the press of the nation, with supporting editorials, these articles aroused the public to action. Opportunely the bill to create the Yosemite National Park within boundaries prescribed by Muir was introduced in Congress. Immediately letters, telegrams, and petitions poured into Washington demanding passage.

Naturally the project stirred up opposition. In California this was voiced in the beginning by an Oakland orator and politician, John P. Irish. In an effort to discredit Muir, "Colonel" Irish bombarded editors and Congressmen with what Johnson called "savage and vulgar letters" that completely overstepped the bounds of truth and decency. One of them was published in the *Oakland Tribune* [20] in answer to an article entitled "As It Appears to John Muir," [21] which seemed to favor the recession of the Yosemite Valley.

Irish in this letter charged Muir and Johnson with a conspiracy to defraud the state. The pride of any Californian, he said, "must be stung to the quick" at this attempt to rob the state of her choicest treasure. As though they were plotting to move the great gorge out of California! Then he exploded this bomb: Muir, he said, "before he abandoned himself to profitable rhapsody and became a pseudo-naturalist, figured among the squatters in the Yosemite. . . . There he cut and logged and sawed the trees of the Valley with as willing a hand as any lumberman in the Sierras. When the State of California became trustee of the grant, Muir and the mill were expelled . . . and his teeth have been on edge ever since. The State got there, however, in time to save the forests from Mr. Muir's lumbering operations, and to prevent the clogging of the Merced with sawdust, to the destruction of its beauty and its trout."

Muir's friends, Colby, Keith, and Professor William D. Armes, sprang to his defense, and Muir himself wrote what was probably the only answer[22] he ever made to libels published against him:

Martinez, September 14, 1890.

To the Editor of the Tribune—Sir: Referring to a discussion of Yosemite affairs in your columns, I would state that twenty years ago I was employed by the month by Mr. Hutchings, to saw lumber from fallen timber, with which to build cottages in the valley. I never cut down a single tree in the Yosemite, nor sawed a tree cut down by any other person there. Furthermore, I never held, or tried to hold any sort of claim in the valley, or sold a foot of lumber there or elsewhere.

At the time of my first visit to the valley, and while I lived there Galen Clark was guardian. He is guardian now, and to that gentleman I would refer you for further information should you require it.

Respectfully,

JOHN MUIR

It would not be worth while to repeat here this old canard, invented, or at least exploited, by Irish in defiance of dates and other easily proved facts, except that it is a sample of the calumny heaped upon Muir through all the years of his conservation work. Whispering campaigns to besmirch his moral standing, and dark aspersions against him as a family man, were spawned by his enemies. Some of these were transferred to Washington to poison the minds of Congressmen, even as late as the Kings Canyon National Park movement of 1939–40, to prevent that park's being named as a memorial to him. Truly, for more reasons than one, Robert Underwood Johnson has rightly said: "California and the Government owe him penance at his tomb."

Fortunate it was for the cause of conservation that John W. Noble was Secretary of the Interior under President Harrison. General Noble, inspired by the writings of Muir, had become convinced of the necessity of preserving the forested watersheds and scenic beauty of America. When, therefore, the Yosemite National Park Bill was introduced in Congress, both he and the President worked for it. As a result it became a law on October 1, 1890, and a cavalry patrol was dispatched to guard the area.

On the same high wave of national enthusiasm aroused by Muir and Johnson, the Sequoia and General Grant National Parks were also created in 1890, for the express purpose of saving valuable stands of sequoia timber.

On the last day of October Dr. Strentzel died. "He died as one falling asleep," said his son-in-law. "How great the loss only those who suffered may know. The family is broken like a house torn asunder and half taken away."

Then because Mrs. Strentzel needed the care and companionship of her daughter, the Muirs moved down the valley to the Big House. The burden of administering the large estate was now added to Muir's other cares. Finally in the spring of 1891 came much-needed relief in the ranch management. John Reid gave up the long struggle to hold his Kansas and Nebraska lands in the face of drought and pestilence and came west with his family, to take charge of the ranch work with vigor and efficiency. And John Muir had the joy of seeing his ailing sister Maggie installed in the old ranch house in the sunny, sheltered valley where he could watch over her for the rest of her life.

With three national parks recently established in California, Muir's fight had now two focal centers: namely, the watershed area north of the Sequoia National Park and the Yosemite Valley itself. While Congress was in the mood, he and Johnson hoped to extend the Sequoia Park boundary northward to include the Kings Canyon yosemites and their tributary basins. This recommendation Muir put into his article "A Rival of the Yosemite," published in the *Century* of November 1891. Secretary Noble, in full sympathy with the plan, recommended it in his Report to Congress late in 1891. But by this time the opposition had made its wishes known to subservient Congressmen, and the report was buried in committee.

Prior to this, however, Secretary Noble had devised an alternative plan by which, if the park project failed, he might set aside the entire watershed area as a forest reserve. Edward A. Bowers, Assistant Land Commissioner, working in accord with Noble, drafted a clause whereby the President could by proclamation "set apart . . . in any State or Territory . . . any part of public lands wholly or in part covered with timber . . . as public reservations." This clause, attached to "A Bill to Repeal the Timber-Culture Laws," was passed by Congress on March 3, 1891, and became known as "The Enabling Act" of that year. This power of the Executive was for a decade and a half to be the most potent single weapon in the hands of the conservationists.

In March 1892 came word from David that the firm of Parry & Muir had failed. Soon thereafter John Muir boarded the train for Wisconsin. He found the whole family desperately beleaguered, and his brother distraught with worry.

The Muir name had been one of the firm's strongest assets. Farmers and townspeople alike, believing in David's rocklike integrity, had entrusted their savings to the firm to be invested in the business. Juliette Treadway, long their faithful bookkeeper, had now become Mrs. David Muir, and she and her husband had done their honest best to make these investments pay dividends, depriving themselves of their own share of the profits to do so.

But the senior partner, Parry, caught up in the get-rich-quick optimism dominating American business during the seventies and eighties, had become involved in Lake Superior real-estate schemes. To bolster up original commitments, he had borrowed from the firm's reserve funds. Then came lean years when things went ill with farmers and merchants. The firm went bankrupt.

Had a bank failed, the populace could hardly have been more aroused. Parry, a legislator, spent most of his time in Madison; so David bore the brunt of their fury. Old friends of a lifetime now turned against him.

John Muir went east prepared to buy out his brother's interest in the store and so save it for him. But finding the business too deeply involved, he gave up the plan.

"David is greatly worn and distressed," he wrote to his wife, "and is threatened with inflammation of the brain. . . . I'll be glad when the end of this miserable business is reached and I can get David away from here . . . there is no saying what some of David's creditors may do. . . ."

Muir had reason to believe his presence helped allay the turmoil. Since the Portage people were proud of him as a local boy who had become "rich and famous," he was willing on his brother's behalf to play upon his reputation. He appeared publicly on every possible occasion with members of the family. This was no time, he told them, for the Muir clan to hide their heads. When Sunday morning came, it was he who suggested to his mother that they go to church. Said Annie in a letter to Louie: "John's coming was a great help and comfort to us all. He cheered us up beyond what seemed possible. . . . I don't know what we would have done without him."

Before leaving Portage, backed by his brother's presence, David came to an understanding with the creditors. Voluntarily he assumed fifty per cent of the firm's indebtedness, pledging himself to repay as rapidly as he could earn the money. Then, although the gossips still wagged their heads, he was allowed to go. John took David with him to Lincoln, Nebraska, where he placed him under Dr. Dan's care. Between them they were able to quiet the fever in his brain so he could sleep once more. When he was out of danger, John went home.

A few weeks later David and his wife arrived in the Alhambra Valley. John, seconded by Louie, offered his brother a portion of the ranch on a share-the-profits basis. A born farmer, David brought the land to new peaks of production and prospered. Although fifty years have passed, the old-timers of Portage still discuss the failure of Parry & Muir as if it had happened yesterday; but the verdict is now wholly in favor of David Muir. "He was the best man I ever knew," declares one venerable citizen. Says another: "He owed me $500, and he paid it back, every cent. And he paid everybody else he owed, too." [23]

Among the events of that tumultuous decade, none was more important for the cause of conservation in California than the founding of the Sierra Club in 1892. Ever since 1889 Robert Underwood Johnson had been urging Muir to "start an association for preserving California's monuments and natural wonders — or at least Yosemite." Muir, shy and distrustful of his own powers of leadership, was reluctant. However, choosing his nucleus carefully, he began to broach the subject to his nature-loving friends. He met with an eager response. Indeed, the idea of a mountaineers' club had already been urged by Professor J. H. Senger of the university. So on May 28, 1892 John Muir met with a small group [24] in the office of Attorney Warren Olney of San Francisco, where together they launched the Sierra Club. Muir was elected president, an office he held to the end of his life. According to the "Articles of Incorporation," the purposes of the organization were: "To explore, enjoy and render accessible the mountain regions of the Pacific Coast; to publish authentic information concerning them; to enlist the support and cooperation of the people and the government in preserving the forests and other natural features of the Sierra Nevada Mountains."

From Samuel Merrill, a young sprig of the Indianapolis family dear to John Muir, and his guest at the time, we learn of his joy over the founding of the club: "He came home jubilant from that meeting . . . and regaled them all with an account of it at the supper table. . . . I had never seen him so animated and happy before. . . . I venture to say it was the happiest day of his life. . . . Hitherto, his back to the wall, he had carried on his fight to save the wilderness. In the Sierra Club he saw the crystallization of the dreams and labor of a life-time. . . . He was hilarious with joy!"[25]

The Club was founded none too soon. For already the lumbermen and stockmen were organizing in California and in Washington a powerful opposition. In 1892 they had a bill introduced in Congress by Representative Caminetti of California, to cut away nearly half the area of the Yosemite National Park, including magnificent timber areas. The bill was rushed through the House by a large vote. But before it reached the Senate, John Muir and the Sierra Club swung into action. The club memorialized Congress to defeat the bill, while Muir gave out interviews to newspapers that were taken up by the Eastern press. He also sent many personal telegrams to men influential in the Government. As a result the bill was tabled for that session, although it hung fire as a threat for three years. This was the first attempt — but far from the last — to destroy the Yosemite National Park.

Samuel Merrill taking up the Boswellian task of his cousin Merrill Moores, has given us charming glimpses of life in the Muir household. Meal-times were periods of relaxation, story-telling, and often uproarious fun led by the naturalist himself. His table-talk fascinated Samuel. Even when scholarly guests were present, he tactfully directed the conversation into light channels. Every evening at dinner — company or no company — Wanda and Helen demanded from their father another installment of Paddy Grogan's adventures — an original tale of an Irish youth and his kangaroo steed. And, according to Samuel, "we were all glad to be quiet and listen." Mrs. Muir from her place at the head of the table, listened too. Quiet herself, "she hung on his words. She was devoted to him."

Frequently Muir's guests urged him to write down Paddy Grogan's story, that all children and grown-ups might share it. "Well, perhaps some day when I have time," he would answer.[26] But he never did, and according to those who heard him, the world has lost a great juvenile classic.

Muir often invited Samuel to his study for an evening talk. To the boy the study was a wonderful place, although somewhat overcrowded: "He was allowed to have his own way in this particular room and no one dared to put it in order. It was so full of his books, manuscripts, and sketches that it was difficult to find a chair unoccupied." "It must have seemed jumbled to anybody else," says Muir's daughter Helen, "but he knew the whereabouts of every article in it." Opposite the door as you entered, you saw a white marble fireplace that always on cool evenings had a cheery blaze. Over the fireplace hung Keith's famous picture *The Oaks,* an especial favorite. The mantel beneath bristled with dozens of brass-framed photographs of friends. At the left of them sprouted a pair of bleached goat's horns picked up on Muir Glacier — "some puir beastie a wolf had killed." High bookshelves covered the walls, crammed with his large library of scientific tomes and the authors he loved best — Carlyle, Scott, Burns, Shelley, Wordsworth, Coleridge, Nansen, Charles Lamb, Emerson, and Thoreau, the last of whom he came in maturity to regard as the wisest of them all. Two large desks were in the room, one of them a flat-topped one by the east window where he could look down over the valley to Suisun Bay. At this desk he did his writing.

Beside the fireplace was a solid oak rocking-chair with a sagging cane bottom, where Muir was wont to sit smoking his clay pipe through an eighteen-inch-long thistle stem garnered from the creek bed. Often on the other side of the hearth sat "our best cat," a gray-and-white Tom, polishing his fur, or quietly humming in his throat. Tom was a mighty hunter, much to the distress of his master, who strove to guard the wrens' nest in the woodpile from his predatory pet, and often snatched a live lizard from his jaws. When Tom caught a gopher and it was quite dead, he would dart with it through an open door and up the stairs to the study to exhibit the fruits of his prowess. After a decent interval — so as not to hurt Tom's feelings — Muir would pick up the corpse and patiently carry it down stairs and out of doors. As his master's constant companion Tom attended him about the ranch like a dog. And following the historic example of Carlyle's cat he sat on the floor beside him at meal time, waiting for morsels of meat or Swiss cheese smuggled down to him, regardless of carpets. But if anything less acceptable was offered, retribution swift and penetrating was applied to Muir's trouser leg.[27]

Alaska was much in the naturalist's thought while Samuel was there, and as he related his adventures, the listening boy could well understand the comment of someone who heard Muir describe a storm: "Our foreheads felt the wind and the rain!" One night Samuel remarked upon the dangers he must have faced. "Yes," mused his host. "I have made a tramp of myself. I have gone hungry and cold. I have left bloody trails on sharp ice peaks to see the wonders of the earth!"

Another evening, being in a mystical mood, Muir related the story of the telepathic message that led him to Dr. Butler in the Yosemite. Also the summons that called him to his dying father. The boy asked him how he accounted for such strange happenings. Muir replied: "Anyone who lives close to the mountains is sensitive to these things."

One night Samuel asked Muir if he had ever found any orchids on his tramps up and down the Pacific coast. "Yes," he replied, "I met two very rare and beautiful species in the wilds of British Columbia." Being an eager student of botany, Samuel asked him their names. Muir, disliking scientific verbiage, answered: "Hush! we won't mention their names, for so rare were they, so delicate, so fragile, and so altogether lovely, that even to mention their names might frighten them away."

According to young Merrill, "Muir was even more delightful out of doors." One day someone called his attention to an oak that was sapping the strength from a stand of grapevines near by. Muir contemplated first the vines and then the tree. Finally he said: "As a farmer I think I should be justified in removing this tree." But he never did. He cut down one of his favorite eucalyptus trees, however, because it shaded his sister Maggie's flower garden, often making it too damp and cold for her to walk there.[28]

Samuel's mother had sent him west to attend Stanford University in the fall. When the term was about to begin, he told his host he would be leaving soon. "Well, Sam," drawled Muir, "it won't do you any harm, I guess. But I'd like to have you stay here." In later years he regretted he had not done so. To be with Muir, to talk with him daily, to see through his eyes the world about him, he felt would have been a far more valuable training than any university could give him.[29]

It must not be supposed from Samuel Merrill's and other accounts of home life in the Big House that John Muir always radiated sweetness and light. "Uncle John was not an easy man to live with," said his niece, May Reid Coleman. "But Aunt Louie knew how to keep everything harmonious." Fundamentally sweet and lovable as she knew he was, she accepted his dour moods and tensions as necessary accompaniments of his Scotch background, his genius, and his work. And her study was to soften them and make them bearable to himself and the family.

Piano-playing was a rock upon which their marriage might have split had she been less wise and selfless. She was an accomplished musician, while to him the very sound of the instrument was a species of torture. This harked back to his winters with the Swett family, when he had to struggle to concentrate and write against four or five hours of daily piano practice in the room below him.[30] This did something to his nerves that he never got over. Louie, finding this out early in their married life, solved the problem simply by keeping her Steinway closed when he was at home.

A few years later, when Helen and Wanda wanted to take piano and violin lessons, she met that problem too, and kept everybody happy by having a sound-proof, brick-walled practice room built on the west end of the house, far from their father's study.

Muir did his writing at a painfully high tension and was easily distracted by any sound. Therefore his wife and the girls, jealously guarding his need for quiet, walked softly and spoke in hushed voices while an article or a book was a-borning. For well they knew that when it was finished and dispatched to the publisher, he would return to them, his old-time boyish, loving self, ready for fun and companionship. He and the girls would then romp over the hills, shouting and laughing, and, as Wanda has said: "Father the biggest, jolliest child of us all!"

Muir had always wanted sons, but in his daughters he found a fine comradeship. Like himself they were eager for every adventure, whether on the hills at home [31] or on mountain rambles taken with the Sierra Club. Helen, the Gael, had his aliveness, his vivid, outgoing spirit and imagination that disregarded the bounds of flesh. Wanda, on the other hand, more sedate, more reserved, had the calm Saxon strength and quietude of Muir's mother and her own. She was the rock upon whom the whole family leaned in times of illness. Thus as living projections of the two components of his own race, they responded to Muir's varying needs and phases, complementing each other and himself into a threefold unity.

As the year 1893 dawned, the future of conservation appeared bright. Grover Cleveland, the President-elect, had assured Robert Underwood Johnson that he would support the cause. Hoke Smith of Georgia, slated for the Cabinet as Secretary of the Interior, also favored it. Moreover, on February 14, 1893, before President Harrison went out of office, he availed himself of the Enabling Act of 1891 to set aside by proclamation more than 13,000,000 acres of watershed land as forest reserves. The most important of these for California was the Sierra Forest Reserve, comprising more than 4,000,000 acres, and extending from the southern boundary of Yosemite National Park to the latitude of Bakersfield.

However, since Congress made no provisions to patrol the reservations with Army personnel, they long continued to be battlegrounds between the Federal Government and the predatory stockmen and lumbermen. In the Sierra Forest Reserve alone, 500,000 sheep continued to be pastured annually in defiance of law, skinning the earth of the fine meadows and forest cover.

In these years of freedom from ranch toil Muir resumed his old close association with William Keith and his circle of illuminati. Keith often came to the ranch, where he and Muir held high revelry with Wanda and Helen. Those who took part or looked on never forgot the pranks and games they played. From the time

Helen was a tiny child, she was "the Mamma" to those two lively lads, Willie and Johnnie. This game was kept up until Helen herself was grown up.[32]

Muir frequently appeared at his friend's "rather dingy but glorious studio" on Montgomery street. Here he met other choice spirits who made it a Mecca. Such as Charles Fletcher Lummis, a California writer "with the bark on"; "that blithe old beaver,"[33] Edward Robeson Taylor, sonneteer and one-time Mayor of San Francisco; and Charles Keeler, the tall, radiant-eyed young poet of Berkeley. "Charlie Keeler looks like a bird," said Keith, appropriately enough since he was also an ornithologist.

Before the session was over, the tall, slender, priestly figure of Dr. Joseph Worcester, Swedenborgian clergyman, would slip shyly but impressively in at the door. The tempestuous Keith had long found a haven in this man's tranquillity, and the somber mysticism of his mature art has been ascribed to the Worcester influence. Keith once said: "My only chance of getting into heaven is by holding on to Worcester's coat tails." Leaving the objective realism of the Muir-Keith period behind him, he had become engrossed in weaving spiritual meanings into his landscapes. Every picture became a visible prayer.

Keeler tells of his first meeting with Muir at the studio:

. . . there entered a lean, bewhiskered farmer. His grizzled beard was rather untrimmed, his hair . . . long and ragged, his face . . . wrinkled and weather-beaten, his gray clothes rather rustic. . . .

"Why, Johnnie!" exclaimed Keith, and the visitor saluted him in quizzical mood. . . . And then I was introduced to John Muir. . . . Soon he and Mr. Keith had started a regular set-to of Scotch banter. . . .

As Keith would show a moonlight scene—an oak grove—Muir would exclaim, "You've got that upside down, Willie!" And Keith would look with a half-resigned, half-disgusted air, and try another. Presently Muir's eyes would fall upon some old, hard mountain scene in which every rock was delineated, and say, "Now, there's a pretty good one, Willie." To which Keith would retort: "Humph! You don't know what a picture is, Johnnie!"[34]

Many such stories, still extant, lend color to the firmly rooted legend that Muir and Keith were at loggerheads in matters of art. But in view of several serious tributes[35] paid to Keith by Muir during this period and later, it seems probable that much of his criticism was sheer banter. Of their heated arguments Keith once said: "Muir is Scotch, and I'm Scotch, and so we always quarrel." Much of their quarreling was grandstand play for the benefit of listeners.

The nub of Muir's real criticism of Keith's subjective, synthetic landscapes appears to have lain in the fact that the artist sometimes ignored the logic of geology. Into a mountain scene with a sweep of his brush he would put a glacier where no glacier could possibly have been; or a river where the topography did not warrant it. To Muir, Saxon and scientist, law and order were fundamental in the universe. Beauty divorced from truth became a discord, an ugly blot.

For ten years Muir and Keith had talked of seeing Europe together. One day in May 1893 Keith sent his friend a telegram saying: "I can't wait any longer. I'm starting tomorrow." Muir, taken by surprise, sent word he'd be ready in a day or two. When he arrived in San Francisco, Keith had gone, leaving a message that he would meet Muir in Chicago. In that city he found a scribbled note: "Couldn't stand the crowd. Will wait in New York." After visiting the World's Fair briefly, and finding it "a cosmopolitan rat's nest," Muir hastened on to New York, only to find his fellow Scot being whirled from one reception to another, staged for him by the elite of society and the art world.

Muir settled down in an obscure hotel to wait for Keith and finish some articles he had brought along. But Robert Underwood Johnson had other plans. Whisking him bag and baggage over to the Players' Club, he began to introduce him to celebrities. There ensued such a succession of luncheons and champagne dinners given in his honor as Muir had never experienced in his life. "I had no idea I was so well known, considering how little I have written," he naïvely told the home folks.

On a blazingly hot day Johnson took him for a cool trip up the Hudson to Castle Rock, the beautiful country home of Henry

Fairfield Osborn, the paleontologist. Thus began one of the closest friendships of his life, with the Osborn family.

Then came visits to Boston, Cambridge, and Concord. In the last-named place he and Johnson tramped about among the homes, haunts, and graves of Emerson and Thoreau. They walked to Walden Pond, where "the blessed crank and tramp" had kept his rendezvous with wild nature and worked out his own "experiment."

On another day they went to Brookline to visit Charles S. Sargent, the Harvard botanist. Here Muir was entertained at dinners formal and informal. For years he had been telling the story of Stickeen, the little Alaskan dog, to children and friends in the West. He had told it to Johnson beside a Yosemite campfire. Now at Johnson's insistence he told it at one of those dinners. After that it was clamored for at every succeeding dinner. "It is curious to see how eagerly the liveried servants listen behind screens, half-closed doors, etc.," Muir wrote home.

He returned to New York "crowded and overladen with enjoyments," to be dined and wined by Dana of the New York *Sun,* who was equally charmed with the Stickeen story. At other affairs he met Mark Twain, Thomas Bailey Aldrich, Charles Dudley Warner, Rudyard Kipling, George W. Cable, and Nicola Tesla. On one occasion he was feasted "in grand style" by Mr. James Pinchot of Gramercy Park, "whose son is studying forestry." He counseled that son in his nature rambles "to go alone, to seek solitude . . . to take plenty of time about getting rich." He seems to have had a strange, prophetic intuition of Gifford Pinchot's ambition — an ambition which was to split the conservation movement into two schools.

Muir took all these social affairs in his stride. Even the food agreed with him. "Last night another champagne supper, and another tonight. But my stomach . . . behaves like a gentleman." As to his own behavior, Johnson says: "Muir bore himself with dignity in every company, readily adjusting himself to any environment." [36]

On a June day he met John Burroughs for the first time. The occasion was not auspicious. Ill from a Whitman dinner the night before, Burroughs was irritable and, according to Muir, "gave no sign of his fine qualities." The course of the Muir-Burroughs friendship never did run smooth. They liked each other best when the continent stretched between them.

Meanwhile Keith and his wife were in a hurry to get off to Europe. They sailed on June 3, leaving Muir to finish his articles and explore the social wildernesses of New York and Boston for another three weeks. There was a tentative plan to meet in London or Paris. But they didn't. Perhaps it was just as well. "Muir is an awful cross fellow to travel with," Keith once said. And Keith, from all accounts, was no lamb. Moreover, an itinerary including both art galleries and glaciers did not augur well for harmony.

After being further wined and dined and "treated like a king" — which, as a novelty, rather tickled the erstwhile Faun, who now viewed society with amused tolerance — Muir sailed on the 26th for Liverpool.

Edinburgh was his first objective. Here he called upon David Douglas, the famous publisher, and they talked all night — "the most wonderful night as far as humanity is concerned I ever had in this world." The next day he traveled to Dunbar, "my own old town." He went at once to the Lorne Temperance Hotel, which had once been his boyhood home, "if for nothing else than to take a look at the dormer window I climbed in my nightgown." The following ten days he spent with his cousin Margaret Hay Lunam and her daughter Maggie. With them or alone he rambled over the old red town and countryside, so full of memories. But always he came back to the rock-bound shore where, as he wrote to Wanda, "The waves made . . . grand songs, the same old songs they sang to me in my childhood, and I seemed a boy again."

On July 20 he was at Trondheim, Norway, and from there sailed down the coast, penetrating the great glacial fiords and yosemites of Hardinger, Romsdale, and Naerdale. Now and then he explored on foot the high walls and hinterlands beyond.

In early August he rode into the English Lake District, Wordsworth's homeland. Traveling by charabanc up the winding, gemlike valleys from Windermere, he reveled in the noble landscape — the lakes and islands and "glacial curving shores, fringed by charming woods . . . mountains and hills green and bosky all around." At Grasmere he visited the ancient Saxon church and spent some hours in the quiet, yew-shaded graveyard where the poet lies beside the tranquil Rothay. "A robin came and sang on the maple as I stood with damp eyes and a lump in my throat. What a pity it is that Wordsworth, with his fine feeling for nature, died without knowledge of the glacial gospel." [37]

A week later he was in London — "a huge and lonely wilderness." Armed with a letter of introduction to the Right Honorable James Bryce, he went to the House of Commons. As he was about to enter the historic chamber, a uniformed flunkey barred his way and waved him off haughtily toward an anteroom. Muir, resentful of his condescending manner, said he had "no time to wait for Lords or anyone else," and strode out of the building.

When the House arose a few minutes later, his card was presented to Mr. Bryce. That statesman, who had been wishing for years to meet the American naturalist, delightedly told those about him that John Muir was outside. It is said there was a concerted rush to find him. But he was gone, and Bryce did not meet him until some years later.[38]

Muir next went to Switzerland, where he stopped at Grindelwald and Interlaken to revel in grand views of the Jungfrau. With true Scotch thrift he did not stay at fashionable hotels, although he walked in their gardens and enjoyed their fountains. "I get the best of such places," he said, "from the outside and *at no cash cost.*"

Ascending the valley of the Rhone to Zermatt, he was tempted to climb the Matterhorn, "a huge savage pyramid . . . piercing the heavens in lonely serene majesty." But compromising upon Gornergrat, he started out astride a mule, "the most stubborn of his race." Tiring of such slow progress, he dismounted and continued on foot.

Two days later he stood at the foot of Mount Blanc, and the mountain royal in its white robes seemed "as near-looking as Mts. Helen and Wanda at our home." [39] Again he was tempted to climb, but his feet, always tender since he had frozen them on Shasta twenty years before, were blistered and wholly unfit after

Gornergrat. "It was hard to hold my legs back, sick or well, old or young," he wrote home.

Returning to Geneva, he made a pilgrimage to Neuchâtel to visit the haunts of Agassiz. Thence he crossed the Jura Mountains through a network of wild limestone gorges and tunnels. From Zürich, "the most beautiful . . . of all the towns of Switzerland," he cut across the country and over the mountains to Lake Como in Italy. He took a steamer trip on the pale green-blue waters, "hemmed in by lofty sharp glaciated mountains. . . . The depth is governed by the down-thrust of many small glaciers. . . . Not a single glacier is visible now from the lake . . . once there were hundreds."

But even in the midst of the sublime scenery his all-seeing eyes scanned people. He observed the "exquisite taste" with which the French and Italian women dressed: "There on the boat sits a lady . . . dressed in mellow cream silk with white embroidery and bits of jet black to match her eyes — perfectly harmonious in color, folds and proportions as any lily. . . ."

Everywhere he was charmed with "the queer mugginses of black-eyed boys and girls." He wanted to talk with them, but they couldn't understand him. French seemed to be a universal language — but not his brand of it. Since boyhood he had read it with facility, but his accent was, as he said, "horrible." "My what a mess I make of it!" he wrote to Wanda. "Even the dogs don't understand it as I speak it, and refuse to wag their tails to my 'Bon chien, bon chien.'"

Arriving once more in London, Muir went out to Kew Gardens to visit his old friend Sir Joseph Hooker, with whom he spent several happy days at the Hooker country home, Sunningdale. Sir Joseph and Lady Hooker also took him to see the sights of London. With them he visited Westminster Abbey. "Heavens what a place!" he wrote Helen. "A grand church full of curious-looking, old-fashioned people made out of stone." The Tower of London he dismissed as "a huge grim old castle full of guns and swords and shields and armor and a thousand queer things that I have no room to write about." Again he went to the Parliament Buildings — this time with Sir Joseph. The Speaker of the House of Commons received them with ceremony, and himself conducted them through the historic pile. One can't help hoping they were seen by the pompous flunkey who had treated Muir with such disdain.

Ever since his visit to Scotland he had dreamed of tramping the Highlands and sleeping on the heather-clad hills. So after a brief sojourn at the Lakes of Killarney in Ireland, he traveled north once more, this time to the town of Thurso on the topmost corner of land jutting into the North Sea. Returning thence he sailed along the Inverness Firth and diagonally down through a chain of lochs to the western coast, thus passing near the home of his ancestral clan. Whether he camped out and slept on the heather — now in glorious purple bloom — is not recorded. But he wrote charming descriptions of it to his girls.

Arriving in Edinburgh he again visited David Douglas. In one of their talks he told him of his adventure with Stickeen. And the publisher and friend of John Brown, who had officiated at the birth of that other great dog story, *Rab and His Friends*, urged Muir in a letter that followed him home: "Do give it to the world."

While in the city Muir ordered a new suit of good Scotch wool, and while trying it on between the mirrors in his room, discovered a round bald spot on the back of his head. Naïvely unconscious that his womenfolk with sharp eyes must have espied it long before and tactfully said nothing, he sat down and wrote a humorous doggerel poem about "The Bald-Headed Scotchman," which he sent home to break the news.

Before leaving Scotland he stopped in Dunbar once more. Here he noted with sadness the perennial wretchedness of the poor. Old people and wan-faced children still roamed the streets and country lanes. He could not forget them, and just before Christmas, after his return home, he sent his cousin a draft for fifty dollars to divide equally between some need of her own, and "the poor of Dunbar." Within a year or two he increased this gift to one hundred dollars, an annual contribution he kept up for twenty-one years — to the last month of his life.

When he landed in New York, he found a telegram from his wife, who in his absence had kept in close touch with conservation affairs. She urged him to go to Washington to talk with the new Secretary of the Interior, Hoke Smith. Following her advice, he spent some days in the national capital, "industriously interviewing everybody . . . likely to be influential in Yosemite and forest affairs — Edward Bowers, Hoke Smith, Farnow, and Senator Perkins."

Doubtless these interviews had much to do with the marked advance of the cause during the Cleveland administration.

John Muir came home with an appointed task — to prepare for publication by the Century Company his first book, *The Mountains of California.* It would consist of articles written over a period of years, including his revised essays on the ouzel, the Douglas squirrel, the Yuba storm, and the sequoias.

Johnson, the experienced editor, was of much help to him in reshaping his material. He advised the elimination of adjectives such as "grand and glorious, used too often for proper effect." This and other counsel Muir took in good part, and proceeded to "slaughter" superfluous words and tone down his tendency to rhapsody. Moreover, as he matured, his manuscripts increasingly reveal the substitution of the word "Nature" or "Beauty" for "God" and "the Lord." Indeed, to him they appear to have been synonymous. He had Wordsworth's pantheistic "sense of animating life in Nature, the dim impersonal personality creating and informing all things." In a journal he wrote: "The pines spiring around me higher, higher to the star-flowered sky, are plainly full of God. God in them. They in God. . . . Oh, the infinite abundance and universality of Beauty. Beauty is God. What shall we say of God, that we may not say of Beauty!"

In matters of style Muir looked mainly to his wife for criticism. Her literary taste was good, and he relied upon her to such a degree that he published nothing until it met with her approval. Unlike John Burroughs, who wrote only when the mood was upon him, Muir wrote daily. He rose early, prepared his coffee and eggs, left ready for him by the cook, then worked at his desk until ten, when he joined the family at breakfast. After this meal he read to his wife his morning's output, often making the changes she suggested. Then he worked until lunch, and again later in the day until dinner.

The Mountains of California, published in 1894, met with immediate and far-reaching success. It rallied and solidified the conservation sentiment of the entire nation, leading directly to a new upsurge of determination to preserve the forests.

It also aroused the opposition, and during the nineties the care and protection of the forest reserves became an increasingly sore problem. Moreover, the timber and mining syndicates kept their own men in Washington as lobbyists or officials in the General Land Office, ready to give advance notice whenever new reservations were contemplated. Immediately there was a rush to establish claims by fake entries. Janitors, barbers, stenographers, and whole crews from visiting ships were sent out, sometimes in lots of fifty or more, to take up land already selected. In due time the tracts thus appropriated were turned over to the corporations employing the claimants, and the land thus acquired was exchanged under the Lieu Land Act for equal tracts of timberland, still unreserved. These rackets became so flagrant that the conservationists saw the need of establishing a strong Government policy.

About this time Gifford Pinchot, trained in the forestry schools of Prussia, had come into prominence in the East for his excellent work with Sargent and Johnson in checking lumbering invasions in the Adirondacks. Having a common desire to save the watershed forests of America, the three men formulated a plan to have a National Forestry Commission appointed to survey the timber reserves of the country, recommend the creation of new reserves, and submit a permanent policy for governing them. Because of Congressional opposition to this, Secretary Hoke Smith in 1896 asked the President of the National Academy of Sciences, as legal adviser to the Government in matters of science, to select such a commission to do the work without salaries. The Commission thus appointed consisted of six members, with Charles S. Sargent as chairman. The others named were General Henry L. Abbot, Professor William H. Brewer, Alexander Agassiz, Arnold Hague, and

Gifford Pinchot. Muir by his own choice was not a member, preferring to be a free lance and adviser. He was urged to join the Commission at Chicago in July and travel with them. Moreover, he had been invited to attend the Harvard commencement in June, to receive an honorary A.M. degree. But being desperately weary, he decided not to take the Eastern trip. As for the Commission jaunt, he would join that on the Pacific coast.

On a June morning, as he was working in his study, a strong premonition was borne in upon him, telling him to go east at once if he would see his mother alive. He had no reason to believe she was ill, but recalling how true had been the summons that called him to his father's death-bed, he took the next train for Wisconsin. On the way he sent telegrams to Dr. Dan at Lincoln, and to Mary at Kearney, Nebraska, telling them to join him on the trip to Portage. Mary, not realizing the urgency and making no plans to leave home, came bareheaded to the station with her husband, Willis Hand, and her little daughter Helen. Muir, standing on the car platform, jumped off before the train stopped, grabbed his sister and her child, and hauled them up the steps and into the car, explaining that they must go at once to see Mother.[40] When the train rolled into Lincoln, Dan was there to meet them, but cynical, as usual, of "hunches," refused to go. If Mother were ill, he said, he would have been the first to be told.

Arrived at Portage, the three walked to the house on Howard Street. Muir entered the yard a little in advance of the others. Sarah, looking out of the front window, suddenly cried out: "Why, there's John!" And rushing out, she exclaimed: "Oh, John, surely God has sent you. Mother is terribly ill!" She was indeed. Taken suddenly a few hours before with an attack of indigestion and heart weakness, she was now apparently sinking into a coma.

Soon they were all gathered about her, Sarah saying: "Mother, John and Mary are here. Wake up and speak to them!" And the old woman, rousing herself out of the mortal fog already enveloping her, murmured happily: "My ain bairns, my ain bairns!"

She began to revive at once, and by nightfall was much improved. The next morning she could sit up. The doctor pronounced her well on the road to recovery. But John, taking no chances, telegraphed Dan the money for his train fare, telling him Mother needed his care.

As the days passed, she continued to gain, and they all had a jolly time together. John poured out his bag of Scotch yarns, and the girls said Mother hadn't laughed so much since he left home in his youth. Dan arrived, adding to her joy and comfort. Six of her children — for Joanna now lived in Portage — she had about her.

More than a week went by, and since she was apparently out of danger, Muir remembered the Harvard commencement on June 24. Both Dan and the Portage doctor thought it safe for him to leave, so he went, leaving addresses where they could reach him by telegram, should she have a relapse. On the 23rd a telegram came to him in New York saying Mother had died in her sleep. Sending back word that he would be there for the funeral, he went on to Cambridge, received his degree, then took the next train for Portage.

When he arrived, they told him of her last conscious hours. Still seemingly holding her gains, and with faculties undimmed, she had suddenly seen her husband. "It's dawn, Father," she cried out. "Now I see you all!" With that she sank into what appeared to be a natural sleep of weariness that deepened into the sleep of death.[41]

Early in July Muir joined the Forestry Commission in Chicago, and with Sargent, Brewer, Hague, and Abbot proceeded to South Dakota to inspect the Black Hills forests of yellow pine. Muir, looking upon the hills denuded by mining operations, fires, and illegal cutting, wrote home: "Wherever the white man goes, the groves vanish." In Wyoming on the Big Horn Mountains they found many of the watershed forests, so essential to irrigation east and west, reduced to blackened stumps. Picking up Gifford Pinchot in Montana, they traveled over the Continental Divide, shrouded in smoke from fires set by the swarming prospectors. In the Priest River basin and on the Bitter Root Mountains they found widespread tree-cutting under the vicious misuse of the Timber and

WANDA *and* HELEN MUIR

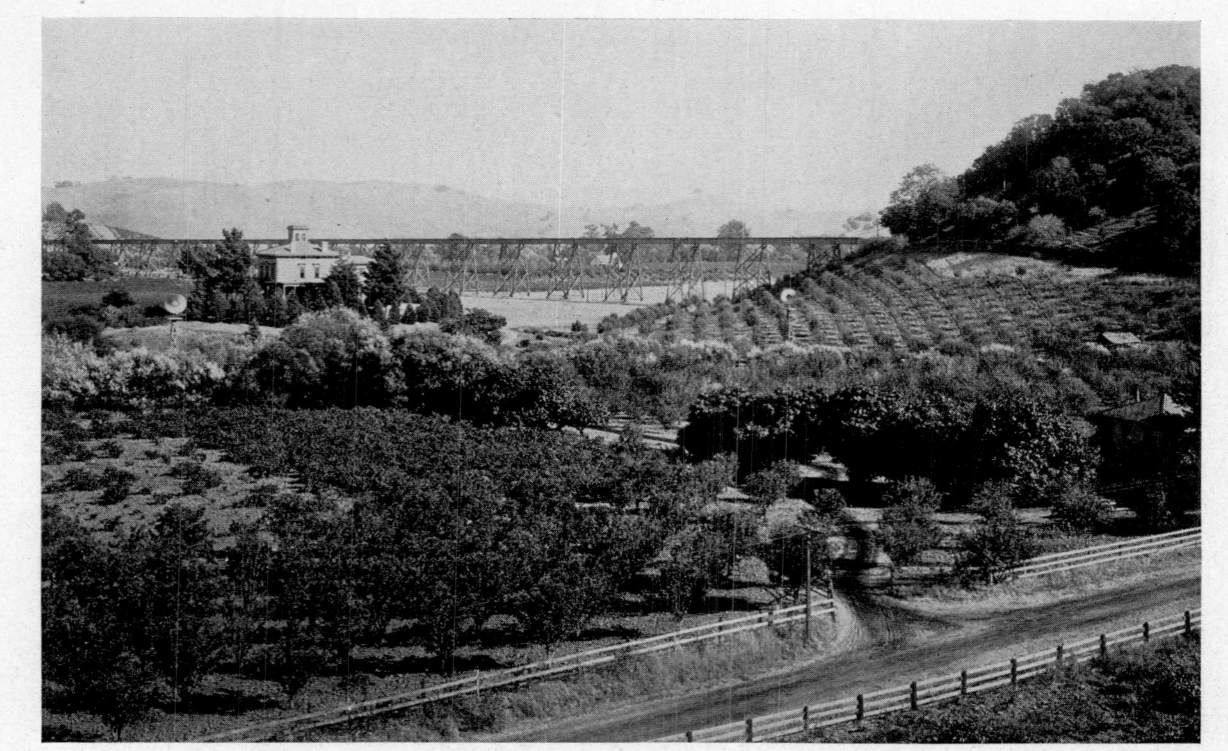

Lower end of the Muir-Strentzel ranch near Martinez, Cal.
The Big House on the knoll was built by Dr. Strentzel in 1881–2. *Lived in by John Muir and his*

Stone Act. The Northern Pacific Railroad, subsidized with a huge land grant stretching westward in a swath one hundred and twenty miles wide, not only had devastated its right of way, but had appropriated enormous bodies of timber north and south.

Similar conditions prevailed among the magnificent forests of western Washington and Oregon.[42] At Crater Lake they witnessed the terrible desolation caused by "hoofed locusts." So thoroughly had the sheep skinned the earth that later, after that region had been under Federal protection [43] for twenty-five years, few of the wild flora that once carpeted the ground had returned.

Proceeding down the coast into California, they passed through cut and burned forests everywhere. Among the redwoods back of Crescent City and Trinidad and in between they found "the work of ruin going on" and huge tracts reduced to "a desolate rugged expanse of black stumps." Making a canvass of the forests of Humboldt and Mendocino Counties, they discovered that not a single section of this valuable timber belt still belonged to the Government. Lumber syndicates had taken it all, in large part by fraudulent means.

After a long course of zigzag surveys of California forested lands and reserves denuded by fire, sheep, and lumbering, the Commission came to the Grand Canyon in Arizona. Although made a reserve by President Harrison, the environing forests were being destroyed, and mines were located within the canyon itself.

When Chairman Sargent got home after investigating the forests of Colorado, he assembled into a Report the Commission's findings and recommendations worked out in many a campfire talk. Rough drafts were sent to Muir for "ideas and inspiration." One instance of Muir's influence had to do with the proposed Stanislaus Forest Reserve. David Starr Jordan and others had urged the creation of this reserve. But it was only after Muir had given his approval that it was added to the list.

In the preparation of the Report a fundamental schism of ideas among the commissioners, began to show itself. Muir, Sargent, and Abbot favored Army guardianship of the reserves, as being more efficient and free from shifting politics; whereas, Gifford Pinchot, wedded to the civilian-guard system of Germany, violently opposed them. Finally for the sake of harmony a compromise was made. Hence the Report recommended military control only until a duly authorized and organized Forest Bureau could be established with officers and subordinates adequately trained to man the reserves, and subject to civil-service regulations.

In February 1897, just before the end of the Cleveland administration, a preliminary copy of the Forestry Commission Report was sent to the President. In essence it recommended:

1. *The creation of thirteen new reservations distributed among eight Western states.*
2. *The repeal or modification of timber and mining laws leading to fraud and robbery.*
3. *The scientific management of forests to maintain a permanent timber supply.*
4. *The creation of two new national parks: the Grand Canyon and Mount Rainier, with adjacent areas.*[44]

President Cleveland, impressed with the logic of this document, celebrated the 165th birthday of George Washington by issuing an Executive Order setting aside the recommended thirteen reservations, totaling more than 21,000,000 acres.

Immediately the lumber, stock, and mining syndicates of the West flew into a mighty rage. Wires sizzled with telegrams. Congress was bombarded with screaming "memorials."

The "Cowboy Senators," hearing from their masters, assembled in hysterical turmoil to undo this "outrage." Wildly they bleated that the whole idea was promoted by "a few zealots, Harvard professors, sentimentalists and impractical dreamers." With like invectives — and many worse — they struggled for two days (including Sunday) to impeach the outgoing President. Failing in this, the Senate passed a rider to the Sundry Civil Bill to annul the Cleveland reservations. But the President, hearing of the rider, declared he would veto the bill if it contained it. So March 4 dawned with no solution, and Congress was automatically adjourned.

Up to this time the *Century* was the only popular periodical working for conservation. But now others joined in the fray.

Walter Hines Page of the *Atlantic Monthly* consulted Sargent as to the best writers. "There is but one man in the United States who can do it justice," declared Sargent, "and his name is John Muir!" Immediately Page was hot on Muir's trail for a series of articles,[45] and the naturalist, putting aside all other work, wrote the first of these, "The American Forests."

The outlook for the Cleveland reserves was black. Cornelius N. Bliss, the new Secretary of the Interior, a deep-dyed politician from New York, held back from public knowledge the Forestry Commission report. In May Congress, called in special session, voted to suspend the Executive Order until March 1, 1898. Then Secretary Bliss opened the reserves to "settlement." A stampede ensued to file claims upon the land. To most of the conservationists the cause seemed lost. But John Muir rallied them to battle once more. To R. U. Johnson he wrote: "Those western corporations with their shady millions seem invincible in the Senate. *But the fight must go on!*"

Muir's "American Forests," appearing in the August *Atlantic*, was doubtless his supreme appeal for the saving of the trees. He performed the remarkable feat of sublimating a Government document (the Forestry Report) into literature. In doing this he went over the heads of Congressmen and struck home to the vital needs and rights of the common people. In the beginning he gave a poetic but historically accurate description of the great primeval forests that had once covered much of America.

"But when the steel axe of the white man rang out on the startled air their doom was sealed. Every tree heard the bodeful sound, and pillars of smoke gave a sign in the sky."

With the deep smoldering anger of a lifetime he went on to write the saga of ruthless tree-slaughter at the hands of the God-worshipping pioneers, continuing down to the present. "Every other civilized nation in the world," he declared, "has been compelled to care for its forests." Our Government, on the other hand, "like a rich and foolish spendthrift," has allowed its heritage "to be sold and plundered and wasted at will."

Muir brought his impassioned plea to a climax in this memorable passage:

"Any fool can destroy trees. They cannot run away; and if they could, they would still be destroyed, — chased and hunted down as long as fun or a dollar could be got out of their bark hides, branching horns, or magnificent bole backbones. . . . Through all the wonderful, eventful centuries since Christ's time — and long before that — God has cared for these trees . . . but he cannot save them from fools, — only Uncle Sam can do that."

Early in August 1897 Muir, together with Sargent and William M. Canby, a botanist of Wilmington, Delaware, were en route to Alaska for a brief holiday. At Victoria they were caught in the surging human river streaming north to the Klondike gold mines. "Not a cool head in the lot," commented Muir. "Gold is the supreme medicine for inaction, but many will be killed in the curing."

At Port Townsend he received a telegram from the Hearst interests, asking him to report the Gold Rush for their papers. His first impulse was to refuse. "Do they think I'm daft like a' the lave o' thae puir bodies?" [46] he exclaimed. Then he reflected that he might be able to slow down this mob of feverish, ill-prepared go-getters by portraying the conditions they would have to meet. So he wired his acceptance. In his articles [47] he declared his purpose was "To calm rather than inflame the present excitement. Be patient and bide your right time. . . . Nearly all the gold of Alaska is still in the ground, and centuries upon centuries of mining will not exhaust it."

Rain was descending in floods when they arrived at Juneau. "New mills on Douglas island. One half million from Treadwell alone per year. $10,000,000 from this one mine. . . ." Muir might have shared in all this. "I camped one night on Douglas island, and noticing the quartz there and on the mainland, across the channel, I said . . . 'If I were hunting gold, I would stop here.' Next summer the Silver Bow and Douglas island mines were discovered near our campground."

At Skagway Muir and his companions got off the boat and walked along the wild, roaring river in the midst of the "grand, splattering, jostling, floundering onrush" of men and pack animals to the foot of the muddy trail that led over White Pass into the Yukon. Everybody was struggling to be first. But only a few "hardy, bespattered pioneers" in the van wallowed through. The others bogged down into hidden holes among the rocks. Pack mules broke their legs and had to be shot, forcing their owners to throw away provisions and tools and scramble on with what they could carry on their backs. "A wild discouraging mess" it was that the calm trees looked down upon from the heights above. After all their toil and trouble what would these poor, soft, bewildered folk find when they got to the Yukon? "All the best ground taken up, every auriferous inch of it — by the smart miners who threw down their picks on all the streams . . . and rushed up there before the crowd could get there." So Muir repeated his warning: "Go slow, count the cost. . . . No reason for killing, pell-mell haste. . . . Be willing to spend ten years to make a showing. Not just one year!"

Stopping in a Seattle hotel on the way home, Muir read in a morning paper that Gifford Pinchot, then in the city, had given out a statement that sheep grazing in the reserves did little if any harm. Now, it happened that the most potent politicians of the state were either sheep and cattle men, or closely allied with live-stock corporations. So along came Mr. Pinchot with his little appeasement policy!

This struck Muir like a blow in the face. Not only did it shake his faith in a man he had trusted, but to his mind it augured ill for conservation, since Pinchot, recently appointed by Cornelius Bliss as Special Forestry Agent, was here to make a survey of the commercial resources of the suspended Cleveland reserves.

During the morning Muir saw Pinchot in the hotel lobby, standing a bit apart from a group of men who — unbeknown to Muir — were newspaper reporters. According to William E. Colby, to whom he related the incident, Muir went up to Pinchot and, thrusting the printed page before him, demanded:

"Are you correctly quoted here?"

Pinchot, caught between two fires, had to admit that he was.

"Then," said Muir, his eyes flashing blue flames, "if that is the case, I don't want anything more to do with you. When we were in the Cascades last summer, you yourself stated that the sheep did a great deal of harm."

Thus the rift opened that swiftly widened between the two schools of conservationists — the strictly utilitarian, commercial group who followed Pinchot, and the æsthetic-utilitarian group who followed Muir — a rift that was to manifest itself deplorably in long years of antagonism between two Government bureaus.

Muir came home in September to find Mrs. Strentzel rapidly failing. She died two weeks later. He was sorely stricken, for he loved her as a son. Now that his friends and dear ones were falling away, he no longer theorized about death as a beautiful phase of life. "This death, disease and pain business of our nature is horrible amid the joy and harmony of our blessed world, and we can only hope and trust that there is a still better world beyond this."[48]

"One life at a time," said the dying Thoreau. "One life at a time" had been Muir's earlier philosophy. In the mountains he had been content with each "big immortal day." Any man who asked for more was "hoggish," he said. It held for him the quality of eternity, and compensated for the loss of an improbable heaven beyond. Only in rare moments of exaltation did he feel a certainty of personal survival; as when in 1872 he had written in his journal: "In full moon, all the horizon is lettered and lifed. I want immortality to read this terrestrial language. This good and tough mountain-climbing flesh is not my final home, and I'll creep out of it and fly free and grow."[49]

But now that the swift years were bearing him on toward old age, he began to hope for a life after this. Keith with his Gaelic other-worldliness, and Charles Keeler with his probings in psychic research, may have had some influence in breaking down old prejudices. He collected articles by Sir Oliver Lodge and Sir Alfred Russel Wallace, pasting some of them into his scrapbook. When Keeler was entertaining in Berkeley the famed psychic researcher Dr. James Hyslop, Muir wrote to him: "I see . . . you . . . are now with a wise man from the east enjoying an outing in ghostland — a good country we are all trying to see and know." [50]

Finally into his paper "Mysterious Things," written in old age, he put this statement: ". . . at the bottom of what is called spiritualism, and what the Scotch call second sight, clairvoyance, telepathy, etcetera, there is . . . a basis of truth, founded on natural laws, which perhaps some day we may discover."

Muir's second *Atlantic* article, "Wild Parks and Forest Reservations of the West," published in January 1898, boldly attacked Pinchot's purely utilitarian concept of conservation. This article was read as avidly as the first. According to Editor Page it increased the *Atlantic* circulation "enormously." Muir's was the authentic voice of conservation, speaking high above the babel of tongues, clearing the public mind of commercial propaganda.

On March 1, 1898 the term of suspension of the Cleveland reserves expired. The Senate passed an amendment to the Sundry Civil Bill to abolish them altogether. But by this time public sentiment in favor of forest preservation, was overwhelming. Therefore the House, more nearly reflecting the will of the people, firmly opposed the Senate amendment. It failed by a vote of 100 to 39!

September 1898 found Muir with his friends Sargent and Canby driving through the hills of North Carolina and Tennessee. For many months he had been ill with grippe and a bronchial cough, but as he reveled in the autumn forests of mountain ash, scarlet oak, beech, and sassafras, he again felt the wine of new life in his veins. "I think I could walk ten miles and not be tired," he wrote to his wife. "The air has healed me." In his zest he persuaded his companions to climb Grandfather Mountain. They trudged up slope after slope, Muir impatiently leading the way. When they reached the bald top, he fell into poetic raptures over the view, while Sargent stood aloof clothed in his "frosty, inherited dignity."

I couldn't hold in, and began to jump about and sing and glory in it all. Then I happened to look around and catch sight of Sargent, standing there as cool as a rock, with a half-amused look on his face at me, but never saying a word.

"Why don't you let yourself out at a sight like that?" I asked.

"I don't wear my heart upon my sleeve," he retorted.

"Who cares where you wear your little heart, mon," I cried. "There you stand in the face of all Heaven come down to earth, like a critic of the universe, as if to say, 'Come, Nature, bring on the best you have. I'm from BOSTON!' "[51]

Five days later they were in Knoxville, and for the first time struck the familiar route of Muir in 1868. He found the whole land still prostrate from the Civil War — the same abandoned farms, worn-out tobacco lands, the earth gutted by water erosion, large areas of forest killed by fire. Little had been done by the prosperous industrial North to rehabilitate the defeated South.

Sargent's sudden illness brought them back to Boston, and while he recuperated, Muir journeyed up into Canada to Montreal, Lake Champlain, and the St. Lawrence River. Returning, he briefly surveyed Maine and the Vermont mountains: "All the scenery . . . robed with glorious leaf colors . . . no one can half tell or even hint at it." On his way through New York he visited the Osborn family on the Hudson.

"What a charming home it is, in the hushed, tranquil woods," he wrote to his wife, "though so near huge Babylon New York." And to Helen he said: "I have the 'blue room' . . . and it has the daintiest linen and embroidery I ever saw. The bed is so soft and fine I like to lie awake to enjoy it. . . . A servant brings in a cup of coffee before I rise. This morning . . . a red squirrel looked in the window at me from a branch of a big tulip tree, and seemed to be saying . . . 'Oh, John Muir, camping, tramping tree-climbing scrambler! Churr, Churr! Why have you left us? Chip Churr, who would have thought it?' "[52]

John Muir was often wondering at himself in these latter years. He who had once heaped scorn upon "soft succulent people" who slept in downy beds had grown to like these and other civilized comforts.

In New York he received a letter from his wife, urging him to go to Washington: "It would be grand if you could preach of God's forests to President McKinley. It does seem to me to be your duty to go. Think of the beautiful woods being left with nothing mightier than Pinchot's *little plan* between them and destruction."

So with the recovered Sargent he went to Washington to interview all and sundry. Whether or not he preached to the President is not recorded. However, he went sightseeing. The Capitol he summed up as "fine grounds, acres of marble." The Congressional Library he described as "gaudy in fresco, but tomby, sepulchral in blue vivid marble outside and in, overdecorated." The Washington Monument he found "the finest of all the stone things hereabouts." But not until he reached the Zoo did he wax enthusiastic: "We saw lots of deer, buffalos, bears, birds. . . . But the queerest and funniest were the kangaroos and a lot of coons . . . sunning themselves in the forks of . . . a big dead tree."

Going on to Florida, he visited his old friends the Hodgson family [53] who had pulled him back from the gates of death so long ago.

Exceedingly homesick by this time, he soon headed toward California by the Southern route. Writing from New York some weeks before, he had told his wife he had "a rendezvous with a tree in Texas." But by the time he reached that state, trees were powerless to delay him. He did, however, have one more temptation. Lying on his bed in the Pullman at night, he raised the curtain and looked out upon a snowy range of mountains. "A noble view. I felt like jumping out of the window to go to them."

In late May 1899 John Muir traveled north with Charles Keeler to join the Harriman Expedition [54] at Portland on a steamer trip along the coast of Alaska. Walking about the streets while they awaited the arrival of the Harriman Special, they passed a men's clothing store. That reminded Muir he wanted to buy a pair of blue jeans. He urged Keeler to do likewise, saying he had always found them the toughest, most satisfactory clothes he could get for glacial work. "Prince Charlie," elegant and well tailored, didn't relish looking like a rustic among these Easterners in their fine sports togs; but so persuasive was Muir that they both went in and bought blue jeans.[55] In the weeks that followed, Keeler smartened his with a pair of high boots, but Muir as usual wore shoes, preferring them to boots since they gave freer play to the ankles.

Promptly at noon on the 30th the special arrived — "the most velvety and superb train I ever saw," said Muir. Out poured more than a score of eminent scientists invited by E. H. Harriman, the railroad magnate, to accompany the expedition. John Burroughs, white-bearded and benign, at once spied John Muir and, grabbing him "like a verra brither," began introducing him. Meeting his host and the charming, friendly Mrs. Harriman, Muir noted that the railroad king was an undersized, somewhat insignificant-looking man, with a cold, almost frigid manner. He felt "rather repelled" at first, but in a final analysis of their relations he said: "I at last learned to love him."

One hundred and twenty-six people were on board the *George W. Elder* when she raised anchor at Seattle and steamed northward. John Burroughs, historian of the expedition, in listing the sciences represented, took his first official jab at his fellow naturalist: "In John Muir we had an authority on glaciers, and a thorough one — so thorough that he would not allow the rest of the party to have an opinion on the subject." [56] From this remark one might surmise there was dynamite on board. However, says Muir: "I soon saw that Mr. Harriman was uncommon . . . scientific explorers are not easily managed . . . are rather inflammable and explosive, especially when compressed on a ship. Nevertheless he kept us all in smooth working order. . . ." [57]

Harriman, the canny manager of men, not only had equipped laboratories on board, but had also provided for informal intercourse, with a large social hall or saloon luxuriously furnished, and a smoking den which, from the first day out, was wreathed in a blue fog of choice tobacco exhalations.

In the midst of this shipboard community, influencing the life about them like climate, was the Harriman family — father, mother, three jolly daughters, Mary, Cornelia, and Carol, and two sons, Roland and Averell — the same Averell Harriman who in 1943 would be appointed Ambassador to Soviet Russia. Among their guests were Mrs. Harriman's brother, W. H. Averell, his wife and daughter, Elizabeth, and Miss Dorothea Draper. Before long Muir had dubbed Mary, Cornelia, Elizabeth, and Dorothea "the Big Four," telling them at the same time of his "Big Two" at home. The small fry—Carol and Roland—he named "the Little Two." His prejudice against the patron himself melted away when he saw the president of the Union Pacific playing on deck with his children, "keeping trot-step with little Roland while helping him to drag a toy canoe . . . with a cotton string."

As they steamed along the inland passage past a majestic panorama of towering mountains clothed in glaciers which Burroughs called "Muir's Mountain Sheep," the scientists were given to understand they could chart their own courses and would be afforded every opportunity for research. For instance, Dr. William Ritter of the University of California, whom Muir nicknamed "Early-bird Ritter," was provided with dredging facilities, and was out on deck or shore at all hours, attending his nets and harvesting marine life.

Father William Duncan's famous Indian mission on Annette Island was the goal of their first land stop. On a Sunday morning Muir and Burroughs called on the genial priest, finding him full of racy Scotch humor and good sense. When the church bells rang, they went along with their shipmates to the beautiful wooden chapel and heard Father Duncan address his charges in native speech.

This appears to have been Muir's only attendance at religious services on the trip. Early on the voyage a near-mutiny was staged over going to hear Chaplain Nelson in the saloon. As Charles Keeler has told the story, Mr. Harriman, upon discovering how few of his guests were present, sent a steward to summon them. When word came to Muir and Burroughs, lounging on the sunny side of the deck, the latter said to his friend: "Well, are you going to obey orders?" "No," growled Muir, "I'll be damned if I do!"

On one occasion, however, Muir was present at a hymn-singing session below decks. When he emerged, Burroughs who had been enjoying the alpenglow from the bridge, hailed him thus: "You ought to have been here fifteen minutes ago, instead of singing hymns in the cabin." "Aye," retorted Muir, "and you, Johnny, ought to have been up here fifteen years ago, instead of slumbering down there on the Hudson!"[58]

Before many days the ship plowed her way into Glacier Bay. With the dim white face of the Muir fronting them, they edged up the inlet choked with rocking bergs, to cast anchor abreast of the stout cabin Muir had built there nine years before. He in his blue jeans, leading the company over the moraine, marked how great were the changes. The great wall of ice had receded two miles since his first visit in '79.

During the five or six days they remained in the bay, groups went out on various pursuits. One was a party of hunters who, as "J. B." said, went "to stir up the bears in Howling Valley . . . a coat-tail pocket of the great glacier."[59] Muir's account of the wolves that besieged him there lured them no end, and they started out with great enthusiasm, attended by a retinue of packers with a huge load of guns, ammunition, alpenstocks, and ropes. Being inexperienced, they walked too fast the first day, and by night were exhausted. Sleeping on the ice under falling rain and snow didn't mend matters. The next day they straggled on through deep snow, roped together to keep out of hidden crevasses. Arriving at Howling Valley tired, lame, and disgruntled, they found it filled with snow—but no wolves! Late the following afternoon they hobbled back, leaning on the arms of packers, and, according to Burroughs, concluding "there might not be any bears in Howling Valley after all—Muir's imagination may have done all the howling." Muir listening to the dolorous tale of their adventures, wrinkled his nose and chuckled deep into his beard.

Among his shipboard companions Muir had formed a warm friendship with Henry Gannett, Chief Geographer of the U. S. Geological Survey. Dr. Gannett was the scientist who later came to the support of Muir's theory of the glacial origin of the Yosemite, with his researches among hanging side-valleys. According to Dr. C. Hart Merriam, Chief of the U. S. Biological Survey, Gannett and Muir were constant companions in walks about the deck. Moreover, they spent much time together in the smoking den. Of the beginnings of their friendship Muir told Merriam "that when he first saw Gannett he was impressed by . . . the 'preternatural solemnity' of his expression. This . . . had convinced him that Gannett, like himself, was fond of humor and he was not long in learning that Gannett, though not a Scotchman, also loved an argument. The result was that the two were always happy together."[60]

When the ship reached Disenchantment Bay at the head of the enclosing Yakutat Bay, the two friends went off gleefully in a boat to visit certain inlets and glaciers. Landing upon some adjacent islands, they found them so delightfully flowery they agreed to leave "Dis" off the name of the bay. Muir did so in his journal account.

On June 24 the *George W. Elder* reached Prince William Sound. Rounding the head of the sound, shaped like a spider with many legs, they ran into difficulties. In trying to pass through a western arm they came face to face with a wall of ice and rocks. The local pilot, taken on at Sitka, refused to proceed. Harriman consulted Muir, who said he felt sure from the trend of the mountains that a passage could be found farther to the west that would open into a fine hidden landscape. Harriman thereupon made one of his fearless decisions: "Go ahead," he ordered. "Rocks or no rocks, I will take the responsibility." So they nosed cautiously ahead, Muir directing the course, until finally they did find the passage he had foreseen. Although "narrow and threatening," it opened into a magnificent fiord fifteen miles long. "Go right ahead up the middle," shouted Harriman, thrilled at their success. "Full speed?" inquired Captain Doran. "Yes, full speed ahead!" answered the man who loved nothing better than a risk. "The sail of this majestic fiord . . . was . . . the most exciting experience of the whole trip," exulted Muir.[61]

That evening near the head of the fiord he and Gannett again put off in a boat. At a late hour they landed in a small cove where they found "a paradise of a camp on a bench covered with Cassiope . . . fifty or sixty feet above the sea," on the edge of a hemlock forest. They went to bed at two a.m. "after a grand exhilarating evening, pitying them on the ship." Muir, in his proper element now and with this most congenial friend, said this was for him "the happiest season of the entire expedition."

As they approached Kodiak Island, south of the Aleutian Peninsula, "the two Johnnies" stood together on the deck, Burroughs delighting in the verdant shores, and Muir in the high glaciers plashing down from the volcanic peaks still plumed with smoke and steam. "J. B.," who hadn't thawed out since they reached Glacier Bay, now began to babble of green fields and running brooks, for Kodiak was "a pastoral paradise."

There was a general exodus at various points along the island coast. The "biological doctors" went out to get specimens, and the big-game hunters, yearning to shoot a Kodiak bear — said to be a regular Paul Bunyan among bears — left for the interior "carrying guns and baggage and plans enough for a Manila campaign." [62] Harriman had even brought along a derrick to hoist the mighty beast on board. In the evening the hunters returned, grinning broadly. "J. B." rejoiced with them that Harriman "had the luck to kill the long-expected Kadiak bear; he shot a mother and cub." Killjoy Muir, commenting upon his host's prowess, said: "Harriman returned last evening after killing two bears — mother and child."

On one of their idyllic days off Kodiak Muir and his shipmates held their variously reported talk on wealth. Muir's version of it follows:

"The scientists, assembled on the forecastle . . . began to talk of the blessed ministry of wealth, especially in Mr. Harriman's case. . . . When these wealth laudations were sounding loudest, I teasingly interrupted them, saying, 'I don't think Mr. Harriman is very rich. He has not as much money as I have. I have all I want and Mr. Harriman has not.' " [63]

Someone reported this speech to their host at the dinner table. Later in the evening the magnate, always straightforward and frank, seated himself by Muir and said: "I never cared for money except as power for work. . . . What I most enjoy is the power of creation, getting into partnership with Nature in doing good, helping to feed man and beast, and making everybody and everything a little better and happier." And Muir, although he held different ideas about "getting into partnership with Nature," sensed the sincerity of this man.

A few days later they anchored in Dutch Harbor, off Unalaska. Here was another paradise. "J. B.'s" longing to escape the trip to

Bering Sea rose to a new high. Walking on shore, listening to the Lapland longspur singing like a bobolink, he made plans. Muir, suspecting what was brewing, kept his eye on him. Charles Keeler relates what happened:

Mr. Muir and I had been strolling about on shore and were just returning . . . when we saw John Burroughs walking down the gangplank with a grip in his hand.

"Where are you going with that grip, Johnny," demanded Muir suspiciously.

Burroughs tried to give an evasive answer, but . . . confessed. He had found a nice old lady ashore who had fresh eggs for breakfast, and he was going to board there and wait for us while we went up into Behring Sea. . . .

"Why, Johnny!" exclaimed Muir derisively. "Behring Sea in summer is like a mill pond. The best part of our trip is up there. . . . Come along! You can't miss it!"

Mr. Burroughs . . . could not withstand Mr. Muir's scorn. He weakened a bit, and was lost. I carried his satchel back to his room, and . . . he returned to the steamer.[64]

Before long they were in Bering Sea, stopping briefly at the Pribilof Islands to see the seal-breeding grounds and the murres flying in myriads about the cliffs. One evening the ship ran aground in the fog, causing the keel to grate horribly on the rocks and creating wild alarm. But, hoisting the jib and reversing the engines, the crew got it free within fifteen minutes.

When they struck the rocks, "J. B." thought they would surely turn about and go home. But, alas, Muir's influence was in the ascendancy, and because he had painted the Siberian coast in such alluring colors to Mrs. Harriman, that lady said she would not be content to go home without seeing it.

So as they plunged ahead through rough seas and a cold pea-soup fog, "J. B." groaned and took to his bed. "Mill pond, indeed!" he probably muttered as he stuffed his ears to keep out "the ferocious whistle . . . tearing the silence and with it our sleep to tatters." Charles Keeler once said of Burroughs that he was "as local as a mud turtle." Certainly he was out of his proper habitat in Bering Sea. The old philosopher, wretchedly seasick most of the time, must have accepted the universe with some reservations just then.

Muir, mentioning Burroughs's illness several times in his journal, was truly anxious about him. But, knowing his own presence would only increase his friend's blood pressure, he often sent Keeler, his cabin-mate, to inquire after him and read Wordsworth's poems to him. Sick as he was, Burroughs could still vent his feelings in doggerel rhymes, dictating them to Keeler and sending him to pin them up in the smoking den:

Snapping, snarling Behring Sea,
Hissing, spitting, as we flee—
Spiteful Sea! . . .

Only murres abide with thee,
Had not John Muir put in his lip,
Thou hadst not found me in this ship,
Groaning on my narrow bed,
Heaping curses on thy head,
Wishing he *were here instead—*
On green hills my feet would be,
'Yond the reach of Muir and thee.[65]

Another poem contained this couplet:

Where every prospect pleases,
And only Muir is vile.[66]

On July 11 they anchored at Plover Bay. "Asia at last," growled "J. B.," "crushed down there on the rim of the world as if with the weight of her centuries and her cruel Czar's iniquities." Muir had something to say about that too. Planting his feet on the shore, he exclaimed: "Now I can shake my fist at the Czar on his own soil, and he can't touch me!" [67]

They sailed as far north as St. Lawrence Island, Burroughs thanking whatever gods there might be for the ice pack that barred them from the Arctic Ocean. Otherwise "Cold-Storage Muir"

Muir Glacier, *in Alaska*

"The Two Johnnies" — JOHN MUIR *and* JOHN BURROUGHS — *in Alaska. Photo taken in* 1899 *on the Harriman Alaska Expedition*

MUIR *with a magnifying glass examining spots in petrified wood*

might have hypnotized the whole crowd into going to Wrangel Land — another of his disgusting paradises!

Leaving the fogs and storms of Bering Sea behind, and once more homeward bound, "J. B." recovered his health and spirits — so much so that one day he danced a jig. Indeed, a general jubilation broke loose as they sailed swiftly down the coast and entered Cross Sound. They shouted, sang, joked, toasted each other with wine at dinner, gave college yells, and danced. But when they passed at night the entrance to Taylor Bay, Muir left the hilarious company, to stand alone by the larboard rail, and there pay silent tribute to the brave little mongrel dog who over there on the back of a dim white glacier had followed him across the icy abyss.[68]

For Muir many strong friendships grew out of the expedition. Before a month had passed, the Big House on the ranch had welcomed and entertained Captain Doran and his wife, G. K. Gilbert of the U. S. Geological Survey, C. Hart Merriam, and Henry Gannett. Gannett spent two days with him, smoking and discussing "everything from earth sculpture to Cassiope and rhododendron gardens, from Welsh rarebit and jam and cracker feasts to Nunatak."[69]

PART VII

1901–1914

FRUITION AND STRUGGLE

HEODORE ROOSEVELT became President of the United States in September 1901. Soon after he took office, he began to invite men of integrity and knowledge in all sections of the country to give him information about existing abuses. In October, C. Hart Merriam, at his instigation, wrote to John Muir:

"The President is heartily with us in the matter of preserving the forests and keeping out the sheep. He wants to know the facts . . . from men like yourself who are not connected with the Government service and at the same time are known and esteemed by the people."

Muir wrote at once, telling the President the facts as he had observed them, and urging that the management of the forest reserves be vested in a Bureau of Forestry under the Department of Agriculture.

On December 3, 1901 Roosevelt sent his first Message to Congress. In this he declared the preservation of the forests to be "an imperative business necessity." "The forest and water problems," he said, "are perhaps the most vital internal questions of the United States at the present time." He advocated the protection of the reserves against fire and livestock, above all against sheep. Finally he recommended the creation of a Bureau of Forestry under the Department of Agriculture.

Theodore Roosevelt wisely chose as his first Secretary of the Interior Ethan Allen Hitchcock of Missouri, who believed in strict law-enforcement. In December 1902 Hitchcock blew the lid off the General Land Office when he demanded the resignation of Commissioner Binger Hermann for suppressing the Halsinger

Report on Arizona land frauds. Now, Hermann of Oregon was a Goliath in the Republican Party. After serving in the House for several terms, he had been, through the machinations of Senator John Mitchell, another Oregon political boss, appointed General Land Commissioner. So when the Secretary asked him to resign, the storm broke. Congressmen, Senators, and syndicate lobbyists — all high in party councils — rushed to the White House with recriminations and threats of vengeance. But the President, standing firmly behind his Secretary, told him to go ahead.

The Halsinger Report, at last uncovered, and others brought in by Hitchcock investigators, revealed a vast octopus-like empire of land frauds controlled by John A. Benson and Frederick A. Hyde, two San Francisco financiers. These partners with monstrous ambitions, beginning as pioneer land-grabbers in California, had extended their tentacles over Arizona, Utah, Nevada, Oregon, and as far east as Minnesota, Kansas, and Nebraska. Their devious methods had been copied by many other land speculators in California, Washington, Oregon, Montana, Wyoming, and Idaho. So it was against a formidable host of Goliaths that Theodore Roosevelt and his Secretary strung their bows for that historic warfare against Western "malefactors of great wealth." In due time the courts began to grind out a long list of indictments against Senators, Congressmen, judges, Land Office officials, lumber, stock, coal, and copper syndicates, and land speculators. Among the indicted were Binger Hermann, Senator Mitchell, Frederick A. Hyde, and John A. Benson.

Things moved fast in Washington. It was soon rumored that the President would visit the West. Robert Underwood Johnson after a conference with him wrote to John Muir that Roosevelt wanted Muir to guide him through the Yosemite. Muir replied: "Should the President invite me, I'll go and preach recession and forestry like . . . a Century Editor." Other intimations to the same effect came from Dr. Chester Rowell of Fresno, and Benjamin Ide Wheeler, president of the University of California, both men in touch with Washington sources.

Hearing that Roosevelt would arrive about the middle of May,

Muir was torn between two loyalties — his duty to the trees, and his promise, long since given, to start at that time with Sargent on a world tour. The President learning of his dilemma, wrote him an urgent personal message: "I do not want anyone with me but you, and I want to drop politics absolutely for four days, and just be out in the open with you." So Muir put the problem up to Sargent, saying: ". . . an influential man from Washington wants to make a trip to the Sierra with me, and I might be able to do some forest good in talking freely around the campfire." Sargent, of course, postponed the date of sailing. But being a stickler for dates and schedules, he applied certain adjectives of the blankety-blank sort to Roosevelt.

On the appointed day the President arrived in San Francisco, and "the city that knows how" turned out with dramatic fanfare to honor him. On the night of the 14th, while he was being feted at the Palace Hotel, Muir came down to join the party for an early start the next morning. Arthur Coleman, his business manager, came with him, and joining Bailey Millard, the journalist, they all walked up Market Street. Muir, bewildered by the tumult and glare, soon declared he was tired and wanted to go to bed. Coleman protested that since he was the President's guest, he should wait up for him. Muir shook his head, saying that not for a President or any man would he lose his sleep. So returning over the ferry to the Oakland Mole, where the Presidential train waited, he went straight to his berth.[1] Millard, commenting upon this incident, said: "This seems a bit strange, but if you knew John Muir, you would know that it was the most likely thing he could have done. Pose? Not a bit of it. He is as incapable of pose as a grizzly and about as hard to tackle if you go at him the wrong way." [2]

In the morning after breakfast he went into the President's car to meet his host. In the course of their very cordial conversation he pulled Sargent's letter from his pocket and, forgetting the blankety-blank adjectives, handed it over to Roosevelt to read. But nothing could ruffle the good humor of T. R. that morning. He fairly howled over the opprobrious words, and Muir's embarrassment as he grabbed the letter back only increased the President's glee. He seems truly to have borne no ill will, since he provided the two travelers with a letter that brought them many courtesies abroad.

At Raymond the party boarded stages for Wawona, Muir sitting directly behind the President to point out the sights. Arrived at the Big Trees, Roosevelt asked for his valise. When told that, contrary to his instructions, it had gone on to Wawona, where he was to be banqueted that night by the Park Commission, a reporter tells us: "His jaws snapped together like a coyote, and the flow of language made even the drivers listen with admiring attention. It put an end to all monkeying with the President's luggage."

That night, regardless of banquets, Muir and the President camped alone in Mariposa Grove under the giant sequoias, Rangers Leidig and Leonard and the cook who prepared their supper making themselves nearly invisible.

The next morning while the main party boarded stages for the valley, Roosevelt, "as happy as a boy out of school," stole away with Muir to the rear of a stable, where they mounted horses and took the trail eastward to Glacier Point. At sunset they camped without tents in a fir-fringed meadow back of the point, where food had been left ready for cooking. Muir and his guest, working together, soon had inch-thick, juicy steaks hissing and sputtering over the flames. As the President washed in the firelight, he sniffed the coffee simmering in the hot ashes and shouted: "Now this is bully!"

Their supper done, they lay down on beds of fir and ferns to talk. When the dark was well advanced, Muir rose up quietly and set fire to a tall dead pine in the meadow. Soon the tree was a roaring tower of flame. "Hurrah!" yelled the President. "That's a candle it took five hundred years to make. Hurrah for Yosemite!"

Kings might be happy, but Citizens Roosevelt and Muir were glorious that night as they reclined and chatted intimately about many things. Muir, telling William Trout about the trip a few years later, admitted that as usual he did most of the talking. "I stuffed him pretty well regarding the timber thieves, and the destructive work of the lumbermen, and other spoilers of the forests." Doubtless, too, Muir urged the need of Federal control for the Yosemite Valley, for Roosevelt emerged from their three-day conference an ardent recessionist. Also, according to Johnson and Colby, Muir, standing in awe of no man, opened his mouth for the dumb. The President began talking about shooting game, whereupon his companion said:

"Mr. Roosevelt, when are you going to get beyond the boyishness of killing things . . . are you not getting far enough along to leave that off?"

To which Roosevelt replied, "Muir, I guess you are right." [3] He went right on hunting after that, but he did it presumably "for museum purposes, rather than for pure sport."

At a late hour they rolled up in their blankets and fell asleep, unaware until they awoke in the dawn that a snowstorm had covered them four inches thick. "This is bullier yet!" croaked T. R. "I wouldn't miss this for anything."

The sun, reddening the summit peaks after the storm, found them standing on the jutting edge of Glacier Point. As they looked down into the valley below them, the President was much impressed with the majestic front of El Capitan, and they plotted to camp yet one more night together, this time beneath the benediction of that great rock. Late in the afternoon, after a trip to the Little Yosemite and back down the Giant Stairway, they entered the valley itself. Few were there to greet the President, since even his own party was ignorant of his route. Most of the huge crowd brought up by the railroads expected him to make his entrance from the lower end.

Meanwhile the Yosemite Park Commission had completed their extravagant plans to entertain the President with a banquet and reception, as well as fireworks, and searchlights to play upon the great fall and mighty rocks. Moreover, the Jorgenson studio had been fitted up with polished Dutch furniture to house him for the night. When Governor George C. Pardee and one commissioner demurred, saying these things would not meet with Roosevelt's wishes, the other members are said to have boasted: "We guess the President will do pretty much what we lay out for him to do."

When about four o'clock five horsemen were seen approaching the village from across the meadows, someone recognized among them that well-known figure in khaki, army hat, and bandanna.

A mighty cheer went up as they surged forward to meet him. Dismounting at the Sentinel Hotel, where he was greeted by Benjamin Ide Wheeler, the President said enthusiastically: "We slept in a snowstorm last night. . . . Just what I wanted!" At the Jorgenson studio — the only building he entered in the valley — he said: "This has been the grandest day of my life! One I shall long remember!" Then looking appreciatively at the furnishings, he remarked: "You know I am Dutch myself!" But when told of the banquet and fireworks planned for him, he shook his head. Not on your life would he miss that last campfire supper and sleeping in the meadow with El Capitan towering above them. When somebody mentioned the searchlights as a final lure, he is said to have vetoed that as "nature faking."

It was all over within an hour. After a brief session by the bridge at the edge of the village, where he spoke to the crowd for ten minutes, shook hands, and cracked jokes, the President mounted his horse and rode on down the street to rejoin John Muir. Curses, not loud, but deep, were muttered that night. Some of the commissioners and frustrated politicians blamed Muir for seducing the President away from them. In the days that followed, face-saving recriminations swelled into a mighty roar that still reverberates when one chances to bring up the subject with certain old-timers.

But little cared these two nature-lovers as they lay on their piny couches in Bridalveil meadow, talking while the dusk deepened into a starlit night.

When the trail-mates shook hands in farewell on the following day, the President said: "Good-bye, John. Come and see me in Washington. I've had the time of my life!" That Roosevelt retained happy memories of Muir's care of him was revealed in a letter some years later:

"I always begrudged Emerson's not having gone into camp with you. You would have made him perfectly comfortable and he ought to have had the experience."

It is certain that their journey together had far-reaching results for conservation. Pausing in Sacramento on his way out from the Yosemite, the President spoke his solemn convictions that "No small part of the prosperity of California . . . depends upon the preservation of her water supply; and the water supply cannot be preserved unless the forests are preserved. . . .

"I ask for the preservation of other forests on grounds of wise and far-sighted economic policy. . . . We are not building this country of ours for a day. It is to last through the ages."

Dr. William Frederic Badè, about to write and compile *The Life and Letters of John Muir,* was invited by Roosevelt to Sagamore Hill in 1916, to hear from his own lips the story of that historic camping trip. He told Dr. Badè also of the impression which Muir's "deep solicitude over the destruction of our great forests and scenery had made upon his mind. Roosevelt . . . came away with a greatly quickened conviction that vigorous action must be taken speedily, ere it should be too late." [4]

On May 24 John Muir was entertained by the Sargents at a formal dinner at their home in Brookline, Massachusetts. He wore, probably for the first time in his life, a dress suit. At Louie's insistence he had had it made. "I was glad for once to be inconspicuous," he wrote her the next day.

In New York he called on Mr. Harriman. Although a wan shadow of himself following a serious illness, the magnate was full of cordial thought for his globe-trotting guest. "I am President of two steamship companies in the Orient," said he. "I'll see that they do everything possible for you when you reach that part of the world." The promise was abundantly fulfilled.

With Sargent and his son Robeson, Muir sailed for Europe, there to begin a dizzy round of sightseeing. By the time they had "done" Paris, he was desperately weary of museums and art galleries — "enough for a life-time."

Not until he crossed the Russian frontier did he begin to enjoy himself. Here were illimitable forests of spruce, silver birch, and pine, interspersed with glacial lakes and bogs gleaming with white lilies. But even here there was too much city sightseeing. St. Petersburg he described as "a huge, semi-dismal old town of enormous yellow buildings, war monuments, barbaric churches and cathedrals, and palaces full of armor, jewelry and some fine paintings." [5] The "fine paintings" were the Rembrandts he saw in the

Hermitage. "Glorious art. One old mother haunts me with her wondrous eyes . . . worth all the beautiful barbaric rubbish."

One day they crossed the Finnish border to view the famous forest of Lindula. After some hours among the larch and pine they stopped at a log farmhouse for lunch. Muir was charmed with the homely peasant and his wife who served them with brown bread, boiled eggs, wild berries, and tea. This was the Europe he had come to see — unspoiled nature and simple, earth-loving folk. "I could live at that home always. I could not help thinking that if ever I was very weary and required a long calm rest, I should like best to go to a Finland farm. No pleasure so fine is to be found in all the Petersburg palaces."

Before long Muir became ill. Hotel foods and worry about things at home were contributing causes. Not a letter had come from his family. Many had been written, but they never caught up with him. When they left for a three weeks' trip to Sevastopol, the Black Sea, and the Caucasus, he had to be carried to the train on a stretcher. But as they sped southward over the fertile black plains of the eastern Ukraine, he was cheered when, lifting himself up, he saw in the distance "blue genuine mountains — the only mountains seen since leaving America." His restoration was furthered when from the Black Sea he faced the Caucasus Mountains, splashed with white descending glaciers. From Tiflis, the lofty capital of Georgian Russia, they traveled north in a post-chaise, past mountain valleys as rich as the Garden of Eden. The primitive peasants living there close to the soil possessed an earth-wisdom by which they planted their crops in strips, rotated them, and used nature's own fertilizers in conserving the life-giving power through centuries of cultivation.

A few days later they arrived at Moscow. Still no letters. Torn with anxiety, Muir cabled home. Back came the heart-warming words of his wife: "All's well. Loving greetings!" "Wondrous quick and comforting," he wrote in his journal. With renewed cheer he set out with the Sargents to see the Kremlin, filled with "endless jewels, crowns . . . and above all guns and other weapons most wearisome to behold." The Cathedral of Ivan the Terrible he noted was "a mass of bulbous domes in barbaric color and grandeur of metal." Bored with these things, in a letter to Johnson he summed up his trip thus far: "I'm still alive after this most monstrous dose of civilization — London, Paris, Berlin, etc., etc., with their miles of art galleries, museums full of old armor and murder implements. . . . Glad to leave holy Moscow, Kremlin, and all."

On August 3 they boarded the train for Siberia. While the Sargents slept, Muir was awake in the dawn to see the valley of the Volga. Looking out upon the vast grain fields that helped to feed the Empire, he saw men cradling wheat as he had done in Wisconsin, others "stooking" it, their bodies bending low over the earth as if belonging to it. Then traveling on over the Ural Mountains, the tundra-like prairies of Siberia, the magnificent rivers flowing north, and through vast forests of "indomitable birch," Muir thought of Russia as a sleeping giant, unconscious of her strength. Nearing Vladivostok, he summed up his prophetic impressions:

"The fertility of the soil extends over vast stretches . . . with scarce a rod of waste. With simple drainage this Ussuri Valley could be made one of the most productive in the world, and support a hundred times as many inhabitants as it does now. Indeed the same may be said of most all Siberia. It is not generally known how vast the agricultural resources of Russia are, and to how slight a degree they have as yet been developed."

After a brief foray into Manchuria Muir returned to Vladivostok, desperately ill with ptomaine poisoning. In his journal he noted: "Still alive. Morphine to stupify pain and brandy to hold on to life." He weighed at this time about ninety pounds.

But as they sailed down the Korean coast, the beauty of the glacial fiords that fringed the land caused the flame of life to burn brighter. Moreover, he had resolved to separate from the Sargents. They planned inland trips into China, while he longed for "the cool sea." "The white Himalayas" and the deodar forests of India had held a lifelong lure for him. But Sargent's time-schedule wouldn't allow for them, so he would go alone.

At Shanghai he slipped away from his companions, cabled to Harriman, and called upon the Harriman steamship agents to aid in planning his route. Before long he was sailing along the Chinese coast, headed for India. "I feel all alive with mountains in sight once more," he wrote to his wife. "Glad to be free. Will never be bound to mortal again on travel."

At Calcutta he entrained for Darjeeling, where he spent several days. Every morning he was up at dawn, climbing Tiger Hill or the ridge back of his hotel, to see the Himalayas in the sunrise. The crisp, snow-cooled air blew new vitality into him, and had he been a few years younger he might have attempted to climb them. But, he said, "I'm thankful God has led me to see his Himalaya, and so soon after it seemed I would see but little more of anything here or elsewhere."

A few days later he was wandering among the deodars near Simla. These "god-trees" standing on a high ridge, etched against the sky, reminded him of the redwoods of California. And a grand view of the Himalayas he had there, too, some of their summits towering nearly 30,000 feet into the heavens.

All that autumn he was disturbed by some fear or premonition about Helen. Even the Indian mourning dove seemed to say: "Baby sick, Baby sick." Homesick and tormented with worry, he cabled his family from Bombay, only to receive back the reassuring "All's well." In his relief he scolded himself as a chronic old fuss-budget, thrust his fears away, and bought a steamship ticket for Egypt. "There are a few more places I should see before I die," he wrote to his wife.

On November 4 he was out on the Libyan Desert inspecting the Pyramids from a mountaineer's point of view:

They don't seem high, and their rough broken, talus-encumbered bases make them look like hills of eroded stratified rocks. . . . But when we go close up and by this exact jointing realize that human hands long gone to dust, have hewn and lifted and placed every stone, then comes wonder. . . .

The Sphinx . . . is so well proportioned, it does not seem in the least monstrous, and the face expression is fine in depth of repose.

Throughout his journey he had made many friends. Now in the dining-room of Shepheard's Hotel in Cairo, where he stayed, he met three young Americans from Philadelphia — the Misses Emily and

Laura Bell and their brother. "The Three Bells" he called them. The young ladies later visited him on the ranch. Miss Emily has related an incident of Muir's behavior at the hotel when he was telling a group about the *Sequoia gigantea:*

Seated at his left was an elderly Englishwoman of the prosaic type . . . she abruptly broke in upon his poetical description . . . with the practical question, "Would they make nice furniture?"

Turning upon her with as fierce a look as his gentle blue eyes could give, "Madam," he replied, "would you murder your own children?"

The climax of his Egyptian sojourn was a steamer trip up the Nile to the First Cataract. Arriving at Assiout on the second day, he mounted a donkey so small his long legs dangled to the ground, and set off to see the town and its environs. "Tombs innumerable . . . the largest carved from the living rock into chambers. Some contain picture writing, here and there a mummy, and many bats. The smell is horrid, strong as the centuries. . . . The hill . . . one vast sepulchre. Near the summit innumerable small tombs. . . . Jackal dogs — the same as we saw living along the Nile — mummied with upright ears, piled at the entrance."

Finally from a terrace above the Nile at Assuan he looked out upon the country covered with drifting sand, and the river divided into channels by "residual granite masses . . . forming islands . . . like those of a glacial lake." He was profoundly impressed by the red granite quarries whence the mighty obelisks and sarcophagi had been carved and transported down the river with titanic labor far back in the auld lang syne. Many of them lay yet among the quarries, rough-hewn and ready for a removal that never came.

Shortly thereafter Muir was at sea once more, glad to get away from the dust and musty smells of antiquity. He was now on his way home via the Orient and the South Seas, "a long, long way that will take two or three months, and I sae weary and fu' o' homesickness. I suppose it will be better, however, to see the parts of the world I have long wanted to see . . . and get done with the wandering Jew business once for all. . . . My health is now quite as good as when I left home . . . my appetite is better than it has been for years."[6]

Christmas Day he spent seventy miles inland from Melbourne, Australia, "in the heart of the forest primeval. . . . A place after my own heart!" It was well for his peace of mind that day that he did not know his beloved Helen was even then critically ill with pneumonia, the first of several attacks that were to overshadow his remaining years with fear.

After another trip inland — this time from the fiord-like harbor of Sydney to the Blue Mountains and the casuarina forests, he set sail for Auckland, New Zealand. "I am beginning botany all over again," he observed gleefully while he classified, dried, and pressed his Australian plants on the sunny deck of the ship.

After botanizing for two weeks on North Island, he crossed to South Island. From Nelson he plunged into the interior. Rain descending in torrents caused most of the stagecoach tourists to huddle inside. But he paid extra fare to be allowed to sit on top and feel the rain and wind in his face. His joy was increased by the fact that cataracts poured down from overhanging cliffs, and wet trees and bushes thrashed him and the driver almost from off their seats. He felt wild and elemental once more. Crossing the island by train and stage from Christchurch, he arrived at the base of Mount Cook, where in a violent storm he explored the lower part of Mueller Glacier. "In jumping on the boulder-clad snout, I found my feet had not lost their cunning!"

Again he went to Australia, this time to see the *Araucaria Bidwellii* and the *Araucaria Cunninghamii* in their native habitat in the mountains of Queensland. The *Bidwellii* he found "the nobler species . . . soaring in magnificent domes above all other trees, outlined on the sky." But nowhere did he find a tree to match *Sequoia gigantea*.[7]

After a brief stay in the Philippines he crossed to the coast of China. At Canton he found a cable from E. H. Harriman, inviting him to journey home on the *Siberia* of the Pacific Steamship Line. With the company's launch to convey himself and his plant-presses and bags bursting with gifts for his womenfolk, he boarded the great liner, to be welcomed as if he were royalty. He was given one of the best staterooms and allotted a large space on deck for his work.

On May 5 they entered the glacial harbor of Nagasaki, Japan. In a ricksha Muir traveled up the terraced hills to a Shinto temple, where he wandered in the sacred gardens.

Here as in every other country he studied the people. He had long had an instinctive distrust of the Japanese. When hordes of them had invaded the ranching communities of California, driving out the Chinese coolies who had served the pioneers, his suspicions were aroused. While most of his neighbors hired them because they thought them faster and more efficient workers, Muir stubbornly refused. "Mark my words," said he, "you'll have trouble with those fellows some day. They are not to be trusted." [8] He continued to employ the Chinese who had worked faithfully for him and the Strentzels before him. But when he saw the Japanese common people on their own soil, his prejudices were softened. Their cities were beautiful and well kept, with "no squalor visible even in the poorest families." When he got home he had much to tell his girls about the little brown-skinned, black-eyed "mugginses" of Nippon.

After a final stop at Yokohama, where from the deck he saw the godlike cone of Fujiyama looming from out of the mist beyond the city, they sailed for Honolulu. With sightseeing done, the twelve hundred passengers settled down for what was to them the monotonous life of a long sea voyage. "How small the talk! Reading and card games. How few do any work with hand or head save the seamen with their eyes on the stars, and the throbbing, tireless engines."

Not a few of the sophisticates, however, were jogged out of their boredom by the leaven of Muir's presence. Leaning over the rail, pointing out the fascinating sea life, or kneeling on the deck as he puttered over his specimens he was daily fringed about by a curious throng, asking foolish questions and laughing at his salty answers. Among them he found a few kindred souls, such as a young Chinese student who loved nature. Midway between Honolulu and California the captain was delegated by the passengers to ask Muir to lecture to them. He declined, but said he would talk informally to a half dozen or so. The news flew about the ship, and when the time came, the big saloon was jammed to the doors.

As they neared the Farallones, just outside the Golden Gate, he was on deck straining his eyes. "Soon the land of Sequoia will be in sight and my wanderings for a time will be ended." It was May 27, a few days more than a year since he had left home.

When he saw Wanda and Helen, tall, smiling, and rosy-cheeked, waiting on the San Francisco dock, he fairly ran down to meet them. "The Big Two" were amazed at the change in their father. His pallor gone, he was bronzed and almost stout. He boasted of 148 pounds — more than he had ever weighed in his life before. And his laugh was the laugh of a boy!

As he got off the train at Muir Station near the ranch, Louie, John Reid, and Sarah Galloway — now living in California — were there "to welcome the wanderer home." In the days that followed, they gave him a great ribbing about being so fat. He played up to them, strutting about, throwing out his chest like a pouter pigeon, and even striding majestically down to dinner with a pillow stuffed inside his clothes.[9]

In the fall of 1904 the movement to re-cede the Yosemite Valley to Federal control began to gather importance. Muir's book *Our National Parks,* made up of the ten *Atlantic* articles and published in 1901, had done much to educate public sentiment. Moreover, the Sierra Club had been working steadily for recession. From its ranks had arisen new leaders, chief among whom was William E. Colby, the son of Gilbert W. Colby of Benicia, whom Muir had once guided in the Yosemite. As a young mining attorney of San Francisco, he had joined the club in 1894, and beginning with 1901 had infused into it new life and cohesiveness by instituting annual mountain trips. As secretary of the large and influential organization, he had worked zealously in the cause of Western conservation.

The time now seemed ripe for a concerted move on the Legislature. Both President Roosevelt and Governor George C. Pardee, since their journey to the Yosemite with John Muir in 1903, had favored recession, and their stand influenced other Republican leaders. Therefore at Muir's request Colby drafted a bill which was introduced in the state Legislature in January 1905.

Nearly all newspapers in California now advocated recession. The *San Francisco Chronicle* was a power in its behalf. Only two — one of wide circulation — led the orgy of bathos staged by the opposition. In the battle of words that ensued, screaming headlines such as these appeared:

THOSE WHO VOTE FOR RECESSION OF YOSEMITE MUST BE TRAITORS. . . . STATE PRIDE SHOULD PREVAIL. . . . YOSEMITE IS THE STATE'S BIG ADVERTISEMENT. WHY GIVE IT AWAY? . . . SHALL CALIFORNIA ADVERTISE THAT IT LACKS MONEY AND CAPACITY? . . . YOSEMITE WOULD BECOME INACCESSIBLE TO MASS OF VISITORS.

The bill came up for a joint committee hearing on January 8. Muir and Colby were there, each making a brief, dignified speech. All together the two of them made nine trips to Sacramento to appear before committees and lobby for the bill.[10] On February 2 it passed the Assembly by a vote of 45 to 20 — a majority that surprised both sides. After that the real tug-of-war dragged on for three weeks in the Senate. According to Muir, many "fluffy, frothy, empty, bellowing speeches" were made against the measure. Senator Charles Shortridge of San Jose waxed sentimental about "golden-haired girls, and the golden poppies in the Golden State," somehow implying that California would be shorn of these glories if the bill was passed.

But the opposition's oratory reached an all-time high in the speeches of that rugged individualist Senator Curtin, Democrat of Sonora, known as "Constitutional John" because of his frequent references to the United States Constitution. As attorney for the hotel and stage-line concessionaires entrenched in the valley under the state Commission, he thundered and raved against a change to Federal administration. Moreover, he had a score of his own to settle. As a predatory stockman he had had personal set-to's with officials in the matter of pasturing his cattle in the Yosemite National Park. One of his "arguments" against recession was that firearms were not allowed within Park boundaries. "I would not live under a Government that would not let me carry a gun!" he shouted. Like his colleagues he spoke as if the Federal Government were a foreign and hostile power. In the course of his flaming oratory he dragged in the hoary old wheeze that Muir himself in early days "was engaged in despoiling the forest growth in the Yosemite until he was forced to close down his mill."

During the dark days while the Senate's action was still in grave doubt, Muir, at Colby's suggestion, appealed to E. H. Harriman for help. As president of the Southern Pacific Railroad, Harriman at once telegraphed to William Herrin in San Francisco, chief counsel for the company, directing him to do everything possible to ensure the bill's passage. Thereupon the powerful railroad lobby went into action. Muir held no brief for railroad lobbies, but, being a realist, he welcomed their aid when they were on the right side.

But even with this help the bill passed the Senate on February 23 by only one vote! At the last moment three opponents voted for it. Senator "Golden-haired" Shortridge explained his shift by saying his constituents had risen up en masse, demanding that he favor the bill. This was due to certain Sierra Club members who had started an avalanche of letters and telegrams. Senator Curtin's constituents, holding mass meetings in Mariposa County, had also demanded that he vote for the bill; but he stood by his guns.

John Muir detested politics as much as he detested war. In it he saw self-interest obstructing every effort toward the common good. "Political Quag" he named the whole dark and treacherous business carried on in the name of government. On the day after their hard-won victory he wrote to "R. U. J." giving him credit as "commanding general" for having started the long fight on that night in the Tuolumne Meadows. He added: "I am now an experienced lobbyist; my political education is complete. . . . And now that the fight is finished . . . I am almost finished myself."[11]

But the fight was not over. It was still necessary for Congress to accept the re-ceded grant. This was held up for more than a year by the opposition. State Senator Curtin, backed by other stockmen, worked to cut a huge slice from the park boundaries for grazing purposes. Lumber companies clamored for a great sugar-pine belt on both sides of the Wawona stage road, extending almost to

Inspiration Point, and another area north of the Merced on the western side. Moreover, the San Francisco water and power interests were trying to seize the Hetch Hetchy Valley and Lake Eleanor for reservoir sites. There wouldn't be much park left if all got what they wanted. Finally Uncle Joe Cannon, in a spasm of economy, held up the acceptance bill in the House, on the ground that appropriations for care, trails, roads, and so on would overburden the Federal Treasury.

If the valley were not accepted within a specified time, the Recession Act would automatically become void. So in the spring of 1906 Muir again appealed to Harriman for aid. Harriman, as powerful in national as in state politics, lost no time in writing to Speaker Cannon, enclosing Muir's letter to himself. There was something so potent in Harriman's letter as to cause Cannon to have an instantaneous change of heart, with the result that the acceptance bill passed the House in May. But in the Senate it had reached another impasse. For the third time Muir called upon Harriman for aid. Through his influence, together with that of Senator Perkins of California, sponsor of the bill, and that of the President, who had announced he would sign no bill with boundary changes, the measure finally passed in June in its original form. Thus on June 11, 1906, with the President's signature, after a fight of seventeen years, the Yosemite Valley became a part of the Yosemite National Park.

During this period of struggle and success, shadows gathered fast about the home life of John Muir. Helen suffered another attack of pneumonia. All through that legislative fight for recession her father was torn with anxiety. Since she failed to rally after her illness, a specialist said she would have to live in the desert for at least a year.

Late in May 1905 Muir, accompanied by Wanda, took her south to Arizona to camp on the Sierra Bonita Ranch near Wilcox. When they arrived in a torrential rain, their host, Henry C. Hooker, took them into his spacious hacienda. This won Muir's eternal gratitude, and because the old pioneer fitted so well into his Spanish surroundings and the feudal scale of his holdings, he nicknamed him "Don Pedro." [12]

On June 21 Louie wrote to her "Beloved Three" that she had been ill, but was " all right now." Three days later came a telegram summoning them to her bedside. Leaving Helen in the desert, John Muir and Wanda came home to learn that a tumor on the lung left little hope of recovery.

Louie died on August 6. After her burial in the ranch plot near her father and mother, Muir and Wanda returned to Adamana on the desert, where Helen was now living. In the weeks that followed, Wanda "so capable and full of brave young life," nursed both her sister and her father. Helen's lungs healed rapidly in the dry desert air, and after a while the two girls, both expert horsewomen, were venturing far over the sands. Sometimes their father, although "deadly, stunningly tired," went with them. In those weeks he moved as in a daze. But on one ride alone with Helen, he discovered and named the "Blue Forest" of petrified wood. And nature once more became his great physician as he set himself to learn all he could of the big trees that in the Triassic period, 160,000,000 years ago, stood on these mesas, and the processes by which they were transformed cell by cell into the beautifully colored rocks that lie prone like great logs on the yellow sands.

That his wife's death was a well-nigh mortal blow to him, only his daughters fully knew. For a time he was lost indeed. In her devotion and understanding his spirit had long found its home, the dual sides of his nature their reconciliation. Not for a year could he adjust himself to her absence and return to his writing. Back in the old home, where he had to spend much time administering the estate, he would allow nothing to be moved — not even a chair — that her hand had placed.

Many tributes came from friends who remembered "her kindly gracious presence." In response to some home photographs Muir sent to James S. Merriam, Dr. Merriam said: "The group at the porch is peculiarly welcome, because it . . . has the face of your wife, and I want never to forget the beauty of a devoted heart which speaks in her motherly care with serene love undying." C. Hart Merriam, who had known the Muir home life intimately for nearly twenty years, paid tribute to her as "a woman of more than ordinary character and ability. . . . She was a clever and noble woman, but so retiring that she was known only to a few. He [Muir] owed much to the sympathetic loyalty of his two daughters, Helen and Wanda, who, like their mother, were devoted to him and the work he was doing." [13]

After a few months publishers were once more hounding Muir for promised articles and books. But with "a mental barrenness" that forbade creative work, he concentrated upon fossilized forests, corresponding with foreign scientists, ordering every available book on the subject, and spending several days each week poring over great tomes in the University of California Library. To Helen he wrote:

"I sit silent and alone from morn til eve in the deeper silence of the enchanted old old forests of the coal age. The hours go on neither long or short, glorious for imagination . . . but tough for the old paleontological body nearing 70. There's no fatness in this work — only leanness. . . ."

But out of Muir's sojourn on the desert and his later researches came one more great triumph for conservation. Congressman John F. Lacey, inspired by John Muir and urged by certain eminent historians and archæologists of America, sponsored in Congress in 1906 a measure empowering the President to set apart areas of historic and scientific value. Muir, with indignation seeing the railroads seizing the Arizona desert lands, and hauling away in car-loads the beautiful stone logs to be carved into souvenirs by private interests, recommended to the President that this region be made into a monument. Thereupon Roosevelt, acting swiftly under the new Lacey Antiquities Act, in December 1906 set aside by proclamation the nucleus of the present Petrified Forest National Monument. In later years were added the Blue Forest, the Black Forest, and other areas explored and recommended by Muir.

In 1908, also upon Muir's advice, President Roosevelt set aside

JOHN MUIR *with his wife and daughters,* WANDA *(left) and* HELEN*, on the porch of the Lower Ranch Home, or Big House*

as a National Monument a portion of the Grand Canyon. This was challenged by private interests and the case went to the Supreme Court, where it was upheld. Eleven years later, in 1919, under President Wilson, the Grand Canyon became a National Park.

With encouraging reports of Helen's health, Muir began in the spring of 1906 to look forward to having his two daughters with him once more. How happy they might still be in the old home! But their plans were somewhat altered by Wanda's return and marriage in June to Thomas Rae Hanna, a young civil engineer, to whom she had become engaged while at private school and university in Berkeley.

In August Muir brought Helen home, apparently healed. The two of them, with a Chinese manservant, settled down in the Big House, while Wanda and her husband went to housekeeping in the old Spanish adobe near the gate, about a quarter of a mile distant. At peace in his mind once more, Muir turned to his writing. Helen learned to use the typewriter so that she might help him. When work hours were over, they with Stickeen, the big shepherd dog, tramped the hills together, searching for flowers in their seasons, imitating bird calls—for they were both good whistlers—and finally ending with a visit to Aunt Maggie or Wanda.[14] Because of her fragile health Muir had always made Helen his special charge and by becoming her playmate had kept her in the open air. He encouraged her in all her interests, even in her enthusiasm for railway mechanics, buying for her technical books and magazines on the subject. Rather proudly he called her "my locomotive daughter." With Sante Fe trains running near their home over a great trestle that crosses the valley and enters a tunnel on the west side of the ranch, she had opportunity to apply her new knowledge. During that year-and-a-half-long alpenglow of happiness in Muir's life, he and Helen played the railroad game together. Often they took rides in the cab, and before long Helen learned to operate the engine. On at least one occasion she made the entire run from Stockton to Muir Station. She and the trainmen became such good friends that when they passed the Big House they made the whistle crow like a rooster to call her out.

One day while they were at dinner with distinguished guests, the rooster crowed, and Muir said: "Midge, don't you hear your friends calling you?" When she jumped up from the table to run out and hail them, Aunt Maggie, who was dining there that day, was horrified that John should encourage such unmaidenly behavior.[15]

During the cherry and grape seasons these two playfellows often took big baskets of fruit to the trainmen as they passed by. One day they cut down a huge bough fairly dripping with ripe cherries, and gleefully, like two youngsters, they nailed or tied it up over the entrance to the tunnel within reach of the cab window. Then when the train came tooting along, they stood in plain view, waving and pointing to the black mouth in the hillside. Engineer and fireman got the idea and, just as they entered the bore, reached out and pulled the bough down and through the window.[16]

Many friends arrived in the valley to visit Muir. Among them were J. E. Calkins, an Iowa newspaper man, and his wife, who were planning to move to California. Calkins has given a vivid picture of the home life he found there. When they drove up from the station, Muir was out in front of the house to greet them.

Bare-headed . . . and smiling a welcome he helped us carry our luggage into the house. Mrs. Muir had gone; only Mr. Muir and Helen were there, attempting to fill those spacious high-ceilinged rooms with the atmosphere of home. . . . The dominant note . . . was simple dignity. No telephone, no electric lights, no domestic gadgets of all the myriad modern inventions. Candles and the open fire gave light by night, and it was by grace of the horse and buggy that one went to town.

As we sat long at the table, the cheerful talk made each meal an event. The conversation was often embroidered with pleasant levity, and amusing anecdote. There were never any jokes at our expense, but Helen was a fair mark for her father's jocundities, which she took with a pleased little laugh. . . .

In the days that followed, Calkins, who wanted to see Muir produce more books, offered his services "to do the useful, unpoetic things," to put down in shorthand what Muir said so easily, thus forming first drafts. The naturalist was somewhat impressed with the idea, but he was even more interested in getting an older woman into the house as a companion for his daughter.

"This house is under-peopled," he said, "with only two poor lonesome bodies in it. Helen is over-young to be so care-laden. Come and content you here, rent free. . . . The Chinese boy here will take care of all the hard menial work, so the house-mother shall not be overburdened. We need a home-maker, not a maid of all work. . . ."

But the plan failed. Before Calkins and his wife could arrange their own affairs, Helen was again banished to the desert.

In October 1907 Muir and Keith went to the Sierra. Muir went reluctantly, for he was worried about Helen. Her old racking cough had suddenly returned, and in spite of diet and medicine it grew worse. On their way in to the Hetch Hetchy Valley by the Big Oak Flat Road, Muir wrote to her: "When I hear you are better I'll care for nothing else in the world. . . . The glory of the woods hereabouts now is the color of dogwood, glorious masses of red and purple and yellow. . . . I can't get the sound of that cough out of my ears. . . ."

Arriving at night in the Hetch Hetchy, they camped near a waterfall that loomed "like a ghost in the dark." They remained for a week, reliving past joys and seeing it all with wonder born anew each day. Keith, for the time being, left behind all his synthetics of the last twenty-five years and humbly, reverently portrayed what he saw, as objectively as in the seventies when Muir first infused into him his own spirit and vision.

Writing afterward of Keith's joy in the valley, Muir said: "The leaf colors were then ripe, and the great godlike rocks in repose seemed to glow with life. The artist . . . after making about forty sketches, declared with enthusiasm that although its walls were less sublime in height, in picturesque beauty and charm Hetch Hetchy surpassed even Yosemite!" [17]

When he came back from the Sierra, Muir found Helen's condition alarming. The specialist called in said she must live on the desert for at least two years; so in December father and daughter once more made their pilgrimage southward. Near the town of Daggett on the Mohave Desert he built her a snug cabin. Finding her a nurse and companion in the person of a Miss Safford, whom he promptly nicknamed "Miss Sassafras," he left Helen comfortably settled, and returned to the lonely old house, now bereft for the second time of all cheer. Unable to resist the pleading eyes of her dog, Stickeen, he sent both him and her riding horse, Sniffpony, south to keep her company.

In these latter years Muir found some appeasement of his own troubles in lessening those of others. As throughout his life, his generosities were boundless. He could squeeze a penny in a business deal as hard as the next Scotchman, but he gave with prodigality. His files are filled with letters of gratitude from organized charities, relatives, friends, and needy people he had merely heard of. In his own neighborhood he chose to make most of his gifts anonymously, through members of his family or through his business manager. Mrs. Coleman relates that he would say to her husband: "Now, Arthur, you get around more than I do among folks. Whenever you find people in want, help them, and charge the bill to me." On one fall day late in his life, however, he asked his niece to drive him around on a tour of "early Christmas giving." Going by way of Martinez, he drew from the bank a supply of gold pieces that seemed to burn holes in his pocket until he got rid of them. An unknown shabby mother and little girl were stopped outside on the street, and while bending down to talk with the child, he slipped a shining cartwheel into her hand. Driving on, they called at a farmhouse here and there where he had heard there was poverty, and while Mrs. Coleman engaged the mother in conversation, he played with the children. When he went away, each child was the richer by a big yellow coin. Still having one or two left, he stopped on the way home at the Swett ranch, where he disposed of them with "the little motherless bairn," the baby daughter of Emily Swett Pankhurst, who had died.

Built on sand hills, the vigorous, growing city of San Francisco had been in a state of perennial panic since its founding, lest in some great calamity it be found waterless. Numerous fires ravaging the city resulted in a public demand for municipal ownership of an unlimited supply. Hence in the late nineties the city's leaders began to look to the Sierra for sites where they could erect dams and impound waters, only to find that water rights had already been parceled out among go-getting capitalists.

James D. Phelan, financier and Mayor of San Francisco during the years 1896–1902, heard from J. B. Lippincott of the U. S. Geological Survey that the Hetch Hetchy Valley, on the main Tuolumne River, was an ideal site for a dam and reservoir that would produce not only water, but what was wanted even more — hydroelectric power; also that in conjunction with the Eleanor Creek branch lower down on the Tuolumne it would supply the city's needs for generations to come. And best of all from a monetary standpoint, these areas, enclosed within the Yosemite National Park, had so far been protected from those seeking water rights.

Phelan thereupon caused surveys to be unobtrusively made and claims filed to the sites involved. Then in February 1901, through the political maneuvering of "certain influential San Franciscans," a bill was put through Congress authorizing the Secretary of the Interior "to permit the use of rights through . . . the Yosemite . . . for . . . water conduits and for water plants, dams and reservoirs. . . ."

Under the ægis of this Act Mayor Phelan twice made formal petition for the reservoir rights he wanted. But Secretary Hitchcock twice denied the petition as being incompatible with public interest since the proposed reservoirs would destroy certain scenic aspects the park had been created to protect.

Following these rebuffs, the city officials appealed in 1905 to President Roosevelt. Roosevelt, by this time much under the influence of Chief Forester Gifford Pinchot, who throughout his career consistently refused to favor national parks, appears to have been won over. At any rate he asked Pinchot's friend Assistant Attorney General Woodruff for a ruling as to the Secretary's authority in the matter. Woodruff promptly came through with an opinion that the Secretary had full power to grant the rights asked for by San Francisco. In spite of this pointed decision, however, Hitchcock for the third time emphatically denied the petition, holding that he was obliged to obey the original mandate, which in creating the park had solemnly dedicated it to "public use, resort and recreation."

The city officials then began to look about for other sources. A commission headed by City Engineer Marsden Manson reported upon certain highly satisfactory sites nearer the city and, although involving the purchase of prior rights, not exceeding the estimated cost of developing the Tuolumne sites and transporting water over the greater distance.

Phelan continued to be a potent influence in city affairs even after his term of office expired. Inspired by him, Engineer Manson corresponded with Gifford Pinchot. The upshot was a letter from the Chief Forester, made public in early June 1906, when the citizens were wrought to the highest pitch of water-famine panic after the earthquake and fire:

May 28, 1906

Mr. Marsden Manson,

San Francisco, California.

Dear Mr. Manson:—

I was very glad to learn from your letter of May 10th that the earthquake had damaged neither your activity nor your courage. I hope sincerely that in the regeneration of San Francisco its people may be able to make provision for a water supply from the Yosemite National Park. . . . I will stand ready to render any assistance which lies in my power.

I was very glad to note that the Attorney General rendered an opinion which agrees with the views held by you and the Forest Service.

Very sincerely yours,

[*signed*] GIFFORD PINCHOT, *Forester.*

So, with the power behind the throne at Washington giving the go-ahead sign, the Board of Supervisors of the City and County of San Francisco, just then about to close a deal for another site, now turned their efforts back to the Tuolumne plan.

About this time Secretary Hitchcock resigned from the Cabinet, and James R. Garfield, another friend of Pinchot's, and also a member of the famed "Tennis Cabinet," was appointed to his place. Soon came another letter from the Chief Forester to Manson, saying: ". . . my advice to you is to assume that his [the Secretary's] attitude will be favorable, and to make the necessary preparations to set the case before him." [18]

After this significant tip the Supervisors lost no time in petitioning the new Secretary for a permit to utilize the Tuolumne sites. On the promise of sharing benefits, Berkeley, Oakland, Alameda, and other Bay cities were persuaded to join in pleas to the Secretary. By the spring of 1908 local newspapers were proclaiming that victory was in sight.

Let no one suppose that John Muir and the other defenders of national park integrity had been silent all this time. On the contrary, they had been fighting successfully until the induction of Garfield. Muir's letters, telegrams, speeches, and pamphlet articles, together with the strong opposition of the Sierra Club to the project, had been rousing conservationists all over America. The press of the East, and indeed of the West outside of the Bay area, had been practically unanimous in condemning what they called "the Hetch Hetchy steal."

On April 21, 1908 Muir wrote a personal appeal to the President, urging that the Hetch Hetchy Valley be saved, even though Lake Eleanor — of less scenic beauty — might be sacrificed. Roosevelt, apparently touched by this letter from his old friend, then tried to back-track or temporize. To Secretary Garfield he wrote:

April 27th, 1908

My dear Mr. Secretary:

Please look over the enclosed letter from John Muir. It does seem to me unnecessary to decide about the Hetch Hetchy Valley at all at present. Why not allow Lake Eleanor, and stop there? . . . there seems to be no reason why we should take action on the Hetch Hetchy business now.

Sincerely yours,

[*signed*] THEODORE ROOSEVELT

But Garfield was too far committed to recede. Muir's telegraphed appeal for a public hearing "on behalf of the people of California and the whole country," and William Colby's request that an impartial Board of Engineers be appointed by the Government to investigate other available sources of water supply, were ignored. Meanwhile the President had been won over again to the other side. And Gifford Pinchot came out with a published statement that the reservoir would do no serious injury to the scenic value of the Sierra.

On May 11, 1908 Secretary Garfield signed the order granting the desired sites to the city of San Francisco. Imposing no conditions of compensation to the Government for property valued at $200,000,000, he asked merely that the Lake Eleanor site be developed first to its capacity.

But John Muir, exhausted and ill at home much of the time with bronchial colds and devastating headaches, girded his remaining strength for the fight ahead and inspired his disheartened followers with new courage:

"Never mind, dear Colby," he wrote, "the present flourishing triumphant growth of the wealthy wicked, the Phelans, Pinchots and their hirelings, will not thrive forever. . . . We may lose this particular fight, but truth and right must prevail at last. Anyhow we must be true to ourselves. . . ."[19]

The fight was by no means over; for according to the terms of the permit the people of San Francisco must still vote to accept it, and Congress must ratify the gift. Otherwise another secretary, not so amenable, might revoke it.

Two days after Garfield signed the permit, the President and Pinchot convened at the White House a much-publicized "Conservation Conference." Robert Underwood Johnson had originated the idea, having suggested it in a letter to Roosevelt. At the time the Chief Forester declared it "impracticable." Later, when the conference convened, the President in a speech fulsomely praised Pinchot, giving him credit for the idea. He also conveyed the impression that to Pinchot belonged the credit for the reserves set aside by President Cleveland. He also failed to mention that conservation as a Government policy stemmed from the Harrison administration and the work of John W. Noble.

The White House conference was a gathering of notables from all over the nation, including governors, university presidents, and a host of other leaders. Charles S. Sargent, General Noble, Edward A. Bowers, and John Muir, however, were not invited. Johnson was able to be present only because of a general bid to the press, and when he protested to Pinchot this neglect of the leaders of conservation, and especially of John Muir, "the pioneer and chief awakener of the people on this subject," he was told there was "no room." [20]

It was noticeable that while the preservation and development of material raw resources, fostered by Gifford Pinchot, was given overwhelming prominence on the program, the conservation of scenic beauty for the health and recreation of the people was given scant hearing. J. Horace McFarland, President of the American Civic Association (now known as the American Planning and Civic Association), and Governor Charles Evans Hughes of New York, alone among the many speakers, urged this form of conservation. Dr. McFarland made a magnificent plea that the Federal Government should safeguard from selfish exploitation the beauty of America, protesting specifically against the commercialism of Niagara Falls and the Yosemite National Park.

Commenting on Pinchot's long-continued opposition to the national parks, and his activities in the Hetch Hetchy deal, Robert Underwood Johnson had this to say: ". . . he felt it more important to get the support of the Pacific slope and other western sentiment for his general conservation policies than that the recreational, hygienic and æsthetic uses of the national parks should be preserved. It was a case of throwing a tub to a whale. He therefore contributed his great influence to the commercialization of the Valley, and but for him I believe the scheme would never have succeeded." [21]

As for Theodore Roosevelt and the extent to which he allowed the Chief Forester to influence him, Johnson relates that on one occasion when he protested to him against damming the Hetch Hetchy, the President replied: "In all forestry matters I have put my conscience in the keeping of Gifford Pinchot." [22]

William Howard Taft was inaugurated as President on March 4, 1909. Literally hoisted into office by his predecessor to carry on "my policies," he was expected to retain the Roosevelt Cabinet. But Taft, revealing an unexpected independence, soon informed all but two members that their services would not be required. In the place of James R. Garfield he appointed Richard A. Ballinger of Seattle as Secretary of the Interior. In a letter to his brother Horace the new President wrote: "The reason why I kept Garfield out of the Cabinet was because I knew him." [23] On another occasion he said he did not retain Garfield because of certain illegal aspects of his conservation policies.[24]

Pinchot was deeply resentful that his friend Garfield had been dropped. He was reported to have called Ballinger "a yellow dog," [25] and to have complained that he had reversed the Garfield policies. This personal feud was to break forth soon in a nationwide scandal that ultimately had much to do with splitting the Republican Party in the election year of 1912.

The change of administrations brought the Hetch Hetchy warfare to a temporary lull. The dam promoters, however, already had a joint resolution before Congress to allow the city and county of San Francisco to exchange outside lands for certain tracts within the park. One of the plots offered in trade for a portion of the sublime Hetch Hetchy Valley was known as Hog Ranch.

Hearings upon the joint resolution were held in Washington early in 1909. The park's cause was ably defended by R. U. Johnson, Harriet Monroe, J. Horace McFarland, and representatives of the Sierra and Appalachian Clubs,[26] so ably, indeed, that several Senators came out for its preservation. James D. Phelan appeared before the Committee in all his cool, suave elegance to speak for the dam project. In the course of his remarks he repeated the old tree-cutting slander against John Muir, and hinted at others: ". . . he began his career . . . as an operator in a sawmill. Verily 'the lover of the tree destroyeth the tree.' . . . He is a poetical gentleman. I am sure he would sacrifice his own family for the preservation of beauty. He considers human life very cheap, and he considers the works of God superior. . . ." [27]

In the course of the questioning both Phelan and Manson were compelled to admit that several other sources — "probably more than a dozen" — could be had "by paying for them." [28] As a result of the hearings Johnson, with resurgent hope, wrote to John Muir: "I believe we are going to win!"

Muir made many trips to the mountains with the Sierra Club in his latter years. Once in the high Alpine air, he threw off his burdens and became his old-time joyous, rollicking self. Stroking his beard and wrinkling his nose, he was an ever gushing fountain of puckish humor. Of his campfire talks Bailey Millard said: "Never was there a naturalist who could hold his hearers so well, and none had so much to tell. Modest and low-voiced, he would set the whole camp in a roar."

Only his daughters, who often went with him before marriage and illness prevented, knew how much it cost him to give those campfire talks. Wanda has related that if he knew he was expected to speak, he would suffer for hours before with nervous chills. His friends, getting an inkling of this, adopted a certain technique in handling him. Nothing would be said to him about making a speech prior to the evening get-together about the blazing fire. The program would proceed with other performers. Then during a lull someone would ask him a question, which he would answer without self-consciousness. This led to another question, and before he knew it, he was launched.

In July 1908 the club made a trip to the Kern River region, where the Fourth was celebrated. Harriet Monroe, the Chicago poet, had written a little play, a forest idyll. Muir had been persuaded with much reluctance, to appear as an invader welcomed by the wild creatures and the trees. It was his one role as an actor and, overwhelmed with bashfulness, he escaped at the earliest opportunity.

A few days later a large party set out for Mount Whitney. Muir was sorely tempted to go with them, but the horse he usually rode was needed to carry a younger man; so he didn't let the others know how much he wanted to go. As their voices faded into the distance, he began to write to Helen:

". . . am taking my ease in my parlor . . . looking at the

trees and lilies, and drinking snow water and its music. . . . I've been lecturing and talking, my tongue sounding on about as ceaselessly as the passing waters. But tomorrow I think I'll step out of camp for a quiet day as of yore. I'm always turning to you wishing you were well enough to be here. . . ."

In August he received a letter from the Harriman family, asking him to join them for a few weeks' outing at Harriman Lodge, their country home on Pelican Bay, Klamath Lake, Oregon. Seeing Harriman in San Francisco, he told him he was too busy writing a book. "Well, you come up to the Lodge and I will show you how to write books," ordered that master of men. "The trouble with you is you are too slow in your beginnings. You plan and brood too much. Begin, begin, begin! . . . Come on, and get something begun." [29] So Muir went.

No one of that house party ever forgot the evenings when family and friends gathered about the big outdoor fireplace to sing and talk under the stars. Muir was in fine form, and one night early in his stay he told them about his boyhood, his stern father, his college days, and his first botany lesson — how that changed all the world for him. "I had been blind before. . . . Now my eyes were opened!"

That night Harriman got an idea, and the next morning he appointed his own expert stenographer, Thomas Price, to follow Muir about and take down every word. From this time on, Price haunted his footsteps. "Might as well try to escape your own shadow as that fellow," grumbled Muir. Since Price took down everything automatically, the result is a strange compost. For instance, as they strolled in the woods, he was telling about the "Dandy Doctors" and the panic that ravaged the children of Scotland lest they be carried off to be cut up in the medical laboratories of Edinburgh. Without pausing in this talk he would suddenly cry out: "By Jove, Price, do you hear that bird?" Or "Listen to that muggins, it's the Douglas squirrel, one of my friends. . . ." Then he went back to the "Dandy Doctors." Moreover, in this first draft of *The Story of My Boyhood and Youth*, sent on to him later typed on more than a thousand pages, he was

William Keith — John Swett — William E. Colby

John Muir with the Sierra Club on the trail to the Hetch Hetchy

often more frank, more revealing about family affairs and his own experiences, than in the published book.

When he had been at Harriman Lodge a few days he wrote to Helen:

"I've . . . been kept so busy, dictating autobiographical stuff, I'm fairly dizzy most of the time, and I can't get out of it, for there's no withstanding Harriman's stenographer under orders. . . . I've never been so task-driven in a literary way before. I don't know when I'll get away from this beneficent bondage. . . . Keith . . . is expected tomorrow evening. I'll tell you promptly how the muggins behaves."

Late in February 1909 John Muir was camping and tramping among the petrified trees of North Forest in Arizona while he awaited the coming of John Burroughs. On the night he arrived, accompanied by his physician, Dr. Clara Barrus, and her friend, Mrs. Ashley, Muir met them at the Adamana station and took them to the Stevenson Hotel. Dr. Barrus, seeing the Western naturalist for the first time, describes him as having "a lonely far-away look in his blue eyes, except when hectoring someone, when he looked like a fun-loving boy. . . . We found him most interesting and the most indefatigable of talkers. Wearied with the journey, Mr. Burroughs finally ventured, 'Muir, I'm sleepy — I'll have to go to bed.'

" 'Sleepy, Johnnie! Why, lad, there'll be time to sleep when you get back to Slabsides, or at least in the grave.' "[30]

After a day spent among the petrified trees, they went on to the Grand Canyon. Arriving tired and hungry in the early morning, Muir jeered at them for wanting breakfast before looking at "the rose-purple abyss a few feet from the hotel." On the last day of their stay Dr. Barrus remarked to Mrs. Ashley: "To think of our having the Grand Canyon and John Burroughs and John Muir thrown in!" Whereupon "J. B." who had been known to complain that Muir was "a little prolix at times," now muttered in his beard: "I wish Muir was thrown in sometimes."[31]

Leaving the Burroughs party in Pasadena, Muir returned north. Later he joined E. H. Harriman in his special car for a trip to

Arizona to consider plans for curbing the annual floods of the Colorado River. The railroad-builder wanted Muir's advice as a geologist upon the best means of achieving this. Had Harriman lived much longer, it is quite possible he would have instituted a river-control project; but as Muir saw him during those days, "weary and pale," and exhausted after the slightest effort, he had said: "there fell a foreboding shadow that I could never shake off." Through his friendship with Muir the magnate had also become interested in saving by purchase a large tract of redwoods on the California coast. But that, too, was left undone.

While they were in Arizona, a belated message reached Muir that Helen, ill with typhoid, had been taken to a Los Angeles hospital. Harriman at once dispatched him with his own physician to her bedside. "Papa rushed into the room pale and frantic," relates Helen, "only to find me getting well and joking with the doctors."

Late April found John Muir playing host in the Yosemite Valley to John Burroughs, the two ladies, and Francis Fisher Browne, editor of the *Dial,* and his warm personal friend. According to Dr. Barrus, the two Johnnies behaved like ten-year-olds.[32]

The first night or two they stayed at a hotel, and on one of these nights Muir and Browne — also a Scotsman — went on "a debauch of poetry." Far into the wee hours they vied with each other in reciting Burns's poems, antiphonally and in concert. As if they had been "elevated"' by some of Burns's own usquabae, they howled with glee over the punches the great Bobbie had taken at Holy Willie and "the unco' gude"; then wept unashamedly over the fate of the "waefu'."

The partitions being thin, Dr. Barrus became concerned for the sleep of Oom John in the adjoining room. Finally she rapped on the wall and shouted: "Noo, bairnies, cuddle doon!" It had the desired effect. The bairnies cuddled doon for the night.

The trails were still blocked with snow, so Muir could not take them to Glacier Point or any other high spot for a wide view; but he persuaded them to camp out with him in the upper part of the valley. From here they walked to see Vernal and Nevada falls. "J. B." was not used to such strenuous exercise. "It was enough to astonish his weary legs," Muir wrote to Helen. "I felt exhilarated and refreshed. Oh, the charm of the mountains!"

He scoffed at them for not wishing to remain several weeks, that they might see the Hetch Hetchy and the Tuolumne Canyon. "I fluttered around here for ten years," said he, "but you expect to see and do everything in four days."

In the Yosemite as elsewhere the two old naturalists wagged their beards in argument upon several subjects. Intelligence versus Instinct in animal behavior was a moot question. Burroughs, of whom Walt Whitman once said: "John goes . . . for usual, accepted, respectable things,"[33] favored the mechanistic theories popular in his day. Animals were "mere animated machines" acting in obedience to "instinct." Only man is "a free lance in nature."

Muir, a lifelong observer of animal behavior, believed instinct to be a body of stored wisdom, a racial memory correlated from the experiences of individuals. It was a heritage common to both men and animals living in the natural state, to be drawn upon in time of need. It did not preclude, on the part of either, the power of reason to meet and solve new problems.

Passionately subscribing to the mechanistic theory, Burroughs had published in the *Atlantic Monthly* of March 1903 an article attacking certain nature-romancers just then flooding the market with stories of wild animals that acted like human beings. His article precipitated an inky fray, into which Theodore Roosevelt leaped, Big Stick and all, denouncing the romancers as "nature fakers." There is not a shred of evidence that either Burroughs or Roosevelt ever classed John Muir as one of these, although Muir's enemies chose to apply the epithet to him. As to the story of Stickeen, Burroughs, who usually damned Muir's writings with faint praise, was fairly enthusiastic, saying it was "almost equal to Rab and His Friends."

But in the Yosemite their main bone of contention was the glacial theory. Burroughs, who had not kept up with recent advances in geology, could not believe that ice had much if any share in excavating the abyss. Muir didn't conceal his scorn. "Aw, Johnnie, ye may tak' all your geology and tie it in a bundle and cast it into the sea, and it wouldna mak' a ripple." Burroughs remained unconvinced and, never able to compete with his brilliant fellow Celt in argument or repartee, eked out a partial revenge in a series of fiery letters and two magazine articles attacking the glacial theory.[34]

One morning in the autumn of 1909 Muir opened his paper to read in big headlines that Harriman was dead. He was shocked and grieved, for he had learned to love him as a brother. So firm was his faith that Harriman had honestly labored to benefit mankind that he decided to write a tribute[35] to him — this in spite of the protests of friends who feared he had gone capitalistic. Dr. Joseph Worcester was one who disapproved; ". . . such accumulations," he said, ". . . are a menace to the integrity of our institutions, and a hindrance to the just ideals of life."

Muir, who was without shadow of turning in his loyalties both to his friends and to his principles, had not gone capitalistic. In his association with Harriman he had made no secret of his lifelong conviction that industrial imperialism was an enemy of democracy. But with the tolerance born of maturity he realized that good as well as evil could be accomplished by monopolistic power. Harriman, taking over the transcontinental lines after the main period of ruthless devastation was past, had organized and improved them, made them safe for public use, established fairer wages and labor conditions, and done much to establish just rates. Under the guiding hand of this man whom he called "the greatest of master builders," Muir, himself a large shipper, saw the railroads now truly developing the West by serving all classes.

In September 1909 Muir was invited by President Taft to accompany him in October to the Yosemite. Seeing here a chance to plead the cause of the Hetch Hetchy, he accepted.

Meanwhile the Pinchot-Ballinger feud flared into the open. Secretary Ballinger was charged by Louis Glavis, apparently acting in accord with Pinchot, with being involved in a conspiracy to turn over certain Alaskan coal lands to the Guggenheim interests. The air was surcharged with explosive elements when President Taft arrived in San Francisco. But hiding his troubled mind behind a smiling face, he went through the elaborate program prepared for him.

On October 6 he was on his way to the Yosemite, accompanied by Governor James N. Gillett, Senator Frank T. Flint, Congressmen William F. Englebright and James C. Needham, and John Muir. Consternation reigned in certain quarters at the inclusion of the last two. Needham, Congressman from the irrigation districts of California, had opposed the Hetch Hetchy dam project in Congress. And as William Colby says: "John Muir was not a man to be whistled down the wind. By their frequent abuse of him they [the dam promoters] revealed the fact that they regarded him as their most powerful opponent."

There was no camping this time, nor, indeed, much chance for Muir to talk alone with the President. Almost every word had to be said in the presence of others, including a flock of newsmen. The second morning found Taft following the old mountaineer on foot down the four-mile trail from Glacier Point to the valley. They hadn't gone far before certain other obese members of the party had to mount horses and mules. Taft, pausing some distance below to watch their descent, came out with one of his great belly laughs as he exclaimed: "Here comes the retreat from Moscow."

At one point where they stopped to rest and look at the valley below, the President, a born tease, remarked slyly to his guide that he thought it would make a fine farm.

"Why!" blazed Muir, "this is Nature's cathedral, a place to worship in. . . ."

"But don't you think," chaffed the President, "that since these valleys are so far from the centers of population, they might just as well be used commercially? Now that," he said, pointing toward the noble gateway to the valley, "would be a fine place for a dam!"

"A dam!" cried Muir, his eyes flashing blue fire. "Yes, . . . but the man who would dam that would be damning himself!"[36]

Taft chuckling as he mopped his perspiring face, was silent a moment, then said gravely: "I suppose you know, Mr. Muir, that several people in San Francisco are very much worried because I asked you to come here with me today."

"Yes," Muir answered, "I know. They call me their enemy, but I didn't know I was so important." After a pause he sighed: "Oh, I guess the rascals will get it in the end." Then he flamed with anger: "It's just like the temple of Jerusalem. They looked at the beautiful place, and said 'Here's a fine place for our money-changers.' That's the only time Christ ever lost his temper!"

If the President appeared to tease Muir more than the other members of his party, it was doubtless because he delighted in drawing his fire and listening to his quaint sallies. But the reporters from local newspapers, puffing along to keep within ear-shot, interpreted it in their favor. One of them wrote to his paper that the President had "shown amused tolerance of Muir's emphatic views" and had twitted him on his "sentimentality."

Just before noon Taft, all hot and drenched with sweat, arrived with his party at the foot of the trail and was whisked away to the Sentinel Hotel. After luncheon they were driven about the valley. Some time during this trip or later the President created an opportunity to talk with his guide alone. Muir showed him some maps and charts he had brought with him, outlining the future development of the entire park, making all parts accessible to the public. He proposed a system of roads and trails to unite the four main features of the area — the Yosemite Valley, Tuolumne Meadows, Tuolumne Canyon, and the Hetch Hetchy Valley — into one of the grandest sightseeing routes in the world.

Taft was enthusiastic over the plan. Moreover, he made plain his opposition to the dam project. Muir wrote down this comment upon their conversation:

"We have much to expect from President Taft. . . . We have good reason to expect that in his message to Congress he will recommend necessary appropriations and legislation that will put to an end such schemes . . . to include the nation's parks for municipal or private purposes."

Acceding to the President's wishes, Muir waited the next day at El Portal to greet Secretary Ballinger and hand him a letter in which Taft urged that he take Muir as his guide to the Hetch Hetchy. With the Secretary on this trip were George Otis Smith of the U. S. Geological Survey, and two eminent Government engineers.

This caused wild alarm among the dam promoters. One newspaper expressed fear lest "Old Professor Muir" had been "drumming into the Presidential ear the other side of the question." But another doing some wishful thinking said it was only to "salve Muir's wounded feelings" that he had been asked to accompany the Secretary.

Muir, however, far from being wounded, seems to have had a very satisfactory trip with Ballinger and his engineers. The reasons appeared later in the fact that throughout the Taft administration the dam promoters pushed their cause in vain.

Soon after President Taft's visit to the park he appointed a board of expert Government engineers, headed by George Otis Smith, to investigate the possibilities of Lake Eleanor's capacity to supply the city of San Francisco. This board reported among other things: ". . . that the Lake Eleanor project is amply sufficient to meet the present and prospective needs of the city. . . ." After studying the Smith Report, Secretary Ballinger set a hearing [37] of the case and called upon the city officials "to show cause why the Hetch Hetchy Valley and reservoir site should not be eliminated from said permit."

Meanwhile in the late fall of 1909 Washington became the hot spot of the nation. With Gifford Pinchot now the known leader of the fight, a series of defamatory articles against Ballinger appeared in *Collier's Weekly*. Norman Hapgood, editor of *Collier's*, Mark Sullivan, and "Marse" Henry Watterson chimed in with their beating of drums, and soon the press of the nation joined the hue and cry, condemning Secretary Ballinger without a hearing. A Congressional investigation absolving him of guilt was denounced as "a whitewash." As a result of his being "at the bottom of the business," President Taft discharged Pinchot from the Forest Service. Thereupon his attacks became more violent than before, and in the uproar the public could not get at the truth.

Urged by his friends and party leaders to throw Ballinger to the wolves to clear himself, the President said: "If I were to turn

Ballinger out in view of . . . the conspiracy against him, I should be a white-livered skunk. I don't care how it affects my administration. . . ."

Space will not allow here a review of the merits of the Ballinger case, except to say that in the calm light of later years this "American Dreyfus" has been adjudged innocent of the charges against him.[38] The only reason for bringing it up here is that, because of Pinchot's large share in the affair, it came to be tied up with the Hetch Hetchy fight and, in the logic of succeeding events, helped to bring about the final victory of the dam promoters and the defeat of John Muir in the last great battle of his life.

In these latter years Muir spent some weeks or months each winter in southern California, to escape northern fogs. Everywhere he was welcomed, for no man ever had more friends. In Pasadena lived an especially congenial coterie — A. C. Vroman, the bookstore man; Colonel A. H. Sellers, father of the Frank Sellers of Yellowstone memories; and T. P. Lukens, a bank president who under Muir's guidance had done much for conservation. The aging naturalist delighted in quietly visiting these friends in their beautiful homes, but he wanted no society fuss made over him. He loathed formal dinners and receptions where he was expected to scintillate. Whenever this "shy bird," as he called himself, suspected such a trap was going to be sprung, he took flight, seeking sanctuary with Helen on the desert, or with Mr. and Mrs. J. E. Calkins in their little country home at San Dimas. Here he would hide away until the celebrity-hunters had quit gunning for him, and the "society weather" calmed down. On one occasion Calkins mentioned to Vroman that Muir had just been visiting him. "So that's where he went, the muggins! We sat up until two o'clock, wondering where he was."

Calkins relates an incident he witnessed in the Sellers home in 1910, that illustrates Muir's homely simplicity and lack of self-consciousness in situations that would have put most folks to the blush:

John D. Hooker's big car and chauffeur arrived to carry him to the Hooker home in Los Angeles for a visit, so he went up to his room to pack. Presently he came down the stately stairway, carrying a shabby, old-fashioned satchel that had come open at one end. Behind him for several feet trailed an exceedingly long gray nightgown of the old school, a wide, woolen flood, cascading down from step to step. His host and hostess and other guests, standing below to bid him farewell, began to show signs of mirth. Glancing back he saw the nightgown. But he was not disturbed, and saw no need for explanation or apology. He simply said: "Ha! I seem to be losing some of my gear," set the satchel down in the midst of the company and proceeded to reel in the vagrant gown, stowing it in by handfuls well-thrust home, utterly unconscious that he was even remotely amusing.

Among the friends who did much to relieve his loneliness and give him the physical care he needed were the members of the John D. Hooker family. Their residence on West Adams street in Los Angeles was one of the "five homes" he called his, where for extended periods he was an honored guest. John D. Hooker, a retired ironmaster and a brother of Henry C. (Don Pedro) Hooker of the Arizona desert, was a lover of nature and an amateur astronomer. Other members of the household were Mrs. Katharine Hooker, their daughter Dr. Marion Hooker, Mrs. Fred Jones, a niece of Hooker's, and her husband. "Alice-hark-the-lark" was Muir's name for Mrs. Jones.

His first long stay with this family was in the spring of 1910, and followed an invitation by Mr. Hooker to attend a stag dinner in Pasadena in honor of Andrew Carnegie. Helen Muir, now married to Buel A. Funk, the son of a cattle rancher on the desert, continued to make her home near Daggett, and when Muir came down to attend the dinner, he brought along a goodly supply of journals and manuscripts, intending to write at her home. But needing more space to spread out his papers, he was persuaded to move to the Hooker home, where a large upper room, which he called "My Palace Garret," was fitted up for his labors. The months he spent in that luxurious home formed a joyous interlude in the stark final years of John Muir. Here he was loved and petted as an old man sometimes needs to be. "Alice-hark-the-lark" brought him a rose for his coat lapel each morning, and Mrs.

Henrietta Thompson, his secretary, supplied him with ties to match his gentian-blue eyes. There were happy evenings spent playing billiards with the men of the household, or smoking and talking with the whole family around the fireplace until the small hours of the morning. One night with an air of great bravado he produced a package of Egyptian cigarettes — the first he had ever smoked. When they heckled him about them, he puffed out his chest and said: "I'm seventy years old." (He seldom remembered his exact age.) "I guess I'm old enough to do as I please. They're mild anyway."

In this period of comfort and relaxation he made greater speed than ever before with his writing. In the space of a few months his first Sierra journal of 1869 was ready for publication. Wisely he made few changes, allowing his text to retain all the fresh spontaneity of his early impressions. When Ellery Sedgewick, editor of the *Atlantic Monthly,* read over the manuscript of *My First Summer in the Sierra,*[39] he wrote to Muir: "I felt almost as if I had found religion!"

In the spring of 1910 Muir received word that Yale University wished to confer upon him at commencement the degree of Litt.D. He accepted, and then, just as he was about to leave for the East to receive it, he heard from the ranch that his sister Margaret Reid was ill. He telegraphed the Yale trustees that he would be unable to attend and hurried home. On June 22 he wrote to Mrs. Hooker: "My dearest, best-loved sister died this afternoon. . . . Glad I was with her to cheer and soothe and comfort while yet she knew me and fondly clung to me. . . . But, oh friends, the last love-glance, last quivering embrace on the edge of the dark. . . ."

In the fall he returned to the Hooker home. Soon he was hard at work revising "the Pelican Lodge auto stuff" into *The Story of My Boyhood and Youth.*[40] Also he was writing *The Yosemite.*[41]

One reason for his happiness at this time was the fact that by the year 1911 he had been "grandfathered thrice by a quarter-dozen youngsters . . . what with Wanda's two and Helen's one." Wanda's Strentzel and John, and Helen's Muir [42] gave their hilarious old grandfather many an excuse to visit the two ranches. An almost miraculous upsurge of new strength came to him in that spring. ". . . the almanac offers startling proofs of age. Yet strange to say, I am almost wholly unconscious of the fast-flying years. . . . This, in part, is the reward of those who climb mountains and keep their noses out of doors."

In March he was invited to a stag dinner given in Pasadena in honor of Theodore Roosevelt, which he described as "a very brilliant and in every way Rooseveltian affair." In spite of all the ex-President had done to give away the Hetch Hetchy, Muir never ceased to love something fine and genuine he had discerned in him during those three days and nights in the wilderness. Although he "did not like the big-stick, hat-in-the-ring political bluster, he always said: 'That is not the real Roosevelt.' "[43] As to the Hetch Hetchy, Roosevelt had been unduly influenced by Pinchot, and once he could be made to see the truth, he might yet defend the valley. Muir got his innings at the dinner by having a long talk with the former President, who "was greatly interested, and promised to help."

But Muir was not too optimistic about that promise. "This playing at politics saps the very foundations of righteousness," he once said. Moreover, he knew the pre-election pot was already boiling, with Pinchot stoking the fires. He knew the one-time Chief Forester, discharged by Taft, had run away to Africa to confer with the returning big-game hunter. As a result Roosevelt came back to America already primed with bitterness against his old friend and chosen successor. And Roosevelt, still young and ambitious, was even then making another bid for the White House.

John Muir was deeply disturbed in that spring of 1911 by the increasingly grave illness of William Keith. In every letter to Colby he begged to be kept informed: "How is Keith. Tell me right off, and give him my love."

Keith died on April 13. The passing of this friend, who along with John Swett had been closer to him than all others, left in Muir's heart a lingering sorrow. He knew, too, that his own sands were fast running out. Meanwhile he would have one more grand adventure!

"Have I forgotten the Amazon, Earth's greatest river?" said Muir in a letter to a friend.[44] "Never, never, never. It has been burning in me half a century, and will burn forever."

His eager young desire to follow Humboldt to the Amazon was his eager old desire demanding fulfillment. Feeling within himself a great resurgence of energy, as if sent to meet this need, and confident that the Hetch Hetchy warfare was stalemated for yet another year, he announced in April 1911 that he would visit South America that summer. His friends called it "a wild excursion" and tried to dissuade him. But with his sense of guidance as strong as in his prime, he calmly replied: "God will take care of me and bring me home safely."

Arriving in New York, he picked up Robert Underwood Johnson and traveled on to Washington. Here he was caught up in a whirl of dinners, speeches, and interviews that had no ill effects: *Had a long, hearty, telling talk with the President, three with Secretary Fisher, lunched with Champ Clark. . . . Smoked and talked over the whole Hetch Hetchy history with . . . Joe Cannon. . . . Saw lots of Senators and Representatives, and made an hour and a half speech on H.H. and parks at a grand dinner of the influential Boone and Crockett Club. . . . I never imagined I could stand so much dining and late hours.*[45]

Back in New York, he was the house guest of Mrs. Harriman and her daughters, and spoke on behalf of the Hetch Hetchy at banquets given in his honor by the Alpine and Appalachian Clubs. He went also to New Haven, where he received his degree from Yale: ". . . we donned our radiant academic robes and marched to the great hall . . . shining like crow blackbirds. I was given perhaps the best seat on the platform, and when my name was called I arose with a grand air, shook my massive academic plumes into finest fluting folds, as became the occasion, stepped forward in awful majesty and stood rigid and solemn like an ancient sequoia while the orator poured praise on the honored wanderer's head — and in this heroic attitude I think I had better leave him." [46]

He had brought east with him for final revision the manuscripts of *The Yosemite,* and *The Story of My Boyhood and Youth.* For

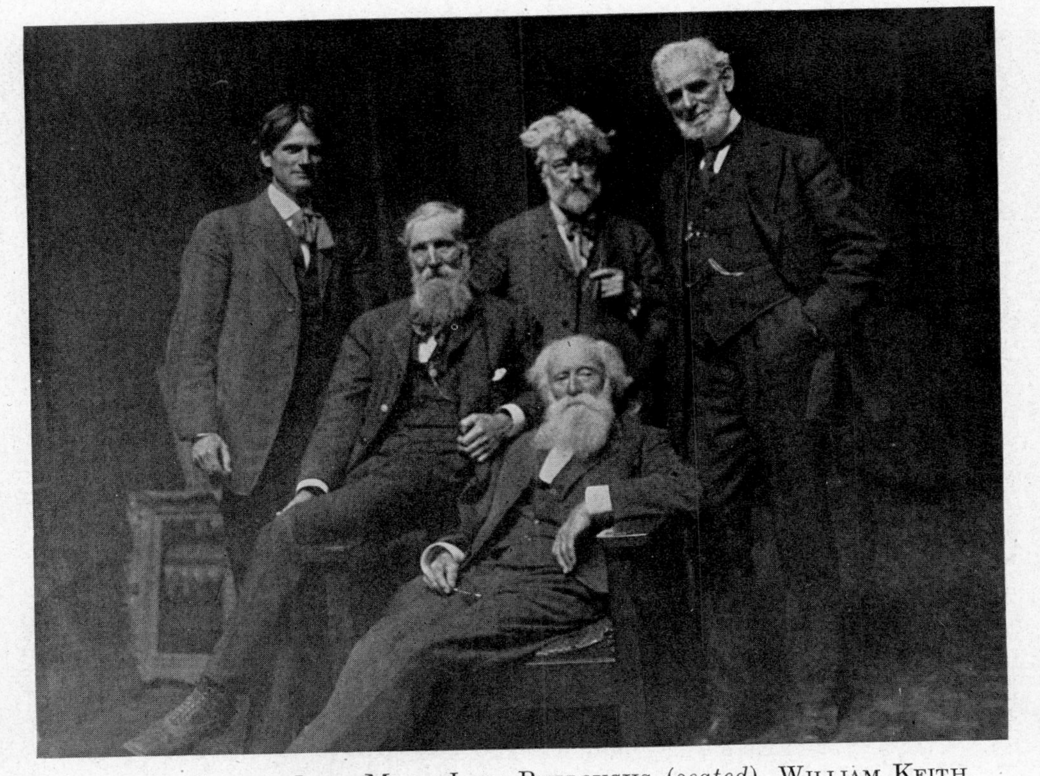

Charles Keeler, John Muir, John Burroughs (*seated*), William Keith, Francis Fisher Browne

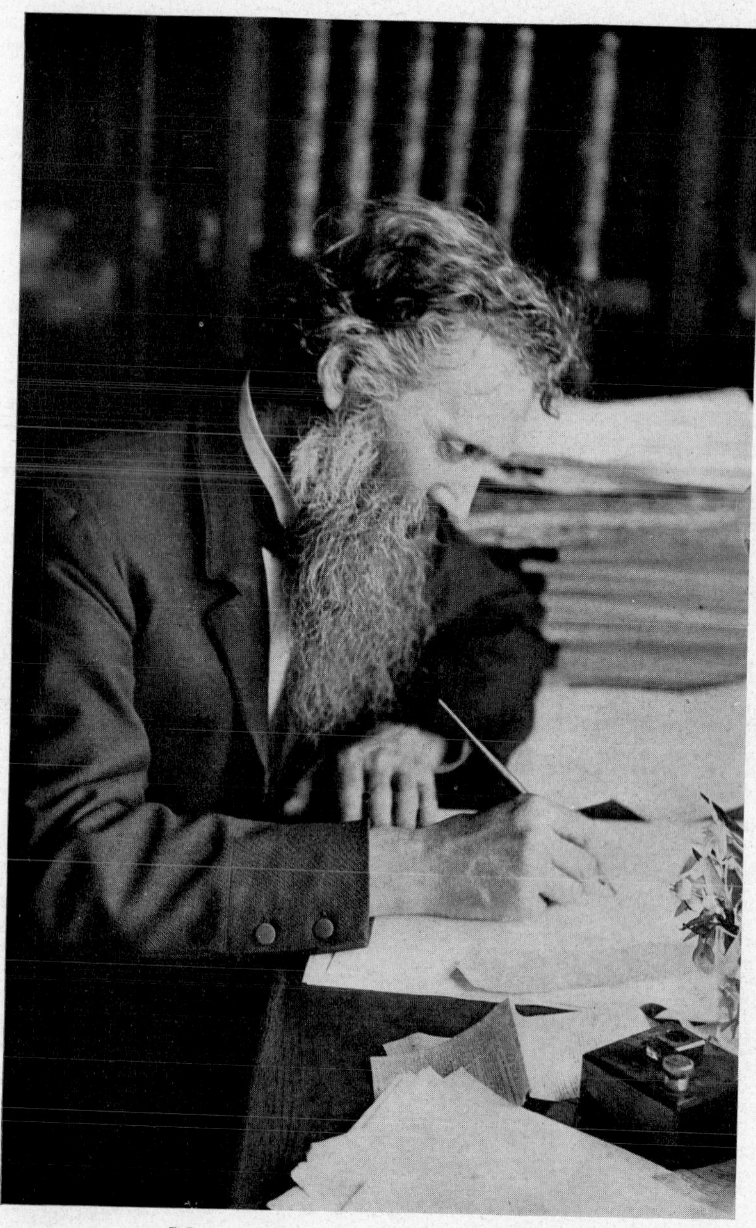

Muir *at work in his "scribble-den"*

some weeks in a little cottage on the Hudson River estate of the Osborns he toiled away at them from dawn to dark. "I have never worked harder in my life," he wrote to John Burroughs. ". . . I do not know what has got into me, making so many books all at once. It is not natural. . . ."[47]

All this in the midst of the gnawing pain of knowing that since he had left home two more dear friends, Colonel Sellers of Pasadena and John D. Hooker, had departed this life. To Helen he wrote: "I wonder if leaves feel lonely when they see their neighbors falling."

When he set sail on August 11, facing a new unknown, it was with the boyish eagerness of his prime. All the protests of his Eastern friends had been in vain. "The world's big," he said, "and I want to have a good look at it before it gets dark." He only chuckled when John Burroughs said he had "gane gite, clean gite" to take such a trip. And when Professor Osborn remonstrated against his going alone, he replied: "I never turn back." Then, quoting Milton, he added: "I have chosen the lonely way. . . ."[48] He didn't tell them he intended to go on to Africa as well. He had long had a rendezvous with a tree in that country — the baobab.

After "a long sublime slide" down to equatorial regions, he embarked on August 31 for a sail up the Amazon. Not wanting to miss a bit of the scenery, he was on deck at four a.m. As they went through "the Narrows," he could almost touch the over-leaning palms. Out in the wider reaches he gloried in the dense vegetation and gorgeous flowers that clothed the banks, and the Indian villages with naked children swarming to the water's edge; while hovering overhead like a canopy were white egrets, ducks, parrots, and buzzards.

On September 5 the ship docked at Manáos, where in the midst of "the rubbery wilderness" he made many friends. "It is perfectly wonderful to me how kind people are to this stranger!" he naïvely exclaimed. With a group he went on a steam tug up a lagoon of the Río Negro into the heart of the jungle. As they crawled up the dark, mysterious waterway, the tall reedy grasses became so dense they had to take to skiffs. Finally they were forced to leave these and creep on hands and knees beneath innumerable ropy lianas and over fallen trees. When the others wanted to turn back, Muir urged going on. He had hoped to find somewhere in that tangled wilderness the *Victoria regia* — a nymphæaceous plant with an enormous white flower and spreading leaves — blooming in her native habitat. But when the way became an impenetrable mesh of vines, even he was compelled to give up and return to the tug.

Coming back to the mouth of the Amazon, he sailed down the coast to Santos. On shipboard he met a party of lumbermen who invited him to go with them into the forests of the interior, where grows the *Araucaria braziliana*. From Port Amazonas they sailed on the Iguassú River into the heart of the mighty woods. "Magnificent primeval forest . . . crowns like umbrella tops rising above each other. . . . Tree ferns fifteen to twenty feet high, fronds five feet long. . . ."

A few days later in Buenos Aires, with Government officials, scientists, and reporters besieging him, he commented wonderingly: "So my fame has travelled this far." He told a newsman he wasn't going to write any more books "until I give up my present occupation."

"And what may that be?"

"Tramp," said he. "I'm seventy-four, and still good at it." [49]

After crossing the great central plateau by train, he was cordially welcomed at Santiago, Chile, by Henry P. Fletcher, the American Minister Plenipotentiary, and taken to the Legation on the famous Avenida. "Never shall I forget the views of the snowy Andes from the balcony of my bedroom window."

The *Araucaria imbricata,* popularly known as the monkey-puzzle tree, was now his quarry, although nobody, not even the Botanical Garden directors, knew where it could be found. But Muir felt certain it must grow along the western slopes of the Andes near the snow line. Following his hunch, he traveled five hundred miles down to Victoria. Then going inland by buggy and later by horseback, he found on a high ridge a whole forest of the trees. That night he camped in a grove with the strange, grotesque trees fringing the horizon all about. His two companions slept in a tent, but the old man of the mountains lay down under the stars, facing the araucarias he had come so far to see. "Guess how happy I was and how I stared at and admired these ancient trees," he wrote to Helen.

New friends turned up everywhere to guide him in a way that seemed to him miraculous. President Taft was the good angel partly responsible for this. Through the far-flung consular service he watched over him on his long journey. But often the friends were civilians who appeared opportunely. His fragile appearance doubtless made everybody want to take care of him. He was vastly amused by an old German lady on the train who insisted upon peeling and cutting up his fruit for him.

While in Montevideo awaiting an Africa-bound steamer, he was inveigled into making a speech. A Mr. Conrad who had been "wondrous kind" promised him a small, informal group to whom he need speak only briefly. When he arrived at the hall, he found a large audience. The American Minister gave him a flattering introduction, then asked him questions to get him started. The night was sultry, but his listeners forgot that in the charm and eloquence of his words. They kept him talking for two hours. "Never was this wanderer more heartily cheered," he recorded. Newspaper accounts following him home reveal that the address created a sensation, being praised as one of the best ever given in that city.

Early in December he was again sailing the tropical seas, bound for Africa. "No sound of wind save a low whispering from small waves brushing the ship's side, and the low heart beats of the engines. . . . The ship glides smoothly like a star."

He soon gauged the caliber of his shipmates. "Not a glint of science visible." But with a second-class passenger who knew the writings of Darwin, Tyndall, and Haeckel he leaned over the rail for hours daily, studying the dragon-like cloud formations, the flying fish, and the dolphins that frolicked in the sea. On Christmas Eve the crew sang carols among the cabins. The old wanderer was a bit lonely and homesick that night, and to comfort himself got out his "favorite letters" and read them over.

Arriving at Cape Town in mid-January 1912, he took the train northward to Victoria Falls, there to enjoy "one of the greatest of the great tree days of my lucky life." At the hotel he stopped only long enough to ask the manager the way to the baobabs. "What are they?" inquired that functionary. Muir described them, but still he did not know. No other tourists, he said, had asked for them. Muir then went out into the street, making inquiries of everybody he saw. Finally a little barefooted Negro boy said he knew where they were. So in the wake of this simple child of nature he was led directly to a large grove of baobabs about a mile from the head of Victoria Falls.

"Kings may be blest," he wrote to Helen, "but I am glorious! Wandered about in the woods that fringe the Falls, dripping with spray, and through the Baobab woods. . . . It is easily recognized by its skin-like bark, and its massive trunk and branches. The bark . . . looks like leather, or the skin of a hippopotamus. . . . The Falls too are grand and novel. . . . Smoke-like spray ever ascending, watering the woods with constant showers. . . ."

At Beira, Muir boarded a Dutch steamer bound north along the eastern coast. From Mombasa he made a trip inland to the sources of the Nile. On the train he found the inevitable friend, a Swiss gentleman named Louis Barbetzat, who, seeing he had brought only dry crackers to eat, shared with him his basket lunch. That night in the cold, berthless compartment he got up and gently laid his own two warm rugs over the sleeping old man. In the middle of the night two Scotchmen entered the compartment, and Muir, hearing one of them pronounce the name John "as naebody but a Scot would speak it," leaped to his feet to greet the strangers. The next day all had a grand time talking and viewing the glacial mountain scenery interspersed with forests and grassy plains. Back of this region Roosevelt and his army of followers had hunted two years before, cutting a wide swath through the wild life with their guns.

From Port Florence, Muir embarked on Lake Victoria Nyanza and, landing at the village of Jinga, went to view Ripon Falls — "a magnificent show of foam." Below the falls stretched the great river of history, starting on its journey down the wide Nile Valley.

Returning to America by way of the Mediterranean and the

Atlantic, he arrived in New York on March 26 after an absence of more than seven months, bronzed and fleshier than he had been for years. Refuting all the dire predictions of his friends, he had not been sick a day on the whole journey. His ageless, unquenchable spirit had once more been master of his body, and his power to wonder undimmed. Pausing only long enough to visit Burroughs on his seventy-fifth birthday, he sped like a homing pigeon toward California. He stopped in Hollywood, where Helen was now living, to see her and his namesake, Muir, and then went north to the ranch to rejoice in Wanda and her third son, Richard, born in his absence.

In a letter to the Osborns he spoke of the "contrast abysmal" between his desolate home and theirs. But abysmal as it was, the old house with its memories and the gardens he and his wife had planted meant more than any other place on earth to him. He knew he had gone on his last long journey. All that remained was work.

Now that the exaltation of his journey had died out, he was more tired than he would admit. Almost immediately he caught a severe cold. "Breathing the dust in my den," he said, had caused it. This cold went deeper into his lungs than ever before, threatening pneumonia. But although hardly able to speak aloud, he was at his desk daily. "Just now from every direction grim work is staring me hard in the face, crying, ' 'Twill soon be dark,' and urging concentration and haste. . . . I'm in my little library den looking over notes, plotting and planning."

Ten years before he had planned to write many books — twenty at least. He made outlines and even rough manuscript drafts of a few of them. Burroughs, visiting him in 1909 and seeing his "barrels of notes," had begged him to hurry and "make them up into loaves." But "the everlasting Hetch Hetchy business" had devoured his time and strength. Two or three books at the most were all he could hope to finish now.

In July 1912 Helen's second son, Stanley, was born, and Grandfather went down to greet the new arrival. Returning to the ranch, he set to work on his Alaska notes. Unable to labor long hours at a stretch, two or three times a day he ambled down to the adobe to play with Strentzel and John. Thomas Rae Hanna relates that the agent of Muir's publisher hovered about for hours one day trying to get his signature to a contract for *Travels in Alaska*. But the boys had captured him, and he had no time for anyone else. Finally they clapped a wicker basket far down over his head, shrieking with glee to see how funny he looked, with his eyes twinkling out like those of a bird in a cage. Not until they grew tired of this sport and ran away did he sign the contract. So he lived every hour to the full. "Even in old age Uncle John was the most alive man I ever knew," says his niece, May Reid Coleman.

Muir's other greatest pleasure when at home was his daily stroll and talk-fest with John Swett. Every morning they met at a certain time on the border line between the two ranches, one hailing the other with some trivial remark such as "It's a fine day, Johnnie," and the other contradicting him. This launched their regular forensic exercise over the merits of the weather and what it would do to the fruit. Their voices rose high and shrill, both talking at once, until some stranger passing by on the road would think the two old white-bearded farmers were having a violent quarrel. This preliminary over, they walked together up to the Swett adobe to sit on the porch and thrash out the affairs of the nation and the world.

John Muir and John Swett had much to discuss that fall of 1912, for the country was in an uproar surpassing that of most election years. Theodore Roosevelt was campaigning up and down the land, preaching his crusade of "New Nationalism" and working the people into a frenzy with his charges of rascality and corruption against the over-patient man in the White House. The Republicans of California, under the lead of Hiram Johnson, had stampeded in the primaries into the shortlived Bull Moose Party, with Roosevelt as their prophet and Presidential candidate.

With Gifford Pinchot as one of the chief financial backers of the campaign, and slated for his old-time influence in the Government if Roosevelt won, the Hetch Hetchy power-and-water project, not killed, only scotched, raised its head once more.

On October 13, while campaigning, Roosevelt was shot and slightly wounded by the fanatic John Shrank. Muir, profoundly shocked, telegraphed to his old friend his sympathy and congratulations upon his escape from more serious harm.

But on November 5 he voted for William Howard Taft.

The country went Democratic, Woodrow Wilson was elected, and President Taft went out of office under a cloud, "the victim of too much Roosevelt." [50]

The Hetch Hetchy hearing, repeatedly postponed over a period of three years at the request of the San Francisco city officials, was finally held in November. Basing his decision upon the Report of the Board of Army Engineers appointed by the President, "that there are several sources of water supply that could be obtained and used by the city of San Francisco and adjacent communities," Secretary Fisher [51] denied the city's request that the Hetch Hetchy be converted into a power-and-water reservoir.

But with the accession of President Wilson on March 4, 1913, a new Cabinet came into being. Franklin K. Lane, former City Attorney of San Francisco, became Secretary of the Interior; and having advocated the dam project while he served the city, he now lost no time in promoting it.

On May 14, Charter Day of the University of California, John Muir and John Swett were the recipients of the degree of Doctor of Laws. Helen Swett Artieda has recalled the occasion: "I can close my eyes today and see that picture of the Greek Theatre on a bright summer day. The two Johns . . . hats off, white hair blown back from their foreheads by the breeze — two stalwarts, for all the world like the trees they both so greatly loved. . . ."

As he conferred the degree upon John Muir, President Wheeler spoke these impressive words:

JOHN MUIR, *Born in Scotland, reared in the University of Wisconsin, by final choice a Californian, Widely travelled Observer of the world we dwell in, Man of Science and of Letters, Friend and Protector of Nature, Uniquely gifted to Interpret unto others Her mind and ways.*

The following day the Swett and Hanna families compared notes. It developed that John Swett, upon being asked what he thought of the new honor, remarked: "I don't care so much for myself. But I'm glad they did it for John!" While down the valley John Muir replied to the same question in identical words: "I don't care so much for myself. But I'm glad they did it for John."[52]

This was a recognition long overdue. But for Muir, honorary degrees, already granted him by Yale, Harvard, and the University of Wisconsin, were an old story.[53] Lack of local recognition of his work he was accustomed to. The main thing was to get the work done, let the credit fall where it would. Other honors had come to him, such as membership in the American Academy of Arts and Letters and the Washington Academy of Science, also a fellowship in the American Association for the Advancement of Science. Moreover, he had served as president of the Sierra Club and of the American Alpine Club. Perhaps no recognition touched him more deeply than the creation in 1908 of the Muir Woods National Monument, on a fine tract of *Sequoia sempervirens* in Marin County, named after him by the wish of the donor, William Kent.[54]

By midsummer the Hetch Hetchy campaign was once more in full swing. Muir, in the face of almost certain defeat, took up the old task of defending the park. With his hand ever upon the pulse of the nation, he sent out from his den a steady stream of letters, telegrams, newspaper articles, and appeals published by the Sierra Club. He had many helpers. Prominent among his California aides were Edward T. Parsons and William Frederic Badè, members of the club. Writing and lecturing indefatigably, they won many to the cause. Dr. Badè made several trips east and to Washington to defend the Hetch Hetchy. In the East the Harrimans and Osborns used all their great influence, interceding with the President himself. Johnson wrote editorials for the *Century* and the *New York Times,* revealing Pinchot's share in the Hetch Hetchy dam plan. The *Boston Transcript,* the *Los Angeles Times,* the *Portland Oregonian,* and many other leading newspapers of the nation fought to preserve the valley. The Mazamas and the Mountaineers of the West, and the American Alpine and

Appalachian Clubs of the East, worked valiantly in the cause, while the American Civic Association, with J. Horace McFarland as president, redoubled its efforts.

But they got nowhere. William Jennings Bryan, who knew no more about the Hetch Hetchy than about certain scientific subjects, was won over to the dam project. And President Wilson, without making an independent investigation, put his "forestry conscience" into the hands of his two Cabinet members Bryan and Lane.

In the midst of the bitter turmoil, on an August day in 1913, John Swett quietly slipped out of life. So fast were Muir's friends going now, like withered leaves in winter winds. Within little more than a decade Mrs. Carr, Catharine Merrill, Keith, Browne, Sir Joseph Hooker, John and Henry Hooker, Colonel Sellers, and Harriman had gone. As Muir turned away from Swett's grave, he felt lost and alone. No more daily communings with this best of friends, this alter ego, who had stabilized and guided him in his young manhood and had labored beside him effectively through all the years.

Late in August when the skids were already well greased for its swift passage, proponents of the Raker bill that would transfer the Hetch Hetchy finally to San Francisco's uses announced in Washington that the measure would not be considered until December. Meanwhile the tariff bill had the floor. When September dawned, many Congressmen opposing the measure were absent from the capital. Then on September 3 the Raker bill was suddenly resurrected and rushed through the House by a vote of 183 to 43, with 205 not voting.

John Muir, toiling at his desk through the blazing summer heat, wrote to Mrs. Osborn: "The Raker Bill has been meanly skulked and railroaded and logrolled through the House, but we are hoping it will be checked in the Senate."

In October, when his strength was well-nigh spent, Mrs. Harriman persuaded him to spend a week with her and her sister-in-law, Mrs. Averell, at their Idaho ranch on the Snake River. From the moment he boarded the train he was cared for by railroad officials delegated for that purpose. At sunrise he was feasting his hungry eyes upon "the blessed pines" of Summit. It was long since he had wandered among them. At Salt Lake he was taken for a drive. He asked to go to the Tabernacle to hear the great organ. "Memorable organ music . . . especially 'Nearer My God to Thee,' so devout, so sweet, so whispering low."

At Island Park Ranch he was welcomed by his two hostesses. After breakfast in a trance of delight he went out to stroll on the "spacious, peaceful meadows embosomed in spiry pines . . . mountains all around. . . ." (To one reading that last slender journal of his wanderings, all his comments seem to bear the accent of farewell.) The following days he spent driving among the firs and spruces, greeting them with his old-time boyish joy, or walking along "the clear, shimmering, whispering, slow-gliding river." On the last night, as if to complete his pleasure, came "a fine thunder-storm with grand display of zigzag, intensely vivid and very near lightning, with keen crashes, grand trailing rain tresses." He sat long on the veranda, enjoying it.

In November the defenders of the Hetch Hetchy marshaled their forces for a last stand in Washington.[55] On the 15th Muir wrote to Helen:

"The H.H. question will probably be decided in the first week of December next and I still think we will win. Anyhow I'll be relieved when it's settled, for it's killing me.

"No matter, for I've had a grand life in these divine mountains and I may yet do something for those coming after me. Do try to make my load as light as possible by keeping well."

During those critical days while he awaited hourly the dire news that would mean the defeat of his long labor, it was characteristic of the many-sided Muir that he offered generous assistance to a friend. Professor Melville Anderson of Stanford University wrote to him from Italy that he feared he could not find a publisher for his new translation of Dante's *Divine Comedy*. Muir replied:

Dear Dante:—I'm delighted to learn that your days of exile re drawing to a close, your grand Dante done according to your wn heart. I . . . make haste to assure you there can be no rouble about the publication . . . for I'll gladly bear all the exense. . . .

Nor did he forget in that midnight hour of his life to send on)ecember 5 his annual draft of a hundred dollars to his cousin ı Scotland, to be divided equally between herself and "the poor f Dunbar."

When the message finally came early in December that the Raker bill had passed the Senate, he wrote to Helen: ". . . we till hope the President will veto it. Anyhow I've done my best, nd am now free to go on with my pen work. The book now on and is Alaska. . . . We are all about as usual. . . . I'm somewhat run down for want of exercise, and exhausting work and vorry. . . ."

That was an extreme understatement, made to keep Helen from vorrying. In truth he was ill with exhaustion and grief. His right ung was seriously infected; and the cough that tore his frail flesh ıe would never be rid of again. Those who visited him in those lays of defeat thought him near the end. One of them, Robert B. Marshall of the U. S. Geological Survey, wrote: ". . . it was sorrowful indeed to see him sitting in his cobwebbed study in his onely house . . . with the full force of his defeat upon him, after the struggle of a lifetime in the service of Hetch Hetchy. It was one of the most pathetic things I ever witnessed, and I could not but think that if Congress, the President, and even the San Francisco contingent, could have seen him, they would certainly have been willing to have delayed any action until the old man had gone away — and I fear that is going to be very soon, as he appeared to me to be breaking very fast." [56]

All who were close to John Muir in those days of his Gethsemane knew that his sorrow was not for personal humiliation and defeat. Rather it was for the cause he loved. He saw in the Hetch Hetchy fight the entering wedge of future efforts to destroy the national parks, to devour them piecemeal. Nothing would be safe from commercialism.

Muir, however, was a prophet of the shape of things to com Like that Thomas Muir of Edinburgh who defended the rights c the lowly, he might have said: "I have devoted myself to the caus of the people. It is a good cause. It shall ultimately prevail. I shall ultimately triumph!"

Even in defeat he had still his indomitable optimism, his belie in the essential goodness of mankind. To Henry Fairfield Osbor he said: "Fortunately wrong cannot last, soon or late it must fal back home to Hades, while some compensating good must surel follow." [57] And again he said in a letter to Bailey Millard: "The will see what I meant in time. There must be places for huma beings to satisfy their souls. Food and drink is not all. There is th spiritual. In some it is only a germ, of course, but the germ wil grow!"

The work of the past twelve years had indeed not been in vain Out of struggle and failure were arising portents of a better day The nation, shocked and aroused by the rape of the Hetch Hetchy would never again allow such an exploitation of the people's her itage of beauty. A letter from Enos Mills about this time mus have been reassuring. Mills, taking the torch from Muir's failing hand, was starting out on his own aggressive campaign for th creation and preservation of national parks.

I shall leave for Washington in a few days to help set thing moving for the conservation of scenery. . . .

As you well know, it is the work that you have done that ha encouraged me . . . in the big work that I am planning to do If you will push along another book or two these books will help the cause more than you can imagine.

And there were others strong and in their prime — Stephen T Mather, Robert Underwood Johnson, C. Hart Merriam, John C Merriam, J. Horace McFarland, William E. Colby,[58] and many more — arising into leadership to carry on the work he had begun Best of all there were thousands of young men and women for whom he had blazed the way, enlisted in the great outdoor clubs of the country, climbing mountains, skiing, learning to know the health and freedom of the wilderness and the love of beauty. These would be the future defenders of nature against the onslaughts of commercialism.

One great piece of "compensating good" was gaining ground. The friends of the parks, headed by J. Horace McFarland, spurred on by threatened invasions, and most of all by the loss of the Hetch Hetchy, were working for the creation of a National Park Service. While the Forest Service under the Roosevelt-Pinchot regime had been well organized and munificently financed, and the reserves extended into a vast empire,[59] the parks, few and comparatively of small area, had been treated like unwanted stepchildren. As Muir had worked to create the Forestry Bureau — now the Forest Service — so he had urged for many years that the parks be placed under one bureau with a fixed policy, adequate funds, and a hedge of laws to protect them. Secretary Ballinger, inspired by Muir and McFarland, had recommended this in his 1910 Report, and a bill was prepared to that effect. But it failed of passage. Secretary Fisher, his successor, commenting that the parks, like Topsy, had "just growed," called a Yellowstone Park Conference in 1911 to promote the movement. In December of that year Senator Reed Smoot of Utah introduced a second bill to create a National Park Bureau.

So powerful was the opposition, however, that not until August 25, 1916 was a measure, introduced by Representative William Kent of California, finally passed by which sixteen national parks and twenty-one national monuments were placed in charge of a director, with the stated purpose: "to conserve the scenery and the natural and historic objects and the wild life therein and to provide for the enjoyment of the same in such manner and by such means as will leave them unimpaired for the enjoyment of future generations."

Franklin K. Lane, we are glad to record,[60] fostered this Bureau by appointing as its first Director that disciple of John Muir, a Californian and a Sierra Club man, Stephen T. Mather. Mather together with his Assistant Director and successor, Horace M. Albright, did the ground work of organizing the park system in accordance with principles so long advocated by Muir for conserving the wilderness life and beauty and making them accessibl to the public for recreation and inspiration. This work has bee faithfully carried on through succeeding years under the Director Arno B. Cammerer and Newton B. Drury.

It is satisfying also to record that the Forest Service, unde chiefs of wise and statesmanlike vision, has increasingly broad ened its functions, not only bringing incalculable benefits to hu manity in reforestation and in redeeming the land from floods an erosion, but also in ministering to the recreative needs of the na tion. Its purposes now approximate the ideals of John Muir o whom Robert Underwood Johnson says: "His work was not sec tional but for the whole people, and he was the real father of th forest reservation system of America."

But as Muir has said: "The battle for conservation will go or endlessly. It is part of the universal warfare between right an wrong." And indeed the battle has gone on relentlessly, every square mile of forest land or scenic beauty having been conserved only after bitter struggle. Truly eternal vigilance is the price o conserving these heritages "unimpaired for the enjoyment o future generations."

Muir felt no bitterness against the people of San Francisco over the Hetch Hetchy. He placed the blame at the door of "three or four ambitious shifty traders and politicians calling themselves 'the City of San Francisco.'" As the years went on, the citizens suffered for the acts of these leaders, but were obliged to make the best of a bad bargain. They had been told that the project would cost not more than $50,000,000;[61] but engineering difficulties brought the total up to the neighborhood of $100,000,000. Long before the system was completed, the adjacent East Bay communities, worn out with waiting to share in the promised benefits, had combined to develop their own project. In the mid twenties they chose the Mokelumne River as a source, purchased the rights, and built the system within four years at a cost of about $36,000,000. Before San Francisco had finished her herculean task, in a year of great shortage (1931), the Mokelumne River was helping to supply that city with pure mountain water at the rate of 25,000,-

ɔo gallons per day. One of the ironies of the situation was that ıe Mokelumne source had been rejected by the San Francisco fficials in favor of the Hetch Hetchy.

With unabated courage John Muir faced the New Year of 1914 nd once more set about his "crystal ice and snow writing." But ith a body mortally stricken by overwork, he was fighting a losıg battle. He knew it was probably only a matter of months now. he two or three books he had hoped a year or two before to write arrowed down to one—his *Travels in Alaska.* Had it not been ɔr a timely suggestion from William Colby, it is doubtful if he ould have done that.

Concerned for his friend Marion Randall Parsons of Berkeley, hose husband, Edward T. Parsons, had recently died, and roubled about John Muir striving in his weakened state to pick p the threads of his writing, Colby suggested they work together. Both rallied to the idea, and Mrs. Parsons henceforth went to the anch on certain days each week.

"The arrangement proved unexpectedly happy and congenial to s both," relates Mrs. Parsons, *"and lasted until within a week of is death. . . .*

"He was living alone in the dismantled old home, unused save or his study and sleeping porch. He went to his daughter's home or his meals, but neither she nor anyone else was allowed to touch he study, overflowing . . . with books and papers. . . .

"By seven o'clock each morning Mr. Muir had breakfasted and vas ready for the day's work, usually lasting . . . until ten at ight. . . . Each sentence, each phrase, each word, underwent is critical scrutiny. . . . His rare critical faculty was unimpaired o the end. So too was the freshness and vigor of his whole outlook n life. No trace of pessimism or despondency, even in the defeat f his most deeply cherished hopes, ever darkened his beautiful hilosophy, and only in the intense physical fatigue . . . was here any hint of failing powers." [62]

In the brief interludes between work periods, Muir went down o Wanda's adobe to play with the children and to see her fourth on, Robert, born in August. "So flourisheth the boy undergrowth," he gleefully wrote. "Interesting mugginses and as live as chipmunks."

Helen, too, had a third son, John, born in June, whom he ha never seen. But he had his absent daughter ever in mind, sendi boxes of choice fruit, and cuttings of jasmine, wistaria, and ros to be planted about her new home on the desert.

In midsummer World War I began. John Muir was so stricke to the heart that he could hardly speak or write of it to his friend But he did talk of it to his daughter Wanda, and it is to her mem ories that we owe some knowledge of his reactions. "Monstrous and "horrible" were the adjectives he applied in anger to the ra ishment of Belgium, and more than once he subscribed liberally the Red Cross and Belgian Relief. Several letters came to him du ing these months from his Swiss friend of African memories, Lou Barbetzat, giving him inside information of conditions in Europ food shortages, and widespread German treachery. All his li Muir had hated war as "the greatest of civilized calamities." Bu now, with his usual clear vision of historical trends, he saw tha here was a savage, demoniac force, unleashed to prey upon weake nations, that must be crushed if the world was to be salvaged fro barbarism. For the first time he believed war could be a righteou thing.

During that summer or fall Muir set about rehabilitating th old house — a strange impulse in view of his opposition to a changes since his wife's death. He liked to wander through th sixteen empty, echoing rooms, reliving the past. But now, wit the help of Ah Fong, his faithful Chinese servant, he cleared awa old furnishings, built new bookcases, and — most amazing of al — installed electricity. Then he went down to San Francisco on buying orgy. Meeting his friend Mrs. Charlotte Kellogg on th way, he asked her to go with him. Mrs. Kellogg has related:

" 'I had thought to go alone,' he said, 'but I should like havin your advice,' adding with a wry smile, 'I'm going to shop to bu some hangings and things.' I hid my astonishment, and once there busied myself with the velvets and rugs spread before us." [63]

Muir never told anyone his motive for putting his house in order t this late date. He did, however, hope his girls would keep the .d home and may have been trying to make it more attractive and .odern for them should either of them decide to live in it. On ecember 3 he wrote his final letter to Helen:

"There is no one in the old house but myself. If I could only ave you and Wanda as in the auld lang syne, it would be lovely. ut such backward thoughts are all in vain. . . . I have got elecic light now in the house and everything has been put in comarative order."

Some time during those last days he told Wanda he wanted to e buried on the ranch beside his wife. After his death some of his dmirers deplored the fact that he was not buried among the ountains, perhaps in the Yosemite. They thought he would have ished it so. But as he often said: "Evenin' brings a' hame," and ome to him was where his loved ones were.

On December 5 he wrote some letters,[64] including one to his cotland cousin, bringing the usual Christmas cheer to herself and the poor of Dunbar." A few days later he told Wanda he wanted visit Helen. And she, sensing the urgency of his desire to see er sister once more, got him ready for the train journey.

So he traveled south for the last time. In his grip he carried the ped manuscript of *Travels in Alaska,* intending to finish it on the esert.[65] As fate would have it, he arrived at Daggett at half ast two in the morning. A bitter wind was blowing over the Iohave, and on the auto ride to the ranch he caught cold. But so eat was his joy at seeing Helen and her children, he appeared most well in the morning. After breakfast he and his daughter rolled out into the desert sunshine. He exclaimed how good it as to breathe the dry, healing air after the cold, damp fogs of e north. They walked for a mile, he stopping often to greet the lant "mugginses" along the trail.

That night he sat by the fire, making some alterations in his anuscript. But when he got up, he staggered with faintness. hey put him to bed, and the doctor who was summoned pro- ounced the case pneumonia.

He was taken to the California Hospital in Los Angeles, and

Wanda was sent for. For a brief time he seemed to improve. H spirit a flaming torch to the end, he joked with the doctor and th nurse, talking eagerly about getting well and going on with h work. At his own insistence his Alaska manuscript lay ready t his hand.

The end came suddenly on Christmas Eve. Neither Wanda nc Helen was with him at the time. The nurse and the doctor ha stepped out of the room. When the nurse returned a momen later, he had crept out of this mortal flesh to "fly free and grow.

Once in those final years — or days — he had written on fragment of paper these words:

"Death is a kind nurse saying, 'Come, children, to bed, and g up in the morning,' — a gracious Mother calling her childre home." [66]

BIBLIOGRAPHY

GASSIZ, LOUIS: *Geological Sketches.* Osgood, 1875.

HERN, G. P.: *Forest Bankruptcy in America.* Shenandoah Publishing House, 1934.

ADÈ, WILLIAM FREDERIC: *The Life and Letters of John Muir.* 2 vols. Houghton Mifflin, 1923, 1924.

ARRUS, CLARA, ed.: *The Heart of John Burroughs' Journals.* Houghton Mifflin, 1928.

—: *The Life and Letters of John Burroughs.* 2 vols. Houghton Mifflin, 1925.

REWSTER, EDWIN T.: *The Life and Letters of Josiah Dwight Whitney.* Houghton Mifflin, 1909.

ROWNE, LEWIS: *Something Went Wrong.* Macmillan, 1942.

HASE, STUART: *Rich Land, Poor Land.* McGraw-Hill, 1936.

ORNELIUS, BROTHER: *Keith, Old Master of California.* Putnam, 1942.

OSBEY, ROBERT C.: "John Muir, a Critical Analysis." Master of Arts Thesis, Columbia University.

ERLETH, AUGUST: *Still Small Voice.* (A biography of Zona Gale.) Appleton-Century, 1940.

LLSBERG, EDWARD: *Hell on Ice, the Saga of the "Jeannette."* Dodd, Mead, 1938.

ERNOW, BERNHARD E.: *Brief History of Forestry in Europe, the United States, and Other Countries.* University of Toronto, 1910.

ARRISON, W. E.: *Religion Follows the Frontier.* Harper, 1931.

RAY, DAVID: *Letters, Poems and Selected Prose Writings of David Gray,* edited by J. N. Larned. The Courier Company, Buffalo, 1888.

AWTHORNE, HILDEGARDE, and ESTHER MILLS: *Enos Mills and the Rockies.* Houghton Mifflin, 1935.

istory of Marquette County, Wisconsin. Acme Publishing Company, Chicago, 1890.

OLMES, FREDERICK L.: *Alluring Wisconsin.* E. M. Hale, Milwaukee, 1937.

UTCHINGS, JAMES M.: *In the Heart of the Sierras.* Pacific Press, San Francisco, 1888.

AMES, HARLEAN: *Romance of the National Parks.* Macmillan, 1939.

HNSON, ROBERT UNDERWOOD: *Remembered Yesterdays,* Little, Brown, 1923.

EELER, CHARLES: "Friends Bearing Torches." Manuscript.

eithiana in Bancroft Library, University of California.

ING, CLARENCE: *Mountaineering in the Sierra Nevada,* edited by Francis P. Farquhar. Norton, 1935.

APHAM, INCREASE A.: *Forest Trees of Wisconsin.* Wisconsin State Agriculture Society, 1855.

—: "The Disastrous Effects of the Destruction of the Forest Trees. . . ." Report to the Legislature, 1867.

E CONTE, JOSEPH: *A Journal of Ramblings through the High Sierra of California.* Sierra Club, 1930.

YMAN, GEORGE D.: *John Marsh, Pioneer.* Scribner's, 1930.

ARSH, GEORGE P.: *Man and Nature.* Scribner's, 1864.

MATTHES, FRANÇOIS E.: *Geologic History of the Yosemite*. U. S. Geological Su vey, Professional Paper 160. Government Printing Office, 1930.

MERK, FREDERICK: *Economic History of Wisconsin during the Civil War*. Wi consin State Historical Society, 1916.

MERRIAM, C. HART, ed.: *Harriman Alaska Expedition*, 2 vols. Doubleday, 1901

MILLS, ENOS: *Your National Parks*. Houghton Mifflin, 1917.

MUIR, JOHN: *Cruise of the Corwin*, edited by William Frederic Badè. Hought Mifflin, 1918.

——: *Edward Henry Harriman*. Doubleday, 1912.

——: *John of the Mountains, the Unpublished Journals of John Muir*, edit by Linnie Marsh Wolfe. Houghton Mifflin, 1938.

——: *The Mountains of California*. 2 vols. Houghton Mifflin, 1917.

——: *My First Summer in the Sierra*. Houghton Mifflin, 1911.

——: *Our National Parks*. Houghton Mifflin, 1901.

——: *Steep Trails*, edited by William Frederic Badè. Houghton Mifflin, 1918.

——: *Stickeen*, Houghton Mifflin, 1909.

——: *The Story of My Boyhood and Youth*. Houghton Mifflin, 1913.

——: "Studies in the Sierra," *Sierra Club Bulletin*, January 1915–January 19 (Vols. IX–XI).

——: *A Thousand-Mile Walk to the Gulf*, edited by William Frederic Bad Houghton Mifflin, 1917.

——: *Travels in Alaska*. Houghton Mifflin, 1915.

——: Manuscripts, Journals, Letters, and Notes.

National Park Files in Washington, D. C.

NEUHAUS, EUGEN: *William Keith, the Man and the Artist*, University of Ca fornia Press, 1938.

OSBORN, HENRY FAIRFIELD: *Impressions of Great Naturalists*. Scribner's, 1928.

PRINGLE, HENRY F.: *The Life and Times of William Howard Taft*. 2 vols. Farr & Rinehart, 1939.

——: *Theodore Roosevelt, a Biography*. Harcourt, Brace, 1931.

RUSSELL, CARL P.: *One Hundred Years in the Yosemite*. Stanford Universi Press, 1931.

Sierra Club Bulletin.

TAYLOR, RAY W.: *Hetch Hetchy, the Story of San Francisco's Struggle to Provi a Water Supply for Her Future Needs*. Ricardo J. Orazco, San Francis 1926.

THAYER, JAMES BRADLEY: *A Western Journey with Mr. Emerson*. Little, 1884.

TURNER, FREDERICK JACKSON: *The Frontier in American History*. Holt, 1920.

WHITNEY, JOSIAH D.: *Geological Survey of California, Geology*, Vol. I. 1865.

——: *The Yosemite Guide-Book. University Press*, Cambridge, 1869.

Wisconsin Alumni Magazine.

Wisconsin Magazine of History.

YOUNG, S. HALL: *Alaska Days with John Muir*. Revell, 1915.

——: *Hall Young of Alaska, "The Mushing Parson," an Autobiography*. Rev 1927.

NOTES

REFACE

[1] Mrs. Wanda Muir Hanna died in July 1942.

[2] Mrs. Helen Muir Funk some time after the death of her husband, Buel A. unk, in 1934, had the family name legally changed to Muir that her sons might rry it on.

[3] *John of the Mountains, the Unpublished Journals of John Muir,* Houghton Iifflin, 1938.

[4] *Remembered Yesterdays,* by Robert Underwood Johnson.

[5] *Sierra Club Bulletin,* X, 25 (January 1916).

ART I

Iany quotations and incidents in Part I, not otherwise specified, are derived om Muir's *The Story of My Boyhood and Youth* and the first draft of the me, here called the "Pelican Bay Manuscript."

[1] So named by Lecky in *England in the Eighteenth Century.*

[2] MS. reminiscences of Clare Blakley Brown, niece of Daniel Muir.

[3] Memories of Helen Funk Muir.

[4] *A Thousand-Mile Walk to the Gulf,* by John Muir, p. 313.

[5] Muir family memories collected by Mrs. Elisha B. Maltbey of Portage, any from the letters of Mrs. Anna Galloway Eastman, daughter of Sarah Muir alloway.

[6] Narrative based on *The Story of My Boyhood and Youth,* the Pelican Bay Ianuscript, and the memories of Mrs. Daniel Brown, niece of Alexander Gray.

[7] Revelation xiv, 10–11.

[8] Memories of Cecelia Galloway, daughter of Sarah Muir Galloway.

[9] For story of Indian wars see *John Marsh, Pioneer,* by George Lyman.

[10] Interview with Sam Ennis. Undated clipping.

[11] See Foreword to "An Autobiographic Letter to Constance Lindsay Skinner," y Frederick Jackson Turner, *Wisconsin Magazine of History,* XIX, 91.

[12] Related by Harry W. Kearns of Hickory Hill Farm.

[13] Memories of Mrs. Jeannie Foster Guidinger, niece of David Galloway.

[14] Muir-Whitehead correspondence, 1913.

[15] *The Story of My Boyhood and Youth.*

[16] Biographical Memoir in *Letters, Poems and Selected Prose Writings of avid Gray,* p. 23.

[17] Ibid., p. 20.

[18] Hickory Hill Farm was purchased from Daniel Muir in 1873 by Thomas earns, father of Harry W. Kearns, the present owner.

[19] In mature life Muir entertained his children with his bagpipe exhibition. Iemories of Helen Funk Muir.

[20] Muir-Duncan narratives are based on Muir's autobiographical fragments, tters, *The Story of My Boyhood and Youth;* and memories of Miss Jessie uncan, daughter of William Duncan.

21 The well dug by John Muir, now made ten feet deeper and surmounted b a modern windmill, still supplies the farm with abundant water.

22 *The Story of My Boyhood and Youth,* p. 219.

23 Related by Chauncey Cairns, son of John Cairns.

24 Related by Harry W. Kearns.

25 To Dr. William Frederic Badè, April 9, 1917.

26 Related by Harry W. Kearns.

27 Letter to Mrs. Edward Pelton, 1861. Muir left many letters partly or whol undated.

PART II

1 Memories of Helen Hand Moore, daughter of Mary Muir Hand.

2 *Wisconsin State Journal,* September 25, 1860.

3 *Evening Patriot,* September 25, 1860.

4 Letter to Mrs. H. J. Taylor, July 1929.

5 To Emily Pelton, February 19, 1872.

6 MS. reminiscences of Milton S. Griswold.

7 Muir's study desk is on permanent exhibit in the Wisconsin State Historic Society Museum at Madison.

8 MS. reminiscences of Charles Vroman.

9 MS. reminiscences of Grace Sterling Lindsley.

10 *Library of the World's Best Literature,* XXIII, 9077–83.

11 Related by Charles E. Brown, Curator of the Wisconsin State Historic Society Museum.

12 Quotations from James Whitehead are from an article in the *Empo* (Kansas) *Gazette,* January 21, 1915, and other clippings and scrapbook rem niscences.

13 The present Lake Harriet School near the town of Oregon, Wisconsin, stan just across the creek from the site of the log hut where Muir taught. Intern evidence reveals this to be the old log schoolhouse of Muir's poem by that nan For selections from the poem see *The Life and Letters of John Muir,* I, 66–8.

14 Reminiscences of John Dreher as told to Mrs. Frank Dreher, Oregon, Wi consin.

15 Dr. Carr's "Inaugural Address to the Wisconsin University Board Regents," January 16, 1856.

16 Letter to Mrs. Carr, September 13, 1865. In *The Life and Letters of Jo Muir,* I, 143.

17 "Ice Period in America," by Louis Agassiz, *Atlantic Monthly,* XIV, 86–9

18 Quotations from Dr. Butler, familiar to his students, are to be found many forms in his manuscripts and "Commonplace Book" in the Wiscons State Historical Society Library.

19 "John Muir," by Jeanne C. Carr, *California Illustrated Magazine,* Ju 1892.

20 Memories of Mrs. McBride Sumner of Madison.

21 A letter from Mrs. Carr to John Muir in 1873 reveals that at that time s was helping to landscape the University of California campus at Berkeley.

22 Quotations from Milton S. Griswold are from his MS. reminiscences.

[23] The Athenæan Society was founded in 1850, and the Hesperian Society in e same decade.

[24] *Voyage aux régions équinoxiales du Nouveau Continent, fait 1799–1804, par lexandré de Humboldt et Aimé Bonpland* (Paris, 1807, etc.).

[25] *The Life and Letters of John Muir,* I, 93–4.

[26] Memories of Helen Funk Muir.

[27] From rhymed letter to Emily Pelton. See *The Life and Letters of John uir,* I, 102–4.

[28] To Emily Pelton, March 1, 1864. In *The Life and Letters of John Muir,* 116.

ART III

[1] Autobiographical notebook.

[2] MS. reminiscences of William Trout.

[3] *The Life and Letters of John Muir,* I, 121.

[4] MS. reminiscences of William Trout.

[5] Letter to Emily Pelton, May 23, 1865.

[6] Autobiographical notebook.

[7] Letter to Mrs. Carr, September 13, 1865. For full text see *The Life and etters of John Muir,* I, 139–44.

[8] Catharine Merrill occupied the chair of English Literature at Butler Unirsity, Indianapolis, being the second woman in the United States to hold a ofessorship.

[9] MS. reminiscences of Merrill Moores.

[10] Autobiographical typed manuscript.

[11] Muir's original charts are in the Wisconsin State Historical Society Library.

[12] Autobiographical fragments.

[13] *John of the Mountains, the Unpublished Journals of John Muir,* pp. 137–8.

[14] Autobiographical notebook.

[15] Related by John W. Smith of Portage.

[16] Ibid.

[17] In Zona Gale's autobiographical manuscript. See also *Still Small Voice,* ugust Derleth's biography of Zona Gale, p. 294.

[18] Autobiographical typed manuscript. For variant form see *The Life and etters of John Muir,* I, 156.

[19] Muir's first extant journal. Most of the quotations used in this narrative e from *A Thousand-Mile Walk to the Gulf* or from unpublished parts of the iginal journal.

[20] For selected portions of this journal see *John of the Mountains,* pp. 1–33.

[21] For Muir's first Sierra journal see *My First Summer in the Sierra.* Quotaons on glaciation are from this source.

[22] The telepathy narrative is based on Muir's manuscript "Mysterious Things"; letter by him to Mrs. J. D. Butler; and *My First Summer in the Sierra,* p. 178–91.

[23] Manuscript. Similar passages are to be found in *My First Summer in the ierra.*

[24] Muir-Randall correspondence, 1901.

[25] The Yellowstone National Park, created in 1872, was the first region plac under Federal jurisdiction as a park.

[26] Muir-Randall correspondence, 1901.

[27] For selections from Muir's first Yosemite journal see *John of the Mou tains,* pp. 36–55.

[28] The prostrate yellow pines were several feet in diameter. Muir sawed the into shorter sections, drove iron pins into the centers, and with chains and ox had them hauled to the mill. Information given by William E. Colby.

[29] Sunnyside Bench, so named by Muir, is a ledge to the east of Yosemi Fall, about 500 feet above the floor of the valley. He approached it by way Indian Canyon. It had earlier been used by the Indians as a retreat, when they shot arrows at the white invaders.

[30] Father of William E. Colby, who in later years was an outstanding ai of Muir's in conservation.

[31] From a brief résumé of glacial processes envisioned by Muir from Sentin Dome, see *John of the Mountains,* pp. 59–60.

[32] *Geological Survey of California,* six volumes, University Press, Cambridg 1865–70.

[33] *The Yosemite Guide-Book,* University Press, Cambridge, 1869. Later ed tions in 1870, 1871, and 1874.

[34] King's explorations and glacial observations in the Sierra were first pul lished in the *Atlantic Monthly,* May to December 1871. Later published in *Mou taineering in the Sierra,* 1872, and subsequent editions.

[35] To Mrs. Carr, April 13, 1870. See *The Life and Letters of John Muir,* 214–16.

[36] Reported by Thérèse Yelverton in her novel *Zanita, A Tale of the Yosemit* p. 29. Mrs. Yelverton was a tourist in the Yosemite in the summer of 1870.

[37] *Journal of Ramblings through the High Sierra of California,* by Josep Le Conte. *Sierra Club Bulletin,* III (January 1900). Published by the Sierra Cl in book form in 1930.

[38] See "The Great Yelverton Case," *Harper's Weekly,* April 6, 1861; and "T Great Yelverton Marriage Case," *Nation,* I, 814 (December 28, 1865).

[39] *Teresina Peregrina,* two volumes, London, R. Bentley & Son, 1874. *Teresi in America,* two volumes, London, R. Bentley & Son, 1875.

[40] *Zanita, A Tale of Yosemite,* Hurd & Houghton, 1872.

[41] Mrs. Yelverton, having lost her own child as a part of her tragedy, want to adopt Floy Hutchings and train her for the stage. Failing to win the conse of the child's parents, she adopted her in her book. In the story, as in life, t girl met an untimely death.

[42] Mrs. Yelverton is reported to have made the same request of Charles Wa ren Stoddard. See Stoddard's essay on Mrs. Yelverton in his *Footprints of t Padres,* A. M. Robertson, 1902 ed. (Essay omitted in later editions.)

[43] Muir's notes. Also Muir-Randall correspondence, 1901.

[44] For text of letter dated "Nut Time," see *The Life and Letters of John Mu* I, 270–3.

[45] According to a woman journalist who accompanied her to the Yosemit Mrs. Yelverton was informed by the British Consul at San Francisco of t Viscount's death and assured of her right to bear the title. See "Summer with

untess," by M. L. Lawrence, *Overland Monthly,* VII, 473–9 (November 1871).

[46] To Mrs. Carr, December 22 (1870). See *The Life and Letters of John Muir,* 237–9.

ART IV

[1] Letter to Dr. William Frederic Badè, January 23, 1923.

[2] Ibid.

[3] For Muir's description of the "hang-nest," see letter to Sarah Galloway, pril 5, 1871, in *The Life and Letters of John Muir,* I, 246–9.

[4] In *A Western Journey with Mr. Emerson,* by James Bradley Thayer, ttle, 1884.

[5] This and other Muir quotations in the Emerson narrative, not otherwise ecified, are taken from *Our National Parks,* pp. 144–50.

[6] to [11] Muir's notes.

[12] Letter from S. S. Forbes to Dr. William Frederic Badè, July 12, 1915.

[13] *John of the Mountains,* p. 436.

[14] Letter to Catharine Merrill, July 12 (1871). For full text see *The Life and etters of John Muir,* I, pp. 288–91.

[15] Father of C. Hart Merriam, Muir's friend of later years.

[16] To Mrs. Carr, August 13 (1871). See *The Life and Letters of John Muir,* 292.

[17] Autobiographical notebook.

[18] To Mrs. Carr, September 8, 1871. See *The Life and Letters of John Muir,* p. 295. Also letter to Robert Underwood Johnson, May 3, 1895. See ibid., , 291–2.

[19] To Mrs. Carr, September 8, 1871. See *The Life and Letters of John Muir,* 293.

[20] A mural in the Boston Public Library.

[21] Published under title "Yosemite Glaciers," *New York Tribune,* December 1871.

[22] See "Living Glaciers of California," *Overland Monthly,* IX, 547–9 (Decem-r 1872); and "Living Glaciers of California," *Harper's Magazine,* LI, 769–76 Jovember 1875).

[23] For journal of this experience see *John of the Mountains,* pp. 79–86.

[24] "Yosemite in Winter" (Letter of January 1, 1872), *New York Tribune* (un-ated clipping).

[25] "Yosemite in Spring" (Letter of May 7, 1872), *New York Tribune* (undated ipping).

[26] Muir's notes. Variant version in *Our National Parks,* p. 287.

[27] and [28] Muir's notes.

[29] "Yosemite Valley in Flood," *Overland Monthly,* VIII, 347–50 (April 1872).

[30] "Twenty-Hill Hollow," *Overland Monthly,* IX, 80–6 (July 1872).

[31] See letter to Robert Underwood Johnson, May 3, 1895, in *The Life and Let-rs of John Muir,* II, 291–3.

[32] To Mrs. Carr (undated fragment), in *The Life and Letters of John Muir,* 261.

[33] and [34] To Robert Underwood Johnson, May 3, 1895.

[35] To Mrs. Carr (undated), in *The Life and Letters of John Muir,* I, 341 (la sentence omitted).

[36] and [37] Muir's manuscript on "Walking."

[38] "Geologist's Winter Walk," *Overland Monthly,* X, 355–8 (April 1873).

[39] "Hetch Hetchy Valley," *Overland Monthly,* XI, 42–50 (July 1873).

[40] "Explorations in the Great Tuolumne Canyon," *Overland Monthly,* X 139–47 (August 1873).

[41] To David Muir, March 1, 1873. For full letter see *The Life and Letters John Muir,* I, 23–5.

[42] To Sarah Galloway, December 2, 1880.

[43] For selections from journal see *John of the Mountains,* pp. 173–88.

[44] Autobiographical notebook.

[45] King's error, discovered in July 1873 by William Goodyear, was report by him to the California Academy of Sciences and published in the August *Pr ceedings.* Meanwhile, two other parties in August and September 1873 climb the real Mount Whitney, one group calling themselves "the Fishermen." Hen for a time the mountain was called Fisherman's Peak.

[46] Letter to John Muir, March 28, 1869.

[47] Quotations in the seance narrative are from Muir's manuscript "Myste ous Things."

[48] The Strentzel ranch home became a refuge for many Polish political ref gees. Mme Modjeska, the Shakespearian actress, remained there six mont while she learned to speak English and prepared for her American debut in a Sa Francisco theater. Her husband, Count Bozenta, and Henryk Sienkiewicz, auth of *Quo Vadis,* were also guests at the ranch.

[49] Mrs. Louisiana Strentzel, born of a Tennessee family migrated to Texa married Dr. Strentzel in that state. In 1849 they came by wagon train to Cal fornia. In 1853 they bought land in the Alhambra Valley near the town Martinez.

[50] For selections from Muir's notes upon returning to the Sierra, see *John the Mountains,* pp. 190–3.

[51] To Mrs. Carr (September 1874). For full text see *The Life and Letters John Muir,* II, 10–27.

[52] To Mrs. Carr, October 7, 1874, in *The Life and Letters of John Mu* II, 28–9.

[53] Manuscript on the Donner Party.

[54] To Mrs. Carr, November 1, 1874, in *The Life and Letters of John Mu* II, 31.

[55] See *Mountaineering in the Sierra Nevada,* by Clarence King, pp. 235–56.

[56] See Muir's letter in the *San Francisco Bulletin,* December 2, 1874. Also " Perilous Night on Shasta's Summit," in *Steep Trails,* pp. 57–67.

[57] For Muir's forest storm experience see "A Windstorm in the Forests," *Mou tains of California,* I, 272–86.

[58] Muir's notes.

[59] See "A Perilous Night on Shasta's Summit," in *Steep Trails,* 67–81.

[60] Muir's journal.

[61] Memories of Norman Sisson.

[62] Muir's journal.

[63] *Harper's Magazine,* LI, 769–76.
[64] *Keith, Old Master of California,* by Brother Cornelius, p. 75.
[65] Information given me by Frank Swett.
[66] "The Kings River Yosemite," *San Francisco Bulletin,* August 13, 1875.
[67] For selections from these journals see *John of the Mountains,* pp. 209–35.
[68] *Our National Parks,* pp. 323–4.
[69] "Tulare Levels," *San Francisco Bulletin,* November 17, 1875.
[70] "Studies in the Sierra," *Overland Monthly,* XII–XIV (May 1874–January 75); also in *Sierra Club Bulletin,* IX–XI (January 1915–January 1920).
[71] "Quaternary History of Mono Valley, California," U. S. Geological Survey port, 1889.
[72] "Systematic Asymmetry of Crest Lines on the High Sierra of California," *urnal of Geology,* XII, 579–88 (1904); also in *Sierra Club Bulletin,* V, 278–86 905).
[73] "Origin of Yosemite Valley," *National Geographic Magazine,* XII, 86–7 901).
[74] Author of *Geologic History of the Yosemite Valley,* U. S. Geological Survey, ofessional Paper 160, Government Printing Office, 1930.
[75] Radio broadcast, NBC, April 17, 1938. Published in the *Sierra Club Bul- in,* XXIII, No. 2, pp. 9–10 (April 1938).
[76] *Geologic History of the Yosemite Valley,* p. 4.

ART V

[1] *Our National Parks,* p. 3.
[2] *The Mountains of California,* II, 286.
[3] and [4] *John of the Mountains,* pp. 252–3.
[5] "John Muir, Pilgrim Soul," by Charlotte Kellogg, *Delineator,* XCII, 2 ugust 1921).
[6] In *The Heart of John Burroughs' Journals,* pp. 192–3.
[7] and [8] Muir's journal. Free verse arrangement by Muir.
[9] *Daily Evening Bulletin* (San Francisco), July 19, 1877; also in *Steep Trails,* . 126–35.
[10] Through the kindness of Mrs. Mabel Young Sanborn of Salt Lake City it s been possible to find a sister of the "Lily," Mrs. Louis Schweitzer of San ancisco.
[11] Muir's old friend Professor Charles H. Allen, formerly of the University Wisconsin faculty, was now principal of the San Jose Normal School. At his quest Muir spoke there several times.
[12] For selections from the journal of the river journey see *John of the Moun- ins,* pp. 236–44.
[13] MS. reminiscences of Mary Tracy Swett.
[14] MS. reminiscences of Helen Swett Arteida.
[15] *Scribner's Monthly,* February 1878.
[16] "John Muir," *Sierra Club Bulletin,* X, 7 (January 1916).
[17] Muir's journal.
[18] Owing to the changing of place names in Nevada, the identity of Mount fferson is unknown.

19 "Glacial Phenomena in the Great Basin," *Daily Evening Bulletin* (San Fran cisco), December 5, 1878; also in *Steep Trails,* pp. 184–94.

20 To Louie Strentzel, April 18, 1879.

21 and 22 Mrs. Strentzel's diary.

23 The Olympic National Park was created in 1938. Enclosing a mountai wilderness on the Olympic Peninsula, it saved from imminent invasion by lum bermen magnificent virgin tracts of Sitka spruce, Douglas fir, Western red ceda and hemlock.

24 *Alaska Days with John Muir,* by S. Hall Young, p. 13.

25 Autobiographical typed manuscript.

26 *Alaska Days with John Muir,* p. 53.

27 "John Muir, Geologist, Explorer, Naturalist," *Craftsman,* March 1905.

28 Known as the Robert Moran State Park.

29 *Hall Young of Alaska,* autobiography of S. Hall Young, p. 189.

30 Based upon Muir's fragmentary notes.

31 Glacier Bay National Monument was created on February 26, 1925

32 Muir's journal. For another account of the same incident see *Travels i* Alaska, pp. 177–9.

33 *Travels in Alaska,* p. 193.

34 Muir's journal.

35 *Hall Young of Alaska,* pp. 211–13. Young disclosed in a letter to Mui January 26, 1897, that the latter taught him in 1879 how to hold his new-bor baby.

36 *Hall Young of Alaska,* pp. 217–18.

37 Muir's journal.

38 After completing a term as State Superintendent of Schools, Dr. Carr wit his wife bought forty-three acres of land on the outskirts of Pasadena along th Aroyo Seco. To this they retired and built a home and established a parklik garden with trees and shrubs from all over the world. Carmelita, as this hom was called, became and is still one of the sights of southern California.

39 To Mrs. Muir, August 2, 1880. For full text see *The Life and Letters o John Muir,* II, 138–42.

40 To Mrs. Muir, August 4, 1880. For full text see *The Life and Letters o John Muir,* II, 145–8.

41 *Alaska Days with John Muir,* p. 126.

42 Muir's journal. Young Glacier is now known as Dawes Glacier.

43 *Travels in Alaska,* p. 277.

44 *Alaska Days with John Muir,* pp. 163–5.

45 Stickeen notebook.

46 *Alaska Days with John Muir,* 183–8.

47 According to a brief sketch of Stickeen written by Young at Muir's reques the dog was stolen from him by a trader. His fate is unknown.

48 *John of the Mountains,* p. 277.

49 For the story of the dog see *Stickeen; Travels in Alaska,* pp. 257, 295, 298 311; *John of the Mountains,* pp. 275–80.

50 For the story of the polar expedition made by the *Jeannette* and her crew see *Hell on Ice,* by Edward Ellsberg.

51 For Muir's story of the relief expedition, see his *Cruise of the Corwin.*

52 *Report of the Cruise of the U. S. Revenue Steamer, Thomas Corwin, in the Arctic Ocean, 1881,* by Captain Calvin Leighton Hooper, Government Printing Office, 1884.

53 Kellett landed on the coast of Herald Island in 1849, but failed to penetrate it.

54 Muir's journal.

55 See *Hell on Ice,* pp. 329–418.

56 Muir's journal.

57 To Mrs. Muir, August 18, 1881. For full text see *The Life and Letters of John Muir,* II, 188–91.

58 "Botanical Notes on Alaska," and "On the Glaciation of the Arctic and Sub-Arctic Regions," both by Muir, were published in Government *Reports* of the expedition in 1883 and 1884. Republished in the Appendix of *The Cruise of the Corwin.*

59 Asa Gray named one of the plants, in honor of John Muir, *Erigeron Muirii.*

60 Working with Muir on this project were Dr. A. Kellogg and Charles C. Parry of the California Academy of Sciences, and Colonel George W. Stewart of Visalia, California, editor and publisher of the *Visalia Delta.*

61 Mrs. Strentzel's diary.

62 Memories of Muir's daughters.

63 Annie Muir remained at her brother's California home for three years, fully regaining her health.

64 Memories of Cecelia Galloway.

65 To Mrs. Muir, September 26, 1885, in *The Life and Letters of John Muir,* II, 207.

66 To Mrs. Muir, October 6, 1885. For full text see *The Life and Letters of John Muir,* II, 208–10.

PART VI

1 *Alaska Days with John Muir,* pp. 205–6.

2 Mount Shasta with the surrounding forests became the Shasta National Forest in October 1905.

3 Philemon Beecher Van Trump accompanied General Hazard Stevens in 1870 on the first ascent of Mount Rainier. He went again in 1883 with another party on the third ascent.

4 For Muir's account of his Mount Rainier trip see *Steep Trails,* pp. 261–70.

5 Memories of A. C. Warner, related to me on a trip to Mount Rainier in 1939.

6 and 7 Muir's notes.

8 According to National Park Service records, successful ascents of Mount Rainier were made in August and October 1870; 1883; 1885; 1885 or 1886. The ascent of the Muir party in 1888 was, therefore, the sixth.

9 *John of the Mountains,* pp. 295–6.

10 See *The Life and Letters of John Muir,* II, 220.

11 See *Enos Mills of the Rockies,* by Hildegarde Hawthorne and Esther Burnell Mills, pp. 75–80.

[12] See *Remembered Yesterdays,* by Robert Underwood Johnson, pp. 278–9.

[13] Quotations are from the poem "With Muir in Yosemite," written by Robert Underwood Johnson three weeks before his death in 1937.

[14] *San Francisco Bulletin,* June 21, 1869.

[15] Chapter xviii in *Travels in Alaska* is based on this journal. For selections from random notes on scraps of paper see *John of the Mountains,* pp. 311–22.

[16] All geographical names used by Muir in the sled-trip narrative were given by himself.

[17] For variant version see *John of the Mountains,* p. 319.

[18] *Travels in Alaska,* p. 376.

[19] *Century,* August and September, 1890.

[20] *Oakland Tribune,* September 8, 1890.

[21] Ibid., September 6, 1890.

[22] Ibid., September 16, 1890.

[23] Statement of Mr. Elisha B. Maltbey of Portage.

[24] This group included, among others, Warren Olney, and Professors J. H. Senger, William D. Armes, and Willis L. Jepson, all of the University of California.

[25] "Personal Recollections of John Muir," by Samuel Merrill, *Sierra Club Bulletin,* XIII, 24–30.

[26] Memories of Wanda Muir Hanna.

[27] Memories of Muir's daughters. Returning from his trip around the world in 1903–4, Muir wrote to his wife that his joy in coming home was marred only by the fact that "poor Tom will not be there to meet me" (letter March 31, 1904).

[28] Memories of Helen Funk Muir.

[29] Conversations with me.

[30] Memories of Helen Funk Muir.

[31] For Muir's journal accounts of walks on the hills with his daughters see "At Home on the Ranch," in *John of the Mountains,* pp. 335–42.

[32] Memories of Helen Funk Muir.

[33] Keith was always seeing resemblances between people and animals, and gave nicknames accordingly.

[34] From the manuscript of an address by Charles Keeler in 1927.

[35] Typical of the tributes paid by Muir to Keith in his mystical period is that written to Bailey Millard, January 1902: "You need not be afraid of over-praising Keith's work. I have known him and his work intimately over thirty years. He is a poet — easily the first of the color poets on this side of the continent." Of Keith's last pictures — the most mystical of all — he wrote to Helen on two occasions: "Keith is painting better than ever before."

[36] *Remembered Yesterdays,* p. 313.

[37] Muir's journal.

[38] The Muir-Bryce incident was related by Annie Muir in a letter of January 16, 1902 to her sister Mary. James Bryce, visiting California in the eighties, tried to get in touch with Muir, but owing to Muir's absorption in ranch duties, failed to meet him. Many years later while Bryce was British Ambassador to the United States, he was entertained at dinner in the Bay region. At his special request Muir was a guest, and the two nature-lovers sat together in rapt conversation. David

Starr Jordan in his *Days of a Man* comments upon the marked resemblance between these two Scots.

39 Twin hills on the ranch, named by Muir.

40 As related by Muir to Samuel Merrill. Also in a letter to his wife, June 11, 1896, he wrote: "I had barely time to rush out and drag Mary and Helen aboard before Willis could say boo."

41 The story of Ann Muir's last illness and her son's premonition is based on the memories of Cecelia Galloway; also on Muir's letters to his wife. Muir administered his mother's estate, dividing the inheritance from Scotland equally among the eight heirs, and then gave his own portion to his widowed sister Sarah. David used his to pay off Portage debts. Mary repaid John for his support of her before marriage, whereupon he invested the money in her name.

42 For Muir's journal of the Oregon-California phase of the Forestry Commission trip, see *John of the Mountains*, pp. 356–64.

43 The Crater Lake National Park was created in 1902.

44 Mount Rainier National Park was created in 1899. The Grand Canyon was made a national monument in 1908 and a national park in 1919.

45 Muir's ten *Atlantic* articles, dealing largely with the Yosemite region, were published in 1901 under the title: *Our National Parks*.

46 *Alaska Days with John Muir*, p. 211.

47 *San Francisco Examiner*, October 1 and 11, 1897.

48 Letter to Charles S. Sargent, October 16, 1897.

49 *John of the Mountains*, p. 89.

50 To Charles Keeler, August 7, 1907.

51 "The Conversation of John Muir," by Melville B. Anderson, in the *American Museum Journal*, XV, 116–21 (March 1915).

52 To Helen Muir, November 4, 1898.

53 For account of Muir's visit to the Hodgson family see *The Life and Letters of John Muir*, II, 315–16.

54 For selections from Muir's journal of the expedition see *John of the Mountains*, pp. 379–426.

55 In manuscript, "Friends Bearing Torches," by Charles Keeler.

56 "Narrative of the Expedition," by John Burroughs, in *Harriman Alaska Expedition*, I, 18.

57 *Edward Henry Harriman*, by John Muir, pp. 10–11.

58 Related by Charles Keeler. For a slightly varied form of the story see *The Life and Letters of John Burroughs*, I, 380.

59 For Burroughs's account of the hunting trip see "Narrative of the Expedition," in *Harriman Alaska Expedition*, I, 38–40.

60 "To the Memory of John Muir," by C. Hart Merriam, in *Sierra Club Bulletin*, X, 148 (January 1917).

61 *Edward Henry Harriman*, by John Muir, pp. 15–16.

62 Letter to Mrs. Muir.

63 *Edward Henry Harriman*, pp. 35–6.

64 In manuscript, "Friends Bearing Torches," by Charles Keeler. Also in *John of the Mountains*, note, pp. 405–6.

65 In mimeographed pamphlet of songs and poems composed on the expedition. Quoted in *The Life and Letters of John Burroughs*, I.

[66] In manuscript, "Friends Bearing Torches," by Charles Keeler.

[67] Related by Charles Keeler.

[68] Muir's journal.

[69] Letter to the "Big Four," August 30, 1899, in *The Life and Letters of John Muir,* II, 331.

PART VII

[1] Memories of May Reid Coleman, niece of John Muir and wife of Arthur Coleman, his business manager.

[2] *Philadelphia Ledger,* May 1, 1910.

[3] *Remembered Yesterdays,* p. 388.

[4] *The Life and Letters of John Muir,* II, 411.

[5] Muir's journals. Quotations in this travel narrative, unless otherwise specified, are from his journals.

[6] To Mrs. Muir, December 1903.

[7] To Bailey Millard, October 1909, Muir wrote: "It is not true that any of the 200 or more species of the Eucalyptus surpasses in height our Big Trees or Redwoods. I failed to find a botanist who had ever seen or measured a tree in all Australia more than 300 feet."

[8] and [9] Memories of Helen Funk Muir.

[10] Narrative of the recession fight in Legislature and Congress is based on conversations with William E. Colby; his article "Yosemite and the Sierra Club," in the *Sierra Club Bulletin,* XXIII, No. 2, pp. 11–19 (April 1938); newspaper reports; and Muir's letters.

[11] To Robert Underwood Johnson, February 24 (1905), in *The Life and Letters of John Muir,* II, 356.

[12] For Muir's tribute to "Don Pedro" see *John of the Mountains,* pp. 432–3.

[13] "To the Memory of John Muir," in the *Sierra Club Bulletin,* X, 146–51 (January 1917).

[14], [15], and [16] Memories of Helen Funk Muir.

[17] *The Mountains of California,* II, 289.

[18] To Marsden Manson, November 15, 1906.

[19] Last two sentences quoted in *The Life and Letters of John Muir,* II, 389.

[20] *Remembered Yesterdays,* p. 305.

[21] and [22] Ibid., p. 307.

[23] To Horace D. Taft, February 1, 1910. Quoted by Henry F. Pringle in his *The Life and Times of William Howard Taft,* I, 386.

[24] See ibid., I, 478.

[25] Ibid., I, 493.

[26] Alden Sampson of New York represented the Sierra Club, Edmund A. Whitman the Appalachian Club, and Miss Harriet Monroe two large outdoor clubs of Chicago.

[27] For Phelan's statement about Muir see *Hearing before the Committee on Public Lands United States Senate on the Joint Resolution* (*S.R. 123*), p. 110.

[28] For statements by Phelan and Manson about sources and cost see *Hearing before the Committee on Public Lands United States Senate on the Joint Resolution* (*S.R. 123*), pp. 112, 123.

[29] *Edward Henry Harriman,* by John Muir, pp. 22–3.

[30] and [31] For account of Muir-Burroughs desert and Grand Canyon trip see *The Life and Letters of John Burroughs,* II, 119–22.

[32] For Muir-Burroughs Yosemite trip see "In the Yosemite with John Muir," by Clara Barrus, *Craftsman,* XXIII, 324–35 (December 1912).

[33] *With Walt Whitman in Camden* (March 28–July 14, 1888), by Horace Traubel, 1908 edition, p. 334.

[34] For an account of the icy controversy between Muir and Burroughs see *The Life and Letters of John Burroughs,* II, 126, 134–8.

[35] *Edward Henry Harriman,* by John Muir, Doubleday, Page, 1912.

[36] The conversation between Muir and Taft is compiled from newspaper accounts written by hovering reporters.

[37] The hearing set for February 25, 1910, and postponed five times at the request of San Francisco officials, was finally held in November 1912.

[38] For a full discussion of the Ballinger case see *The Life and Times of William Howard Taft,* by Henry F. Pringle, I, 470–514; II, 558, 731–3, 758, 952. See also "Not Guilty," by Harold L. Ickes, in *Saturday Evening Post,* CCXII (May 25, 1940).

[39] *Atlantic Monthly,* CVII (January to April 1911). Published in enlarged form as a book by Houghton, Mifflin in 1911.

[40] Published by Houghton, Mifflin in 1913. Muir, reluctant to write his autobiography, was finally persuaded to do so by his wife, Robert Underwood Johnson, and Richard Watson Gilder. His brother David and his sister Sarah strongly disapproved of his revelation of their father's harshness. But his sister Joanna wrote to him: "The portion relating to yourself and the family was read in tears, and I wished with all my heart it had not been so true." Muir intended to write the remainder of his life story, but never got beyond some rough typed drafts.

[41] Published in book form by the Century Company in 1912. Republished in 1917 by Houghton, Mifflin in *Mountains of California,* Vol. II.

[42] Muir Funk's given name was changed to Wayne when the family name was legally changed to Muir.

[43] Memories of Helen Funk Muir.

[44] To Elizabeth Averell, March 2, 1911.

[45] To William E. Colby, May 8, 1911.

[46] To Mrs. Katharine Hooker, June 26, 1911, in *The Life and Letters of John Muir,* II, 365–7.

[47] To John Burroughs, July 14, 1911, in *The Life and Letters of John Muir,* II, 366–7.

[48] "John Muir," by Henry Fairfield Osborn, *Sierra Club Bulletin,* X, No. 1, p. 31 (January 1916).

[49] *Buenos Aires Herald,* November 15, 1911.

[50] *New York Times,* March 5, 1913.

[51] Secretary Ballinger, ill and broken in spirits, resigned from the Taft Cabinet in March 1911. He was succeeded in the Department of the Interior by Walter L. Fisher of Illinois.

[52] Related by Thomas Rae Hanna.

[53] A.M., Harvard, 1896; LL.D., University of Wisconsin, 1897; Litt.D., Yale, 1911.

[54] The John Muir Trail, financed by legislative appropriation, is still in the process of being completed as a state memorial to Muir. According to William E. Colby, who originated the idea, the trail is about 185 miles in length. Beginning in the north at the Le Conte Memorial Lodge in the Yosemite Valley, it follows the Sunrise Trail into the Tuolumne Meadows and thence extends south to Mount Whitney, following as near the crest of the Sierra as feasible, mainly on the western slopes of the summits. Walter A. Starr, Jr., a young nature-lover after Muir's own heart, prepared before his own death among the Minarets the excellent *Guide to the John Muir Trail and the High Sierra Region,* which has been published by the Sierra Club.

[55] For an account of the last days of the Hetch Hetchy fight in Washington, see *Remembered Yesterdays,* pp. 307–13.

[56] To Dr. William Frederic Badè, February 10, 1914.

[57] To Mr. and Mrs. Henry Fairfield Osborn, January 4, 1914. For full text of letter see *The Life and Letters of John Muir,* II, 385–6.

[58] In addition to his great influence in the cause of national conservation William E. Colby served nine years on the California State Park Commission, during all of which period he was chairman. While he was in office, $12,000,000 were expended in the purchase of between fifty and sixty new parks to be added to the state system, including important ones such as Point Lobos, Calaveras Big Trees, Bull Creek Flat, and other outstanding redwood areas.

[59] Theodore Roosevelt created by proclamation 150 national forests, thus increasing the reserved areas from 46,000,000 acres to 194,000,000 acres. He also created five national parks and twenty-three national monuments. See *Sierra Club Bulletin,* X, 431–2 (January 1919).

[60] In fairness to James D. Phelan, it should be recalled that as United States Senator he introduced in Congress in 1919 a bill to enlarge the Sequoia National Park to include the Kings and Kern Canyons, the whole to be named the Roosevelt National Park. Opposed by special interests, the bill failed of passage.

[61] Phelan stated at the Senate Committee hearing in Washington that the Hetch Hetchy project would cost "from $40,000,000 to $50,000,000." See *Hearing before the Committee on Public Lands United States Senate on the Joint Resolution (S.R. 123),* p. 113.

[62] "John Muir and the Alaska Book," by Marion Randall Parsons, in *Sierra Club Bulletin,* X, No. 1, pp. 33–6 (January 1916).

[63] "John Muir, Pilgrim Soul," by Charlotte Kellogg, *Delineator,* XCII, 2 (August 1921).

[64] Among Muir's final letters was one in support of a campaign to save the cypress trees on the Seventeen-Mile Drive along the Monterey coast, and another to the Berkeley Chapter of the Red Cross, enclosing a generous check to aid in Belgian relief.

[65] The final editing of the manuscript of *Travels in Alaska* was done by Marion Randall Parsons after Muir's death. The book was published by Houghton, Mifflin in 1917.

[66] *John of the Mountains,* p. 440.

INDEX

INDEX

INDEX

A NOTE ON THE TYPE

The text of this book is set in Caledonia, a Linotype face which belongs to the family of printing types called "modern face" by printers — a term used to mark the change in style of type-letters that occurred about 1800. Caledonia borders on the general design of Scotch Modern, but is more freely drawn than that letter.

The book was composed, printed, and bound by The Plimpton Press, Norwood, Massachusetts. The typography and binding design are by W. A. Dwiggins.